America's Forgotten Colony

America's Forgotten Colony examines private U.S. citizens' experiences on Cuba's Isle of Pines to show how American influence adapted and endured in republican-era Cuba (1902–58). This transnational study challenges the notion that U.S. territorial ambitions ended after the nineteenth century. Many Americans, anxious about a "closed" frontier in an industrialized, urbanized United States, migrated to the Isle and pushed for agrarian-oriented landed expansion well into the twentieth century. Their efforts were stymied by Cuban resistance and reluctant U.S. policymakers. After decades of tension, however, a new generation of Americans collaborated with locals in commercial and institutional endeavors. Although they did not wield the same influence, Americans nevertheless maintained a significant footprint. The story of this cooperation upsets prevailing conceptions of U.S. domination and perpetual conflict, revealing that U.S.–Cuban relations at the grass roots were not nearly as adversarial as on the diplomatic level at the dawn of the Cuban Revolution.

Michael E. Neagle is an assistant professor of history at Nichols College in Dudley, Massachusetts. His work has appeared in *America in the World* (Cambridge University Press), *A Companion to Woodrow Wilson*, *The Journal of the Gilded Age and Progressive Era*, and *Latino America: A State-by-State Encyclopedia*. He has won grants from the Society for Historians of American Foreign Relations, the Tinker Foundation, the University of Connecticut Humanities Institute, and the University of Connecticut Center for Latin American and Caribbean Studies.

Cambridge Studies in US Foreign Relations

Edited by

Paul Thomas Chamberlin, *University of Kentucky*
Lien-Hang T. Nguyen, *University of Kentucky*

This series showcases cutting-edge scholarship in US foreign relations that employs dynamic new methodological approaches and archives from the colonial era to the present. The series will be guided by the ethos of transnationalism, focusing on the history of American foreign relations in a global context rather than privileging the United States as the dominant actor on the world stage.

Also in the series

Elizabeth Leake, *The Defiant Border: The Afghan–Pakistan Borderlands in the Era of Decolonization, 1936–1965*
Renata Keller, *Mexico's Cold War: Cuba, the United States, and the Legacy of the Mexican Revolution*

America's Forgotten Colony

Cuba's Isle of Pines

MICHAEL E. NEAGLE

Nichols College

CAMBRIDGE
UNIVERSITY PRESS

One Liberty Plaza, 20th Floor, New York, NY 10006, USA

Cambridge University Press is part of the University of Cambridge.

It furthers the University's mission by disseminating knowledge in the pursuit of education, learning, and research at the highest international levels of excellence.

www.cambridge.org
Information on this title: www.cambridge.org/9781316502013

© Michael E. Neagle 2016

This publication is in copyright. Subject to statutory exception and to the provisions of relevant collective licensing agreements, no reproduction of any part may take place without the written permission of Cambridge University Press.

First published 2016

Printed in the United States of America by Sheridan Books, Inc.

A catalogue record for this publication is available from the British Library.

Library of Congress Cataloging-in-Publication Data
Names: Neagle, E. Michael.
Title: America's forgotten colony: Cuba's Isle of Pines /
Michael E. Neagle, Nichols College.
Description: New York, NY: Cambridge University Press, 2016. |
Series: Cambridge studies in US foreign relations |
Includes bibliographical references and index.
Identifiers: LCCN 2016014927| ISBN 9781107136854 (hardback) |
ISBN 9781316502013 (paperback)
Subjects: LCSH: Isla de Pinos (Cuba) – History. | United States – Relations – Cuba. |
Cuba – Relations – United States. | BISAC: HISTORY / United States / 20th Century.
Classification: LCC F1799.I8 N43 2016 | DDC 972.91/25–dc23
LC record available at https://lccn.loc.gov/2016014927

ISBN 978-1-107-13685-4 Hardback
ISBN 978-1-316-50201-3 Paperback

Cambridge University Press has no responsibility for the persistence or accuracy of URLs for external or third-party Internet Web sites referred to in this publication and does not guarantee that any content on such Web sites is, or will remain, accurate or appropriate.

For Susan,
my wife, partner, and friend

Contents

Illustrations

Acknowledgements

Although I have spent a lot of time by myself working on this book over the years, I could not have done it alone.

I began this project as a graduate student at the University of Connecticut, where I was fortunate to have an abundance of financial, scholarly, and collegial support. The Department of History, under the leadership of Shirley Roe and Chris Clark as well as the invaluable administrative assistance of Dee Gosline, provided me with summer grants and travel monies that enabled me to begin research. Fellowships from UConn's Center for Latin American and Caribbean Studies as well as the Graduate School helped to sustain my research in the United States. I am particularly indebted to the UConn Humanities Institute, which awarded me a year-long Graduate Student Dissertation Fellowship that provided me valuable time to write and think more deeply about my project at a formative stage. I benefited greatly from conversations with my fellow Fellows, particularly Miloje Despić, Kenneth Gouwens, Margo Machida, Joanne Pope Melish, Gustavo Nanclares, and UCHI Director Sharon Harris.

Archivists and librarians are an historian's best friend when it comes to research. I was fortunate to have the help of many, including Steve Batt and Marisol Ramos at UConn, Jim Douglas and Rosalba Onofrio at Nichols College, David Langbart at the U.S. National Archives, Suzanne Gehring and Anna Mozley at Asbury University, Greta Mickey at the Yates County (NY) Genealogical and Historical Society, Nick Speth at the Indiana Historical Society, as well as the dedicated staffs at the Library of Congress, New York Public Library, Connecticut State Library, Ohio Historical Society, Fond du Lac Historical Society, and Wisconsin

Historical Society. Beyond the professional archives, I was able to tap into many private sources as well. Eli Swetland graciously allowed me into his home to comb through his father's papers. My research there led me to a variety of other treasure troves – including an Isle of Pines page on Facebook established by William Stimson – that helped fill key gaps in the story. I am thankful to all those individuals who kindly shared with me their memories, pictures, letters, and family stories.

Grants from the Tinker Foundation and the Society for Historians of American Foreign Relations afforded me the opportunity to do archival work in Cuba. Elizabeth Mahan in UConn's Office of International Affairs, Mayra Alonso at Marazul Charters, and Belkis Quesada at Cuba's Instituto de Historia helped me navigate the labyrinthine bureaucratic process. I never could have made it, though, without the kindness and hospitality shown by Adriana González, Alina González, and Augusto Glez, who treated me like family while I was in Havana. Likewise, I am grateful to Daniel Rodríguez, Linda Rodríguez, and Joanna Elrick for helping me get my bearings in Cuba. On the Isle, Elda Cepero Herrera shared not only her home but also her memories of the American presence in the 1950s. Her son, Rigoberto, was a fantastic tour guide who cheerfully took me around the Isle in his Soviet-made car. The archivists and staff I encountered in Cuba could not have been more helpful and accommodating. I am particularly appreciative of the assistance offered by Julio López Valdés, Lisset Guardia Parlá, and Silvio S. Facenda Castillo at the Archivo Nacional de Cuba; Michel at the Biblioteca Nacional "Jose Martí"; Yanelys Plasencia Padrón at the Isle's Museo Municipal; Zaily Secourt Amador, Yaneysi Manzo Durán, and especially Yaquelín Ramírez Olivero at the Archivo Histórico Municipal de la Isla de la Juventud.

Many scholars and friends also helped me to find sources, develop ideas, and sharpen my focus. Louis A. Pérez Jr. offered sage research advice that paid great dividends. Before he passed away in 2012, eminent Isle historian Juan Colina la Rosa and I enjoyed an *intercambio* of material that I hope was mutually beneficial. At various stages of the project, I enjoyed constructive conversations and exchanges with Peter Baldwin, Patrick Blythe, Richard D. Brown, Chris Clark, Adrián López Denis, Michael Donoghue, Raúl Galván, Tony Goins, Antonio Hernández-Matos, Lisa Jarvinen, John Kincheloe, Jana Lipman, Dennis Merrill, Mark Overmyer-Velázquez, Thomas Paterson, Kelly Shannon, Blanca Silvestrini, Bruce Stave, Catherine Thompson, Rob Venator, and Sherry Zane.

I'm grateful to those who helped make me a better writer and historian before I even knew it's what I wanted to do with my life. At Holy

Cross, professors Robert Brandfon, Noel Cary, Gary Phillips, and Steve Vineberg all helped nurture me at a formative time, the dividends of which I would not fully appreciate until years later. And when I was a newspaper reporter in a past life/career, Dean Russin was a terrific editor and an even better friend.

In my new professional home at Nichols College, I have been warmly welcomed by many administrators and colleagues who spurred me on as I finished this book. President Susan Englekemeyer, Provost Alan Reinhardt, and Associate Dean of Liberal Arts Mauri Pelto have been enthusiastic supporters of my research efforts. Andrea Becker, Maureen Butler, and Chris Wojnar have consistently gone above and beyond with their administrative assistance. Hans Despain and History Program Chair Paul Lambert have been outstanding mentors whom I can always count on for smart advice. Likewise, I have appreciated the good cheer and support from fellow faculty members Boyd Brown, Erin Casey-Williams, Jim Deys, Kellie Deys, Jeff Halprin, Michael Lajoie, Libba Moore, Jay Price, and Erika Smith among many others.

At Cambridge University Press, I am deeply indebted to my editor Debbie Gershenowitz for championing this project from an early stage and seeing it through. Her unflagging enthusiasm was a source of inspiration. Editorial assistants Kristina Deusch and Dana Bricken greatly helped to streamline the path to publication. I remain grateful to series editors Paul Chamberlin and Hang Nguyen for including my work among such esteemed company. The two anonymous reviewers for the press provided uncommonly constructive feedback that made the end result stronger. I am also thankful to editor Alan Lessoff and two anonymous reviewers for their incisive feedback to my October 2012 article in the *Journal of the Gilded Age and Progressive Era*, parts of which appear in Chapters 1 and 2 of this book.

I owe a special thanks to those who helped shepherd this project from its genesis. Chief among them is Frank Costigliola, my graduate advisor, whose model scholarship, teaching, and mentorship continue to inspire me. I will be forever appreciative of his confidence in my abilities and his constant encouragement, which has enriched my professional development in ways beyond measure. Melina Pappademos consistently challenged me not to lose sight of Cuban perspectives. Her trenchant feedback enabled me to complicate and clarify my arguments more effectively. Graduate colleagues and friends Dominic DeBrincat, Chad Reid, and Tom Westerman – my "informal committee" – patiently read through early drafts when this project was still in development;

Dominic, in particular, selflessly read through chapters many times over. Their dependably incisive feedback has made this a much better book.

I am also mindful of those who supported me along the way with whom I wish I could have shared this finished product: Courtney "C-Bass" Erickson, who never missed an opportunity to express his pride in my accomplishments; Nancy Comarella, who helped guide me through graduate school bureaucracy; my father-in-law, Lewis Silverman, who was a great audience to talk to about my work; *mi abuelita*, Tarcila Rojas, with whom I burnished my Spanish watching silly Peruvian TV shows; my grandfather, William E. Neagle Jr., who made reading and writing a family trait and would have made a first-rate historian; and J. Garry Clifford, an advisor and master wordsmith whose sharp eye and encyclopedic knowledge helped to enliven this story.

Finally and most importantly, I have been blessed with the love and generosity of my family throughout this entire process. My parents, Thomas and Elda Neagle, made this all possible in more ways than one. Their support was not only emotional and financial, but also tangible: Dad worked on the index and Mom helped with some translations. Moreover, their boundless encouragement, along with that of my brother, Robert, has sustained me as I have pursued a career of teaching and scholarship. Although they were not yet here when I began this project, my children, Olivia and Ethan, have made its completion that much sweeter. I look forward to them reading Daddy's book someday. Last, my wife, Susan, has been an exceptional model of kindness, patience, and understanding throughout my academic career. Dedicating this book to her is but a small token toward a debt that I am much richer for incurring.

Abbreviations

ACS	American Central School
AHM	Archivo Histórico Municipal de la Isla de la Juventud
ANC	Archivo Nacional de Cuba
CSL	Connecticut State Library
IHS	Indiana Historical Society
LOC	Library of Congress
NARA	U.S. National Archives and Records Administration
SFA	Swetland Family Archives
TDC	Tropical Development Company
YCGHS	Yates County (NY) Genealogical and Historical Society

Introduction

The American Cemetery on Cuba's Isle of Youth is a largely forgotten place. No sign, no marker, no memorial identifies the site holding the remains of some 200 U.S. citizens who lived on what was once called the Isle of Pines.[1] The cemetery lies in a pastoral area nearly eight miles from Nueva Gerona, the Isle's largest town. A bus line runs past it, but little else. Time and nature have eroded one of the few relics of the sixty-year U.S. presence. Although the cemetery is maintained by the Isle's municipal government, many of the headstones are chipped, cracked, or faded. Animal droppings dot the landscape. Most of the wooden fence posts that mark the boundary between the cemetery and the road have rotted away.

The cemetery's sad twenty-first-century condition contrasts starkly with how it once appeared and the attention locals gave it. Founded in 1907, the cemetery was located in the town of Columbia, the first settlement created by U.S. citizens who moved to the Isle after the War of 1898. For decades, private American clubs financed and landscaped the cemetery. It was a point of pride to U.S. settlers because it marked the final resting place for the pioneers who had created an American community there. An English-language newspaper on the Isle in 1932 boasted, "This has become one of the most perfectly kept cemeteries to be found

---

[1] Fidel Castro changed the island's name in 1978. One writer, citing the work of Cuban historian Juan Colina la Rosa, states that 280 Americans are buried at the cemetery. Luis Sexto, "El Cementerio de los Americanos," http://luisexto.blogia.com/2006/080101-el-cementerio-de-los-americanos.php (accessed May 1, 2016). That number could not be confirmed. My own count in April 2010 found nearly 175 headstones. For a video of the cemetery as it appeared in 2008, see http://youtu.be/p3WGeUOoGMA (accessed May 1, 2016).

FIGURE I.I. The American Cemetery on the Isle of Youth as it appeared in 2010. Created in 1907, it holds the remains of some 200 U.S. citizens who lived on the Isle.
Source: Author's photo.

anywhere and holds the remains of many others who came here to find fortunes and, most of them, found the greater riches of contentment and peace in this fairest land of perpetual springtime."[2]

The newspaper's claim notwithstanding, many of the early settlers found neither wealth nor leisure. Clearing, planting, and building were more taxing and more expensive than they had anticipated. Most businesses failed. Natural disasters wreaked havoc on their properties. In short, living as pioneers was a more difficult proposition than they had expected. Settlers who remained for more than a few years often struggled to make ends meet. Most returned to the United States disillusioned. Those who stayed for the long term, however, developed a deep affinity for the Isle, its people, and its customs. In contrast to the self-isolation and annexationist aims of turn-of-the-century settlers, Americans at mid-century demonstrated a greater willingness to engage socially and commercially with their island neighbors. The onset of the Cuban Revolution,

[2] "Ira Asa Brown," *Isle of Pines Post*, April 25, 1932.

though, changed that dynamic. The American Cemetery, then, stands as an enduring reminder of settlers' hopeful expectations of social and financial prosperity, and its abandonment fittingly embodies a forgotten chapter in the history of U.S. expansion and U.S.–Cuban relations.

Geographically, Cuba is more than just one island. While the main body encompasses most of the country, Cuba is also comprised of archipelagos and keys. The largest of these other islands is the presently named Isle of Youth (Isla de la Juventud) located about forty miles off mainland Cuba's southwest coast. At 934 square miles, it is roughly three-fourths the size of Rhode Island. Most of the population clusters on the northern half of the island, where the land is low, flat, and dry. The Lanier Swamp runs like a belt around the Isle's midsection and virtually divides it. South of the swamp, the lower portion of the island is dense forest that is a national park accessible only by special permit with a licensed guide. Surrounding the north, east, and west of the Isle, the Gulf of Batabanó is only ten to fifteen feet deep in some stretches. To the south, however, the Isle sits on a shelf that leads out to deep water popular among divers.

Throughout most of its history, the Isle of Pines was sparsely populated. Little is known about its pre-Columbian inhabitants. One scholar surmised that the native population never reached more than 200.[3] Christopher Columbus is widely credited as the first European to set foot on the Isle of Pines, arriving in June 1494 during his second westward voyage. Spain's attempts to populate the Isle thereafter went through fits and starts. A late sixteenth-century Spanish settlement was reportedly wiped out by Sir Francis Drake in 1596 and for decades thereafter colonization stalled. Most of the land later was divided into seven *haciendas* (large estates) owned by descendants of a Spanish noble who had received a royal title to the Isle in 1630.[4] Succeeding generations further subdivided title to property so that by the late eighteenth century, an estimated twenty estates dominated the Isle.[5] Aside from cattle raising and farm production for local consumption, little industry or export activity took place.

The Spanish crown renewed efforts to organize the Isle more formally in 1830, when it founded the Reina Amalia colony while establishing a

---

[3] Morton D. Winsberg, "The Isle of Pines, Cuba: A Geographic Interpretation" (PhD diss., University of Florida, 1958), 35.

[4] Irene A. Wright, *Isle of Pines* (Beverly, MA: Beverly Printing Company, 1910), 20–2.

[5] Irene A. Wright, *The Gem of the Caribbean* (Nueva Gerona: Isle of Pines Publicity Company, 1909), 16–18.

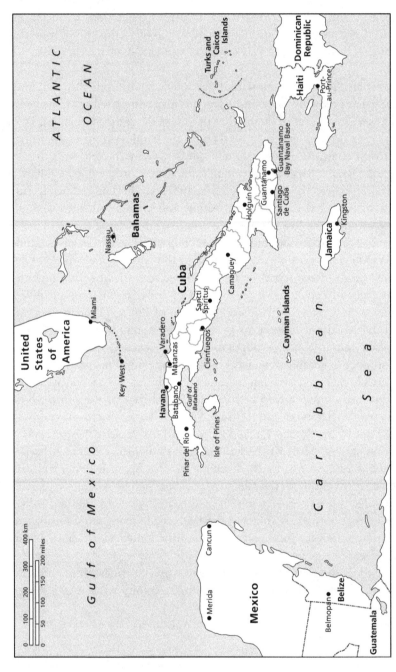

FIGURE I.2. Map of the Isle of Pines, Cuba, and Florida (provided by Cambridge University Press).

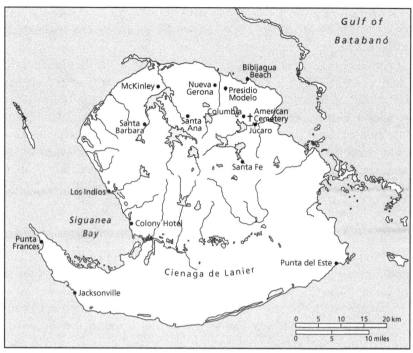

FIGURE I.3. Map of the Isle of Pines (provided by Cambridge University Press).

garrison to protect Cuba's southern flank from pirates. That garrison, in turn, spurred the foundation of Nueva Gerona, which by the end of the century would become the Isle's largest town.[6] According to one author, the colony initially struggled because public lands were scarce, so the crown came to depend on *hacendados* (large landowners) to donate property for settlement. Few *hacendados* or settlers took up the offer, however, and the Isle's population remained in the hundreds a decade later.[7] As a result, the Spanish crown sent common criminals and political prisoners there. The move backfired as it created the popular perception that the island was nothing more than a penal colony and pirate lair, a reputation that would stifle Spanish efforts to transform it into a flourishing colony and tourist destination.[8] Journalist Irene A. Wright, who wrote two histories of the Isle, argued that this negative association

[6] Wright, *Gem of the Caribbean*, 23–4.
[7] Jane McManus, *Cuba's Island of Dreams: Voices from the Isle of Pines and Youth* (Gainesville: University Press of Florida, 2000), 3.
[8] Winsberg, "Isle of Pines, Cuba," 54–5.

extended into the twentieth century with the view "that the people of the Isle of Pines are necessarily (by nature or by acclimation) a lawless and turbulent lot."[9]

Although Cuba was ravaged by rebellions in the late nineteenth century – including the Ten Years' War (1868–78), *la Guerra Chiquita* (1879–80), and the War of Independence (1895–8) – the Isle of Pines remained largely unaffected. This isolation from mainland Cuba was also evident during the country's republican era (1902–58). For the most part, news from the Isle drew scant attention from the Havana press, save for instances in which U.S. settlers threatened annexation. Cuban writer Eduardo Lens, for example, titled his 1942 study of the Isle *La Isla Olvidada* – the forgotten island.[10] He was not the only writer to use the phrase. Ofelia Rodríguez Acosta in 1926 wrote a short travelogue about her trip from Havana and referred to her destination as both a "forgotten Isle" and a "sleeping beauty."[11] Other scholars, including Waldo Medina and Antonio Núñez Jiménez, gave the Isle another sobriquet – the Siberia of Cuba.[12] The title not only suggested the Isle's physical and emotional detachment from the heart of Cuba, but also that it was a place of banishment. Moreover, Medina and Núñez Jiménez agreed that *pineros* (Isle natives) historically had been treated like second-class citizens within Cuba. Medina wrote that *pineros* generally felt overlooked and unappreciated by more cosmopolitan *habaneros*. He blamed this dynamic on Cuban politicians who ignored the Isle's common heritage with mainland Cuba.[13] Such attitudes help to explain the relative ease with which U.S. settlers entered the Isle during the early twentieth century.

The Imperial Project

U.S. interest in the Isle began as the country was taking tentative steps toward becoming a global power. If Latin America was an "Empire's

---

[9] Wright, *Isle of Pines*, 24.

[10] Eduardo F. Lens, *La Isla Olvidada: Estudio Físico, Económico y Humano de la Isla de Pinos* (La Habana: 1942).

[11] Ofelia Rodríguez Acosta, *Apuntes de Mi Viaje a Isla de Pinos* (La Habana: Montiel y Co., 1926), 30, 36.

[12] Waldo Medina, "Isla de Pinos en el XXII Aniversario de la Ratificación del Pacto Hay-Quesada," *Aquí, Isla de Pinos* (La Habana, 1961), 35; Antonio Núñez Jiménez, *Autobiografía de Isla de Pinos* (La Habana: 1949), 18. Both writers credited José de la Luz y Caballero for coining the phrase in the mid-nineteenth century but suggested that the sentiment remained much the same among Cubans in the mid-twentieth century.

[13] Medina, "Amor y Dolor de la Isla," *Aquí, Isla de Pinos*, 121.

Workshop" for the United States, then Cuba was one of its key laboratories.[14] U.S. actions in Cuba foreshadowed other engagements in the region and the world throughout the twentieth century. Amidst the various U.S. occupations of Cuba (1899–1902, 1906–9, 1917–22), the United States landed troops elsewhere in the Caribbean basin, including Haiti, the Dominican Republic, and Nicaragua. These actions produced long-standing occupations that ushered in new leaders and systems of government subject to U.S. approval. The U.S. naval base at Cuba's Guantánamo Bay – a location established after the Theodore Roosevelt administration rejected the Isle of Pines – also set a precedent. A century later, the United States would have hundreds of overseas bases around the world.[15] U.S. commercial expansion into Cuba, both as a market for American products and as a place from which to extract resources, set the stage for similar engagements elsewhere. Finally, the U.S. cultural incursion into Cuba, by way of goods, schools, technology, and other forms, presaged the penetration of U.S. styles and customs in virtually every corner of the globe.

The U.S. presence on the Isle of Pines illustrated these elements in microcosm. Historians in the United States and Cuba, however, have given this illuminating story short shrift. This book aims to rescue this overlooked story of American imperialism from obscurity to both elucidate and complicate our understandings of the United States and U.S.–Cuban relations during the early twentieth century.

U.S. hegemony – that is, the manipulation of a country's politics and economy to the disproportional benefit of U.S. interests – was evident in three forms. First, settlers colonized the Isle with the aim of annexing it to the United States. The drive for landed expansion through purchase or conquest had been a hallmark of U.S. imperial growth during the nineteenth century. The U.S. engagement on the Isle of Pines shows that the quest for territory continued into the twentieth century. Although geostrategic considerations and Cuban resistance prompted the Roosevelt administration to eschew annexation, the question would linger for nearly a quarter-century. Secretary of State John Hay and Cuban Foreign Minister Gonzalo de Quesada in 1904 signed a treaty that recognized

---

[14] Greg Grandin, *Empire's Workshop: Latin America, the United States, and the Rise of the New Imperialism* (New York: Henry Holt, 2006). William Appleman Williams makes a similar argument about Cuba and U.S. imperialism. Williams, *The Tragedy of American Diplomacy*, New Edition (New York: W.W. Norton, 1972), 1–13.

[15] Chalmers Johnson, *Nemesis: The Last Days of the American Republic* (New York: Metropolitan Books, 2006), 137–70.

Cuban sovereignty on the Isle. The U.S. Senate, however, did not ratify the agreement until 1925. During this diplomatic limbo – in which Cuba administered the Isle – private U.S. citizens purchased an estimated 90 percent of the island's arable land, founded a dozen towns, and developed a community of Americans perhaps 2,000 strong at its height in the 1910s.

The second form U.S. expansionism took was commercial. Over six decades, settlers and entrepreneurs commodified economic activity on the Isle. What had been an insulated, largely pastoral economy during the Spanish colonial era changed into an economy grounded in export-oriented capitalism. Settlers introduced citrus fruits and winter vegetables for sale in U.S. markets. Entrepreneurs presumed this activity would finance their livelihoods. Moreover, U.S.-based landholding companies depicted the Isle as an exotic tropical paradise to attract migrants, tourists, and land buyers. This activity was not wholly unwelcome by Cubans. Havana policymakers gave their tacit approval in the hopes that U.S. settlers and entrepreneurs would develop a place once generally ignored under Spain. Meanwhile on the Isle, *pineros* and other foreign nationals, particularly Jamaicans and Cayman Islanders, relied on U.S. business- and grove-owners for work.

Third, Americans on the Isle exerted a profound cultural influence throughout their sixty-year presence. Settlers at the turn of the century looked to Americanize the island, not necessarily to uplift their neighbors but rather to strengthen their case for annexation. As historian Brooke Blower has argued, the United States was not only rooted in physical geography, but also in the values, customs, and social institutions it projected abroad.[16] Examples of such American-ness evident on the Isle included promotion of export-oriented capitalism, proliferation of schools and social clubs, introduction of American goods, products, and technology, and widespread use of the English language and the U.S. dollar. Even after 1925, when the question of the Isle's sovereignty was resolved and most settlers returned to the United States, U.S. cultural influence persisted. The most notable example was the American Central School, a private institution that provided English-language instruction to children from grades one to twelve. While serving as a key space for mutual cooperation and sociability, the school was partly financed by the U.S. government and followed a U.S.-based curriculum taught by

---

[16] Brooke L. Blower, *Becoming Americans in Paris: Transatlantic Politics and Culture between the World Wars* (New York: Oxford University Press, 2011), 3.

American teachers and run by American administrators. This distinctly American flavor, moreover, was a key draw for students, a majority of whom were Cubans wanting to learn English.

Rather than a deliberate system imposed by Washington or by wealthy elites, this hegemony was more of a process that featured ebbs and flows of influence based on a variety of factors. Multiple actors such as politicians, businessmen, landowners, settlers, and laborers – all with their own interests and contingent authority – shaped the contours of the imperial relationship in ways that belie a static center-periphery dynamic. This complex arrangement was evident in how Cubans accommodated and frustrated Americans' designs. Policymakers in Havana, as well as elites and locals on the Isle, mostly supported the U.S. presence. Settlers' infusion of capital helped to grow the local economy, generating commercial interest in a place largely considered a backwater. This activity included the proliferation of stores, banks, transportation networks, and infrastructure. The U.S. presence created a market for real estate that had been virtually nonexistent, which benefited the *hacendados* who had dominated the Isle for generations. Many elites were only too happy to see Americans – and U.S. dollars – flood into the Isle. There were limits to this welcoming spirit, however. Class differences aside, *pineros* shared a resentment against settlers' quest for U.S. annexation, and occasionally they mobilized in public protest. Cubans also gathered to hold public celebrations when the U.S. Senate ratified the Hay-Quesada treaty, a spectacle that demonstrated *pineros'* Cuban nationalism. Nevertheless, Americans depended on *pineros* for the success of their pioneering enterprises. They needed *hacendados* to be willing to sell their land – and they did, often in large parcels. Settlers who initiated export-oriented commercial farming also relied on local labor to establish and maintain their groves. In short, Americans could not have maintained a presence on the Isle without locals' active participation. It is an important distinction that reveals the limits of U.S. hegemony.

Uncontrollable elements also hemmed the hegemonic project on the Isle: geography, soil conditions, dearth of deep harbors, market forces, and tropical storms. U.S. settlers could do little to control these variables, which forced them to adapt. Some intensified their lobbying of the U.S. and Cuban governments. Some pursued commercial alliances with locals. Some put more money into their ventures. Some gave up and returned to the United States. These contingencies help to demonstrate how U.S. power and influence adapted and ultimately eroded in the years well before the Cuban Revolution.

Nevertheless, the U.S. presence on the Isle endured, undergoing a remarkable shift over roughly six decades. The first generation of settlers, spurred by fears of a "closing" continental frontier, sought to Americanize the island in preparation for annexation and showed little affinity for local customs. Later generations, however, showed a much greater willingness to integrate socially and commercially with their Isle neighbors, among whom were Europeans, Asians, and West Indians. This changing attitude produced deeper intercultural exchanges as well as a détente between Americans and Cubans that contrasted with the growing anti-Americanism in mainland Cuba on the eve of the 1959 Cuban Revolution.

U.S. foreign relations scholarship in the early twenty-first century has tended to gravitate toward the transnational, examining trends and ideas that transcend the boundaries of the nation-state. I maintain that the nation-state is still an important area of study, particularly as a marker of identity. U.S. national identity – in addition to considerations of class, race, and gender – was critical to settlers' self-perceptions, especially those of the first generation at the dawn of the twentieth century. Early settlers' connection to the United States helped to set them apart from native Cubans and other foreign nationals. That is not to say those ideas were immutable. Indeed, by mid-century, U.S. citizens were socially engaging their Isle neighbors more often and some were even calling themselves "*pineros*." Being a U.S. citizen was still an important marker, though, and no instances are on record of Americans renouncing their U.S. citizenship. But the long-term trend illustrates the fluidity of identity and the importance of nationality.

The Sovereignty Question

The U.S. presence on the Isle of Pines can be divided into two periods. The first, from 1898 to 1925, I call the Hay-Quesada era after the treaty that formally recognized Cuban sovereignty yet remained unratified for more than twenty years. It constituted the period when Americans flocked to the Isle in the belief that they were colonizing a new territory for the United States. Sovereignty over the Isle remained an open diplomatic question stemming from Article VI of the Platt Amendment, which read: "That the Isle of Pines shall be omitted from the proposed constitutional boundaries of Cuba, the title thereto being left to future adjustment by treaty." U.S. entrepreneurs widely interpreted this clause as proof that the U.S. government would eventually annex the Isle. After the

Hay-Quesada treaty made clear the Roosevelt administration's disinterest, settlers lobbied the U.S. Senate to reject it.

Settlers' steadfast belief that the Isle should become U.S. territory affected not only their attitudes toward the U.S. government – Washington's general disinterest had them feeling misled and abandoned – but also their relationship with *pineros*. Americans resented submitting to Cuban authority, which they largely viewed as ineffective (at best) or illegitimate. By virtue of their nationality and status as prime property holders and employers, many settlers presumed the top rung on the social hierarchy. *Pinero* officials, meanwhile, chafed at settlers' contempt toward them. Many were locals of Spanish descent or transplants from mainland Cuba who often had more wealth and property than some of the Americans who looked down on them. The incongruity frustrated them.

Nevertheless, during this period, U.S. settlers and entrepreneurs were indeed the most significant drivers of the Isle's economy. Many estimates suggest that Americans owned most of the Isle's arable land and they introduced commercial, export-oriented farming. Despite the Isle's rapid Americanization, settlers socially isolated themselves from the rest of the island's population. Documented instances of relationships or marriages between Americans and native Cubans or other foreign nationals were few. Americans tended to socialize only with other Americans, lived in towns founded by or consisting of mostly U.S. citizens, and resisted learning local customs, such as speaking Spanish.

The second era, 1925 to 1960, proved markedly different. With the Hay-Quesada treaty ratified and the sovereignty question resolved, the U.S. presence on the Isle was less overt, in terms of both population and influence. By 1925, most Americans had returned to the United States. The U.S. population on the Isle fell from a high of around 2,000 settlers in 1914 to fewer than 400 by the early 1930s. They were discouraged by the end of the annexationist dream, widespread business failures, and property damage from periodic hurricanes. Some of these settlers remained until mid-century, when a new influx of Americans arrived. Many of these later newcomers were retirees, teachers, missionaries, and tourists who were far less interested in money-making entrepreneurial activities than their early-century forerunners.

Relations among Americans, Cubans, and other foreign nationals during this period were far less contentious, owing mostly to the resolution of the sovereignty issue. Indeed, the era saw a great deal more collaboration and social integration among the national groups, which included people not just from Cuba and the United States, but also from Jamaica, the Cayman Islands, Canada, England, Sweden, Germany, Hungary, China, and Japan. Economically, Americans found themselves in a less dominant position; Cuban entrepreneurs had taken up the mantle as the prime real estate brokers and economic drivers. Still, a significant number of Americans remained and retained economic, social, and cultural influence. As Cuban officials and entrepreneurs developed the tourist industry, they sought Americans as their primary foreign clients. Meanwhile, with the collapse of American colonization, remaining settlers lived much more closely among their Isle neighbors. The Isle's multinational population enjoyed a spirit of cooperation and cordiality that its denizens fondly recalled years later.

A Changing Nation

Although Cuban territory provides the setting, the story of Americans on the Isle of Pines sheds light on life in the United States, as well. The historiography of U.S. expansion generally posits that the United States expanded territorially in the nineteenth century and then focused exclusively on acquiring commercial markets overseas in the twentieth. This book illustrates that the delineation was not quite so neat. Rather, the U.S. experience on the Isle of Pines shows a blending of the two methods during the early twentieth century. Settlers' desires for U.S. annexation demonstrated that the zeal for territorial growth remained strong among some citizens. The rhetoric of Manifest Destiny – the 1840s justification for U.S. landed expansion – may have been passé by the turn of the century, but its last gasps were audible on the Isle of Pines. Landed expansion was not an end unto itself, however. Settlers and entrepreneurs also had a commercial incentive. It was not necessarily in search of foreign markets, as many turn-of-the-century U.S. policymakers and business leaders desired. Instead, U.S. migrants saw the Isle as a place to grow export commodities, with the United States as the preferred market. Annexation to the United States would have eliminated tariffs imposed on their goods. Although annexationists often couched their arguments in patriotic terms, their underlining motivation was to scale the prohibitive tariff wall that hurt their businesses.

Settlers' interest in the Isle also reveals middle-class Americans' discontent with conditions in the United States, though not necessarily with American life. At the dawn of the twentieth century, the United States was becoming a more urbanized and industrialized society dominated by corporations and oligarchs. Life on the Isle promised to preserve an idealized agrarian ethic, inspiring cooperation among settlers and rewarding individual hard work with improved standards of living. Most settlers were farmers from agricultural areas in the U.S. Northeast and Midwest. Landholding companies' literature heavily emphasized the so-called closing of the American frontier, suggesting that such opportunities to maintain traditional ways of life were becoming scarce. Moving to the Isle provided the opportunity not only to replicate American ways but to perfect them as well. To this end, settlers founded towns, created institutions, and developed an economy that reflected the values and customs they held most dear.

This story emphasizes the experiences of these non-state actors – that is, private citizens who did not formally represent the U.S. government – rather than policymakers. This approach illustrates two important elements. First, a view of grassroots-level engagements illuminates complexities in U.S.–Cuban relations that are not necessarily evident from the vantage point of state-to-state interactions. Settlers' views of Cubans were not monolithic and were greatly shaped by class and cultural distinctions. For example, many settlers expressed admiration for the Spanish-descended (i.e., white) landholding elite, praising them for their gentility. Such acclaim contrasted sharply to the negative views many Jim Crow-era whites held of the predominantly mixed-race population in mainland Cuba, a perspective that played a large part in eroding the long-held popular zeal for Cuban annexation. Nevertheless, settlers criticized these same *pinero* elites, many of whom were cattle ranchers, for their ineffective use of the land. To U.S. entrepreneurs, transforming the Isle into a land of export commodities proved that they had a more modern and sophisticated sensibility. This sense of hierarchy – with Americans at the top by virtue of their nationality and associated customs – also was evident in settlers' relationships with the Isle's working-class denizens. Americans who cultivated large groves or started their own businesses often turned to the local labor force to support their ventures. This dynamic reinforced a social hierarchy that placed settlers in a superior position vis-à-vis laborers by virtue of their status as employers and property owners. Working-class *pineros* tacitly embraced the U.S. presence. They worked on the farms and in the houses of U.S. landowners and enjoyed cordial relations with settlers. But they held some resentments. One was Americans' use of English-speaking Afro-Caribbean laborers. Although this trend was somewhat ironic given settlers' satisfaction with the Isle's (mostly white) racial makeup, the use of West Indian workers increased competition for unskilled work and depressed wages to the consternation of native-born *pineros*. The second resentment, which stretched across all classes of *pineros*, came from settlers' calls for U.S. annexation. Cubans generally accepted the introduction and proliferation of American capital, customs, and institutions, but they made clear their belief that the Isle of Pines was sovereign Cuban territory.

Second, emphasis on non-state actors also illustrates tensions in the U.S. imperial project at the turn of the century. In many important ways, private citizens carried out the work of U.S. expansion, as colonists, entrepreneurs, teachers, and missionaries. But in the case of the Isle of Pines, the U.S. government placed limits. As historian Emily Rosenberg has argued, the years between the 1890s and World War I were the era of the "promotional state," when government officials supported efforts to expand U.S. interests around the world while allowing private enterprise to take the initiative.[17] This encouragement included non-state actors' commercial endeavors on the Isle of Pines. The Roosevelt administration, however, displayed little zeal for further territorial expansion. Officials were discouraged by the insurgency in the newly acquired Philippines, uncomfortable with adding non-Anglo-Saxons to the national polity, and concerned about the global perception that it was behaving like a traditional European colonial power. As a result, it rejected annexationists' pleas. Settlers succeeded, however, in keeping the question alive for more than two decades. The annexationist debate pitting U.S. citizens against their own government illustrated tension among proponents of expansion about the most effective means for pursuing U.S. interests abroad. While non-state actors played an important part in shaping Washington's policy, that policy also affected their experience on the Isle.

The Settlers

U.S. settlers are the primary actors in this story. They were a mixed lot. Many first-generation settlers were small-scale entrepreneurs. It was not uncommon for settlers to sell their homes and possessions to finance the journey to the Isle and the land on which they moved. Another subgroup was large-scale farmers and businessmen, those who could afford to build a second home and return frequently to the United States. Although most U.S. citizens had left the Isle by the time the Hay-Quesada treaty was ratified, during the 1950s the Cuban government promoted the Isle as

---

[17] Emily Rosenberg, *Spreading the American Dream: American Economic and Cultural Expansion, 1890–1945* (New York: Hill and Wang, 1982).

a tourist destination and a new group of settlers entered. Many of these mid-century migrants were retirees and those looking for a winter home. There were also teachers and missionaries who worked at the American Central School. Unlike early-century settlers, this later generation was less concerned about acquiring wealth, starting businesses, or lobbying for landed expansion.

Estimates of the U.S. population on the Isle varied widely. Landholding companies and settlers tended to inflate the numbers to attract more U.S. investment. For example, one settler in 1906 reported to his local newspaper that 5,000 Americans lived on the Isle.[18] Cuban officials, particularly in the country's census, generally undercounted U.S. citizens because many of them were only part-year residents; most tallies numbered only a few hundred. U.S. consuls on the Isle, who were charged with registering U.S. citizens, consistently estimated 10,000 American landowners and roughly 2,000 settlers at the peak of U.S. involvement around 1914. As one consul noted, however, accurate counts of the U.S. population during the early twentieth century were based "entirely on guesswork" because of poor record keeping by both U.S. and Cuban officials.[19] Regardless of their precision, the number of U.S. settlers was significant considering that the 1899 census had counted only 3,199 people on the Isle.[20]

Settler backgrounds varied but certain similarities prevailed. Although migrants came from across the United States, the great majority originated in rural areas of the Northeast and Midwest. Many of the first-generation settlers came in clusters from the same towns: Fond du Lac, Wisconsin; Duluth, Minnesota; Watertown, Iowa; Penn Yan, New York. Settlers tended to be farmers or middle-class professionals such as salesmen or small business owners. The overwhelming majority were white Americans of European descent, including a significant number of those who were children of recent immigrants to the United States. There were a few African Americans, as well, but sources that speak to their experiences are scant.

---

[18] "Fertile Isle of Pines," *(Oshkosh) Daily Northwestern*, May 31, 1906.
[19] William Bardel to Wilbur J. Carr, December 5, 1918, 1910–29 Central Decimal File, General Records of the Department of State Relating to the Internal Affairs of Cuba, NARA Microcopy 488, Roll 27, File 837.014P/153.
[20] The Isle's population slowly increased over the years before spiking after the Cuban Revolution. There were 4,228 residents in 1919, 6,791 in 1931, and roughly 10,000 in 1959. According to the most recent Cuban census in 2002, the Isle had more than 86,000 residents.

Regardless of race, most settlers engaged in a rural, agrarian life-style, one that seemed to be vanishing as the pace of industrialization and urbanization quickened at the turn of the century. Their endeavors came at a time in which the spirit of "rebirth" permeated the American cultural ether. Historian T.J. Jackson Lears has argued that between the Civil War and World War I, "a widespread yearning for regeneration ... penetrated public life."[21] Such rhetoric was certainly evident among turn-of-the-century settlers and entrepreneurs. They often framed their excursions as opportunities to recapture a Jeffersonian society, one anchored by the independent-minded yeoman farmer who was at risk of disappearing along with the frontier in an over-civilized United States. To a generation scarred by depressions in each decade between 1870 and 1910, the opportunity to preserve such a way of life in what was potentially American territory was surely attractive.

The Isle offered not only social and cultural regeneration, but physical rejuvenation as well. Its warm climate – usually between seventy and ninety degrees Fahrenheit year-round – stood in stark contrast to the punishing winters that afflict the U.S. Northeast and Midwest. The Isle's abundant mineral springs and the absence of mosquito-borne illnesses endemic to other tropical locations made the Isle an ideal place to ease one's ailments. Some Americans who feared losing their U.S. citizenship because of their prolonged departure from the United States signed affidavits citing health issues as the primary reason for their lengthy foreign residency. One fourteen-year settler in 1921 wrote, "I suffered from laryngitis, bronchitis, and catarrh in the U.S. and am entirely free from these ailments while here." Another longtime resident of Nueva Gerona echoed those sentiments: "I suffered from rheumatism in my right arm while living in the United States and was unable to lift the arm.... I have been entirely free from these ailments since I came to the Isle of Pines."[22]

An element of adventure also attracted Americans to the Isle. This appeal came at a time when middle-class whites were mired in what historian Kristin L. Hoganson has called a "crisis of manhood."[23] Uneasy

[21] T.J. Jackson Lears, *Rebirth of a Nation: The Making of Modern America, 1877–1920* (New York: HarperCollins, 2009), 1.

[22] Affidavits of Fred W. Stiegele and Richard W. Nesbitt, respectively, contained in Nueva Gerona – Isle of Pines, Cuba, Vol. 24, Correspondence, 1921 – Part I, Record Group 84, NARA.

[23] Kristin L. Hoganson, *Fighting for American Manhood: How Gender Politics Provoked the Spanish-American and Philippine-American Wars* (New Haven, CT: Yale University Press, 1998), 12. See also Gail Bederman, *Manliness & Civilization: A Cultural History of Gender and Race in the United States, 1880–1917* (Chicago: University of Chicago Press, 1995).

with both the rise of women's political activism and competition from immigrants and African Americans for jobs and influence, white men generally sought out virile pursuits to reassert their dominance. As Hoganson has shown, one outlet for that anxiety was war. Another was living what Theodore Roosevelt famously referred to as "the strenuous life." U.S. promoters and travel writers piqued American men's interest in such action and excitement. For example, they often referred to the Isle as "Treasure Island," claiming somewhat speciously that it was the locale that had inspired the classic Robert Louis Stevenson novel of the same name. Some stories maintained that the Isle, a reputed pirate haven during the Spanish colonial era, was rife with buried treasure.[24] Although there were no credible reports of booty, the Isle nevertheless captured the imaginations of those who made the journey. As one descendant of a landholding company executive asked: "[W]ho of us is wholly immune to the siren voice; what snowbound, crabbed grocer cannot be lured to the land of the lotus-eater?"[25] While exuding a sense of wonderment about an unfamiliar land, the reference to Homer's "Odyssey" also revealed much about settler attitudes toward the Isle. It showed how settlers exoticized the land, suggested a view of *pineros* as simple and languid, and implied an abundance of the Isle's natural resources that would sustain those willing to take a chance there.

While most advertisements and opportunities were geared toward men, women were important participants in developing this American colony. They not only played supporting roles in the home as wives and mothers, but they also served as workers, teachers, missionaries, travel writers, club members, and delegates who lobbied the Cuban government for development and the U.S. government for annexation. Some women were enthusiastic agents of empire because it allowed them to step out of traditional domestic spheres. Others were less exuberant. But just as *pineros* and Cubans gained varying degrees of negotiating space within this hegemonic process, so too did women settlers.

At the start of the U.S. engagement on the Isle, some entrepreneurs claimed to be interested in commercially developing it not merely for their own benefit, but for that of the country as well. "Besides my friends

[24] For a brief synopsis of the pirate influence on the Isle, see Winsberg, "The Isle of Pines," 35–43, and Wright, *The Gem of the Caribbean*, 13–15. This trope still resonates in the twenty-first century, as shown in a November 2013 article in the British newspaper *The Guardian*: www.theguardian.com/travel/2013/nov/29/cuba-isla-de-la-juventud-diving (accessed May 1, 2016).

[25] Memorandum of Frederick Swetland Jr., March 7, 1961, 1, SFA.

and myself," one settler wrote in 1901, "there are a number of other American Citizens who have also invested their Capital in that Island, believing there would be no question but that our beloved Stars and Stripes would ever float over this most healthful and beautiful little Tropical Island."[26] As the comment intimated, nationalist sentiment often fed the annexationist argument. Some went so far as to suggest that settlers who did not sufficiently lobby for it were an "unpatriotic clique" while those who actively opposed the Hay-Quesada treaty were the "real Americans."[27] Although the annexationist debate revealed fissures within the American community, it also showed that patriotism was a driving force in compelling settlers to migrate to, invest in, and claim the Isle of Pines for the United States.

Colonial Connections

While colonization has long been a part of U.S. history, what happened on the Isle of Pines marked one of its rare instances in the twentieth century. Colonists made a prolonged effort to secure and develop new territory for the United States after the annexationist zeal had ebbed elsewhere. In most instances of nineteenth-century landed expansion – such as the Louisiana Purchase and the Mexican Cession – the United States had acquired the territory before its citizens migrated in appreciable numbers. Moreover, interest in the Isle was an example of colonization initiated at the grassroots level. In that sense, Americans' activities on the Isle of Pines resembled the filibusters of the nineteenth century. But they were different in significant ways. For example, rather than trying to conquer through force of arms, these colonizers invaded with private capital. As historian Robert May defines the term, filibusters were private ventures of conquest that had neither the explicit nor implicit permission of the federal government.[28] Those on the Isle, by contrast, received mixed signals from policymakers; some officials supported settlers' ventures, others

[26] Charles Raynard to Elihu Root, April 21, 1901, General Records, General Classified Files: 1898–1945, Box 72, Record 377, Record Group 350, NARA.

[27] T. J. Keenan to Philander Knox, January 30, 1913, 1910–29 Central Decimal File, General Records of the Department of State Relating to the Internal Affairs of Cuba, NARA Microcopy 488, Roll 27, File 837.014P/106; F. S. Hervey to Charles Evans Hughes, January 24, 1924, 1910–29 Central Decimal File, General Records of the Department of State Relating to the Internal Affairs of Cuba, NARA Microcopy 488, Roll 28, File 837.014P/231.

[28] Robert E. May, *Manifest Destiny's Underworld: Filibustering in Antebellum America* (Chapel Hill: University of North Carolina Press, 2002), preface.

vehemently opposed them. That powerbrokers even considered annexing the Isle of Pines, though, can largely be attributed to private citizens' actions and thus illustrates their substantial influence on U.S. policy.

During the Hay-Quesada era, when the Isle's sovereignty remained in question, those Americans who went to the Isle engaged in settler colonialism. The concept has become a burgeoning area of study that considers the phenomenon globally, not just in U.S. history. According to one of the field's leading theorists, Lorenzo Veracini, settler colonial studies examine "the permanent movement and reproduction of communities and the dominance of an exogenous agency over an indigenous one."[29] In such cases, settlers endeavor to establish a more ideal society, claim a "higher use" for the land they acquire (whether it be to uplift the local population or commodify natural resources), and presume a lastingness to their efforts.[30] These aspects were evident among Americans on the Isle, at least up to 1925.

Several important distinctions of this story, however, depart from settler colonial studies theory. First, such studies focus primarily on violence against indigenous societies in the conquest of land, the removal of native peoples, and the construction of new ethnic, national communities. Historian Walter L. Hixson, for example, emphasizes this aspect in his synthesis of U.S. settler colonial history.[31] Such violence was not evident on the Isle of Pines, though. In fact, rather than being run off the island, *pineros'* presence and accommodation as laborers, business associates, and land sellers was essential to the success of the American colony. Another key difference is the relationship with the metropole. In the case of the Isle, settlers' support from Washington was ambivalent, at best, despite their sustained lobbying. Tensions came not because there was too much metropolitan oversight and direction but rather because there was a lack of it. Finally, rather than establishing a permanent presence, American settler colonialism ultimately failed on the Isle of Pines. After the ratification of the Hay-Quesada treaty, the phenomenon morphed into another form of colonialism, one predicated less on settlement and more on commercial and cultural considerations.

---

[29] Lorenzo Veracini, *Settler Colonialism: A Theoretical Overview* (New York: Palgrave Macmillan, 2010), 3.

[30] Ibid., 4, 20, and Veracini, "Introducing Settler Colonial Studies," in *Settler Colonial Studies* 1 (2011): 6.

[31] Walter L. Hixson, *American Settler Colonialism: A History* (New York: Palgrave MacMillan, 2013).

Historically, Isle colonization efforts are also notable because they cut against a significant contemporaneous trend: migration *into* the United States. The early twentieth century featured a vast expansion in the number of foreign-born peoples in the United States, owing largely to improvements in transportation and the need for industrial labor. The case of the Isle of Pines presents a contrasting study: that of U.S. citizens emigrating *from* the United States in search of opportunity. These migrants, however, did not renounce their U.S. citizenship; indeed, some men even returned to the United States to volunteer for service during the world wars. Settlers instead maintained American customs as best they could and presumed the flag would eventually follow them. This pattern was not totally unique in U.S. history. Some nineteenth-century settlers had done likewise, most notably in the case of Texas when it still belonged to Mexico.[32]

U.S. settlement on the Isle of Pines was not a complete anomaly for its time. Other migrations were taking place in domestic and foreign locales. In the United States, migrations into Florida and California offer the clearest comparisons. In both instances, settlers from colder climates relocated to a place that offered warmer weather, improved health, and promises of wealth to those who engaged in agribusiness. Like the Isle, both states had their share of boosters that played on agrarian-oriented, middle-class Americans' fears of a closing frontier. These entrepreneurs pitched primarily to Northeast and Midwest audiences the prospect of a homogenous, republican society of equals, one defined by wealth, independence, and self-directed labor.[33] In Florida, where the land boom was contemporaneous to the Isle's, developers published brochures and travel books promoting the state's virtues, much like U.S.-based landholding companies had done for the Isle to entice settlers.[34] One account noted that Florida developers made an "extravagant use of advertising" that touted its climate and prospects for prosperity while portraying it "at once [as] the last frontier and the source of eternal growth."[35] One key

---

[32] Timothy J. Henderson, *A Glorious Defeat: Mexico and Its War with the United States* (New York: Hill and Wang, 2007), 24–101; William C. Davis, *Lone Star Rising: The Revolutionary Birth of the Texas Republic* (New York: Free Press, 2004), 54–76; David M. Pletcher, *The Diplomacy of Annexation: Texas, Oregon, and the Mexican War* (Columbia: University of Missouri Press, 1973), 64–88.

[33] Henry Knight, *Tropic of Hopes: California, Florida, and the Selling of American Paradise, 1869–1929* (Gainesville: University Press of Florida, 2013), 7–10.

[34] Samuel Proctor, "Prelude to the New Florida, 1877–1919," in *The New History of Florida*, Michael Gannon, ed. (Gainesville: University Press of Florida, 1996), 272.

[35] Homer B. Vanderblue, "The Florida Land Boom," *Journal of Land and Public Utility Economics* 3 (May 1927): 121–2.

difference between the Isle and Florida was that the Isle's land boom did not crash as infamously as Florida's. Whereas Isle settlers usually retained the land they bought even if they did not develop it, land in Florida typically was not held for long. As a result, the Florida real estate market suffered from overspeculation and outright fraud before it crashed in the mid-1920s. In California, meanwhile, most of the efforts were linked to the burgeoning citrus industry. Agents issued advertisements that promoted the warm climate, available land, and potential for profits to attract new growers using much of the same rhetoric as U.S. boosters of the Isle, though there is no evidence to suggest that these were the same entrepreneurs.[36]

Migration movements outside the continental United States also were taking place at the turn of the twentieth century. For example, Americans moved into Hawai'i and successfully secured annexation to the United States just as the Isle of Pines was entering the American consciousness. As on the Isle, U.S. settlers in Hawai'i – many of whom were descendants of missionaries who had arrived during the 1830s – were largely inspired by economic incentives, in that case to grow sugar and fruit on a commercial scale for sale to U.S. markets. To that end, U.S. settlers and investors lobbied for annexation primarily to eliminate the tariff placed on their goods, which similarly motivated Isle settlers.[37] The circumstances of U.S. settlement in Panama, meanwhile, were radically different. The United States had secured a 553-square-mile swath of territory – roughly half the size of the Isle of Pines – to build a trans-isthmus canal and filled the area with workers, technicians, support staff, security personnel, and their dependents, nearly 40,000 people in all. Like the Isle of Pines, Americans in Panama had a tremendous effect on the local population's politics, economy, society, and culture.[38] But Americans' presence there was sanctioned by the state and in service of a geostrategic interest;

[36] Studies that examine these promotions include Knight, *Tropic of Hopes*, Douglas Cazaux Sackman, *Orange Empire: California and the Fruits of Eden* (Berkeley: University of California Press, 2005), and Matt Garcia, *A World of Its Own: Race, Labor, and Citrus in the Making of Greater Los Angeles, 1900–1970* (Chapel Hill: University of North Carolina Press, 2001).

[37] Studies that explore U.S. settlement, annexation, and the social ramifications thereof in Hawai'i include Judy Rohrer, *Haoles in Hawai'i: Race and Ethnicity in Hawai'i* (Honolulu: University of Hawai'i Press, 2010) and Noenoe K. Silva, *Aloha Betrayed: Native Hawaiian Resistance to American Colonialism* (Durham, NC: Duke University Press, 2004).

[38] The study that most ably examines the depth of this influence is Michael E. Donoghue, *Borderland on the Isthmus: Race, Culture, and the Struggle for the Canal Zone* (Durham, NC: Duke University Press, 2014).

settlement was a secondary concern. Last, U.S. citizens were moving to Mexico in substantial numbers during this time. As historian John Mason Hart has shown, U.S.-based landholding companies bought vast tracts across Mexico and advertised available land to American audiences in much the same vein as U.S. pioneers on the Isle. Their work contributed to a flood of U.S. migration there that reached an estimated 40,000 settlers in 1910, some of whom renewed calls to annex Mexico, or at least portions thereof.[39] The turmoil and backlash arising from the ensuing Mexican Revolution, however, blocked further such expansion and U.S. influence, much like the Cuban Revolution would do a half-century later.

The Isle of Pines also was not the only place in Cuba where U.S. citizens migrated at the turn of the twentieth century. By 1920, Cuba featured dozens of distinct U.S. settlements, many of which were on or near sugar plantations.[40] Many U.S. settlements in the province of Oriente closely resembled those on the Isle. Colonies like Omaja, for example, featured American-run groves, schools, churches, stores, and hotels. The town of La Gloria in the province of Camagüey stood as the largest of these settlements. Boasting up to 1,000 Americans at its peak, this was one of the first U.S. settlements established after 1898, a time when annexation of all Cuba still appeared to be a distinct possibility. James M. Adams, who lived in the colony for six months in 1900, reported that settlers went to La Gloria for many of the same reasons others went to the Isle: to enjoy a warmer, healthier climate amid a picturesque landscape; to start up citrus groves and plantations for profit; and to create local institutions to solidify a U.S. presence. They also had similar experiences. Settlers in both locations struggled with the lack of material comforts, had to improvise as a result of a poor infrastructure, and suffered through swarms of insects. They also established cordial relations with the local population that was largely considered docile and friendly.[41]

The Isle of Pines, however, differed from other U.S. settlements in Cuba in three important respects. First, Americans on the Isle were

---

[39] John Mason Hart, *Empire and Revolution: The Americans in Mexico since the Civil War* (Berkeley: University of California Press, 2002), 167–267.

[40] Carmen Diana Deere, "Here Come the Yankees! The Rise and Decline of United States Colonies in Cuba, 1898–1930," *Hispanic American Historical Review* 78 (November 1998): 729–65; José Vega Suñol, *Norteamericanos en Cuba: Estudio Etnohistórico* (La Habana: Fundación Fernando Ortiz, 2004), 50–84.

[41] James M. Adams, *Pioneering in Cuba: A Narrative of the Settlement of La Gloria, the First American Colony in Cuba, and the Early Experiences of the Pioneers* (Concord, NH: Rumford Press, 1901).

concentrated closely together rather than spread out as was the case in mainland Cuba. By 1919, the Cuban census showed that the Isle had the second-most U.S.-born citizens living in its municipality, behind only the province of Havana.[42] Although U.S. colonies on the Isle usually had no more than 100 people per town, the next settlement was within a reasonable distance, normally within five to ten miles. Towns developed their own identities, even with a hint of rivalry among some settlements. But Americans from different towns still socialized with relative ease, thanks to a common language, heritage, and interests, which, in turn, reinforced their national identity. Second, settlers came to the Isle believing it was or would soon become U.S. territory. It was a key selling point for the land-holding companies. Many settlers struggling financially during the early years persevered in the hopes that the Isle would become U.S. territory. Finally, the duration of the U.S. presence set it apart from other colonies in Cuba. Most U.S. colonies in Oriente began to dissipate after 1917 because of Cuban political instability, property damage from hurricanes, and prohibitive tariffs on exports to the United States.[43] U.S. citizens on the Isle faced similar challenges, especially with hurricanes and tariffs. But they retained a considerable presence, albeit in fewer numbers, until the Cuban Revolution. Americans maintained many of the customs and ways of life they had enjoyed in the United States, and they were still a significant economic, social, and cultural force by the time Fidel Castro came to power.

Many private U.S. citizens at the turn of the twentieth century looked to the Isle of Pines as a place of opportunity – to advance their economic standing, to preserve an agrarian way of life, to improve their health, to display their patriotism, and to find adventure. Given the U.S. government's lukewarm attitude toward the Isle, though, private entrepreneurs were the primary drivers of this interest. They did so by appealing to rural and middle-class Americans' hopes and fears, shaping the discourse and expectations of what settlers were to find in an alien land. These promotional efforts generated enough attention, investment, and settlement to produce a nearly sixty-year presence of what would become a forgotten colony of Americans.

---

[42] *Census of the Republic of Cuba, 1919* (Havana: 1920).
[43] Deere, "Here Come the Yankees!" 764.

PART ONE

THE HAY-QUESADA ERA

I

Promoting a New Frontier

Like other elected officials at the turn of the twentieth century, Sen. Orville Platt fielded many inquiries from his constituents about Cuba. U.S. entrepreneurs had been interested in the island dating back to the eighteenth century. With Cuba as an independent state under the watchful eye of the United States, opportunities for commercial prosperity seemed ripe for enterprising Americans. Eager to take advantage of the situation, W. H. Putnam of Bridgeport, Connecticut, wrote his senator to ask for advice about living and investing in Cuba. Platt was familiar with Cuban affairs. As chairman of the Senate Committee on Relations with Cuba, he was the sponsor of the so-called Platt Amendment that had made Cuba a U.S. protectorate. Although Platt favored close commercial ties between the United States and Cuba, he was tepid about middle-class entrepreneurs' prospects for success; he surmised that only financiers with large amounts of cash could prosper. But Platt recognized that U.S. businessmen already engaged there were working to get other Americans to follow their lead. "This new phase of business which is called 'promotion' seems to be the popular one with regard to Cuba just now," he wrote.[1]

That "promotion" was especially evident on the Isle of Pines. At the dawn of the twentieth century, U.S.-owned companies advertised throughout the United States to entice Americans to buy land. As with any good sales pitch, these landholding companies accentuated the Isle's attractive features while minimizing, or altogether ignoring, factors that

---

[1] Platt to Putnam, December 5, 1904, Orville Platt Papers, Box 2, Official Correspondence: 1900–1905 – Various Subjects, Vol. 1, 190, Record Group 69, CSL. Putnam's professional background is not clear from the correspondence.

complicated the picture. Later experiences would bear out that companies often exaggerated physical, political, commercial, and social conditions to enhance the Isle's appeal. These enterprises, however, insisted that their descriptions were not too good to be true. "Mindful of the fact that exaggerations and misleading statements are all too frequent in the average prospectus," the Cleveland-based San Juan Heights Land Company wrote, "it is the purpose here to be conservative." This from a company that referred to the Isle as "A Veritable Garden of Eden."[2]

Among Cubans, particularly in Havana, the Isle of Pines largely was viewed as a backwater. In the 1890s, it was home to only about 3,000 people, mostly cattle ranchers, wage workers, and subsistence farmers. To American entrepreneurs, however, the Isle seemed something else: an opportunity. Shortly after the War of 1898, U.S. businessmen began buying tens of thousands of acres from Spanish and Cuban landowners. These businessmen then subdivided the land into smaller parcels with the aim of reselling it at modest prices that would appeal to middle-class Americans.

Much of the Isle's promotional literature reflected white Americans' changing attitudes toward the tropics around the turn of the twentieth century. As Catherine Cocks has shown, popular racist beliefs that the tropics were places of disease, sloth, and moral degeneracy gave way to new considerations of these regions as areas of opportunity and rejuvenation.[3] Boosters, entrepreneurs, and tourism promoters drove this shift, which was evident in the ways landholding companies portrayed the Isle of Pines. They framed the Isle in four ways. First, they described the Isle as an exotic tropical paradise. This allure included not only the promotion of the year-round warm climate and proximity to beaches, but also its mythology as a colonial-era pirate haven. By implication, the Isle was laden with riches, both figuratively (in the form of its agricultural potential) and literally (buried treasure).

Second, companies depicted the Isle as attainable and tamable by Americans who were willing to work hard. Its relative proximity to the United States gave the comforting impression that something so alien and exotic was actually close to home. Moreover, companies often portrayed *pineros* as pliable. They described *pineros* as unsophisticated, yet lauded them for being courteous, welcoming to foreigners, and a source

[2] San Juan Heights Land Company, "The Isle of Pines: The Garden Spot of the World" (Cleveland, OH, 1914), 7, 1.

[3] Catherine Cocks, *Tropical Whites: The Rise of the Tourist South in the Americas* (Philadelphia: University of Pennsylvania Press, 2013).

of inexpensive labor that could help settlers convert their land into groves and farms.

Third, the Isle offered physical and financial rejuvenation. Companies hailed the mineral springs for their healing powers and cited the warm climate as a place to recuperate from chronic illness. Developers also stressed that the Isle was free from the tropical diseases prevalent in other Caribbean islands, including mainland Cuba. Financially, the Isle promised to be a place where Americans could make their fortune, either through investment in the landholding companies or moving to the Isle to start their own farms or businesses. Advertisements depicted the Isle as "the modern El Dorado," the mythological city of gold that Spanish explorers had searched for in South America.[4] Such promises of wealth surely resonated during an era of economic boom and bust.

Finally, the Isle of Pines promised a new frontier for U.S. expansion. The 1890s signaled the so-called closing of the frontier in the U.S. West. The Isle was depicted as a means to revive territorial expansion. Many companies and settlers harkened back to the pioneer spirit of the nineteenth century. For example, one letter-writer to the *New York Times*, who claimed to have lived on the Isle for ten years, asserted that Americans who settled there were akin to those who went west during the Gold Rush and "fought a fight against tremendous odds of distance and nature that will compare most favorably with what our old Forty-niners did in years gone by."[5]

These elements helped frame U.S. perceptions of the Isle for the next half-century and spurred Americans to settle and invest there. Private companies and individuals, rather than officials and policymakers, drove this phenomenon. Military reports were typically lukewarm about the Isle's prospects for U.S. interests. While recognizing that the Isle had modest potential for agricultural commodities and tourism, such reports also downplayed its capability to sustain a military base, which curbed U.S. officials' enthusiasm. The potential for commercial growth, however, lured private U.S. entrepreneurs who communicated that promise through advertisements aimed at middle-class Americans. Their message helped inspire as many as 10,000 Americans to buy property there – some 2,000 of whom may have owned a residence – and ushered in a U.S. presence and influence on the Isle that endured for more than sixty years.

---

[4] The Isle of Pines Investment Company, "The Pineland Bulletin" (Cleveland, OH, 1908), 4–5.
[5] J. Earl Finnigan, "Whose Isle of Pines?" *New York Times*, February 11, 1923.

Entering the American Consciousness

Although U.S. interest in Cuba had existed for years – Benjamin Franklin and Alexander Hamilton had called for increased commercial ties going back to the eighteenth century – the Isle of Pines had not attracted much attention in the United States. That changed during Cuba's War of Independence, particularly after an uprising in Nueva Gerona on July 26, 1896, in one of the rare instances of combat on the Isle during the conflict.[6] Seventeen-year-old Evangelina Cossio, whose father had been sent to the Isle for helping Cuban *insurrectos* the year before, led a revolt of other exiled rebels against a Spanish garrison. Their hope was to quell the small Spanish force by capturing the Isle's governor, Lt. Col. José Bérriz, and secure passage to the main island to rejoin the rebellion. Despite briefly detaining Bérriz by using Cossio as bait (the colonel was said to be infatuated with her), the uprising ultimately failed. Cossio was sent to a women's prison in Havana, where she remained for the next year. That is, until her story caught the attention of renowned publisher William Randolph Hearst and the U.S. press. Cossio's tale was widely reported to American audiences, more so after Hearst's correspondents freed her from jail and whisked her to the United States in October 1897. Her exploits attracted widespread sympathy, in large part because of the powerful gendered dimensions to her story. While often portrayed as brave and patriotic, akin to a modern-day Joan of Arc, her femininity was unquestioned. Described as attractive and delicate – the *New York Times* referred to her as "picturesquely beautiful"[7] – she also exemplified the perfect damsel-in-distress, rebuffing the unwanted advances of Bérriz and languishing in Spanish captivity. Much of this sympathy also resonated in U.S. support for the cause of *Cuba Libre*, particularly evident in political cartoons of the day that personified Cuba as a threatened female.[8] Cossio's notoriety and her story's setting helped to introduce the Isle to Americans.

[6] Details taken from the following syntheses: Louis A. Pérez Jr., *Cuba in the American Imagination: Metaphor and the Imperial Ethos* (Chapel Hill: University of North Carolina Press, 2008), 77–80; Jane McManus, *Cuba's Island of Dreams: Voices from the Isle of Pines and Youth* (Gainesville: University Press of Florida, 2000), 6–16; Kristin L. Hoganson, *Fighting for American Manhood: How Gender Politics Provoked the Spanish-American and Philippine-American Wars* (New Haven, CT: Yale University Press, 1998), 58–61; Wiltse Peña Hijuelos, et al., *Con Todo Derecho: Isla de la Juventud* (La Habana, 1986), 33–5; Antonio Núñez Jiménez, *Isla de Pinos: Piratas, Colonizadores, Rebeldes* (La Habana: Editorial Arte y Literatura, 1976), 525–38.

[7] "Senorita Cisnero's Tale," *New York Times*, August 25, 1897.

[8] For examples, see Pérez, *Cuba in the American Imagination*, chapter 2, and John J. Johnson, *Latin America in Caricature* (Austin: University of Texas Press, 1980), 72–95.

Once the United States formally entered the conflict against Spain in 1898, the Isle of Pines proved only a minor theater of operations. One colonel suggested using the Isle to hold Spanish prisoners of war because it would require a minimum of resources to guard and maintain them.[9] Although the U.S. military did not pursue such a policy, the Isle posed a source of some concern as a base for blockade runners. U.S. newspapers noted that the Isle served as a station from which smugglers could evade the U.S. naval perimeter around Cuba because warships were too big to patrol the shallow waters of the Gulf of Batabanó between the Isle and mainland Cuba.[10] This anxiety did not last long, however, as U.S. Marines captured the Isle in August 1898 when Spanish forces on site surrendered after light resistance.[11]

With control of the Isle – indeed, all of Cuba – secure by the end of summer, the U.S. military began producing on-site reports about conditions there. Although the military informed U.S. officials, such as Secretary of War Elihu Root, that the Isle offered little strategic utility for the United States, these studies also suggested potential commercial benefits. The first of these reports came in November 1898, when a three-man military delegation spent four days on the Isle. Upon arrival, the group reported an emotional reception of "nearly the whole male population of [Nueva Gerona], about 350 people, who were most enthusiastic in their greeting, shouting 'Viva la Comission Americana,' 'Viva Cuba Libre,' etc., waving their hats, throwing themselves into each other's arms and fairly going wild with enthusiasm."[12] The report offered few demographic details

---

[9] Col. C. C. Byrne to Surgeon-General, U.S. Army, May 11, 1898, in *Isle of Pines: Papers Relating to the Adjustment of Title to the Ownership of the Isle of Pines*, 68th Cong., 2d sess., 1924, S. Doc. 166, 177–8.

[10] "Havana Fed from Progreso," *New York Times*, June 21, 1898.

[11] "Marines Will Capture the Isle of Pines," *New York American*, August 11, 1898; "Move Against Havana," *Tacoma Daily News*, August 12, 1898. The only first-person account of combat came from a published letter that indicated the USS *Maple* had engaged in a firefight against resistance near Siguanea Bay. "Walter Hiatt – Writes an Interesting Letter from Isle of Pines," *Lexington Morning Herald*, August 16, 1898. Some Cuban historians have noted that the United States secured the Isle by positioning two ships at the mouth of the Río Las Casas to block the main port of Nueva Gerona. Roberto Únger Pérez, et al., *Americanos en la Isla* (Nueva Gerona: Ediciones El Abra, 2004), 11; Peña Hijuelos, et al., *Con Todo Derecho*, 35. One report stated that Gen. Nelson Miles wanted to invade the Isle in July to move against blockade runners. But President William McKinley and Secretary of War Russell Alger rejected the plan, presumably to focus on taking Santiago in eastern Cuba, which proved the decisive conflict in the Cuban theater. "Alger's Story of the War," *New York Times*, December 3, 1898.

[12] Maj. William E. Almy, et al., to Brig. Gen. J. W. Clous, November 25, 1898, in *Isle of Pines*, 68th Cong., 2d sess., 1924, S. Doc. 166, 179–80.

about the Isle's people but rather focused on resources and military utility. The delegation noted the Isle's limited potential for agriculture – "The soil is not rich, being sandy and arid, the country resembling somewhat the scrub-oak country of the Indian Territory or Wyoming" – but also its abundance of timber, marble quarries, and medicinal springs.[13] It also suggested that the Isle might be a good way station for U.S. troops to acclimatize them to tropical conditions.

Gen. Fitzhugh Lee, U.S. consul general in Havana before the war and nephew of famed Gen. Robert E. Lee, offered another report in February 1899 after a four-day trip to the Isle. He was more skeptical about the Isle's utility. "The Isle of Pines is disappointing in its appearance, [the] number of its inhabitants, and the fertility of its soil."[14] Although tobacco and timber might be good export products, sugar – one of the principal export crops in Cuba – did not grow well on the Isle, at least in the abundance it would take to be profitable. Nor were the marble quarries quite as promising as the November 1898 report had indicated. Moreover, Lee questioned the placing of U.S. military personnel on the Isle considering the slow speeds of the shallow-water boats that could travel between the Isle and mainland Cuba.[15]

Later that month, Capt. Frederick Foltz made a three-week visit to the Isle. His subsequent report provided the most detailed description of the Isle during the three-and-a-half-year U.S. military occupation of Cuba. Foltz found the Isle disorganized with a poor infrastructure owing to a Spanish-era tax structure in which only about one-fourth of the money collected had been reinvested locally. "As a consequence," Foltz wrote, "the bridges are in need of repair, the schools are closed, the clerks [are] living from hand to mouth without any remuneration."[16] Economically, Foltz suggested that the Isle held some promise for its agricultural commodities. He predicted that tobacco had the best chance for export success. But he saw another industry as having even more potential: "The exploitation of the island as a sanitary resort is, however, the enterprise which seems to promise the greatest return to the capitalist, as well as

---

[13] Ibid., 180.
[14] Lee to Adna Chafee, February 9, 1899, in *Isle of Pines*, 68th Cong., 2d sess., 1924, S. Doc. 166, 185.
[15] Lee's trip to the Isle was reported in U.S. newspapers, suggesting U.S. audiences were aware of activity on the Isle. For example, see "Lee on a Visit," *Birmingham Age-Herald*, February 7, 1899.
[16] Foltz to Lt. Col. Tasker H. Bliss, February 22, 1899, in *Isle of Pines*, 68th Cong., 2d sess., 1924, S. Doc. 166, 192.

the greatest benefit to the island itself."[17] In the months that followed, U.S. entrepreneurs took up Foltz's suggestion, indicating that business-men were closely attuned to these reports.[18]

The following year, Capt. H. J. Slocum reported substantial progress on the Isle in terms of civil society and the local economy, but with still more room for improvement. He stated that health and order in Nueva Gerona were "excellent," with clean streets and neat schools – "much better than any I have seen on the island of Cuba."[19] Yet infrastructure remained poor, particularly roads and bridges that were still in disre-pair. Slocum's report also hinted at divisions among Cubans on the Isle, particularly officials against the general population. On one hand, he noted "some feeling on the part of the people about the alcalde [mayor] and some of the officials not being the people of the isle, these officials having been sent to the island from Cuba."[20] Yet "the alcalde informed me that the people are very lazy. I learned incidentally that they won't even raise their own garden truck or catch their own fish." After not-ing that the local police in Santa Fe had not made an arrest for more than four months – and even that was for public drunkenness – Slocum stated, "From all appearances the people were too lazy even to get into trouble."[21] Slocum concluded his report with a generally positive reflec-tion about the Isle and its economic potential: "From all I saw on the island I am satisfied that it is capable of being quite productive, there being immense mountains of marble and fine timberland, and the warm springs and abundance of excellent cold water make it attractive as a health resort."[22] Such optimism foreshadowed some of the promotional literature that landholding companies developed in the ensuing years.

Spreading the Word

Reports assessing the Isle's commercial potential coincided with linger-ing questions about the status of Cuba after the War of 1898 and stoked renewed calls for formal annexation to the United States. Throughout the

---

[17] Ibid., 194.

[18] For example, Foltz's inspection was reported in "The Isle of Pines," *Boston Evening Transcript*, March 23, 1901.

[19] Slocum to Adjutant-General, April 20, 1900, in *Isle of Pines*, 68th Cong., 2d sess., 1924, S. Doc. 166, 169.

[20] Ibid., 170.

[21] Ibid., 171.

[22] Ibid., 171–2.

nineteenth century, U.S. policymakers had looked to Cuba as a potential addition to the Union. Thomas Jefferson once wrote, "Cuba's addition to our confederacy is exactly what is wanting to round our power as a nation to the point of its utmost interest."[23] During the height of Manifest Destiny, the U.S. government made two bids to purchase Cuba from Spain: the James K. Polk administration offered $100 million for it in 1848; six years later, the Franklin Pierce administration increased the bid to $130 million.[24] But Spain refused to sell, partly because of Cuba's profitability, partly out of a sense of national pride as Cuba, the "ever faithful isle," was one of the last remnants of Spain's vast empire in the Western Hemisphere. With Spain out of the picture after 1898, the notion of Cuba's formal incorporation within the United States seemed ripe for reconsideration.

Such ideas continued throughout 1899 despite the passage of the Teller Amendment the year before, as well as the formal signing of the Treaty of Paris ending hostilities between the United States and Spain. The Teller Amendment, attached to the U.S. declaration of war against Spain, stated that the United States would not exercise sovereignty over Cuba but would merely maintain control over it until its "pacification" was secured and it became ready for self-government. Specific benchmarks for what constituted pacification or readiness for self-government, however, were left vague. Likewise, the wording of Article II of the Treaty of Paris led some to question whether the Isle of Pines rightfully belonged to the United States. It stated: "Spain cedes to the United States the island of Porto Rico and other islands now under Spanish sovereignty in the West Indies." Confusion persisted, both publicly and privately, which led some Americans to address the question directly to U.S. officials.

One of the earliest inquiries about sovereignty and settlement came from a private citizen in Philadelphia, Philip Kern, who requested a land grant in order to found a colony on the Isle. Kern had read that the U.S. government was preparing such grants for U.S. citizens.[25] Although reports about impending grants may have been exaggerated, stories about the Isle of Pines had been appearing in newspapers across the country since the summer of 1898. Kern's hometown newspaper, *The Philadelphia*

[23] Jefferson to James Monroe, June 23, 1823, in *The Writings of Thomas Jefferson*, H. A. Washington, ed., Vol. 7 (Washington, DC: Riker, Thorne, 1854), 300.

[24] Louis A. Pérez Jr. *The War of 1898: The United States and Cuba in History and Historiography* (Chapel Hill: University of North Carolina Press, 1998), 5.

[25] Philip Kern to Sen. Boies Penrose, February 3, 1899, General Records, General Classified Files: 1898–1945, Box 73, Record 393, Record Group 350, NARA.

Inquirer, published a feature-length piece about sunken pirate ships laden with gold and silver lying off the Isle's coast, reinforcing the "Treasure Island" mythology.[26] A widely published travel article that first appeared in the *New Haven Journal* reflected such exotic visions. The uncredited writer described the weather as "near absolute perfection," which helped with chronic illness. Aside from the nuisance of "Fleas, roaches, spiders, a thousand wriggling, crawling, stinging creatures [that] beset you continually," the writer portrayed the Isle as a tropical paradise. He continued by stating that "The natives of Isla de los Pinos [are] a simple, kind-hearted people, whose greatest pleasure seems to be chatting with strangers and listening to their accounts of the outer world.... The young children go about entirely naked and the universal innocence, combined with the utmost dignity and punctilious courtesy, is charming to behold."[27]

These depictions attracted U.S. citizens' attention. Many of them wrote to officials asking for more information about the Isle. Writers often operated from the assumption that the Isle of Pines was U.S. territory acquired from Spain, not a part of the political body of Cuba.[28] They asked for reports about the Isle, including details about its native population, topography, climate, and availability of land. Initially, individuals independently wrote these letters. But as more Americans were settling on the Isle, letter-writing campaigns became coordinated efforts, looking less for information about the Isle and more to express arguments on behalf of annexation. For example, in April 1901, Charles Raynard, who

---

[26] "Millions and Millions of Treasure," *Philadelphia Inquirer*, January 15, 1899. Similar stories continued to emerge a decade later. For example, a travel writer told the story of a "Mr. Johnson of Pennsylvania" who had come to the Isle in the 1880s. He obtained a treasure map from one of the last surviving pirates and found two barrels of gold on the sparsely inhabited South Coast. After evading Spanish authorities, he made his way back to Pennsylvania with his riches. Frederic J. Haskin, "The Real Treasure Island," *The State (Columbia, SC)*, January 20, 1909.

[27] "Isle of Pines," *Butte Weekly Miner*, September 15, 1898. Reprinted from *New Haven Journal*. Other contemporary travel articles in popular national magazines portrayed the Isle in a similar light. John Huston Finley, "The Isle of Pines," *Scribner's* 33 (1903): 174–81; "The Isle of Pines," *National Geographic* 17 (1906): 105–8.

[28] Newspapers frequently reported that the Isle was or would become U.S. territory, undoubtedly shaping or reinforcing popular perceptions about the issue. For examples, see "Tiny Lands to be Marked 'U.S.'" *Kansas City Star*, August 30, 1898; "Belongs to the United States," *Grand Rapids Herald*, January 14, 1899; "The Isle of Pines," *Duluth News-Tribune*, February 27, 1899; "An Isle of Pines Colony," *Kansas City Star*, March 13, 1899; "Isle of Pines," *Dallas Morning News*, August 6, 1899; "The Isle of Pines Is Ours," *Kansas City Star*, November 27, 1900; "To Hold the Isle of Pines," *(Oshkosh) Daily Northwestern*, November 27, 1900; "Isle of Pines Will Be Retained," *Fort Worth Morning Register*, November 28, 1900.

had bought land on the Isle and later formed the American Club there, wrote to Secretary of War Root lobbying for the United States to maintain possession of the Isle. He noted that he and some friends already had invested $25,000 there with the understanding it was to be U.S. territory and that others were doing likewise.[29] Over the next month, at least four other men submitted letters offering virtually the same points, suggesting a coordinated effort. These letter-writing campaigns began at roughly the same time that American entrepreneurs started pooling their resources to form landholding companies, which quickly were becoming the dominant brokers on the Isle.

Enter the Landholding Companies

The first U.S. citizens to buy land on the Isle of Pines were individuals, acquiring property for themselves by the tens or hundreds of acres. Claims regarding the first U.S. property owner on the Isle are in dispute. Journalist Irene A. Wright, a contemporary of the era, wrote that C. M. Johnson was the first American to buy land on the Isle; he had an option for 17,500 acres in Santa Rosalia in March 1901.[30] Another scholar has contended that Johnson was the first U.S. settler after the War of 1898, but that Capt. H. Haemal in 1899 was the first American to receive title to land, in Los Indios.[31] Neither writer provided sources for their information. The first American on record to have bought land on the Isle was Henry Haener, who purchased 133 acres for $250 in July 1900.[32]

U.S. records indicate that no other Americans bought land on the Isle until after the United States passed the Platt Amendment in March 1901. Best known as the U.S. congressional act that made Cuba a protectorate of the United States and gave the United States the right to a naval base in Cuba, the Platt Amendment also contained a clause regarding the Isle of Pines. Article VI stated that the Isle was to be omitted from the constitutional boundaries of Cuba and that sovereignty would be determined by a future treaty. While Root is often credited as the progenitor of the

[29] Raynard to Root, April 21, 1901, General Records, General Classified Files: 1898–1945, Box 72, Record 377, Record Group 350, NARA.

[30] Irene A. Wright, *Isle of Pines* (Beverly, MA: Beverly Printing Company, 1910), 44.

[31] F. A. Carlson, "American Settlement in the Isla de Pinos, Cuba," *Geographical Review* 32 (January 1942): 28.

[32] Herbert G. Squiers to John Hay, March 18, 1903, in *Isle of Pines*, 68th Cong., 2d sess., 1924, S. Doc. 166, 189. An American-owned, English-language newspaper referred to him as Henry Haenel and claimed he was "the first American to buy land on the Isle of Pines" in Los Indios. "Oldest Oldtimer Returns," *Isle of Pines Post*, August 15, 1930.

Platt Amendment, Sen. Orville Platt, the amendment's titular sponsor, privately took credit for Article VI. Although Platt believed that the Isle was part of Cuba and not among the islands ceded to the United States from Spain, he argued that it held great value as a potential naval base and should be purchased. "I inserted a clause to the effect that the title should be subject of treaty negotiations," he wrote in 1902. "I feel that it is of the utmost importance that it shall be ours. It will give us the most advantageous point from which to defend the entrance of the isthmian canal."[33] To Americans interested in the Isle, Platt's clause seemed a signal that the Isle would one day formally become U.S. territory and spurred further U.S. investment.

This development greatly concerned many *pineros*. Some took their pleas to Havana. Just a month after Cuban independence was established in May 1902, the Isle's *alcalde* and *ayuntamiento* (town council) sent a letter to Cuban President Tomás Estrada Palma. Referring to themselves as "good Cubans," the writers, supported by the signatures of more than 170 *pineros*, argued that leaving the Isle's sovereignty in question undermined Cuba's territorial integrity. Moreover, they argued that if incorporated by the United States, *pineros* risked losing their customs, laws, and even their religion. They implored Estrada Palma not to let that calamity happen.[34] When given the opportunity, some *pineros* voiced their opinion directly to U.S. officials. In the spring of 1900, a U.S. officer on routine inspection spoke with local authorities concerned about U.S. designs. According to the report, the officials "expressed a strong preference toward belonging to the island of Cuba if any issue should arise."[35]

Large landowning Cubans, however, welcomed the prospect of a greater U.S. presence because it created a market for real estate that had been virtually nonexistent during the colonial era. *Hacendados* owned most of the land in estates that had been passed down or divided over generations since the seventeenth century. U.S. entrepreneurs' post-1898 interest in land gave Spanish and Cuban landowners reason to sell.

[33] Platt to J. C. Lenney, November 5, 1902, in *Isle of Pines*, 68th Cong., 2d sess., 1924, S. Doc. 166, 285. In an undated handwritten draft of the amendment, one version states that "there shall be secured to the United States the following rights and privileges: One, a recognition of the title of the United States to the Isle of Pines." Record Group 69, Orville Platt Papers, Box 2, Official Correspondence: 1900–1905 – Various Subjects, 11, CSL.

[34] Juan M. Sánchez, et al., to Tomás Estrada Palma, June 30, 1902, Secretaria de la Presidencia, 1902–1958, Legajo 75, Expediente 66, ANC.

[35] Capt. H. J. Slocum to Adjutant-General, April 20, 1900, *Isle of Pines*, 68th Cong., 2d sess., 1924, S. Doc. 166, 170.

Although undeveloped land sold for only about $2 an acre, *hacendados* earned a tidy sum by selling in large quantities, often by the thousands or tens of thousands of acres.[36] José M. Tarafa was one such *hacendado*. Before the U.S. Senate passed the Platt Amendment, Tarafa, who claimed to own up to 40,000 acres on the Isle, wrote to Root to ask him to clear up the ambiguity over the Isle's sovereignty. "You will readily understand how important it is to me, as the largest landowner on the Isle of Pines, to know under what flag that island is going to remain," he wrote. "I hesitate before investing more capital in my estates on the Isle of Pines until I can know how this matter stands."[37] Two years later, Tarafa sold an indeterminate number of acres to American buyers for $38,000.[38]

Those transactions were just the beginning. According to U.S. Minister to Cuba Herbert G. Squiers, Americans spent more than $265,000 to acquire property on the Isle between March 1901 and March 1903.[39] Landholding companies made a great majority of these purchases. American entrepreneurs in the Northeast and the Midwest formed these businesses and bought land by the tens of thousands of acres, then subdivided the land into smaller parcels, usually ten-, twenty-, or forty-acre plots, for resale at up to $50 an acre for undeveloped land. These companies became the predominant marketers of real estate on the Isle of Pines during the early twentieth century.

---

[36] Estimates of land prices taken from Academia de Ciencias de Cuba, "Serie Isla de Pinos No. 23: Latifundismo y Especulación," Delfín Rodríguez, et al., eds. (La Habana, 1968), 4.

[37] Tarafa to Root, August 10, 1900, General Records, General Classified Files, 1898–1945, Box 72, Record 377, Record Group 350, NARA.

[38] *Isle of Pines*, 68th Cong., 2d sess., 1924, S. Doc. 166, 198. In September 1902, Tarafa made a $30,000 transaction with the Almacigos Springs Land Co. He made four additional $2,000 transactions with individuals, including Robert I. Wall and C. M. Johnson, both of whom were involved with landholding companies. Tarafa's land deals would not be his last transactions with U.S. entrepreneurs. He was one of the leading railroad magnates in Cuba and in the 1920s merged his Cuba Northern Railroad with the U.S.-based Cuba Company that virtually monopolized the country's railways. Juan Carlos Santamarina, "The Cuba Company and the Creation of Informal Business Networks: Historiography and Archival Sources," *Cuban Studies* 35 (2004): 75–6; Robert F. Smith, *The United States and Cuba: Business and Diplomacy, 1917–1960* (New Haven, CT: College and University Press, 1960), 31.

[39] Squiers to Hay, March 18, 1903, in *Isle of Pines*, 68th Cong., 2d sess., 1924, S. Doc. 166, 189. This amount was just a fraction of what American land buyers purchased in all of Cuba. According to one estimate, some 13,000 Americans spent more than $50 million to acquire land in Cuba by 1905. Leland Hamilton Jenks, *Our Cuban Colony: A Study in Sugar* (New York: Vanguard Press, 1928), 144.

This activity was not unique to the Isle. Similar transactions among American entrepreneurs were taking place all across Cuba as potential settlers and investors looked to take advantage of depressed property values in the wake of Cuba's devastating War of Independence.[40] On the Isle, however, much of the activity occurred while sovereignty remained in question. Annexation to the United States appeared a distinct possibility just as zeal for incorporating all Cuba seemed on the wane. Entrepreneurs wanted to take advantage of this ambiguity. Some hoped that a flurry of American activity would compel U.S. officials to annex the Isle; others wanted to buy and sell land before Cuban sovereignty could be formally established. They assumed Americans would lose interest if the Isle was officially declared Cuban territory.

Landholding companies took great pains not to appear as speculators. Such a stigma carried a pejorative association.[41] In promotional literature, company officials claimed their activities on the Isle had higher aims than simply to turn a profit. For example, the Buffalo, New York–based Tropical Development Company stated that its purpose was "to systematize and stimulate the work of colonization and improvement already inaugurated by the numerous **American** population of the Island."[42] Another enterprise, the Cañada Land & Fruit Company based in Marinette, Wisconsin, claimed that the work of these landholding enterprises benefited average Americans. "American syndicates have purchased large tracts of land, surveyed and platted the same, thereby making it possible for the man of moderate means to buy and own a piece of land commensurate with his means."[43] The Cleveland-based Isle of Pines Investment Company justified buying so many acres, ostensibly to avoid the appearance of speculation. According to its prospectus, former Spanish and Cuban landowners "refused to sell part of their lands unless the purchaser was willing and able to take the whole tract; consequently

[40] Louis A. Pérez Jr., *On Becoming Cuban: Identity, Nationality, and Culture* (Chapel Hill: University of North Carolina Press, 1999), 104–25; Carmen Diana Deere, "Here Come the Yankees! The Rise and Decline of United States Colonies in Cuba, 1898–1930," *Hispanic American Historical Review* 78 (November 1998): 738–52.

[41] Robert P. Swierenga, "Land Speculation and Its Impact on American Economic Growth and Welfare: A Historiographical Review," *Western Historical Quarterly* 8 (July 1977): 283–302.

[42] Tropical Development Company, "McKinley, Isle of Pines: A City of Orange Groves in the American District of Cuba" (Buffalo, 1906), 5. Emphasis in original.

[43] Cañada Land & Fruit Company, "Isle of Pines: Land of Fruit and Flowers" (Marinette, WI, 1903), 29.

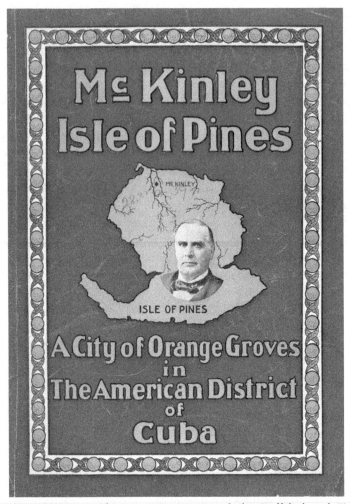

FIGURE 1.1. Cover to the 1906 prospectus of the Buffalo-based Tropical Development Company. The TDC founded the town of McKinley on the northwest side of the Isle in the name of the slain president. The patriotic gesture enabled the company to blunt criticism that it was merely engaged in real estate speculation. Courtesy of the Yates County (NY) Genealogical and Historical Society.

a large capital was required before one could buy land in the Isle of Pines."[44]

Company executives also denied to U.S. officials that they were profiteers, a charge that some newspapers had suggested. Albert B. Young, one

---

[44] Isle of Pines Investment Company, "The Pineland Bulletin," 1.

of the Tropical Development Company's directors, insisted to Sen. John T. Morgan, who was part of the Senate Foreign Relations Committee, that his enterprise was not involved in speculation. "Misled by the false statements given to the press, you may be induced to believe that all Americans interested in the Isle of Pines are operating as real-estate speculators. Let me assure you that this is not the case."[45] George Hibbard of the El Canal Company told Morgan likewise. "This howl by some of the papers that the island was bought up and *held* by speculators is the worst kind of rot."[46]

Landholding companies also cited the rather undeveloped state of the Isle to justify their activity. They suggested that Spanish misrule during the colonial era had prevented the Isle from reaching its full agricultural and commercial potential. As a result, the Tropical Development Company asserted, "thousands of acres of virgin soil now await the thrifty and energetic American to make it the most productive spot in the world."[47] Another company stated that "it is doubtful if the indolent Spaniards appreciated [the Isle's] possibilities as a field for citrus culture."[48] U.S.-based landholding companies implied they would not make that same mistake. Wright argued that these companies were doing the Isle a favor by bringing order and development, a subtle nod to the contemporary idea of the "White Man's Burden" to help civilize non-Anglo-Saxon peoples. "These companies ... rendered the Isle a great service in accurately surveying and in clearing titles to the same," she wrote.[49]

Companies invoked their activities within a larger continuum in U.S. history: pioneering work in the nineteenth century. The timing of this rhetoric was important. By the turn of the century, the notion of a "closed" continental frontier was widely accepted. There was a great deal of anxiety about what the United States would do now that this frontier feature, which had been part of Americana since inception, was apparently no more.[50] With land in their possession in abundance, landholding

[45] Young to Morgan, January 20, 1906, in *Isle of Pines*, 68th Cong., 2d sess., 1924, S. Doc. 166, 293.

[46] Hibbard to Morgan, March 1, 1906, in *Isle of Pines*, 68th Cong., 2d sess., 1924, S. Doc. 166, 27. Emphasis in original.

[47] Tropical Development Company, "McKinley, Isle of Pines," 22.

[48] Isle of Pines Company, "McKinley, Isle of Pines: A City of Orange Groves in the American District of Cuba" (New York, 1911), 3.

[49] Irene A. Wright, *The Gem of the Caribbean* (Nueva Gerona: Isle of Pines Publicity Company, 1909), 36.

[50] Walter LaFeber, *The New Empire: An Interpretation of American Expansion, 1860–1898*, 35th ann. ed. (Ithaca, NY: Cornell University Press, 1998), 62–101; David M. Wrobel, *The End of American Exceptionalism: Frontier Anxiety from the Old West to*

companies underscored a closing domestic frontier to steer land-buyers in their direction. "**The era of golden opportunities in Southern California, for instance, is a thing of the past,**" the Tropical Development Company stated.[51] If the average American was to continue to look to the frontier for farming opportunities, they would have to look beyond U.S. shores to find it. U.S. businessmen argued that the Isle of Pines could supply this extended frontier through its cheap, plentiful land, prospects for growth and wealth, and a pliant native population who would not interfere with American designs.

The extent to which landholding company executives truly believed in the agrarian ethic they were promoting is certainly questionable. Post-1898 American expansion provided established elites with new commercial opportunities, particularly for profitable investment abroad.[52] The availability of land on the Isle of Pines provided such a potential benefit for U.S. businessmen. But those entrepreneurial ambitions – to reap the financial benefits of investing in foreign real estate – were often masked in the rhetoric of nineteenth-century agrarianism, a language that often featured opposition to urbanism and industrialization.

The largest and longest-lasting of these landholding companies was the Isle of Pines Company, which plainly stated its mission: "Our purpose is to systematize and stimulate the work of colonization and improvement already inaugurated by the numerous American population of the Island, and to engage in the buying, selling, improving, and cultivating of land in the Isle of Pines."[53] Samuel H. Pearcy was the driving force behind the enterprise. A Confederate army veteran from Tennessee, Pearcy owned shipping and manufacturing interests in Havana before he turned his attention to the Isle in 1899.[54] Within two years, Pearcy and a

---

the *New Deal* (Lawrence: University Press of Kansas, 1993); Richard Slotkin, *Gunfighter Nation: The Myth of the Frontier in Twentieth-Century America* (New York: Atheneum, 1992); Slotkin, *The Fatal Environment: The Myth of the Frontier in the Age of Industrialization, 1800–1890* (Norman: University of Oklahoma Press, 1985); Richard Hofstadter, *The Age of Reform: From Bryan to FDR* (New York: Vintage Books, 1955), 46–59; William Appleman Williams, "The Frontier Thesis and American Foreign Policy," *Pacific Historical Review* 24 (November 1955): 379–95.

51 Tropical Development Company, "McKinley, Isle of Pines," 56. Emphasis in original.

52 T.J. Jackson Lears, *Rebirth of a Nation: The Making of Modern America, 1877–1920* (New York: HarperCollins, 2009), 169.

53 Isle of Pines Company, "McKinley, Isle of Pines," 24.

54 One sympathetic account of Samuel and his brother, Josiah, referred to them as the George Washington and Benjamin Franklin of the Isle of Pines. The report also noted that Josiah Pearcy was one of the original members of the Ku Klux Klan, but that he had "condemned" the group's radicalism of its later years. Frederic J. Haskin, "Personal Stories," *Omaha World Herald*, March 19, 1907.

group of New York investors bought more than 106,000 acres from former Spanish landowners for roughly $174,000. The company's holdings
spread across five former Spanish estates, including Santa Barbara, which
would eventually have the highest concentration of Americans. The company also bought tracts in small towns as well as in sparsely populated
areas on the South Coast, typically paying about $1.75 to $2 an acre.[55]
Squiers in 1903 referred to the company as "purely speculative," as it had
yet to resell any land but was instead waiting for the prices to increase.[56]
By the end of the decade though, the Isle of Pines Company became the
prime seller of Isle real estate to Americans, selling tracts for up to $50 an
acre, and advertising in newspapers all across the United States.[57] At the
same time, Pearcy emerged as one of the most vocal and visible members
of the budding American community, largely in an effort to persuade the
U.S. government to annex the Isle. Although Pearcy died in 1913, his son,
Edward, continued to serve as the company's manager on the Isle until he
closed the business in 1950.

In an example of cooperation among landholding companies, the
Tropical Development Company was born out of the Isle of Pines Company,
from which it had purchased 5,200 acres on the north end of the Isle. James
A. Hill, a New York–based publisher, served as treasurer of the Isle of Pines
Company as well as vice president of the Tropical Development Company.
The Tropical Development Company was best known for founding the
town of McKinley, named for the slain U.S. president. As described in its
company literature, the Tropical Development Company designed the
town to help support and sustain the American presence on the Isle. To
finance this development, the company sold bonds. It was expected that
these bonds would mature in ten years, specifically on "McKinley Day,"
January 29, 1914. At that point, it planned to sell its 500-acre company
citrus grove in five-acre plots to the highest bidder (the company expected
to fetch $1,000 per acre by then), the proceeds of which would then be
divided among all bondholders.[58] Although the town of McKinley endured
for many years, no records indicate if the company successfully sold off its
groves on "McKinley Day" or how long it stayed in operation.

Landholding company executives came from a variety of industries.
The Isle of Pines Company featured publishers and shippers. Among the

[55] Academia de Ciencias de Cuba, "Serie Isla de Pinos No. 23," 4.
[56] Squiers to Hay, March 18, 1903, in *Isle of Pines*, 68th Cong., 2d sess., 1924, S. Doc.
     166, 188.
[57] *Philadelphia Inquirer*, March 30, 1909; *Kansas City Star*, February 21, 1910.
[58] Details from Tropical Development Company, "McKinley, Isle of Pines."

FIGURE 1.2. A 1914 map showing the various tracts on the Isle of Pines, many of which were owned by U.S. landholding companies who had bought them from Cuban or Spanish *hacendados* after the War of 1898. Shaded areas represent tracts owned by the Santa Fe Land Company and the Isle of Pines United Land Companies, which were incorporated in Iowa and Illinois, respectively.

Source: Santa Fe Land Company and the Isle of Pines United Land Companies, "Marvelous Isle of Pines: That Magnificent Land of Sunshine, Health and Wealth" (1914).

Tropical Development Company's directors were former Buffalo mayor Erastus Knight and bookseller Frederik A. Fernald, who sold his business to become an investor in the company.[59] The Isle of Pines Investment Company was mostly a family affair. Real estate mogul Truman Swetland

---

[59] Harvard College Class of 1882, *Sixth Report of the Secretary* (Boston: E.O. Cockayne, 1908), 65–6.

started the company in 1908 when he bought nearly 10,000 acres at San Francisco de las Piedras, the largest undivided tract at the time, from the Sarda family for $55,000. Among the company's directors were three of Swetland's sons, who were integral to the tract's development. Frederick Swetland Jr. noted that "After my grandfather signed the contract, the rest of the family finally dug up the purchase money to bail him out ('after all, how can you go wrong on land at $5 an acre'?)."[60] Over the next half-century, the Swetland family engaged in a variety of business enterprises, including land sales, citrus production for export, resort development (the family converted part of its house into an inn for tourists), and cattle raising. The family soon emerged as one of the most prominent on the Isle. They retained their property in San Francisco over four generations up to the Cuban Revolution, and would be one of the last American families to leave.

Selling the Isle

In addition to word of mouth, perhaps the most effective way in which news spread about the Isle of Pines and its available land was through advertisements. Companies produced notices not only in newspapers and magazines, but also through prospectuses that touted the benefits of living on the Isle and the abundance of opportunity. At the turn of the century, advertisements increasingly were becoming a feature of American business.[61] Landholding companies found them indispensable to operating on the Isle. For example, the Isle of Pines Company produced a glossy, picture-filled, easy-to-read prospectus, a feature that surely reflected the fact that two of its directors, J. C. Tichenor and James A. Hill, were publishers in New York City. In general, companies portrayed the Isle as an untapped commodity, ripe for exploitation by savvy, hard-working Americans who, through ingenuity, industriousness, and know-how, could maximize its latent potential. But companies also often exaggerated, obfuscated, or suggested grandiose development plans that never came to fruition.

---

[60] Memorandum of Frederick Swetland Jr., March 7, 1961, 2–3, SFA.

[61] Stuart Ewen, *Captains of Consciousness: Advertising and the Social Roots of the Consumer Culture*, 25th ann. ed. (New York: Basic Books, 2001); Pamela Walker Laird, *Advertising Progress: American Business and the Rise of Consumer Marketing* (Baltimore, MD: *Johns Hopkins University Press*, 1998); James D. Norris, *Advertising and the Transformation of American Society, 1865–1920* (New York: Greenwood Press, 1990); Roland Marchand, *Advertising the American Dream: Making Way for Modernity, 1920–1940* (Berkeley: University of California Press, 1985).

Most conspicuously, landholding companies drew interest in the Isle by citing its prospects for wealth. The Cañada Land & Fruit Company, for example, was rather blunt in its assessment. In a section of its prospectus titled "What Could I Do in the Isle of Pines?" the company stated: "Among other things you could get rich.... You do the work properly, and fortune will follow as certainly as day follows night. And no beggarly pittance either, but wealth ample even for these days, and it can be vast wealth, if you have sufficient energy and push."[62] The pronouncement tapped into a trope familiar to turn-of-the-century Americans: the Horatio Alger code – the idea that success and upward mobility were possible, but would have to be earned through struggle and hard work. Companies presented the Isle as a place in which to achieve independence and self-sufficiency. The Isle of Pines Company, for example, implored potential settlers to "Stop working for other people. Join us and become an independent citizen of this sturdy American Colony in the Isle of Pines. You can take possession of your property at once and be working for yourself instead of toiling for a mere existence day in and day out."[63] At the same time, companies claimed to be targeting "high class Americans" and "America's most progressive citizens" as potential customers.[64] The Tropical Development Company mentioned the names of notable men who invested on the Isle, including prominent politicians, bankers, financiers, and railroad magnates. **"These are the men who are making the adjacent tropics a safe and profitable field for investment."**[65] Not only did such an association give the Isle an image of exclusivity, but it also was meant to assure skeptical investors of average means that their money would be in good company.

Landholding companies most often cited the development of citrus fruit as the way to wealth. This fruit included grapefruit, oranges, and pineapples that because of the favorable climate and soil could grow in abundance. Companies claimed that the Isle produced high-quality fruit, better than that from Florida and California. "The Isle of Pines grape fruit has been tested by fruit experts in New York and European markets and has been pronounced absolutely the finest that has ever reached these markets," one company boasted.[66] Moreover, citrus fruit production on

---

[62] Cañada Land & Fruit Company, "Isle of Pines," 32.
[63] Isle of Pines Company, "McKinley, Isle of Pines," 58.
[64] San Juan Heights Land Company, "The Isle of Pines," 18–19.
[65] Tropical Development Company, "McKinley, Isle of Pines," 96. Emphasis in original.
[66] Santa Fe Land Company and the Isle of Pines United Land Companies, "Marvelous Isle of Pines: 'That Magnificent Land of Sunshine, Health, and Wealth'" (Chicago, 1914), 11.

the Isle had a competitive advantage over rivals in the domestic United States because of the warmer climate. Citrus trees could escape the early-season frosts that occasionally blighted production in Florida. This also meant that Isle producers could get their product to market earlier than Florida growers and thus receive a better price. Fruit from the Isle had another advantage over similar products from California: because Isle growers shipped by steamer rather than by railroad, they could get their produce to eastern markets more quickly and less expensively.[67]

Although citrus fruit was the most heavily promoted export commodity, landholding companies cited other products that promised to bring settlers and investors a handsome profit. Befitting its name, the Isle of Pines boasted a significant timber industry. One estimate suggested the Isle had up to sixty varieties of wood with high export potential, including pine, cedar, and mahogany, constituting "the most valuable tract of timber to be found in the West Indies."[68] Saw mills did, in fact, emerge throughout the Isle over the years, mostly to make crates in which to ship citrus. The Isle also featured marble quarries, most of which remained largely untapped during the Spanish colonial era, as well as deposits of gold and silver – or so the claim went.[69]

In mainland Cuba, sugar and tobacco were the two biggest export commodities that long attracted U.S. investment. Landholding companies promoted both products as sustainable industries on the Isle as well. "The Isle of Pines will produce better tobacco than any known section on the globe, except for a few favored localities in Cuba," the Cañada Land & Fruit Company declared.[70] The Isle of Pines Company made a bolder claim, suggesting that "the tobacco raised on the Isle of Pines was as good as the Cuban stock." It also claimed that "Sugar cane ... grows luxuriantly on the Isle of Pines and will be extensively cultivated and constitute a profitable crop."[71] Despite such assertions, sugar never developed as an export industry. Early settlers quickly found that the conditions on the Isle – particularly the sandy soil, smaller plantations,

---

[67] Isle of Pines Company, "The Isle of Pines: Uncle Sam's Latest Acquisition of Territory" (New York, 1901), 6; Cañada Land & Fruit Company, "Isle of Pines," 19; Tropical Development Company, "McKinley, Isle of Pines," 61; "No Frost in Isle of Pines," advertisement in *Duluth News-Tribune*, January 14, 1913.

[68] Isle of Pines Company, "The Isle of Pines." The company claimed that the value of timber on land it owned was approximately $9.05 million.

[69] Cañada Land & Fruit Company, "Isle of Pines," 18.

[70] Ibid., 14.

[71] Isle of Pines Company, "The Isle of Pines," 12–13.

and lack of refineries – could not sustain sugarcane on the same scale as on the main island.

Landholding companies also pitched the Isle as a resort location. This discourse suggested that the Isle could be a place for physical and mental rejuvenation. "[The Isle] has been a health resort for more than a century and is one of the oldest known," the Cañada Land & Fruit Company stated. "The sea air, pure water, the mineral springs and equitable temperature are all conducive of long life."[72] Company literature cited the mineral waters, in particular, as having healing properties for a variety of ailments, including stomach and kidney disease, rheumatism, and asthma. Mineral waters from the Isle were so desired in Cuba that it was bottled and shipped to Havana for those who could afford such a luxury. The Tropical Development Company stated that one settler, T. J. Keenan, so highly regarded the healing powers of the mineral springs that he spent $3,000 to build a private bathhouse around one.[73] Company literature also noted that the mineral springs in the interior of the Isle "are constantly visited by many invalids, who find speedy relief."[74]

Stories about the Isle's healing prowess were not new to American audiences. Samuel Hazard wrote about the Isle's mineral springs in an 1871 travelogue. Plagued by a respiratory ailment while in Havana, Hazard was instructed to do one of two things: quit smoking, or go to the Isle and "take the miraculous waters of its mineral baths." He chose the latter option. Although underwhelmed by the lack of material comforts around the springs at Santa Fe, Hazard nevertheless expressed amazement at being "completely cured" after a ten-day regimen of two baths and four glasses of water per day. He concluded that his trip to the Isle provided "much pleasure and some few discomforts, with lasting benefit in health."[75] Three decades later, landholding companies promised the same thing to settlers.

In addition to appeals for self-improvement, landholding companies piqued the imaginations of settlers and investors. Prospectuses portrayed the Isle in exotic terms, as a land significantly more alien and mysterious than any found in the familiar Northeast or Midwest. Images commonly depicted the Isle as precious and pristine. The Isle, the Tropical Development Company stated, "has been compared to 'a jewel pendant

---

[72] Cañada Land & Fruit Company, "Isle of Pines," 9.

[73] Tropical Development Company, "McKinley, Isle of Pines," 39.

[74] Cañada Land & Fruit Company, "Isle of Pines," 9.

[75] Samuel Hazard, *Cuba with Pen and Pencil* (Hartford, CT: Hartford Publishing Company, 1871), 382–97.

from the throat of Cuba, blazing in the tropic sun.' "[76] A sense of adventure and excitement – even a subtle hint of danger – seemed to pervade the Isle. Prospectuses cited the Isle's mythical heritage as a pirate hideout during the colonial era as well as its status as a destination for political prisoners during the nineteenth century, including, most famously, José Martí in 1870.[77]

While evoking a sense of mystery, excitement, and derring-do in their depictions of the Isle, companies also sought to reassure potential customers that it was not *too* far away, literally and figuratively. To that end, companies showed that the Isle was, in fact, easily reachable, its potential benefits attainable, and its exotic nature capable of being tamed by the average American. One of the key selling points was the Isle's relative proximity to the United States. The Isle of Pines Company stated that the Isle was within four days' travel from any major city in the United States.[78] The Tropical Development Company put it another way: the Isle of Pines was as far from New York City as St. Paul, Minnesota – although in the distinctly opposite climatic condition.[79] To get there, of course, one needed sufficient financial means. As of 1911, the round-trip cost of first-class travel from New York to the Isle was $100.70; an "intermediate"-class ticket cost $58.60.[80] To rural and middle-class U.S. settlers, these costs likely prohibited frequent returns to the United States.

Based on the glowing descriptions of the Isle's climate, however, the trip was worth it for the weather alone. The Isle was warm during the winter, but not too uncomfortably hot in the summer, contrary to most tropical climates. "The Isle of Pines enjoys one continuous summer," the Isle of Pines Company hyped. "No heavy overcoats or expensive clothing [is necessary]."[81] Considering landholding companies advertised mainly in the Northeast and Midwest, with their cold winters, depictions of the warmer climate on the Isle surely had an appeal. Frederick Swetland Jr. believed that was the case for his grandfather. Envisioning what Truman Swetland thought when he first came to the Isle in 1908, Frederick Swetland Jr. wrote, "How fragrant, warm, clear and quiet it must have seemed to him, straight from the snows and grime and huddled cold of

[76] Tropical Development Company, "McKinley, Isle of Pines," 30.
[77] Isle of Pines Company, "The Isle of Pines," 1.
[78] San Francisco was listed as the lone exception; travel from there took an unspecified longer amount of time. Isle of Pines Company, "The Isle of Pines," 4.
[79] Tropical Development Company, "McKinley, Isle of Pines," 13.
[80] Isle of Pines Company, "McKinley, Isle of Pines," 31. The trip consisted of a steamship to Havana, railroad to Batabanó, a steamer to the Isle, and included three daily meals.
[81] Isle of Pines Company, "McKinley, Isle of Pines," 41, 46.

Cleveland, with the wind off the crumpled ice floes of the lake. Of course he fell in love with it as all Northerners coming down into winter sun and color must do."[82] The Tropical Development Company conspicuously referenced not only the warmer temperatures on the Isle, but also its consistency, in contrast to the fluctuations typical in Buffalo, the company's headquarters.[83] The Isle of Pines Company starkly described the difference between the climate on the Isle and what was typically found in the Northeast and Midwest: "When Snows, sleet and blizzards hold this country in their icy grip, McKinley with its orange blossoms, birds, flowers, sunshine and blue sky is a picture of summer, a paradise for those seeking to escape coughs, colds, bronchitis, pneumonia, catarrh, consumption and rheumatism which are so prevalent here [in the United States]."[84]

There was one important caveat, however, to the Isle's ideal climate: hurricanes. Every prospectus either ignored or overlooked tropical storms. Some companies claimed that such storms did not affect the Isle despite a 1902 U.S. government report that stated they had occurred periodically over the years.[85] According to the Cañada Land & Fruit Company, "Hurricanes, cyclones and tornadoes have never visited the island. No crops are ever injured by storms, overflows or frosts."[86] The Isle of Pines Investment Company made a similar prevarication. "Natives claim that there has never been a single visit of either a hurricane or cyclone to the Island.... No other place in the West Indies is so free from storms."[87] This was certainly not the case during the period of American involvement. Over the next half-century, the Isle experienced devastating hurricanes that significantly damaged crops, property, and infrastructure. The storms of 1917 and 1926 were particularly catastrophic.

---

[82] Memorandum of Frederick Swetland Jr., March 7, 1961, SFA.

[83] Tropical Development Company, "McKinley, Isle of Pines," 14–15.

[84] Isle of Pines Company, "McKinley, Isle of Pines," 61.

[85] The Division of Insular Affairs in the U.S. Department of War reported that although "hurricanes are less frequent [on the Isle] than in Cuba ... damaging hurricanes occurred in 1774, 1844, 1846, 1865, 1870, 1876, 1885, 1894." "The Isle of Pines (Caribbean Sea): Its Situation, Physical Features, Inhabitants, Resources, and Industries" (Washington, DC: Government Printing Office, 1902), 15.

[86] Cañada Land & Fruit Company, "Isle of Pines," 9.

[87] Isle of Pines Investment Company, "The Pineland Bulletin," 6. The company made one of the only allusions to hurricanes, citing a "severe wind storm" in 1906 that was the worst there in thirty years, "but the damage to the island was so slight as to be hardly worth mentioning."

Nevertheless, landholding companies promoted the notion that the Isle of Pines was safe for American settlement – specifically, for white American settlement. The Isle of Pines Investment Company declared that the island "may be regarded as strictly a white man's country, a condition almost impossible to find in the Southern States and unknown in any other part of the West Indies."[88] Landholding companies sought to reassure Americans who considered moving that they would not meet a hostile reception in a foreign land from uncivilized tropical peoples. To that end, prospectuses emphasized *pineros'* whiteness and sophistication, suggesting that they wholeheartedly welcomed Americans. "The natives are of Spanish descent ... and they are now almost to a man gratified that the island is United States territory," the Isle of Pines Company stated. "The natives are an intelligent, hospitable people and welcome emigration from the States."[89] Likewise, the Cañada Land & Fruit Company claimed: "The native of the Isle of Pines is not lazy. He is very much of a gentleman and prefers not to do much manual labor, but enjoys riding around on horseback to look after his stock, and they are for the most part from their own standards well fixed, having simple tastes easily satisfied."[90]

This depiction ignored deep divisions within *pinero* society, particularly between the minority *hacendados* and the vast majority who made a living as wage laborers or subsistence farmers. In 1899, the U.S. military government conducted a census that found the Isle had 3,199 residents, a 63 percent increase from the previous Spanish census in 1887. Although still one of the smallest population densities in the country, the increase was exceptional in light of the fact that Cuba's population declined during the twelve years between censuses mainly because of the toll of war. More than 80 percent of the Isle's population in 1899 was considered "white," the precise definition of which presumably referred to people of Spanish descent. Nearly 56 percent of the overall population was male. Economically, *pineros* were not quite as well off as landholding companies suggested. Indicators show that 1,916 people were "without gainful occupation," including all but thirty-seven of the enumerated women. Of those employed, the most popular occupations were in "domestic or personal service" (647 people) and "agriculture, fisheries, mining" (403 people). In terms of education, only twenty-two *pineros* were considered

---

[88] Isle of Pines Investment Company, "The Pineland Bulletin," 16.
[89] Isle of Pines Company, "Isle of Pines," 5.
[90] Cañada Land & Fruit Company, "Isle of Pines," 20–1.

to have "superior education," while less than one-third of the population was said to be literate.[91]

Some companies suggested *pineros* would make good employees, eager to work for U.S. landowners. The Tropical Development Company stated that locals were "not remarkably industrious, because they don't have to work hard, [but] they are not so lazy nor so much given to holiday making as are the people of many Spanish-American countries.... [T]hey learn quickly and prove good farm laborers under proper supervision."[92] The Isle of Pines Investment Company echoed that contention, describing *pineros* as "full-blooded Spanish people – hard-working, law abiding, peaceable, hospitable, and honest – who invariably command the respect, after acquaintance, of all Americans.... In fact, the native population on the Isle of Pines is distinctly different in character and disposition from the average native of Cuba."[93] By emphasizing *pineros'* Spanish, European heritage, landholding companies made a clear distinction that the natives were not Afro-Cuban, as was more common in mainland Cuba. Therefore, settlers would not have to worry about consorting with non-whites, a fear prevalent in the United States that spurred the rise of Jim Crow segregation.

Companies looked to alleviate another concern often associated with tropical regions: disease. This was a long-held concern among Anglo-Americans anxious about traveling to the tropics for fear of contracting ailments such as yellow fever or malaria. During the War of 1898, some U.S. soldiers stationed in Cuba were uneasy about staying on the island longer than necessary. Most notably, Theodore Roosevelt appealed to get his Rough Riders out of Cuba soon after hostilities ended out of fear that his soldiers would contract tropical diseases.[94] Landholding company executives clearly remained alert to this concern. Citing U.S. government reports, the Isle of Pines Company asserted that the Isle had no record

---

[91] *Report on the Census of Cuba, 1899* (Washington, DC: Government Printing Office, 1900).

[92] Tropical Development Company, "McKinley, Isle of Pines," 43.

[93] Isle of Pines Investment Company, "The Pineland Bulletin," 16. U.S. newspapers widely echoed these depictions of *pineros* as friendly, cooperative, and simple. For examples, see "Isle of Pines," *Grand Rapids Herald*, June 19, 1898; "About the Isle of Pines," *Lexington Herald*, July 20, 1898; "'Paradise of the Atlantic': The Isle of Pines," *Biloxi Herald*, April 6, 1903.

[94] In August 1898, Roosevelt requested to have the Rough Riders relieved and returned home. In a letter to his friend Sen. Henry Cabot Lodge, Roosevelt feared his troops would contract malaria and "die like rotten sheep." Quoted in David F. Trask, *The War with Spain in 1898* (New York: Macmillan, 1981), 330.

of yellow fever or cholera.[95] Indeed, in the years that a U.S. consul was stationed on the Isle (1910–29, 1942–4), health reports indicated no instances of yellow fever or malaria.

Landholding companies also typically obfuscated the sovereignty question. While U.S. and Cuban officials deliberated about such claims, U.S.-based landholding companies and private U.S. investors rarely, if ever, recognized Cuban interests or authority, even though the Cuban government had been administering the Isle since independence in May 1902. Instead, U.S. settlers and investors often referred to the Isle in prospectuses, company stationary, and personal correspondence as "Isle of Pines, W.I." – West Indies. This designation not only denied Cuban sovereignty but also implied that it was among the islands Spain had ceded to the United States under the Treaty of Paris. Some companies went further by suggesting that the Isle of Pines belonged to the United States unconditionally. The Tropical Development Company referred to the Isle as the "American District of Cuba"; the Isle of Pines Company stated that "The Isle of Pines is the very latest of Uncle Sam's territorial acquisitions."[96] Even after the Hay-Quesada treaty was signed (but before the U.S. Senate formally ratified it), landholding companies continued to suggest that the U.S. government was an active player in the Isle's affairs and that it would guarantee the physical and financial protection of settlers and entrepreneurs. In 1911, the Isle of Pines Company claimed, "The United States government has absolutely pledged itself to see that an orderly government is maintained and there is to-day in the Isle of Pines as perfect security of life and property as in any part of the United States."[97]

Such promise of security was critical in light of some companies' pledge to construct a deep-water port and a railroad.[98] Although neither project ever came to fruition, the idea of development was an integral part of the landholding companies' sales pitch. They promised significant returns on investment to the settler who bought land sooner rather than later so they could reap the benefit of the inevitable increase in land values. Or, as the Isle of Pines Investment Company put it: "Buy Land Now, It's Like Taking Out an Insurance Policy [–] the Longer You Put It Off the More

[95] Isle of Pines Company, "McKinley, Isle of Pines," 40.
[96] Tropical Development Company, "McKinley, Isle of Pines"; Isle of Pines Company, "The Isle of Pines," 1.
[97] Isle of Pines Company, "McKinley, Isle of Pines," 33.
[98] Isle of Pines Railroad Company Inc., "Isle of Pines Railroad Company Prospectus" (New York, 1910).

Expensive It Gets."[99] In the first years of the twentieth century, landhold-ing companies generally sold undeveloped land for up to $50 an acre. They promised that once developed, the value of land would increase exponentially. The Isle of Pines Company asserted that "Every available acre of tillable land in the Isle of Pines is, in our opinion, worth $100, uncultivated, to-day. Cultivated (in grapefruit or oranges, for instance) it should be worth $1,000 in full bearing."[100] Advertisements attributed this increase in value to the efforts of settlers, whose industry and effi-ciency made the Isle more productive and valuable than it ever was under Spanish rule. According to the Isle of Pines Company, "the activity of the Yankee settler [brought] an era of prosperity – and of increase in land values vastly greater in five years than in the five centuries preceding."[101]

Another tactic of landholding companies was to cite testimony from existing settlers, investors, and experts to support its claims. One of these experts, Dr. William Browning, wrote in November 1910 about the Isle's prospects as a health resort. Although lukewarm in his assessment – "Cuba hardly equals [the U.S. South], certainly not yet for lack of suitable accommodations" – he nevertheless argued that it was a place physicians should consider for its potential to improve patients' health.[102] That was sufficient endorsement for the Isle of Pines Company, which quoted his report at length in its 1911 prospectus.[103] A decade earlier, the company reprinted a letter in full from independent inspectors of its property that reported that its tract was "the best I have found for growing Tropical fruits and winter vegetables" and that "the leaf grown on [the] Isle of Pines is of good quality."[104] It likewise reprinted letters from settlers who were said to be thriving on the Isle. J. A. Lattin of Farmingdale, New York, wrote the Isle of Pines Company to say that he and his fam-ily were enjoying life on their forty-acre farm in West McKinley so much

---

[99] Isle of Pines Investment Company, "The Pineland Bulletin," 14.

[100] Isle of Pines Company, "McKinley, Isle of Pines," 28.

[101] Ibid., 4.

[102] William Browning, "The Isle of Pines as a Hibernaculum," *Long Island Medical Journal* (November 1910), 10.

[103] Isle of Pines Company, "McKinley, Isle of Pines," 7–12.

[104] Isle of Pines Company, "Isle of Pines," 19–20. Similar letters testifying to the Isle's potential were reproduced by other companies, including: the Tropical Development Company, with a 1904 letter from Squiers, "McKinley, Isle of Pines," 8; the Isle of Pines Investment Company, with a note from the president of the Cuban National Horticultural Society, "The Pineland Bulletin," 22; and the San Juan Heights Land Company, which offered excerpts of five letters from fruit shippers testifying to the quality of Isle citrus, "The Isle of Pines," 31–2.

that "Mrs. Lattin did not care to come North on a visit, stating that she enjoys the summer climate there as well as the winter. In fact, nothing could induce us to move back to the States. The island undoubtedly has a great future."[105]

Cultural Representations

The landholding companies' sales pitch evidently caught Americans' attention. An estimated 10,000 Americans eventually bought land. Another sign was how the Isle of Pines resonated in U.S. popular culture, where its image both reflected and reinforced landholding companies' portrayals. Descriptions of the Isle as a tropical paradise, a place for rejuvenation, an opportunity for prosperity and social mobility, and an untapped commodity ripe for exploitation all were evident in contemporary books, poetry, and even a play.

Irene A. Wright, who spent nearly a decade in Cuba, became the most notable chronicler of the Isle of Pines in the early twentieth century. A native of Colorado, she served as a writer and an editor for various Havana-based publications before later working for the U.S. National Archives and Department of State.[106] She wrote two books about the Isle, *The Gem of the Caribbean* and a revised and expanded version, *Isle of Pines*. The project began as a report undertaken at the behest of the Provisional Government of Cuba, which the United States administered during a twenty-eight-month reoccupation beginning in September 1906. Both publications were similar in form and style to the landholding company prospectuses published around the same time. In *Gem of the Caribbean*, for example, pictures included panoramas of Nueva Gerona and Santa Fe as well as various farms, beaches, dwellings, and groves in their early stages of development. Such images, particularly of the young groves, left the powerful impression of future growth to come. Like the company prospectuses, Wright's works read like promotional literature, emphasizing the benefits and attractive features of the Isle. About settlers she wrote, "On one point, however, everybody agrees: that the Isle of Pines is the greatest place on earth. No view to the contrary is tolerated."[107] This laudatory tone is perhaps not surprising considering

---

[105] Lattin to J. D. Potts, September 30, 1910, in Isle of Pines Company, "McKinley, Isle of Pines," 20.

[106] http://encyclopedia.jrank.org/articles/pages/4812/Wright-Irene-Aloha-1879–1972.html (accessed July 18, 2015).

[107] Wright, *Isle of Pines*, 92.

Wright had sought editorial and financial help from U.S. businessmen to get *Isle of Pines* published.[108] Nonetheless, whereas company prospectuses touted a particular tract, Wright's works promoted the Isle in its entirety, including attractive descriptions of its climate and topography, its citrus and vegetable potential, as well as its native people, plants, and animals.

While the works by Wright and the landholding companies depicted the Isle of Pines as a new frontier for U.S. settlement, other writers promoted elements of the island as having a place *within* the United States. This idea was offered most notably in Mary Estelle Franklin's *Isle of Pines Cook Book*. Published in 1914 by the Boston-based Isle of Pines Co-Operative Fruit Company, an agent for the United Fruit Company, the cookbook offered a collection of recipes featuring grapefruit, which the company grew on the Isle. Franklin suggested a variety of uses of the fruit, including for beverages, salads, sandwiches, entrees, and desserts, some 250 recipes in all. She portrayed the Isle's citrus fruit as of the highest quality to generate interest among potential investors in the Isle of Pines Co-Operative Fruit Company.[109] Like the landholding company prospectuses, Franklin used third-party testimonials to establish the quality of the Isle's produce. "[T]here is no question as to its flavor being far superior to that of any other grapefruit grown," Franklin quoted one shipper. "We have disposed of a large quantity of Isle of Pines grapefruits at $6.00 a crate, and have received nothing but the highest praise in regard to it from our customers," she cited another.[110] Moreover, Franklin emphasized the U.S. presence and influence on the Isle to show it was not a totally foreign land and to suggest that investments in the fruit company's efforts were a safe bet. To that end, she asserted that 4,500 Americans, including many New Englanders, lived on the Isle, who owned 99 percent of the land.[111]

---

[108] Ibid., foreword.

[109] U.S. growers in Hawai'i also used a cookbook to promote an American-run enterprise, in this case to draw attention to the pineapple industry in the newly annexed territory. Gary Okihiro, *Pineapple Culture: A History of the Tropical and Temperate Zones* (Berkeley: University of California Press, 2009), 143–50.

[110] Testimonials quoted from C. S. Alden, president of the Cleveland-based Alden Adams Brokerage Co., and Thomas F. Galvin of Boston, respectively. Mary Estelle Franklin, *Isle of Pines Cook Book*, (Boston, MA: Isle of Pines Co-Operative Fruit Company, 1914), 30. Wright also attested to the high quality of the fruit produced on the Isle. "It is not possible to produce anywhere better pineapples than grow on the Isle of Pines." Wright, *Isle of Pines*, 79.

[111] Franklin, *Isle of Pines Cook Book*, 31.

The quality of the Isle's produce also offered a selling point for grocers in the United States. In May 1913, the Hartford, Connecticut, grocer Newton, Robertson & Company promoted having just received pineapples from the Kopf Nursery Company, one of the prominent U.S.-owned citrus enterprises on the Isle. "No fruit could be more delightful and healthful to eat than these perfectly ripened Isle of Pines Pineapples," the advertisement stated.[112] Just two months earlier, however, it was apparent that Newton, Robertson & Company did not have this Isle pineapple. Instead, the company promoted its stock by favorably comparing it to that from the Isle. "Solid, ripe, beautiful eating fruit," the advertisement stated. "Equal to the Isle of Pines fruit at about half the price."[113]

The Isle of Pines also inspired poetry from American writers. In 1905, W. H. Merritt wrote "Isle of Pines," an ode to the favorable climate and conditions on the island. Referring to the Isle as the "fairest gem," Merritt's poem contained three themes. The first was the stark contrast between the weather on the Isle and the climate in Merritt's hometown of Bolivar in western New York, a place notorious for its punishing winters and lake-effect snow. On the Isle, Merritt wrote, there are "No withering vines with frost bit leaves … No chilly winds with icy breath; No winter storm with its shroud of death." The second theme depicted the Isle as a place for relaxation and rejuvenation. "And my heart grows young," he wrote, suggesting the healing powers of the serene surroundings. This was followed closely by "And my soul is filled with peace and rest," which, in addition to crediting the Isle's calm nature, offered a heavenly allusion. That leads to the third theme in the poem, a religious or spiritual quality to the Isle. Merritt compared the Isle to the biblical "promised land" and portrayed the Isle as a "gift from the hand divine." Nowhere did he allude to the competing claims of sovereignty or lobby the U.S. government for annexation. Rather, Merritt referred to the Isle as "home" and "the land for me," suggesting that it was so marvelous a place as to be worth leaving the United States.[114]

Merritt's work, however, did not achieve the same level of notoriety as the most famous U.S. poet associated with the Isle of Pines, Hart Crane. Best known for his poem, *The Bridge* (1930), the Ohio-born Crane wrote

---

[112] Advertisement in *Hartford Courant*, May 20, 1913. Additional advertisements appeared in the editions of June 5 and 11, 1913. The company was still promoting Isle of Pines produce as of 1941. See *Hartford Courant*, November 18, 1941.

[113] Advertisements in *Hartford Courant*, March 6, 1913; March 8, 1913.

[114] W. H. Merritt, "The Isle of Pines" (1905).

much of his renowned opus while living on his family's property on the Isle in 1926. That stint was his second visit to the Isle; his first occurred as an adolescent in the winter of 1915, an experience, one scholar wrote, that "sank plummet-wise into the depths of his being, where it lived and grew secretly, later to put forth in his poetry curious and moving images of tropical seascapes."[115] While writing *The Bridge*, he lobbied his mother and grandmother to stay in the house his grandfather had built. Echoing some of the selling points from landholding companies, he wrote that the fresh air and recreation on the Isle – in contrast to that of his home in New York City – would reinvigorate him. Moreover, he did not want the family's property to go to waste. "It's a clean home with beautiful surroundings and sunshine with quiet and tranquility – compared to this metropolitan living with its fret and fever – it's a paradise."[116] Crane's mother, Grace, however, refused his repeated requests, suggesting that problems with the property would prevent him from finding the peace and quiet he sought. "I never want you to plan to go to the Island or give it another thought – it is too absurd to consider," she wrote. "If you knew the troubles & complications that are constantly confronting me with that property, you would want to stay as far as possible."[117] She eventually relented and he stayed on the Isle with the family's housekeeper for nearly six months, during which he channeled his energies not only into his writing, but also into the daily upkeep of the family property.

Although he had idealized the Isle as a retreat from which he could focus on his writing, his letters suggest that his opinion of the Isle varied in proportion to his productivity. During his most creative burst in late July and August, when he wrote significant portions of *The Bridge* as well as other short poems, he called the Isle "the most ideal place and 'situation' I've ever had for work."[118] Just weeks earlier, however, during an ebb in his writing, he complained that the Isle's conditions were stifling him and made it difficult to work: "I have not been able to write one line since I came here – the mind is completely befogged by the heat

[115] Philip Horton, *Hart Crane: The Life of an American Poet* (New York: W.W. Norton, 1937), 26. See also, José A. Taboada and Enrique O. González, *Hart Crane: El Poeta Perdido en Isla de Pinos* (Nueva Gerona: Ediciones El Abra, 2001).

[116] Hart Crane to Grace Hart Crane, October 20, 1926, *The Letters of Hart Crane, 1916–1932*, Brom Weber, ed. (New York: Hermitage House, 1952), 153.

[117] Grace Hart Crane to Hart Crane, April 17, 1924, in *Letters of Hart Crane and His Family*, Thomas S. W. Lewis, ed. (New York: Columbia University Press, 1974), 304.

[118] Crane to Grace Hart Crane, July 30, 1926, *Letters of Hart Crane*, 269. One Crane biographer argued that Crane's creative burst during this period came while he was battling insomnia, brought on by the heat of the Isle's summer months. Horton, *Hart Crane*, 212.

and besides there is a strange challenge and combat in the air – offered by 'Nature' so monstrously alive in the tropics which drains the psychic energies."[119] Even after his return to the United States, Crane suggested that his sojourn did not live up to his expectations. "The result has been that there was only about four weeks on the Isle of Pines that I managed to accomplish any work at all; my mother's unrestrained letters, the terrific heat and bugs, etc., nearly killed me."[120]

Crane's work, though, clearly bore an imprint of his time on the Isle. *The Bridge* contains many scenes and allusions to coastline and beachfront. As does the posthumously published *Key West* (1933), which contains some short poems that he wrote during his 1926 stay. In "O Carib Isle!" for example, Crane writes:

> To the white sand I may speak a name, fertile
> Albeit in a stranger tongue. Tree names, flower names
> Deliberate, gainsay death's brittle crypt. Meanwhile
> The wind that knots itself in one great death –
> Coils and withdraws. So syllables want breath.[121]

In this passage, Crane describes the process of giving words and descriptors to objects and settings, some of which – like the "white sand" or the "wind that knots itself" – he surely encountered while on the Isle. Crane's experience living through the powerful October 1926 hurricane also is evident in "Eternity," which he wrote after his return to New York. He describes a scene of utter devastation at his family's house, where he survived with the housekeeper:

> After it was over, though still gusting balefully,
> The old woman and I foraged some drier clothes
> And left the house, or what was left of it;
> Parts of the roof reach Yucatan, I suppose.
> She almost – even then – got blown across lots
> At the base of the mountain. But the town, the Town!

There, he finds "Wires in the streets and Chinamen up and down With arms in slings ... Everything gone – or strewn in riddled grace – Long tropic roots high in the air, like lace."[122] The poem concludes with reference to talking with American sailors who brought relief aid to the island

---

[119] Crane to Unknown, July 1926, *Letters of Hart Crane*, 264. The recipient and exact date of the letter are redacted in this edition.

[120] Crane to Charlotte Rychtarik, November 1, 1926, *Letters of Hart Crane*, 276.

[121] "O Carib Isle!" in *Key West: An Island Sheaf* in Hart Crane, *Complete Poems and Selected Letters*, Langdon Hammer, ed. (New York: Library of America, 2006), 77.

[122] "Eternity" in Crane, *Complete Poems and Selected Letters*, 131. See also McManus, *Cuba's Island of Dreams*, 44–7.

aboard the USS *Milwaukee*. Considering Crane wrote as much as half *The Bridge* as well as shorter works like "O Carib Isle!" and "Eternity" while living on the Isle of Pines, his retreat certainly had its desired effect in spurring him to write.

Most cultural reflections of the Isle of Pines celebrated the virtues of U.S. settlement, but that sentiment was not universal. Nowhere was this more evident than in the two-act play *The Isle of Pines: A Musical Comedy*, written by three playwrights in 1906, which satirized Americans' drive for land and desires for annexation. One of the main characters, Thad Thompkins, manufactures a phony cablegram from the Roosevelt administration stating the United States was assuming sovereignty over the Isle and sending a governor to take command. This governor, Billy Norcott, is actually a low-level State Department clerk in on Thad's ruse. Thad's motivation is to secure 30,000 acres, the title to which was in dispute with Kitty Curtis, an American woman who also claimed ownership of the land through inheritance of an old Spanish deed. Thad's plan is to have Billy, as governor, install Ben Bingham as a territorial judge who will surely rule the land dispute in Thad's favor. From there, Thad says, "I will sell the lands on the strength of his decision. We go half on the proceeds, and by the time Uncle Sam gets on to the fake, we can be any old place enjoying the fruits of our honest toil."[123]

Although the second act devolves into a farcical romantic comedy (wherein a variety of love triangles enmeshes each of the story's ten main characters) and the misadventures of mistaken identity, the play nevertheless offers some criticisms about contemporary events on the Isle. The first is powerbrokers' proclivity for scheming and corruption. This element is most clearly evident in Thad's plot to bolster his property claim. If Thad is representative of the U.S. landholding companies, his scheme can be read as a critique of the companies' own land claims, especially since there were few formal titles at the turn of the century. Also, in one scene Ben, Nellie (Thad's daughter), and Don Pedro (a prominent Spaniard) lobby Billy for preferential benefits in his new government, specifically kickbacks. "We want Graft!" they declare.[124] In response, a disgusted Billy throws them out of his office. Finally, the play lampoons the habit of powerbrokers to call for rebellions when matters do not go their way.

---

[123] Collin Davis, Max Rosenfeld, and Hilding Anderson, *The Isle of Pines: A Musical Comedy* (1906), Copyright Office, Drama Deposits, 1901–1944, Reel 209, Act I, 16, LOC.
[124] Ibid., 31.

This tendency is evident in both Thad's scheme, as well as characters' talk of staging a counter-revolution against Billy. Such talk of revolution among these characters reflected many reports at the turn of the century that settlers were on the verge of revolting against Cuban authority to secure U.S. annexation. Amid the talk of counter-revolution against Billy, the play's powerbrokers suggest that manipulating the general populace would be fairly easy. Don Pedro says, "The people are ready to rebel. We have incited them to revolt."[125] Such views of *pineros* presents another common theme that runs through the play, that the natives are naïve and simplistic, easily manipulated by more sophisticated Americans and Spaniards (as represented by Don Pedro). Indeed, there are only two Cuban characters by name, Lt. Garcia and Lolita, suggesting *pineros* were inconsequential to the Isle's power struggles. Early in the play, Ben refers to the natives as "simple-minded," easily distracted by the pomp and circumstance of welcoming a new governor.[126] In fact, the only issue of concern to Lt. Garcia is his desire to have the new governor, Billy, change the law to allow him to marry seventeen-year-old Lolita (the law in the play allowed for marriages after eighteen). The suggestion here is that the older, lecherous Lt. Garcia was trying to take advantage of an innocent young girl.

The play opens with a nod to the contested political status of the Isle, particularly the question over sovereignty. In the first scene, *pineros* – described as "Citizens of the Island [in] (Spanish costume)" – gather for the opening song:

> We first were subjects of Sunny Spain
> 'Till they blew up the Main [*sic*];
> And then we went under Cuba's flag,
> But found it all the same.
> So now we call on the U.S.A.,
> Just over across the way,
> Between them all, it's a game of tag,
> We're waiting to hear them say:
>
> Come, come, into the fold, into the U.S.A.,
> For that's the only country on the face of the globe to-day,
> Come, come give us your hand, we'll send a governor down,
> But you must vote for Teddy when election comes around.
>
> Have you received the cablegram?
> Have you heard from Uncle Sam?

---

[125] Ibid., 35.
[126] Ibid., 3.

We're sick of revolutions,
Sick of Cuba's flim, flam, flam,
We can't find among the Spaniards,
Any man we care to love.
Send us down some chaps from Broadway,
We will be their turtle Dove.[127]

The song suggests that *pineros* were looking to the United States to provide political stability and would welcome annexation. Indeed, it ignores any notion that *pineros* may have felt ties to, or identified with, mainland Cuba. Instead, it more aptly reflects the sentiments expressed by annexationists who appealed to the Roosevelt administration to make the Isle U.S. territory. These efforts are referenced later in Act I as Thad explains the backdrop to his annexation ruse saying, "Cabled Uncle Sam to take us under his wing as a territory. Root sent his refusal – expected it. He didn't want the Isle of Pines as a gift."[128]

Like other contemporary literature, reports, and advertisements, *The Isle of Pines: A Musical Comedy* took a condescending tone toward *pineros*, portraying them as ignorant and simple-minded. Yet unlike most other writings of the era, the play also satirized entrepreneurs and investors. It revealed a counter-narrative that slowly emerged after the first few years of the U.S. presence. Some settlers who returned to the United States complained that the notion of the Isle as a tropical paradise was a sham; it was not as picturesque as they had been led to believe, nor could it support the kind of lifestyle they expected to enjoy. They vilified landholding companies as profit-driven speculators who had dishonestly mischaracterized the Isle and duped Americans of modest means into sinking their money into a losing enterprise. The play reflected a growing undercurrent of discontent among those who found that the Isle of Pines was not all it had been portrayed to be.

By 1910, U.S. interests had acquired more than 90 percent of available land on the Isle of Pines. It was a startling figure considering that ten years earlier only one American with a little more than 100 acres was on record as a property owner. Private interests largely facilitated this development, with only modest support from the U.S. government. Indeed, in a January 1904 report Elihu Root flatly stated that "The executive department of the Government does not deem the isle of value to the

---

[127] Ibid., 1. The scene description notes that the play takes place in Nueva Jeroma – presumably a misspelling of Nueva Gerona – on the Isle of Pines.
[128] Ibid., 16.

United States."[129] Nevertheless, private U.S. citizens continued to buy and sell land. Landholding companies' advertising and publicity campaigns greatly spurred this activity. These efforts successfully appealed to Americans of sufficient means who continued to look to the frontier for adventure and opportunity. But U.S. entrepreneurs were not alone in crafting this appealing vision. While they supplied the advertisements and prospectuses that drew Americans' attention, their depictions of "Treasure Island" were reflected and reinforced in U.S. popular culture, particularly among writers who described the Isle using many of the same themes. They established an image of *pineros* as simple, yet friendly and welcoming, as well as a set of assumptions about the Isle that many settlers carried with them. Depictions of the Isle as an exotic tropical paradise, a place for rejuvenation, and an area ripe for American development not only resonated in the early 1900s, but would continue to be used for the next half-century.

For the first U.S. landowners, however, simply having property was not enough. Their goal was to ensure that the Isle would be U.S. territory, not Cuban. Landholding company executives and investors looking to sell the hundreds of thousands of acres they owned feared that Americans would have little interest in buying land in a foreign country. Moreover, if the Isle was indeed foreign territory – a question that would remain in diplomatic limbo until 1925 – those entrepreneurs looking to sell their goods and produce in U.S. markets would be subject to tariffs and undermine their bottom line. To achieve annexation, then, a distinctly American presence had to be established. So began the proliferation of American settlements and communities across the Isle during the early twentieth century.

---

[129] Report of Secretary of War to U.S. Senate, January 14, 1904, *Isle of Pines*, 68th Cong., 2d sess., 1924, S. Doc. 166, 211.

2

Going South

For more than a century, U.S. citizens searching for opportunity had traveled west. They looked to exploit a frontier that promised cheap, plentiful land, a submissive or nonexistent native population, and the chance for a better way of life. By the start of the twentieth century, though, the prevailing wisdom maintained that the frontier had "closed." But old habits persisted as Americans continued to look for landed opportunity. While some settlers continued to go west – indeed, historian David M. Wrobel points out that more homesteads were settled in the first decades of the twentieth century than in all of the nineteenth century – other frontier seekers turned their gaze south.[1] Inspired by the attractive depictions that landholding companies, newspapers, and townsfolk offered, many U.S. citizens went to the Isle of Pines with their families and neighbors in ways reminiscent of the covered-wagon trains that crossed the continental United States throughout the nineteenth century. One of the first of these Isle-bound parties left from Iowa in 1901, taking a route that became typical for many turn-of-the-century settlers. The 1,000-mile trip to New Orleans was just the first leg of the journey; a boat to Havana and a train to Batabanó followed, and the trek concluded with an overnight ferry

[1] David M. Wrobel, *The End of American Exceptionalism: Frontier Anxiety from the Old West to the New Deal* (Lawrence: University Press of Kansas, 1993), 143. Note that U.S. citizens also considered frontier settlement to the south during the nineteenth century. During the mid-century height of Manifest Destiny, expansionists looked to Cuba and all of Mexico as potential additions to the United States, mostly as slaveholding territory. See Louis A. Pérez Jr., *Cuba and the United States: Ties of Singular Intimacy.* 2nd ed. (Athens: University of Georgia Press, 1997), 34–54, and David M. Pletcher, *The Diplomacy of Annexation: Texas, Oregon, and the Mexican War* (Columbia: University of Missouri Press, 1973).

to Nueva Gerona. The group consisted of twenty-three farming families from the towns of Fairfield, Spencer, Ottumwa, and Creston. They were on their way to meet with thirteen other families, from Spirit Lake, who already had established a citrus-fruit colony. News of the Iowans' efforts spread across the country.[2] Soon, parties of other Americans followed to buy property and establish farms and homes. To these settlers, the Isle of Pines became the new frontier.

Remarkably, this migration of U.S. citizens into "foreign" territory came at a time when immigration *into* the United States was on the rise. During the first decade of the twentieth century, some 8.8 million migrants arrived on U.S. shores.[3] Many of these new arrivals to the United States came in search of opportunity and to find some semblance of social mobility. They took advantage of improvements in transportation – primarily steamships and railroads – to facilitate faster and easier passage. Some, particularly those from Canada or Mexico, would often engage in circular migration in which they lived and worked in the United States for a time before returning to their countries of origin depending on the season. Many U.S. settlers who went to the Isle of Pines did so for similar reasons and followed like patterns. They came to the Isle to start up their own farms and businesses and to improve their standards of living. They traveled on new transportation networks and periodically returned to the United States. One important distinction, however, was that Americans did not consider themselves emigrants or expatriates. Rather, many of them presumed that the Isle was or would eventually become U.S. territory; living in "Cuban" territory would only be temporary.

The rapid increase of settlers marked the first decade of the twentieth century on the Isle. Frederick Swetland Jr. recalled his father's description: "It was, in the early days, like an Alaskan Gold Rush; people poured in by the boatloads, my father told me, and hostelries … were so crowded that people slept on the ground, in tents, and in wagons."[4] Thus began what some Cuban historians have termed the "neocolonial" era of the Isle's history, because while the United States did not wield formal political

[2] "An Iowa Colony Off Cuba," *Kansas City Star*, January 4, 1902; "Emigrate to Isle of Pines," *Dallas Morning News*, January 4, 1902; "Colonizing the Isle of Pines," *Pawtucket Times*, January 4, 1902; "Settling Isle of Pines," *Philadelphia Inquirer*, January 5, 1902; "The Isle of Pines," *(Eau Claire) Sunday Reader*, January 5, 1902; "Isle of Pines," *New York Times*, December 27, 1903.

[3] Roger Daniels, *Guarding the Golden Door: American Immigration Policy and Immigrants since 1882* (New York: Hill and Wang, 2004), 5.

[4] Frederick Swetland Jr. letter, March 7, 1961, 2, SFA.

control, it still came to dominate economically.[5] Yet that first generation of U.S. citizens on the Isle more closely resembled traditional colonists. These residents considered themselves pioneers who presumed that the Stars and Stripes would follow them to the Isle of Pines. They bought property, established groves and homes, and developed institutions like those they had left behind. Although their efforts to bring about annexation would ultimately fail, settlers nevertheless transformed the physical and social landscape in dramatic ways. They planted thousands of acres of citrus groves, built new towns, and spurred a population boom that would come to attract a disparate group of nationalities.

Not all settlers were pleased with what they found. In contrast to the promised tropical paradise, many settlers instead found an arid climate that made farming difficult. Although diseases such as malaria and yellow fever were virtually nonexistent, settlers commonly complained about the number of mosquitoes, flies, and other insects. Moreover, the dearth of roads and ports made importing and exporting a difficult, time-consuming, and costly process. These perceived shortcomings fueled settlers' animosity toward landholding companies for misleading portrayals that oversold the Isle's potential and Cuban officials for not doing their share to improve the island.

Indeed, settlers made clear from their first arrivals that they held Cuban authority in low regard. This contempt had multiple roots. Since many settlers believed that the Isle was or would soon belong to the United States, they were uneasy submitting to a foreign authority. The fact that it was not an Anglo-Saxon authority – most officials were of Spanish descent – certainly made many white Americans uncomfortable. Settlers also harbored a list of grievances against what they very quickly determined to be inefficient and incapable rule. They viewed most local officials as corrupt and unable to maintain order and security. Americans further decried a lack of deference from *pinero* authorities, a galling sign of disrespect given the lofty racial, national, and socioeconomic status that settlers presumed. Settlers also complained that the Cuban government did not do enough public reinvestment in the Isle's infrastructure and education system, which undermined their commercial and cultural designs. Such shortcomings exposed Cubans' unfitness for self-government.

For their part, Cuban officials were ambivalent about the U.S. presence. On one hand, politicians both in Havana and on the Isle desired

---

[5] Wiltse Peña Hijuelos, et al., *Con Todo Derecho: Isla de la Juventud* (La Habana, 1986), 36–80.

U.S. capital to develop the Isle. U.S. settlers and investors provided wages for farmhands and helped to spur a land boom that generated a great deal of revenue for Spanish and Cuban *hacendados*. On the other hand, officials were leery of Americans enjoying too much influence and power in Cuban territory, particularly with the issue of sovereignty still in question. As a result, the difficult living conditions and tension with Cuban officials produced a contentious first decade of U.S. settlement.

Carrying on the Pioneer Tradition

Contemporary writings about the Isle showed that the pioneer tradition remained a potent force in the American consciousness. In framing the Isle as the next land of opportunity, observers and advertisers drew explicit comparisons to previous frontiers. For example, journalist Irene A. Wright argued that settlers were the "legitimate heirs to the spirit, courage, health, and ability of those other pioneers, their forebears, who hewed the American Union out of the wilderness of North America, and wiped even the Great American Desert off the map."[6] Landholding companies used these comparisons as a selling point. One company wrote that "A description of these [opportunities] reads like a fairy tale and as it is told one is reminded of the pointing finger directing so many footsteps to the distant West fifty years ago and to the equally alluring call from the gold fields of Alaska."[7] In accentuating the rewards of the frontier while minimizing the risk, the Isle of Pines Company suggested that settling the Isle would be an easier task than pioneers had faced in the eighteenth and nineteenth centuries, in part because of modern improvements in technology, farming techniques, transportation, and communications. "The early settlers of Tennessee, Kentucky and the Western Reserve of Ohio had far more difficulties to surmount than you will have in the Isle of Pines. The settlers who go to Canada and the West to-day are far less fortunate than you will be in the Isle of Pines."[8] The company also maintained that settlement would be easier in Cuba because of the warmer climate, which eliminated concerns about home heating in the winter, frosts on produce, and the expense of heavy clothing.

---

[6] Irene A. Wright, *Isle of Pines* (Beverly, MA: Beverly Printing Company, 1910), 92.

[7] Cañada Land & Fruit Company, "Isle of Pines: Land of Fruit and Flowers," (Marinette, WI, 1903), 5.

[8] Isle of Pines Company, "McKinley, Isle of Pines: A City of Orange Groves in the American District of Cuba," (New York, 1911), 46.

Most settlers at the turn of the century came from the same towns, often in the U.S. Northeast or Midwest. As of 1906, the U.S. towns with the highest concentration of Isle property owners were in Wisconsin, including Fond du Lac (thirty-six landowners), Marinette (twenty-seven), and Watertown (twenty-five).[9] Duluth, Minnesota, with twenty-two registered property owners, had the next-highest concentration outside of Wisconsin. Such clustering can be attributed to several factors. First, local newspapers frequently published stories about the Isle that kept it in the public consciousness. These reports often highlighted former residents who had gone to the Isle or reprinted letters from them about their experiences. Second, classified advertisements from local landholders helped maintain local interest. Announcements touting available land were frequent staples, especially during the U.S. reoccupation of Cuba beginning in September 1906. In the *Duluth News-Tribune*, for example, H. L. Shepherd ran advertisements, usually during winter, pitching available land under headings such as: "Life Income Assured"; "No Frost in Isle of Pines"; and "Everyone Happy in the Isle of Pines."[10] Shepherd's emphasis on profit, warmth, and happiness on the Isle suggests a contrast between life there and in Duluth that may have appealed to readers.

Local agents were a third factor in the clustering of interest. Many of the smaller landowners – those who owned less than forty acres – bought their property sight unseen. Often, sales agents were their neighbors, presumably someone a buyer trusted. For example, much like Shepherd in Duluth, E. Ben Knight sold land to his neighbors in and around Penn Yan, New York. Knight, a farmer by trade, served as an agent for the Tropical Development Company and the Whitney Land Company.[11] He made frequent trips to the Isle that established his bona fides among his neighbors. Earning a commission of 15 percent plus $1 per acre, Knight sold plots to at least two dozen of his neighbors, some of whom traveled

---

[9] U.S. Congress, Senate Committee on Foreign Relations, *Isle of Pines: Papers Relating to the Adjustment of Title to the Ownership of the Isle of Pines*, 68th Cong., 2d sess., 1924, S. Doc. 166, 5–12. This list includes nearly 300 landowners in the following tracts: La Cañada; San Juan; El Canal; El Hospital; and Calabaza. It does not include other tracts popular among Americans such as McKinley, Santa Barbara, Santa Fe, Santa Rosalia, or Los Almacigos, where the aforementioned group of Iowans had settled in 1902. Such limitations testify to the incompleteness of available records that makes a precise count of U.S. property owners and settlers virtually impossible. Cuban government registries of U.S. property owners on the Isle could not be found in Cuban archives.

[10] *Duluth News-Tribune*, January 3, 1909; January 14, 1913; December 25, 1913.

[11] B. F. King to E. Ben Knight, September 10, 1912, E. Ben Knight Papers, Box 1, Folder 1, YCGHS.

with him. For instance, in 1908 Knight went to the Isle with Herman Bullock, a fellow neighbor of the Finger Lakes region, who bought a plot near Santa Fe to serve as his family's winter home.[12]

Naturalized U.S. citizens or their children made up a significant portion of the first settlers. Some had only lived in their towns for a generation or less. This trend suggests that some settlers were accustomed to migrating or looking far afield for opportunity. They also may have lacked deep roots in their local communities and thus were less hesitant to leave. Biographies of the first settlers are scant, but those available show that the trend appeared strongest in Wisconsin, home to many first- or second-generation German immigrants. One historian of the German-American experience has noted that German migrants had an "inherently expansive" culture in which "each new generation required new land."[13] If so, then this observation may explain why German-American migrants were attuned to business and real estate opportunities in far-flung places like the Isle of Pines. Two of the most notable examples were the Schultz brothers, whose father, August, was a native of Germany. Emil W. Schultz owned a furniture store and a factory before forming the Calabaza Land Company with his brother, William, in the southeast-central portion of the Isle. Max H. Gaebler, one of Emil Schultz's partners in the Watertown Table-Slide Company, also was the son of a German immigrant. One biography referred to him as a "leading manufacturer" in the area.[14] Gaebler owned thirty acres on the Isle, far less than the Schultz brothers, yet still a sizable plot.

The trend of naturalized U.S. citizens migrating to the Isle continued into the 1910s. Of the nearly 200 U.S. citizens the U.S. consulate in Nueva Gerona registered in 1913, about 35 of them were naturalized.[15]

---

[12] Philip Bullock, "This is My Life" (2006), unpublished autobiography, courtesy of Paul Bullock. Herman Bullock was Philip and Paul's grandfather.

[13] Kathleen Neils Conzen, "Phantom Landscapes of Colonization: Germans in the Making of Pluralist America," in *The German-American Encounter: Conflict and Cooperation between Two Cultures, 1800–2000*, Frank Trommler and Elliott Shore, eds. (New York: Berghahn Books, 2001), 13–16. Another scholar has argued that German-American farmers tended to be mobile, particularly the adult children of immigrants, and that they were "eager to own rather than to rent their farms." These trends also were evident among German-Americans who bought land on the Isle. Frederick C. Luebke, *Germans in the New World: Essays in the History of Immigration* (Urbana: University of Illinois Press, 1990), 166.

[14] John Henry Ott, *Jefferson County, Wisconsin and Its People: A Record of Settlement, Organization, Progress and Achievement* (Chicago: S. J. Clarke, 1917), 96.

[15] The number of registered citizens is far fewer than many of the prevailing contemporary estimates, although the ratio of native-born to naturalized citizens appears roughly

August C. Kopf was among the most notable of this group. Born in Germany, Kopf became a naturalized U.S. citizen and for a time lived in New York City before emigrating to the Isle in October 1910. Kopf, part owner of the Kopf Bros. citrus company, became a member of the Isle of Pines Chamber of Commerce, a group that for many years consisted almost exclusively of Americans. Over the course of nearly forty years on the Isle, he owned a number of groves and sold fertilizer; one U.S. consulate report stated that roughly 70 percent of the Isle's fertilizer sales went through him.[16] Carl F. Holmberg was another prominent naturalized U.S. citizen. A native of Sweden, he became somewhat of a *cause célèbre* among settlers in October 1906 when local authorities sentenced him to a $21 fine and twenty-one days in jail for cutting down a tree on his own property line. Annexationists complained to the provisional governor, Charles Magoon, then head of the U.S. administration of Cuba, that the episode was "a fair sample of Cuban 'graft' and their treatment of American Citizens."[17]

Support for Holmberg and Kopf illustrated that place of birth did not preclude their acceptance among the larger community of Americans. Two elements may help explain this phenomenon, which came at a time when immigrants to the United States were struggling for wider acceptance. First, their northern European heritage made other white Americans more comfortable. Second, as one scholar has noted, Germans were widely considered to have integrated well into American life and were thus seen as a desirable group, at least before World War I.[18] These factors explain why the larger American community on the Isle accepted naturalized U.S. citizens and why first- and second-generation

accurate based on a general survey of settler biographies. Nueva Gerona – Isle of Pines, Cuba, Vol. 58, Isle of Pines Certificates of Registration, 1913–1917, Record Group 84, NARA. At 15 percent, the number of naturalized U.S. citizens on the Isle as a portion of the overall U.S. settler population was more than twice that in the United States. According to the earliest available data through *Historical Statistics of the United States*, in 1920 only about 6 percent of the total U.S. population were naturalized citizens. See http://hsus.cambridge.org/HSUSWeb/table/seriesfirst.do (accessed August 7, 2013).

[16] World Trade Directory Report, A. C. Kopf, Nueva Gerona – Isle of Pines, Cuba, Vol. 54, 1943 (File No. 125–811.11), Record Group 84, NARA.

[17] S. H. Pearcy and Charles Raynard to Charles Magoon, November 1, 1906, Provisional Government of Cuba, "Confidential" Correspondence, 1906–1909, Box 1, Folder 003, Record Group 199, NARA.

[18] Luebke, *Germans in the New World*, 113. During the war, however, the U.S. consulate kept close tabs on anyone of German descent on the Isle, including U.S. citizens. For reports about suspected subversives, see George Makinson to U.S. Secretary of State, July 7, 1918, Nueva Gerona – Isle of Pines, Cuba, Vol. 16, Correspondence, 1918 – Part II, Record Group 84, NARA.

U.S. immigrants were willing to take a chance in a new land under presumed American auspices.

Settler Testimonials

What U.S. settlers found on the Isle and how it compared to landholding companies' alluring portrayal often depended on migrants' socioeconomic status. One group, consisting mostly of farmers and the middle class, stayed on the Isle year-round with the intention of making it their permanent home. They were not necessarily expatriates since they presumed the Isle would one day become part of the United States, if it was not already. Those who eventually returned to the United States disillusioned by what they found – or did not find – tended to come from this group. They blamed the landholding companies for exaggerating the Isle's promise, raising unrealistic expectations, and duping settlers. Moreover, they found *pineros* less agreeable than they had been led to believe and the living conditions more primitive than they were willing to tolerate.

In contrast, a second group generally only stayed part of the year, returning to their homes in the United States during the summer months when temperatures on the Isle became appreciably warmer. These settlers tended to be better off financially and could afford traveling to and from the Isle multiple times a year. This group often claimed that the Isle was just as it had been described to them; their perspectives echoed landholding companies' promotions. Apart from varnishing tales of frontier adventures to their townsfolk, these reports also served a tangible purpose. Settlers and entrepreneurs widely presumed that as more Americans took a financial interest in the Isle, as residents, tourists, or entrepreneurs, their property values would increase. This interest might also compel U.S. officials to annex the Isle, which would be a further boon to their property values and business ventures.

Among settlers who gave the Isle glowing reviews, testimonials generally addressed at least one of five points. The first enthused about the Isle's favorable climate. Temperatures ranged between seventy and ninety degrees Fahrenheit throughout the year, with humidity tempered by cooling sea breezes. Such a climate was a far cry from the oppressive heat often associated with tropical regions. It also was considered more favorable than anything found in the continental United States, especially in Florida or California, rival areas to the Isle's burgeoning tourist and citrus industries. E. T. Wheelock, a former editor at the *Milwaukee Sentinel* who was part of a landholding company that controlled a tract called

La Esperanza on the west coast, wrote that "The Time is coming I firmly believe, when the Isle of Pines will be the most popular winter resort for citizens of the United States."[19] After a brief return to his home in New Jersey, George A. Cole told his local newspaper that he was anxious to get back to his citrus grove. "He declares he will not remain north longer than is absolutely necessary for him to complete his business, for he prefers life in the balmy air and sunshine of the south," the *Trenton Evening Times* reported.[20] That also was the case for Edgar Bullock, Herman's son. A former resident of upstate New York who also had bought land from E. Ben Knight, Bullock told Knight's widow, Catherine, that he was only too happy to stay on the Isle during the winter months. "As usual the weather has been the best from the living standpoint and when we read of the storms and cold that have been going through the North, we are glad that we do not have to put up with these things the way you people up there do."[21]

A second general point referenced the Isle's soil, which was favorable to citrus fruit, vegetables, and tobacco. Such news surely resonated with farmers, who were the most common settlers. L. J. Noble, a native of Oshkosh, Wisconsin, who owned a small plantation on the Isle, expressed the soil's relationship to the bottom line most plainly. He stated that most settlers were "enterprising investors who seek to cultivate the rich soil and make use of the golden opportunities which the island affords."[22] J. H. Worst, a professor at an agricultural college in Fargo, North Dakota, echoed those sentiments, noting the Isle's "fertility."[23] Worst's description conjured an image of a feminized Isle. While adventurous Americans sowed their entrepreneurial seeds, Cuba's "Mother Earth" would bear their fruit. It was not an isolated remark; Cuban writers also often portrayed the Isle in feminine terms.[24] Such a portrayal supported the image of the Isle as nurturing and familiar rather than harsh and alien.

That the Isle yielded good produce was a third common refrain. "Isle of Pines is a Fruit Paradise," one Duluth headline read.[25] Citrus was said

[19] "Tells about Isle of Pines," *Monroe Weekly Times*, April 8, 1907.

[20] "Trenton Men Do Well on Island," *Trenton Evening Times*, October 18, 1909.

[21] Edgar Bullock to Catherine Knight, February 27, 1929, E. Ben Knight Papers, Box 1, Assorted Correspondence: 28-226-8, YCGHS.

[22] "Isle of Pines," *(Oshkosh) Daily Northwestern*, February 21, 1905.

[23] "Isle of Pines Is Described," *Grand Forks Herald*, September 1, 1910.

[24] For example, noted revolutionary-era scholar Antonio Núñez Jiménez called the Isle a "fascinating lover" (*novia fascinante*). Núñez Jiménez comment in Waldo Medina, *Aquí, Isla de Pinos* (La Habana: Instituto Nacional de la Reforma Agraria, 1961), 5.

[25] *Duluth News-Tribune*, August 16, 1906.

to be larger, more flavorful, and more abundant than any produced in Florida or California. Settlers returned to the United States with samples for their neighbors. Equally important, promoters claimed that crops grew plentifully, suggesting a good return on investment. One newspaper reported about an Oshkosh man, appropriately named Frank Grove, who estimated that he could earn between $500 and $600 an acre from his fruit trees.[26] Wheelock offered a more generous estimate: he said full-bearing groves could earn up to $1,000 an acre for their produce.[27] Despite the varying estimates, these reports trumpeted the same message: the Isle of Pines was a place of impending commercial prosperity.

Settlers' testimonials offered a fourth common point, that anyone interested in exploiting the Isle's commercial potential should act soon since property values were rapidly increasing. During the first decade of the twentieth century, settlers reported that undeveloped land sold for up to $50 an acre; cleared land with planted fruit trees sold for as much as $200 an acre. Settlers willing to put in the time and effort to improve their plots would surely reap a financial windfall. Walter Neville of Oshkosh insisted that farming on the Isle was a sound investment. "All things considered, I think like all who have visited the Isle of Pines that it is just the place for a young man with a little capital to come to and get a good start in life."[28] Frank S. Kleinkauf of Trenton, New Jersey, apparently enjoyed such a benefit. According to his hometown newspaper, he went to the Isle in 1908, bought twenty acres with his wife, Dora, to start a grapefruit grove, and "fell completely in love with the country." Six years later, the fruits of their labor were evident. "Since they started their farm, the land has doubled in value and is still increasing. The island is everywhere being cultivated and everyone there is enthusiastic about his work."[29]

To quell concerns about going to a foreign land, settlers commonly raised a fifth point: many fellow Americans already lived there, with surely more to come. "Americans are going to the island rapidly and will soon greatly outnumber the natives," Ludwig Sudlack reported to his hometown of Duluth.[30] William Schultz wrote that when he arrived on

[26] "Ideal Place to Live," *(Oshkosh) Daily Northwestern*, March 19, 1904.

[27] "Tells about Isle of Pines," *Monroe Weekly Times*, April 8, 1907.

[28] "Oshkosh Young Man's Impression of Isle of Pines," *(Oshkosh) Daily Northwestern*, February 18, 1905.

[29] "Went to the Isle of Pines for His Health, Liked it and has Since Made Home There," *Trenton Times-Advertiser*, November 8, 1914.

[30] "Isle of Pines Is a Paradise," *Duluth News-Tribune*, May 28, 1906. Sudlack apparently was a part-year resident who returned to the United States during the summer months.

the Isle from Fond du Lac in 1902, he was just one of fifteen Americans and the only one from Wisconsin. Five years later, he reported more than 2,000 Americans living there.[31] Schultz's report typified the varied estimates settlers offered about the U.S. population, little of it supported by the Cuban census. In May 1906, for example, Sudlack claimed that 1,200 Americans lived on the Isle.[32] That same month, Neville wrote that 5,000 Americans lived there.[33] According to the 1907 Cuban census that the U.S.-run provisional government conducted, the Isle had 3,276 inhabitants. That included 438 people born in the United States as well as 169 others born elsewhere.[34] Regardless of their precision, though, the numbers settlers offered suggested that more Americans were in fact coming to the Isle and that their arrivals were registering a distinct impression on those already there.

But not all settlers were satisfied with what they found. Indeed, many returning U.S. citizens offered a contrasting portrait, one that featured a harsh landscape, poor conditions, and little governance. For example, months after Cuba's independence in May 1902, some settlers complained about its ineffective government that put U.S. investments and settlements at risk. T. J. Keenan, one of the most ardent annexationists, said Cubans had done little to ensure order and stability as it had been under U.S. military occupation. He declared: "The Isle of Pines is on the verge of anarchy, having no governor, no courts, no magistrates, no schools and no revenue."[35] Although a bit hyperbolic – there were, in fact, schools, courts, and a local government featuring an *alcalde* and *ayuntamiento* – Keenan's primary contention was that taxes and duties collected on the Isle were not reinvested there by the Cuban government. As a result, he argued, the Isle's infrastructure remained deficient and local bureaucracy was underfunded and ineffective.

Other issues soon emerged. After a few days on the Isle in 1904, Charles Greve returned to his home in West Duluth, Minnesota, and declared: "Whatever others may say the Isle of Pines is the biggest swindle on earth." While conceding that the Isle had an attractive climate, he lamented that the landholding companies had already bought the best

---

[31] "Land of Fruit and Flowers," *Stevens Point Gazette*, January 30, 1907.

[32] "Isle of Pines Is a Paradise," *Duluth News-Tribune*, May 28, 1906.

[33] "Fertile Isle of Pines," *(Oshkosh) Daily Northwestern*, May 31, 1906.

[34] *Censo de la República de Cuba Bajo la Administración Provisional de los Estados Unidos, 1907* (Washington, DC: Oficina del Censo de los Estados Unidos, 1908). It is unclear if the census included settlers who only spent the winter months on the Isle.

[35] "Situation on Isle of Pines," *Hartford Courant*, November 11, 1902.

property; the only available land remaining for small farmers had poor soil and was unlikely to yield much produce. Even if a farmer had an abundant crop for sale, the problem of transportation and infrastructure meant selling crops back to the United States would be cost-prohibitive. The problems of commercially developing the Isle, Greve said, were well known in mainland Cuba. "At Havana they laugh at you if you say that you intend to buy land in the Isle of Pines.... I do not hesitate to say that the Isle of Pines is a fraud."[36]

William Murray of North Fond du Lac echoed these sentiments. He pointed out a host of inadequacies on the Isle that contrasted with the prevailing narrative. Murray cited a high cost of living – driven up largely by the cost of shipping goods and materials to the Isle – scarcity of accommodations, and a land covered in brush that was not worth the time and effort to clear. Moreover, unlike many other settlers' accounts, Murray claimed he rarely saw Americans. One exception was his encounter with R. M. Jacks, a fellow Wisconsinite. Although Jacks did not offer Murray his impression about the Isle, "Mrs. Jacks thought it no place for Americans."[37]

Julius Kuehn agreed, at least as far as Americans of modest means were concerned. He argued that the cost of clearing land, most of which was "barren," was prohibitive to the small farmer. Kuehn maintained that the Isle was perfectly fine as a winter resort, "but [was] a mighty bad place for a poor man to go and try to raise anything." Upon returning to his home in Wisconsin, he relayed to the *Eau Claire Leader* that a settler had told him "it was a crime to get Americans to locate on the island with a promise that they could get good returns from the raising of fruit."[38]

Even after U.S. citizens had spent more than a decade on the Isle, contrarian views to the Isle's popular depiction continued to emerge. Oregon native A. J. Craig offered one of the most impassioned refutations. "The land is nearly all a sand bed, with streaks of coarse gravel," he wrote in June 1914. "There is hardly any soil worthy of the name." He continued that many American families had abandoned their homes after failing to turn a profit on their small groves. Craig complained that potable water was in short supply, as were basic foodstuffs such as meat and dairy products. "The land is covered with a wild sour wire grass that stock

[36] "Says Available Land Is All Taken," *Duluth News-Tribune*, December 30, 1904. Greve claimed he traveled across the Isle for two days in search of a good plot of land, but to no avail. His primary occupation is unclear.

[37] "Not Well Pleased," *Stevens Point Daily Journal*, January 21, 1905.

[38] "Says Isle of Pines Is a Barren Land," *Eau Claire Leader*, February 14, 1906.

can't eat; a goat turned loose on the isle would starve to death." He also disputed the image of the Isle as a safe tropical paradise. He cited fifteen-foot snakes that attacked livestock, swarms of insects, tropical storms, a shortage of good schools, and a cost of living nearly double that of the United States. Not only was the Isle cost-prohibitive to the small farmer, he argued, but "it is not a fit place for white people to live."[39]

Craig's account did not go unchallenged. Robert Dunning, another Oregonian who had spent six years on the Isle, rebutted Craig's portrayal. Dunning suggested that Craig was "spiteful" because his physician's practice failed to get off the ground and argued that conditions were not as bleak as Craig described. He wrote that citrus indeed grew abundantly and was in demand in eastern U.S. markets. Homes may have appeared abandoned because most settlers returned to the United States during the summer months. Potable water was widely available in the various mineral springs around the island. And anyone who had seen fifteen-foot snakes "must have imbibed freely on 'aguardiente' (Cuban whisky)." Dunning also cited the variety of hotels, shops, social clubs, schools, and roads as proof that the Isle was far more developed than Craig had acknowledged. "The doctor has probably listened to the Havana hotel men and real estate 'sharks' who knock the Isle of Pines in order to keep tourists and investors from going there; they want them to remain in Cuba."[40]

One travel writer in 1914 assumed a balanced view between the Craig and Dunning accounts. A. Hyatt Verrill, a writer of some renown in the early twentieth century with more than 100 works to his credit, recognized that the Isle had been "widely advertised and immoderately praised." He conceded that the island had many natural attractions, including its climate, beaches, and fishing, and that settlers had done much to develop its commercial potential. "On the other hand," Verrill wrote, "the island has been grossly overestimated and overadvertised and its possibilities, resources and fertility have been greatly exaggerated by unscrupulous land-sharks and promoters." He estimated that up to one-third of the Isle was "worthless" – swampy, mountainous, or barren land that required expensive fertilizer to produce good crops. Moreover, many settlers who went to the Isle "filled with rosy hopes" found their lots below their expectations and learned "too late that they have been duped, swindled and ruined." But it was not all bad. He acknowledged

[39] "Place Not Fit for White Men," *The Oregonian*, June 19, 1914.
[40] "Isle of Pines Defended," *The Oregonian*, June 21, 1914.

that some settlers were doing well and that some land was yielding valuable produce. Verrill wrote that life on the Isle for Americans was "no 'get-rich-quick' proposition and foolish indeed is he who buys land he has not seen or who burns his bridges behind him and emigrates to a new land until he knows the truth of its resources, conditions and future at first hand."[41] Verrill's account illustrated that those settlers with insufficient capital who went "all-in" tended to meet with disappointment, while those who could afford to be patient with start-up costs more often found the Isle to their liking.

Living Conditions

With promises of paradise awaiting them, many settlers left for the Isle with a sense of excitement. Frederick Swetland Jr.'s father told him that "when he arrived sometime in 1908 or 1909, the boat disgorged full loads of immigrants; they came down the gangplank feverish with haste to build and plant."[42] But when the first settlers arrived at their destination, that enthusiasm was considerably tempered. Once off the boat, many had difficulty finding critical amenities such as shelter, food, and tools, to say nothing of luxury items. Although the Isle had been widely portrayed as a paradise ready for development, it nevertheless lacked certain comforts, which posed an immediate challenge to the first generation of settlers. Swetland recalled that even after his family was already well established, his father would pack suitcases and trunks full of household goods and tools that could not be obtained on the Isle.[43]

Settlers also encountered a persistent nuisance in pests and unfamiliar wildlife. Jim Tracy remembered an episode from his childhood in which his father, U.S. vice consul George B. Tracy, found a chicken in the family barn with a six-foot snake wrapped around it. Tracy also recalled finding tarantulas, scorpions, and voracious ants. In one instance, his father had stored some sandwiches under a tree and "when he retrieved the sandwiches that evening and took a bite he found they were covered with viviagua [*sic*] ants – ugh!!!"[44] Millie Giltner – whose father, Ira Brown, was among the first settlers – also recoiled at the Isle's insects.

---

[41] A. Hyatt Verrill, *Cuba Past and Present*, Revised Edition (New York: Dodd, Mead & Company, 1920), 162–6. Verrill originally wrote his account in 1914.

[42] Frederick L. Swetland Jr., *Isle of Pines*, 32.

[43] Ibid., 9–10.

[44] Jim Tracy, "Random Thoughts on Growing Up," (2005), unpublished memoir, courtesy of April Jean Tracy.

FIGURE 2.1. The boat landing at Nueva Gerona, the Isle's largest town and the primary port in which people and goods traveled to and/or arrived from mainland Cuba, as it appeared in the early twentieth century.
Source: The Isle of Pines (1913).

Her first impression of the Isle was being "eaten up with ants and with sand flies. You couldn't walk out across the field without being covered by fleas. The mosquitoes and sand flies. We slept with cheese cloth over our beds."[45]

The adequacy of shelter marked another hardship the first settlers endured. The Isle had few hotels and many of those who cleared land on their plots had to sleep in tents for weeks until they could build their new homes, an expense that could run anywhere from $300 to $800, according to one estimate.[46] Once they had cleared their land, settlers with modest plots tended to have small homes. For example, in 1919 Homer Bullock and his family left upstate New York and went to the Isle to work with his brother, Edgar, on a saw mill. Homer's son, Phil, recalled that the family's first house was little more than four walls and a roof.

---

[45] Millie Giltner oral history interview with Frederick Swetland Jr., March 13, 1969, tape 1, 2, SFA.
[46] Isle of Pines Company, "McKinley, Isle of Pines," 63.

"It was extremely primitive," he wrote. "The 'windows' were mere openings in the walls with covers that were hinged at the top so they could be propped open in good weather. They contained no glass but must have had netting to keep out the insects. When the 'windows' were closed, it would be dark inside."[47]

As settlers became more established on the Isle, their homes reflected their status. Many homes boasted a lavish two stories; some had indoor fireplaces and plumbing. Cuban writers noted that these features were hallmarks of "American homes."[48] Jim Tracy's home in the early 1920s had "two stories with verandahs on both floors facing the [Las Casas] river and extending partly around to the north (on the town side). There was a large living room on the river side with carbide lamp fixtures on the walls. They were never used but there was plumbing and a carbide gas generator on an outside wall. Kerosene lanterns & candles provided lighting at night."[49] The largest landowners and landholding company executives tended to have the biggest, most ostentatious homes. Phil Bullock remembered that Robert I. Wall, who was associated with two landholding companies and owned a Santa Fe hotel popular with U.S. tourists, had a "palatial" home.[50] T. J. Keenan was said in 1902 to have spent more than $50,000 to build a house, ice plant, and bathhouse, along with other property improvements; his residence was made of brick, cement, and marble.[51] By the late 1920s, the Swetland family had one of the most impressive homes on the Isle. Rebuilt and reinforced after a hurricane, the house consisted of twelve bedrooms, five bathrooms, a sixteen-seat dining room, a swimming pool, tennis court, and water fountain.[52] These homes not only marked settlers' wealth and status, but the styles and layouts starkly illustrated cultural differences between Americans and *pineros*.

---

47 Bullock, "This Is My Life."
48 Medina, *Aquí, Isla de Pinos*, 64; Eduardo Lens, *La Isla Olvidada: Estudio Físico, Económico y Humano de la Isla de Pinos* (La Habana, 1942), 17; Roberto Únger Pérez, et al., *Americanos en la Isla* (Nueva Gerona: Ediciones El Abra, 2004), 23–4; Hijuelos, et al., *Con Todo Derecho*, 50.
49 Tracy, "Random Thoughts on Growing Up."
50 Bullock, "This Is My Life"; Personal Notes on Americans Interested in the Isle of Pines, October 11, 1923, Nueva Gerona – Isle of Pines, Cuba, Vol. 32, Correspondence, 1923 – Part II, Record Group 84, NARA.
51 S. H. Pearcy, J. H. H. Randall, T. J. Keenan to John Hay, November 8, 1902, in *Isle of Pines*, 68th Cong., 2d sess., 1924, S. Doc. 166, 153; Tropical Development Company, "McKinley, Isle of Pines: A City of Orange Groves in the American District of Cuba" (Buffalo, 1906), 39.
52 Eli Swetland oral history interview with author, July 10, 2009, 9–10.

FIGURE 2.2. One of the Isle's most ardent annexationists, T. J. Keenan was said in 1902 to have spent more than $50,000 to construct his home out of brick, cement, and marble. Known as Brazo Fuerte, it was a marked architectural contrast from most of the other homes on the Isle.
Source: The Isle of Pines (1913).

First Encounters

Historian Ada Ferrer has argued that U.S. soldiers entering Cuba during the War of 1898 had to "determine, invent, construct" their understanding of Cubans.[53] So, too, did settlers when they arrived on the Isle. Based on their correspondence and interviews, settlers seemed to have a hard time fitting *pineros* into neat categories. Settlers' views of *pineros* remained ambiguous and inconsistent. Their assessments usually were intimately linked to class. *Pineros* who came from wealth were more often seen as white and civilized. Working-class *pineros*, however, tended to be viewed as less white and less civilized, though still a distinct cut above Afro-Cubans and West Indian migrants.

Cubans from all walks reacted to the U.S. presence with ambivalence. Policymakers in Havana generally tolerated if not tacitly encouraged

---

[53] Ada Ferrer, *Insurgent Cuba: Race, Nation, and Revolution, 1868–1898* (Chapel Hill: University of North Carolina Press, 1999), 190–1.

U.S. settlement if it meant developing the Isle's economy, which had been largely ignored during the Spanish colonial era. *Pineros*, meanwhile, sold land or worked on the farms and houses of U.S. settlers while enjoying cordial relations. Politicians and *pineros*, however, drew the line at U.S. annexation. They accepted American capital, customs, and institutions but made clear their belief that the Isle of Pines was sovereign Cuban territory. That debate led to sporadic tensions over two decades.

Most of the first U.S. reports about *pineros* were unflattering. Samuel H. Pearcy, vice president of the Isle of Pines Company and its on-site manager, expressed a jaundiced view of the native population in light of the Isle's earlier history as a penal colony. "[Q]uite a large percentage of the people here, even some that are well to do, are ex-convicts, who were exiled here years ago and have become residents and raised families. It is, therefore, not to be expected that they are the best class of citizens, and it seems to us it would not be out of place to watch them carefully."[54] But more so than fear for one's personal safety and property, the typical view of the first settlers was revulsion at *pineros'* living conditions, particularly regarding how some locals shared their quarters with animals. These portrayals reiterated the stereotype of tropical people as unrefined. After a three-week stay on the Isle in 1902, Willard H. Butts reported that "most of the people live in little shacks with palm thatched roofs. The whole family seems to live in the same room – old folks, children, cats, dogs, pigs, etc."[55] H. T. Mork of Duluth, who owned a hotel on the Isle, offered a similar account. With a distinct tone of disgust, he told the *Duluth News-Tribune* that *pineros* were "a lazy, shiftless, dirty breed and many of them would rather starve than work. They are the filthiest people on the face of the earth. I have seen dogs, pigs, chickens all living in the same room as the family. They seem to revel in dirt."[56] Certainly, such conditions did not apply to all *pineros*. Indeed, most eked out a modest living. According to the 1907 census, farming and fishing were the Isle's most popular occupations, but nearly 60 percent of the population was considered "without gainful employment."[57]

[54] S. H. Pearcy to Governor-General Leonard Wood, May 8, 1902, in *Isle of Pines*, 68th Cong., 2d sess., 1924, S. Doc. 166, 175.

[55] "Tells about Isle of Pines," *Omaha World Herald*, March 3, 1902.

[56] "Is a Fine Place; Natives Filthy," *Duluth News-Tribune*, June 15, 1907.

[57] *Censo de la República de Cuba Bajo la Administración Provisional de los Estados Unidos, 1907* (Washington, DC: Oficina del Censo de los Estados Unidos, 1908), 511. According to the census, 677 people worked as "farmers, fisherman, miners" and 1,946 had no "gainful occupation." Louis A. Pérez Jr. points out that most of the latter

FIGURE 2.3. Landholding company promotions and U.S. settlers often portrayed *pineros* as distinctly less modern than Americans. Such unflattering depictions, which used living conditions as supposed evidence, were typical of early twentieth-century white American stereotypes of people in tropical regions. *Source: The Isle of Pines* (1913).

Another element that made U.S. observers uncomfortable was *pineros'* clothing, or lack thereof. This view fed another stereotype that people in the tropics were less civilized, slothful, and sexually promiscuous. Ignoring mitigating factors such as climate and economic standing, Mork said: "Another feature – and one that often proves embarrassing to Americans and Europeans – is that the natives wear as few clothes as the law allows, and sometimes fewer. Out in the country men, women and children frequently go around clothed only in a pleasant smile and the Venus at the bath effect is most startling."[58] Such views were noted not only from the sparsely populated countryside but in town centers as well. Irene A. Wright described Nueva Gerona as a sleepy town where "women and children [are] idle ... and naked babies play in and out of open doors."[59] Butts said the skimpy clothing was just a phase that the

category typically were women. Pérez, *Cuba: Between Reform and Revolution*, 4th ed. (New York: Oxford University Press, 2011), 158.
[58] "Is a Fine Place; Natives Filthy," *Duluth News-Tribune*, June 15, 1907.
[59] Wright, *Isle of Pines*, 35.

young experienced. "The children run around without any clothes but as they grow up they begin to dress up as well."[60]

To some settlers, *pineros'* backward customs easily could be modernized with a little Americanization. In their promotional literature, landholding companies asserted that *pineros* welcomed the U.S. presence and were eager to learn from American tutelage. Neville's experience reinforced this view. In 1906, he reported that his grove on twenty acres was producing so well that he could entrust the "natives" with maintaining it while he returned home to Wisconsin in the summer months. His confidence in them stemmed from the fact that "they are all faithful and are striving to become thoroughly Americanized."[61] Neville's assuredness seemed to assume that because *pineros* were willing to work for him, an American, that must mean they desired Americanization. In actuality, such a relationship was unremarkable. *Pinero* wage laborers frequently worked for Spanish landowners during the colonial era. The influx of U.S. landowners at the dawn of the century meant that *pinero* laborers in search of wage-based farm work increasingly had little choice but to work for Americans.

Aside from the annexationist debate, private *pineros'* perspectives about the U.S. presence are largely absent from the archival record. The level of cooperation from both the working and landowning classes, however, suggests that *pineros* favorably greeted settlers. Local Cuban farmhands – as well as those from the West Indies, who were preferred because they spoke English – proved indispensable to settlers looking to clear their new land and plant citrus groves. Local businessmen also worked closely with Americans. Many *hacendados* sold their land to U.S. investors, which helped to create a real estate boom. Some locals also joined U.S. entrepreneurs in business ventures. Benito Ortíz did both. A native of Spain, Ortíz owned property throughout the Isle and was one of the prime sellers of real estate to U.S. investors. In 1904, he sold approximately 74,000 acres on the South Coast to the Isle of Pines Company for an undisclosed sum.[62] A year later, he joined a group of wealthy Americans to form the Isle of Pines Bank. One U.S. military report noted that settlers admired Ortíz "to such an extent that his advice is even asked by Americans on business propositions."[63] In 1908, he was

[60] "Tells about Isle of Pines," *Omaha World Herald*, March 3, 1902.
[61] "Fertile Isle of Pines," *(Oshkosh) Daily Northwestern*, May 31, 1906.
[62] Academia de Ciencias de Cuba, "Serie Isla de Pinos No. 23: Latifundismo y Especulación," Delfín Rodríguez, et al., eds. (La Habana, 1968), 4.
[63] Robert Tittoni to Charles Magoon, July 24, 1907, Secretaria de la Presidencia, 1902–1958, Legajo 9, Expediente 48, ANC.

appointed the Isle's *alcalde* and during his five-year term was one of the few Cuban officials whom settlers highly regarded. Wright wrote that Ortíz "presides to the complete satisfaction of 'natives' and Americans alike. He is a man who knows what justice is, and acts in accordance with that knowledge."[64] That his interests seemingly aligned with settlers' appeared to have much to do with this conciliation.

Tensions with Cuban Officials

Settlers' cooperation with Ortíz in his capacity as an administrator was an anomaly during the Hay-Quesada era. Americans and Cuban officials clashed frequently. Records of deliberations within the Tomás Estrada Palma administration are scarce, but indirect evidence suggests a decided wariness among officials in Havana about the growing U.S. presence. For example, U.S. Minister to Cuba Herbert G. Squiers reported in January 1903 that Cuban Minister of Foreign Affairs Carlos de Zaldo "considers there is a great danger in permitting the settlement of Cuba by communities or colonies of Americans, who may not make the most law-abiding citizens, particularly in the cases in which they may consider their interests are threatened."[65] Zaldo apparently worried about Americans who might challenge Cuban authority, especially when it came to enforcing local taxes in an area whose sovereignty remained in diplomatic limbo.

Another indication of Cuban suspicion of U.S. influence came a few years later in Wright's account of the Isle. Her work had been commissioned during the U.S. reoccupation, but was not completed until Cuban authorities had returned to power. The new Cuban government then refused to print Wright's work. She had to solicit private funds, mostly via advertisements, to publish it. The Cuban government did not want to cooperate, she wrote, because it did not want "to issue any descriptive literature of a nature nor in a language likely to attract to any section of its jurisdiction, least of all, to the Isle of Pines, more American, or other English-speaking, settlers."[66]

Yet additional evidence shows that Havana officials welcomed U.S. settlers and investors and sought to assuage Americans' concerns. Settlers feared that the Isle under Cuban jurisdiction would wither and aired their grievances before the U.S. and Cuban governments. For example, rumors

---

[64] Wright, *Gem of the Caribbean*, 31–3.
[65] Squiers to John Hay, January 22, 1903, in *Isle of Pines*, 68th Cong., 2d sess., 1924, S. Doc. 166, 165.
[66] Wright, *Isle of Pines*, Foreword.

persisted that the Cuban government planned to create a leper hospital or penal colony. Settlers also wanted a new port of entry with a customs house, a property registry, and a guarantee that at least one of the public schools would have an English-language teacher.[67] Cuba's Acting Foreign Minister José M. García Montes pledged to Squiers that Havana would accommodate settlers.[68] Although some settlers later complained that the Cuban government was slow to fulfill its pledges, Secretary of War Elihu Root strongly disagreed: "The Government of Cuba is showing every disposition to comply with all reasonable requests of the citizens of the United States on the island."[69] Indeed, it behooved the Cuban government to keep settlers happy since they provided the largest influx of capital the Isle had ever seen. U.S. investors helped to alleviate the debts of bankrupt Spanish and Cuban landowners and were pledging to turn the Isle into a tourist destination and land of export commodities that stood to provide a substantial windfall to the Cuban government in taxes and commercial development. Moreover, encouraging Anglo-American migration to the Isle supported Havana elites' aim to "whiten" Cuba as they sought to minimize the influence of Afro-Cubans and keep an independent Cuba from becoming "another Haiti."[70]

Some settlers, however, resisted partnership with the Cuban government. They were leery about working with a government that many viewed as unable or incapable of providing the support they needed for their enterprises in the form of infrastructure, bureaucratic institutions, and public works. In March 1904, Keenan assailed the Cuban government, claiming that it was not living up to its agreements, failures that were "a new demonstration of bad faith on the part of Cubans." He asserted that that customs house was a "farce," the sanitary inspector a

---

[67] James C. Lenney to Sen. Nelson Aldrich, October 31, 1902, Nelson W. Aldrich Papers, Reel 23, General Correspondence, Manuscript Division, LOC.

[68] García to Squiers, July 2, 1903, in *Isle of Pines*, 68th Cong., 2d sess., 1924, S. Doc. 166, 216–17.

[69] Elihu Root to President Pro Tempore United States Senate, January 11, 1904, in *Isle of Pines*, 68th Cong., 2d sess., 1924, S. Doc. 166, 211.

[70] The term, used in both the United States and Cuba, pejoratively suggested the potential for chaos, disorder, and economic failure. For studies about racial politics in the early Cuban republic, see Melina Pappademos, *Black Political Activism and the Cuban Republic* (Chapel Hill: University of North Carolina Press, 2011); Alejandra Bronfman, *Measures of Equality: Social Science, Citizenship, and Race in Cuba, 1902–1940* (Chapel Hill: University of North Carolina Press, 2004); Aline Helg, *Our Rightful Share: The Afro-Cuban Struggle for Equality, 1886–1912* (Chapel Hill: University of North Carolina Press, 1995).

"crank," the new judge refused to hear testimony in English, and the only English teacher on the Isle was "wholly incompetent."[71]

Two years later, settler antipathy toward the Cuban administration of the Isle continued. George Hibbard, head of the El Canal Company, argued that U.S. investment was the only reason the Cuban government had any interest in the Isle. "The moment the Cubans found that the Americans were likely to settle and improve the island they began to want it. Until that time they considered it of no account, as they had ten times more land in Cuba than they ever could make use of; but here was an opportunity to get something for absolutely nothing, and an opportunity to collect taxes from us Americans." He suggested that the Cuban government was purposely delaying badly needed infrastructure improvements because "they are so jealous of the superiority of American methods and push that they throw every obstacle our way, thinking they will discourage our people so they will leave the island with all our improvements to them."[72] Clearly, many Americans who went to the Isle for commercial purposes considered the Cuban government an unsuitable business partner.

The language barrier exacerbated this acrimony. Military observers noticed this tension during the U.S. reoccupation. In November 1906, Maj. Frederick Foltz reported that settlers "honestly tried to conform to existing laws," but that ignorance and misunderstandings, mostly because of unfamiliarity with the Spanish language, had been the primary source of conflict with Cuban authorities.[73] Another report echoed Foltz's findings. It argued that relations between settlers and *pineros* were improving and "as the Cubans and Americans learn to know each other better, misunderstanding will disappear. I believe that many of the past complaints are due to a lack of knowledge of Spanish by Americans as well as a lack of knowledge of the law of the Country."[74] Over the next decade, some settlers showed greater willingness to learn the local tongue. One American, who had lived in Havana for ten years before moving to the Isle, told a fellow U.S. traveler that "the trouble with most Americans is

---

71 "American Alleges Bad Faith in Cuba," *Trenton Times*, March 1, 1904.

72 George E. Hibbard to Sen. John T. Morgan, March 1, 1906, in *Isle of Pines*, 68th Cong., 2d sess., 1924, S. Doc. 166, 28, 32.

73 Foltz to Charles Magoon, November 12, 1906, Provisional Government of Cuba, "Confidential" Correspondence, 1906–1909, Box 1, Folder 003, Record Group 199, NARA.

74 J. A. Ryan to Frederick Foltz, January 31, 1907, Provisional Government of Cuba, "Confidential" Correspondence, 1906–1909, Box 1, Folder 003, Record Group 199, NARA.

that they don't understand the Cubans, can't speak their language. When I first came down I could only speak a little…. But that didn't worry me, and I just kept plugging away until I could *ablar* [*sic*] with the best of them. Now I get their viewpoint."[75] Indeed, many Americans who lived on the Isle picked up at least a rudimentary understanding of Spanish, although complaints persisted from Cubans about Americans speaking grammatically incorrect Spanish, or "Spanglish."[76]

Language barriers aside, settlers harbored many other grievances with Cuban authority. They generally pointed to at least one of six sources of discontent. The most-often cited reason was Cubans officials' alleged inefficiency or corruption, which offended Americans' conception of good governance. Settlers bemoaned the scarcity of government services that compelled them to go to the main island to resolve administrative matters. Samuel H. Pearcy in 1902 listed the lengths he had to go to register property with the Cuban government. In the absence of a registry on the Isle, he had to travel to Bejucal, ten miles south of Havana. According to Pearcy, due to Cuban officials' "procrastination," it took four months to execute the paperwork, during which he made ten trips from the Isle that cost $300. In addition, the Cuban notary demanded a $500 fee to draw up the deed. The recorder fee was $1,160. Taxes on the property amounted to more than $1,300. In all, he spent nearly $4,000 merely to register his property.[77] It is unclear whether the lands in question were Pearcy's personal property or (more likely) the vast acreage that the Isle of Pines Company had purchased. Although this was perhaps an atypical or exaggerated case, it does suggest why most U.S. property holders avoided the process, which made future land claims and boundary disputes difficult to verify.[78]

Settlers considered the apparently arbitrary nature of fees and fines a sign of government corruption. Eugene Lee, a teacher from Indiana who

[75] William D. Boyce, *United States Colonies and Dependencies* (Chicago: Rand McNally, 1914), 528.

[76] "Un Gran Farsa: Lo de Isla de Pinos," *La Discusión*, November 17, 1905.

[77] S. H. Pearcy, J. H. H. Randall, T. J. Keenan to John Hay, November 8, 1902, in *Isle of Pines*, 68th Cong., 2d sess., 1924, S. Doc. 166, 150.

[78] In 1906, another settler stated that it cost $30 to $50 to register property on the Isle, compared to a $2 to $3 fee in the United States. Ed Ryan to Senate Committee on Foreign Relations, January 24, 1906, in *Isle of Pines*, 68th Cong., 2d sess., 1924, S. Doc. 166, 50. One chronicler noted that up to March 1903 no Americans had officially registered their property with the Cuban government and that no landowners had paid taxes until 1904. Leland Hamilton Jenks, *Our Cuban Colony* (New York: Vanguard Press, 1928), 147.

came to the Isle in 1902, reported being shaken down by local officials at seemingly every turn. An officer threatened to arrest him for owning a shotgun, but relented when Lee resisted and the officer failed to produce a warrant. Another officer wanted Lee to pay a tax on a farm wagon, but declined to pursue the matter when Lee refused to pay. Lee also interpreted for a U.S. merchant who was on the verge of being doubly taxed for his grocery store. The tax collector claimed that since the merchant also carried tools, he should be taxed as a hardware store as well. Lee concluded that Cuban officials were trying to take advantage of the ignorant, a tactic, he said, that would ultimately lead to confrontation between settlers and *pinero* officials. "This manner of procedure has the effect to shake the faith of the Americans in the executive department of their Government ... so we are forced to the conclusion that the only sure test is to try them on."[79] Lee's comments underscored a key cultural difference between the United States and Cuba in terms of acceptable behavior of bureaucrats and officials. Whereas public workers in the United States were expected to do their jobs without additional remuneration lest they be labeled corrupt, in Cuba such patronage was more the norm than the exception, in part to supplement officials' often meager salaries.[80]

Claims of corruption eroded settlers' confidence in the fairness of the Cuban government. Ed Ryan in January 1906 told the Senate Foreign Relations Committee that he believed Cuban officials were extorting money from settlers. Such suspicion undermined trust in the authorities. "We who have had abundant experience fear to trust ourselves to the administration of Spanish and Cuban laws, either by the courts or the executive officers, as they now exist in Cuba and the Isle of Pines."[81] Charles Raynard, one of the most vocal annexationists, told Sen. John T. Morgan that U.S. citizens were growing restless living under capricious Cuban authority that was preventing them from taking full advantage of the Isle's opportunities. Calling for the U.S. government to step in and assume authority, Raynard wrote that U.S. citizens there "never will silently submit to being ruled by an incompetent government, administering ancient and obnoxious laws calculated only to retard progress and check development."[82]

---

[79] Eugene Lee to Charles Raynard, February 10, 1904, in *Isle of Pines*, 68th Cong., 2d sess., 1924, S. Doc. 166, 283.

[80] Pérez, *Cuba*, 162–4.

[81] Ed Ryan to U.S. Senate Committee on Foreign Relations, January 24, 1906, in *Isle of Pines*, 68th Cong., 2d sess., 1924, S. Doc. 166, 52.

[82] Raynard to Morgan, November 19, 1904, in *Isle of Pines*, 68th Cong., 2d sess., 1924, S. Doc. 166, 280.

The second significant source of U.S. discontent with Cuban governance derived from the desire for publicly funded infrastructure improvements. By the close of the nineteenth century, the Isle had few roads and two small ports of entry. Settlers who came to the Isle to grow export commodities were counting on improvements in roadways and ports to get their produce to market faster, cheaper, and easier. The slow progress frustrated settlers and suggested to them that Cubans were not up to the task of self-governance. Wright focused her criticism squarely on the Estrada Palma administration, claiming that under the Cuban republic's first president, "the Isle of Pines chafed under the complete neglect of her interests."[83]

Settlers had hoped the Cuban government would make substantial improvements to ports and roads. In terms of the former, Nueva Gerona and Jucaro served as the Isle's ports of entry, but they could only accommodate shallow-water vessels. Large ships could not dock, so goods had to be transported on lighter vessels to Batabanó and taken by train or truck to Havana, before they could go on oceangoing ships for points abroad. This path not only added to transportation costs, but ensured that produce would be less fresh when they arrived at market. As a result, U.S. grove and business owners called on the Cuban government to develop a deep-water port so that goods could be shipped directly to and from eastern U.S. markets. Such public projects, however, were virtually nonexistent in the early twentieth century. Private efforts tried to fill the void with little to show for it. The Whitney Land Company, for example, looked to develop such a port near Los Indios on Siguanea Bay, on the Isle's less-populated west coast. It never came to fruition, presumably because of a lack of funds. For a brief time beginning in 1909, the Isle of Pines Transportation and Supply Company, known as the Isle Line, began schooner service between Nueva Gerona and Mobile, Alabama. This enterprise also did not last long, presumably because of minimal traffic.

Settlers' more enduring complaint focused on the poor quality of roads. Most existing roads turned to mud during the rainy season, often leaving them impassable during critical times of the year. Bridges also washed out in poor weather. With appeals to the Estrada Palma administration falling on deaf ears, settlers made renewed requests to Charles Magoon, Cuba's provisional governor during the U.S. reoccupation. Magoon approved nearly $30,000 in road repairs as well as an

[83] Wright, *Gem of the Caribbean*, 33.

additional $146,647.62 to construct three major roadways.[84] Within a few years, improvements were evident. A traveler to the Isle shortly after the resumption of Cuban sovereignty reported that roads were "the equal of the best anywhere. They rarely show much grade, and of course are admirable for autoing."[85] In the decade after the provisional government's road projects, American-owned automobiles proliferated. In 1911, there were only about forty cars on the Isle. Four years later, nearly 200 sped along on some forty miles of government-maintained roads.[86]

Settlers' efforts to compel Havana to make infrastructure improvements reflected and reinforced their skepticism about Cubans' ability to govern, a third common complaint. Raynard in June 1902 referred to "the chaotic state of affairs on this island – no governor, no courts, no constitution, and no law." The situation was made worse, he wrote, because the Isle's *alcalde*, Juan M. Sánchez – whom the U.S. military appointed to the position in 1899 – was a man who had an "averseness to Americans, or anything which is American."[87] The virtual absence of law enforcement also unnerved settlers, suggesting that they did not feel entirely secure. An appeal to U.S. Secretary of State John Hay in 1902 mentioned that there were only seven policemen on the Isle and no court; all judicial proceedings at the time took place in Havana.[88]

Settlers saw the lack of quality schools as another sign of the Cuban government's ineptitude, a fourth common complaint made to U.S. officials. This concern was apparent even before Cuban independence. The first Americans had a rather dim view of the Spanish educational system they found. One U.S. military officer wrote: "Schools: None in operation

---

[84] These roadways included one from Nueva Gerona to McKinley; an extension of the Nueva Gerona–Santa Fe line to Columbia and Jucaro; and a road from Santa Fe to Los Indios, including a bridge. Wright, *Isle of Pines*, 88; N. M. Bush to Charles Magoon, May 28, 1907, Secretaria de la Presidencia, 1902–1958, Legajo 69, Expediente 61, ANC.

[85] William Browning, "The Isle of Pines as a Hibernaculum," *Long Island Medical Journal* (November 1910), 5.

[86] Vervie Sutherland to James L. Rodgers, January 17, 1911, Nueva Gerona – Isle of Pines, Cuba, Vol. 9, Correspondence, 1910–1911, 52, Record Group 84, NARA; Sutherland to E. S. Wordsworth, February 17, 1915, Nueva Gerona – Isle of Pines, Cuba, Vol. 13, Correspondence, 1914–1915, 214, Record Group 84, NARA.

[87] Charles Raynard to T. J. Keenan, June 12, 1902, in *Isle of Pines*, 68th Cong., 2d sess., 1924, S. Doc. 166, 140. See also Raynard, et al., to U.S. Minister to Cuba Edwin V. Morgan, October 24, 1906, Provisional Government of Cuba, "Confidential" Correspondence, 1906–1909, Box 1, Folder 003, Record Group 199, NARA.

[88] S. H. Pearcy, J. H. H. Randall, T. J. Keenan to John Hay, November 8, 1902, in *Isle of Pines*, 68th Cong., 2d sess., 1924, S. Doc. 166, 149.

FIGURE 2.4. One of U.S. settlers' biggest complaints was the conditions of roads. During the U.S. reoccupation of Cuba from 1906 to 1909, provisional governor Charles Magoon approved more than $175,000 in road construction and repairs. Automobiles, such as this one near the American town of Columbia, proliferated during the mid-1910s as a result.
Source: The Isle of Pines (1913).

now. Schoolmasters were ignorant and incompetent."[89] The U.S.-directed census of 1899 revealed that most *pinero* children did not go to school; only 38 of 822 children under age ten did so. Furthermore, just 22 of the Isle's 3,199 enumerated residents were said to have "superior education."[90] To reverse that trend, the U.S. government established primary and secondary schools across Cuba, including the Isle, during the U.S. military occupation.

The Cuban government pledged to provide for English-language instruction in its schools to placate settlers anxious about the Isle's school system.[91] But a little more than a year after Cuban independence,

[89] Capt. Fred S. Foltz to Lt. Col. Tasker H. Bliss, February 22, 1899, in *Isle of Pines*, 68th Cong., 2d sess., 1924, S. Doc. 166, 193.

[90] *Report on the Census of Cuba, 1899* (Washington, DC: Government Printing Office, 1900).

[91] José M. García Montes to Herbert G. Squiers, July 2, 1903 and Carlos de Zaldo to Squiers, December 9, 1903, in *Isle of Pines*, 68th Cong., 2d sess., 1924, S. Doc. 166, 216, 220.

U.S. residents complained that schools were not being properly maintained. Specifically, they were not providing sufficient English-language instruction, or following any U.S.-established curricula. In November 1904, Raynard wrote that the "Spanish-English school ... teaches only Spanish, and is in session but two and a half to three hours on such days of the week as the teacher feels so disposed as to be in attendance." He continued that "the discipline and instruction [was] so unsatisfactory as to cause Americans to withdraw their children from such schools and to employ, at their own expense, governesses and teachers wherever it is possible to do so."[92] Raynard pressed his case against the Cuban school system the following year in a letter to the *Washington Post*. Citing the "deplorable condition" of the school system, he argued that the Cuban government was reneging on its agreement to hire teachers who could speak, read, and write in English. As an example of how much education conditions had deteriorated, he cited one teacher who not only habitually arrived to school late and left early, but also smoked in class and used vulgar language in front of the students.[93] Squiers, though, was sympathetic to Cuban officials in this matter. He recognized that with the Isle's sovereignty in diplomatic limbo, the Cuban government was reluctant to pour resources into the educational system there.[94]

The absence of quality schools, government services, law enforcement, and infrastructure led settlers to question how the Cuban government allocated their taxes, a fifth common complaint. Many were upset that the monies from their property taxes – which only applied to improved properties, that is, lands cleared for groves, businesses, and residences – were being sent to Havana with little of it reinvested into the Isle. As Josiah L. Pearcy, Samuel's brother, summarized: "The Cuban authorities have been levying and collecting taxes upon property and privileges in the island, but have never spent as much as one dollar that I have ever heard of for the benefit of the people from whom they collect these taxes."[95] Protests in this vein stressed that settlers were suffering "taxation without representation." In a November 1902 appeal to Hay, Samuel H. Pearcy,

[92] Raynard to John T. Morgan, November 19, 1904, in *Isle of Pines*, 68th Cong., 2d sess., 1924, S. Doc. 166, 279.
[93] Raynard to *Washington Post*, August 7, 1905, in *Isle of Pines*, 68th Cong., 2d sess., 1924, S. Doc. 166, 281–2.
[94] Squiers to John Hay, March 18, 1903, in *Isle of Pines*, 68th Cong., 2d sess., 1924, S. Doc. 166, 187.
[95] J. L. Pearcy to John T. Morgan, December 18, 1905, in *Isle of Pines*, 68th Cong., 2d sess., 1924, S. Doc. 166, 274.

T. J. Keenan, and J. H. H. Randall wrote that "As it is now, Americans owning property on the island are taxed without representation, and money extracted from them is used in no way for their benefit."[96] This argument powerfully harkened back to the roots of U.S. independence and what it meant to be an American. Their pleas struck a sympathetic chord with some in the United States. In a December 1903 editorial, the *Philadelphia Inquirer* drew attention to settlers' plight, writing that "the tax-payers never received any value for their money. No effective arrangements were made for the maintenance of order, for the construction and repair of roads, for the institution of schools or for the supply of any other of the various facilities required by a civilized community."[97]

A sixth issue settlers raised suggested that Cuban authorities did not grant them the proper respect or deference. Certainly these feelings stemmed, in part, from having to submit to the authority of a foreign government in a land that many settlers believed belonged to the United States. As one longtime settler reflected, "You must understand that when we were on the Isle of Pines as Americans we were on American territory and understood it would be American territory in the future."[98] Turn-of-the-century racial conceptions also merit consideration. Although virtually all *pinero* officials were well-to-do men who were considered "white," the fact that they were of Spanish descent – some were even natives of Spain – nevertheless put them a rung below Anglo-Saxons on the hierarchy of whiteness.[99] Submitting to the authority of "lesser" peoples who governed ineffectively surely chafed at Anglo-Americans, who comprised the vast majority of settlers.

Some settlers charged Cubans with incivility and offending their sense of propriety. In one complaint from "the American people of the Isle of Pines," Cuban officials were accused of acts that were a "disgrace to civilization." One egregious affront was the burial of a deceased American in an open cemetery, his body allegedly dismembered by authorities before it was cast into a mass grave. The act was a demonstration of "officials'

---

[96] S. H. Pearcy, J. H. H. Randall, T. J. Keenan to John Hay, November 8, 1902, in *Isle of Pines*, 68th Cong., 2d sess., 1924, S. Doc. 166, 150. The archival record does not offer any precise indication of tax rates.

[97] "Will Open a Port and a School for Them," *Philadelphia Inquirer*, December 14, 1903.

[98] Ernest Gruppe oral history interview with Frederick Swetland Jr., June 21, 1971, tape 18, 3, SFA.

[99] Matthew Frye Jacobson, *Whiteness of a Different Color: European Immigrants and the Alchemy of Race* (Cambridge, MA: Harvard University Press, 1998); David R. Roediger, *Working Toward Whiteness: How America's Immigrants Became White* (New York: Basic Books, 2005).

bitter contempt of the Americans."[100] In another incident, *pinero* authorities arrested Eugene Lee for burying his deceased brother unlawfully. After being held for four days on the Isle, he was transferred to a jail in Bejucal, where conditions were decidedly less pleasant. Lee's cell was "infested with vermin and festooned with cobwebs" and already occupied by "a Cuban woman of ill fame and unsavory odor, who had been placed there on a charge of drunk and disorderly conduct." To his great discomfort, Lee shared the cell's lone cot with the woman, but only for a night before she was released. Later in his thirty-one-day sentence, he shared his cell with another woman "who was at once the filthiest and noisiest specimen I have ever seen. She annoyed me very much, and I would have liked to have had her removed, but I suppose she was put in my cell on purpose to humiliate me.... I had the pleasure and honor of the company of my colored female chum for about a week, when she was taken to the lunatic asylum."[101]

Both tales reveal a range of personal and societal offenses that would have reinforced settlers' views of Cuban unfitness for self-government. Reports of the disinterment and treatment of the dead were retold with tones of revulsion. The unsigned letter gives additional explicit details about the condition of dead bodies that clearly were meant to persuade the reader of Cuban officials' disrespect and incivility. Lee's story suggests the same, particularly in his points about sharing space with non-white inmates. Sharing a cell with a woman also violated his sense of gender propriety, not just in sharing such close quarters, but also in literally lying down with a woman he did not know. That his latter companion was non-white and, allegedly, insane only added to the insult of the situation.

For *pinero* officials, class dynamics surely affected their approach to settlers as well. Most of the Isle's administrators, including the *alcalde* and members of the *ayuntamiento*, were men of Spanish descent who maintained significant property holdings. Some officials belonged to the coterie of politically well-connected elites in Havana and were appointed to administrative positions on the Isle. Settlers typically decried these men as "carpetbaggers."[102] Financially, they were well off. Settlers who owned

---

[100] "Compliments of the American People of the Isle of Pines," undated, in *Isle of Pines*, 68th Cong., 2d sess., 1924, S. Doc. 166, 275.

[101] Lee to Raynard, February 10, 1904, in *Isle of Pines*, 68th Cong., 2d sess., 1924, S. Doc. 166, 283–4.

[102] For examples, see Charles Raynard to *Washington Post*, September 3, 1906, General Records, General Classified Files, 1898–1945, Box 72, Record 377, Record Group 350, NARA; Lt. Robert Tittoni to Chief of Staff, Army of Cuban Pacification, January 19,

ten- to twenty-acre lots typically were not, at least to the same extent. To these *pinero* officials, then, showing undue deference to foreigners below them on the socioeconomic ladder would have been discomfiting.

Others grew tired of the grief Americans gave them. Judge Alberto Diago was one such official. Named the Isle's first magistrate in 1904, Diago recalled the appointment as a trying time in his career. "I endured all kind of trouble as the political situation there is very hard to deal with: the Americans in that Island do not abide our laws or authority; I had to stand many inconveniences against me as Judge, for the sake of avoiding greater friction and complaints, and I stood it two years, daily asking for my relief." When his transfer to Matanzas came through in 1906, Diago remembered it as "one of the happiest days of my life."[103] During the reoccupation, U.S. officials approached Diago about returning to the Isle. But he made clear that he had no desire to go back, not just because of his reluctance to deal with Americans again, but also out of concern for the poor conditions of the schools and their effect on his children.

Indeed, tensions between settlers and Cuban officials – especially judges – ran particularly high whenever Americans were arrested. Most incarcerations were for minor offenses, usually when settlers refused to comply with Cuban authorities. Some, like Lee, were arrested for violating court orders. Others were fined and sometimes jailed for refusing to pay taxes. In one instance, *pinero* authorities arrested A. W. Moerke for not paying taxes on his store; he had refused on the grounds that the Cuban government had no authority on the Isle. Moerke's arrest made headlines in the United States – the *New York Times* referred to him as a "Martyr" – although it remains unclear how the matter was resolved.[104]

1907, Provisional Government of Cuba, "Confidential" Correspondence, 1906–1909, Box 1, Folder 003, Record Group 199, NARA; T. B. Anderson to Woodrow Wilson, September 15, 1913, 1910–29 Central Decimal File, General Records of the Department of State Relating to the Internal Affairs of Cuba, NARA Microcopy 488, Roll 27, File 837.014P/116; "Isle of Pines Natives Must be Re-Cubanized," *Isle of Pines Appeal*, May 10, 1924.

[103] Alberto Diago to Frank Steinhart, December 8, 1906, Provisional Government of Cuba, "Confidential" Correspondence, 1906–1909, Box 1, Folder 003, Record Group 199, NARA.

[104] "Isle of Pines Martyr," *New York Times*, March 1, 1906. The man in question was probably August E. Moerke, a native of Mason City, Iowa, who U.S. records show lived on the Isle with his wife and two children from 1903 through at least 1922. He also worked as a postmaster in Columbia.

The arrest in July 1906 of three Americans for operating an unauthorized telegraph line spurred some of the most serious tension between settlers and Cuban officials. The dispute stemmed from a telegraph line that Louis C. Giltner, H. L. Augustine, and Millie Brown (Giltner's future wife) had set up in Columbia. Upon discovery, the Isle's Judge of First Instance, Vicente Moreno y Díaz, ordered the trio to pay a $500 fine – the maximum allowed – for violating a statute against unauthorized telegraph lines, a law established during the first U.S. occupation. When they refused to pay the fine, Moreno sentenced each to thirty-three days in jail. The swiftness with which Moreno handed down the sentence suggested to the conspiracy-minded *Philadelphia Inquirer* that it was "as though the Cuban officials were anxiously awaiting just such a chance" to arrest Americans.[105]

The most egregious offense, however, was Moreno's sentencing of Brown, a nineteen-year-old woman, to a common jail. The *Havana Post* reported: "Some of the Americans seemed at first simply stunned with surprise that the new judge could be so inconceivably narrow minded, not to say vindictive, as to impose any real penalty on a young lady for such a purely nominal offense. Surprise developed into indignation – and as the news spread through the island anger grew into universal condemnation, and in many cases ominous threats of vengeance were heard."[106] As most U.S. citizens did when they ran afoul of Cuban authorities, Brown appealed to U.S. officials for help. She wrote to Morgan that "beside the indignity of arrest and imprisonment without cause are added the outrages of compelling a young girl of 19 years to pass 33 days and nights in the close companionship of some twenty guards and male prisoners."[107] Thanks to the public pressure as well as U.S. *chargé d'affaires* Jacob Sleeper's lobbying, Estrada Palma commuted the trio's respective sentences after twelve days. But the damage already had been done, because it further inflamed settlers' opposition to Cuban authority. The *Havana Post* incisively assessed the implications of the affair, citing Moreno's sentence as a mistake that played into the hands of annexationists: "A judge who would be so narrow minded ... will simply be playing right into the hands of the most radical of the American 'revolutionists.' The latter

---

[105] "Americans Jailed in the Isle of Pines," *Philadelphia Inquirer*, July 18, 1906.

[106] Quoted in *Isle of Pines Appeal* Supplement, July 23, 1906.

[107] Ibid. According to one report, Brown turned down *alcalde* Juan M. Sánchez's offer of confinement to his home rather than the jail. "Palma Pardons Isle of Pines Prisoners," *Hartford Courant*, July 26, 1906.

are looking for trouble – a kind of trouble big enough to excite sympathy in the United States, and, as they hope, hasten American control."[108] Brown's mother, who had been in the United States when the incident unfolded, insisted on paying her daughter's fine when she returned to the Isle. Isabel Brown wanted to pay the fine "on the ground that she could not permit her daughter to be used by American revolutionaries for the purpose of creating sympathy with their cause."[109] Indeed, the incident had occurred during the height of the annexationist movement that sowed discord not only between Americans and *pineros* but also between settlers and the U.S. government. This friction would linger until the sovereignty question was settled in 1925 and would be a hallmark of the first quarter-century of U.S. settlement.

Despite mixed reviews of the Isle's potential, difficult living conditions, and tensions with Cuban officials, Americans continued to migrate to the Isle of Pines at the turn of the twentieth century. The pioneering ethos that compelled Americans to travel westward in the nineteenth century still resonated with those who went south. The lure of opportunity on a new frontier remained strong, as did the idea that a settler could make a new and better life for himself on the Isle through hard work and pluck. While the popular pioneer myth credited rugged individualism for taming the frontier, the federal government had played a critical role in developing the West's infrastructure and facilitating the movement of people, goods, and resources. On the Isle, U.S. settlers recognized the importance of government assistance. That Havana-directed improvements were so slow in coming – presumably because Cubans did not have the foresight, expertise, or wherewithal for such development projects – frustrated settlers.

A great deal of settlers' irritation stemmed from the Isle's underdeveloped infrastructure, which undermined their commercial endeavors. Promoters maintained that the exploitation of the Isle's natural resources, especially commercial farming of citrus fruit and vegetables, would finance settlers' ventures. The promise of high returns on investment inspired many settlers to come to the Isle and try their hand at what for most Americans was a new type of farming. As a result, during the early twentieth century the Isle's landscape was transformed into a collection

---

[108] Quoted in *Isle of Pines Appeal* Supplement, July 23, 1906.
[109] "Palma Pardons Isle of Pines Prisoners," *Hartford Courant*, July 26, 1906. The roots of Isabel Brown's antipathy toward annexationists are unclear.

of groves and gardens that grew produce primarily for U.S. markets. The size and strength of the U.S. community on the Isle was often directly proportional to its commercial endeavors – or at least the optimism that such efforts *would* be productive and profitable. Indeed, settlers of the early twentieth century largely enjoyed slow and steady growth in their farms and businesses. It was amidst this sense of optimism and commercial activity that the American colony reached its apex.

3

Squeezing a Profit

Like other Americans of modest means who went to the Isle of Pines at the turn of the twentieth century, Frank Kleinkauf was accustomed to struggle. As a young man, the Trenton, New Jersey, native was afflicted by throat problems. Doctors recommended he go to a warmer climate to ameliorate his condition, so he went to the Isle. Once there, Kleinkauf not only found relief, but, according to his hometown newspaper, he "fell completely in love with the country."[1] He desperately wanted to return, but he still had to figure out a way financially to sustain himself and his new wife, Dora. The answer, upon which many other like-minded settlers arrived, involved growing citrus fruit for export. In 1908, the Kleinkaufs scraped enough money together to return to the Isle and buy twenty acres in Santa Ana to start a grapefruit grove. That was just the beginning of their new hardship, though. Frank and Dora had to clear, plant, and maintain the grove until it bore fruit. For a year, the couple lived in a tent. To generate income while they waited, Frank managed an automobile garage in Nueva Gerona and sold vegetables. As the *Trenton Times-Advertiser* explained in 1914, "the past six years have been extremely hard ones for the Kleinkaufs." But that year, the grove came into bearing and the couple started selling fruit to merchants in New York City, the major market for Isle citrus. The Kleinkaufs' fortunes apparently were changing. "Kleinkauf soon expects to devote his entire time to his farm and retire from all other kinds of work," the *Times-Advertiser* stated. "He has now constructed a good-sized bungalow on his farm and is considered

---

[1] "Went to the Isle of Pines for His Health, Liked It and Has since Made Home There," *Trenton Times-Advertiser*, November 8, 1914.

one of the future big cultivators on the island."[2] The Kleinkaufs' good fortune did not end there. In February 1914, they also bore something else: a son, George.

The Kleinkaufs' tale of struggle and success was similar to other settler narratives that appeared in U.S. newspapers during the 1910s, a decade that marked the high tide of American settlement. Promoters almost uniformly suggested that settlers could support themselves through the commercial exploitation of the Isle's natural resources – chiefly, citrus groves (especially grapefruit) and vegetable gardens for export back to the United States. Those who started the process at the turn of the century were just beginning to see their first fruits in the early 1910s.

The idea of making a living off the land appealed to farmers, who were the target audiences for most promotions. The Isle of Pines Company claimed in its 1901 prospectus that farmers in the United States got an average of $8.26 an acre for their crops. In contrast, it maintained that farmers could fetch at least $100 an acre for what they grew on the Isle.[3] Some Americans who went to the Isle trumpeted the same promises. J. H. Worst, who taught at an agricultural college in North Dakota, surmised in 1910 to his hometown *Grand Forks Herald* that growing commercial citrus could cover the cost of moving to and living on the Isle: "Many families are purchasing a few acres with a view to their improvement as a winter residence, anticipating sufficient revenue from their citrus fruit groves to pay for their transportation and living expenses."[4] Spurred by this optimism, U.S. settlers in the first two decades of the twentieth century transformed the Isle's landscape into a land of commercially oriented citrus groves and vegetable gardens.

Such schemes, though, went against commercial trends in the early twentieth-century United States. Industrialists were the primary drivers of the U.S. economy. These entrepreneurs were looking for markets abroad in which to sell factory-made goods that were being produced in greater quantity and efficiency. The desire to sell products abroad more easily was one of the reasons for the reciprocity treaty the United States and Cuba signed in 1903 that reduced up to 40 percent the Cuban tariff on U.S. goods. In contrast, Americans on the Isle of Pines shunned this industrializing (though not necessarily its technology). Instead, they were looking to grow agricultural products and preserve an agrarian-oriented

[2] Ibid.

[3] Isle of Pines Company, "The Isle of Pines: Uncle Sam's Latest Acquisition of Territory" (New York, 1901), 14.

[4] "Isle of Pines Is Described," *Grand Forks Herald*, September 1, 1910.

economy. What's more, these settlers envisioned the United States as the principal marketplace for their commodities. This approach was not unique. The U.S.-based United Fruit Company, for example, was establishing plantations in the Caribbean region to sell produce primarily to U.S. markets. And historian Kristin Hoganson points out that imports were an important hallmark of the burgeoning U.S. empire at the turn of the twentieth century.[5] But U.S. policymakers at the time were in the midst of trying to reverse trade imbalances. Elihu Root in 1906 took the first trip to South America by a sitting secretary of state in large part to ameliorate the yawning U.S. trade deficit with the region.[6] U.S. settlers' efforts on the Isle of Pines, then, seemed to go against the grain of Washington's commercial policy.

While export commodities were the most notable commercial activity among settlers, they also engaged in other ventures that allowed them to make a living and grow the Isle's economy. Some entrepreneurs provided goods and services to other settlers and *pineros*. Such businesses included banks, hotels, shipping, and general stores. Some enterprises looked to stimulate tourism, though it was often in service of compelling travelers to buy land. By the early 1920s, U.S. citizens had invested an estimated $15 million on the Isle and their property was valued at $21.75 million, nearly half of that in citrus groves.[7] While these figures represented only a tiny fraction of total U.S. investments in Cuba – which U.S. officials in 1924 estimated at $1.36 billion, nearly half of which was in the sugar industry – it was a significant sum on the Isle, which the Spanish had generally ignored during the colonial era.[8]

Although the first generation of settlers prided themselves on their self-reliance, their businesses depended on local labor and Cuban government

[5] Kristin L. Hoganson, *Consumers' Imperium: The Global Production of American Domesticity, 1865–1920* (Chapel Hill: University of North Carolina Press, 2007).

[6] *Speeches Incident to the Visit of Secretary Root to South America* (Washington, DC: Government Printing Office, 1906).

[7] Population of Cuba and Isle of Pines and United States Investments Therein, undated, 1910–29 Central Decimal File, General Records of the Department of State Relating to the Internal Affairs of Cuba, NARA Microcopy 488, Roll 28, File 837.014P/313; Charles Forman to U.S. Secretary of State, January 11, 1922, 1910–29 Central Decimal File, General Records of the Department of State Relating to the Internal Affairs of Cuba, NARA Microcopy 488, Roll 27, File 837.014P/164. Forman estimated that U.S. citizens owned 460,800 acres of land, including 10,470 acres of citrus worth an average of $1,000 an acre.

[8] State Department Memorandum, December 10, 1924, 1910–29 Central Decimal File, General Records of the Department of State Relating to the Internal Affairs of Cuba, NARA Microcopy 488, Roll 28, File 837.014P/310.

assistance. This dynamic illustrated the symbiotic relationship between Americans and the local population. Settlers needed *pinero* cooperation for everything from buying and clearing land to packing fruit and domestic work. By the same token, American-led investment and development projects faced little resistance from Cubans. Politicians tolerated, if not tacitly encouraged, private American activity because settlers were commercially developing a place once used primarily for cattle ranching or subsistence farming. For *pineros*, U.S. commercial enterprises, particularly citrus groves, meant jobs. Isle natives, however, often faced competition for farm and domestic work from other Caribbean islanders, especially those from Jamaica and the Cayman Islands. U.S. farm and business owners preferred workers from the British West Indies because they spoke English and worked for lower wages. Nevertheless, Cuban essayist Waldo Medina credited U.S. economic activity for creating what he called "prosperity" on the Isle during the early twentieth century.[9]

The success of settlers' enterprises – or, more accurately, the *optimism* for success – sustained the U.S. community during the first two decades of the twentieth century. The opportunity to make a comfortable living, whether through export commodities or running a local business, was the biggest draw for most Americans. Sen. Orville Platt understood this attraction, in general, but he was nevertheless skeptical. Writing to a Connecticut constituent in 1904 who had asked him about business opportunities in Cuba, Platt wrote, "I think it is a natural characteristic of mankind to look for business opportunities far away from home, feeling that they may do better in another state or country than where they reside – the usual result is disappointment."[10] For most Americans who went to the Isle of Pines, his words would be prescient.

Export Industries

U.S. settlers' cultivation and extraction of natural resources for export back to the United States was hardly unique to the Isle. Other American entrepreneurs had been doing likewise elsewhere in Cuba since the Spanish

---

[9] Waldo Medina, "Isla de Pinos en el XXII Aniversario de la Ratificación del Pacto Hay-Quesada," in *Aquí, Isla de Pinos* (La Habana: Instituto Nacional de la Reforma Agraria, 1961), 39. Medina, however, was not an uncritical supporter of the U.S. presence on the Isle. In another essay, he argued that the Isle's era of prosperity was the result of U.S. "imperial" expansion of colonists and capital. See "Isla Profanada," in *Aquí, Isla de Pinos*, 64.

[10] Sen. Orville Platt to W. H. Putnam, December 5, 1904, Orville Platt Papers, Box 2, Official Correspondence: 1900–1905 – Various Subjects, 190, Record Group 69, CSL.

colonial era, mostly in the sugar and tobacco industries. This activity continued into the twentieth century. At the conclusion of the U.S. military occupation in May 1902, U.S. capitalists had invested approximately $45 million in Cuban tobacco and an additional $25 million in sugar.[11] Thanks to growing demand in the United States and a reciprocity treaty in 1903, U.S. entrepreneurs began pouring even more money into Cuban sugar. By World War I, American companies – including corporations such as Coca-Cola, Hershey, and Hires Root Beer – owned up to 50 percent of the sugar mills in Cuba.[12] In fact by 1918, the New York–based Cuba Cane Sugar Corporation became the largest sugar enterprise in the world.[13]

Neither sugar nor tobacco grew in abundance on the Isle because of soil conditions, but settlers had their eye on other produce. Citrus fruit quickly emerged as the top enterprise, growing to a more than $500,000-a-year industry by the early 1920s.[14] Vegetables such as peppers, cucumbers, and eggplant later proved another key export. Interest in these products reflected the growing demand for imported foods in the late nineteenth- and early twentieth-century United States.[15] Americans, however, had limited involvement in timber and marble, the Isle's other main commercial trades; Cuban- and Spanish-owned enterprises dominated those industries and sent most of their production to Cuban markets. Nevertheless, before the arrival of Americans, there is no evidence to suggest that any produce or resources from the Isle had been exported to the United States, at least on any appreciable commercial scale; *pineros'* crops mainly had been used for subsistence or local trade. Migrating

[11] Jules Robert Benjamin, *The United States and Cuba: Hegemony and Dependent Development, 1880–1934* (Pittsburgh: University of Pittsburgh Press, 1974), 8.

[12] César J. Ayala, *American Sugar Kingdom: The Plantation Economy of the Spanish Caribbean, 1898–1934* (Chapel Hill: University of North Carolina Press, 1999), 78; Hugh Thomas, *Cuba, or the Pursuit of Freedom*, Updated Edition (New York: Da Capo, 1998), 541.

[13] Muriel McAvoy, *Sugar Barons: Manuel Rionda and the Fortunes of Pre-Castro Cuba* (Gainesville: University Press of Florida, 2003), 81–103; Ayala, *American Sugar Kingdom*, 87–9. See also Gillian McGillivray, *Blazing Cane: Sugar Communities, Class, and State Formation in Cuba, 1868–1959* (Durham, NC: Duke University Press, 2009), 34–6, 75–80; Thomas, *Cuba*, 289–90, 466–70, 536–43; Louis A. Pérez Jr., *Cuba and the United States: Ties of Singular Intimacy*, 2nd ed. (Athens: University of Georgia Press, 1997), 17–28, 59–63; Leland Hamilton Jenks, *Our Cuban Colony: A Study in Sugar* (New York: Vanguard Press, 1928), 18–40.

[14] See data in Nueva Gerona – Isle of Pines, Cuba, Vol. 1, Record of Fees and Declared Exports, Record Group 84, NARA.

[15] Hoganson, *Consumers' Imperium*, 105–15.

Americans saw the Isle then as an untapped commodity ripe for commercial exploitation and the fastest way to personal wealth.

By the early twentieth century, citrus production had become a burgeoning industry in the United States. Given their subtropical climates, Florida and California were the two main centers of domestic production. In a search for investors, industry leaders made appeals to potential growers in the Northeast and Midwest similar to those landholding companies offered about the Isle. In southern California, the citrus industry's advertisements promoted the warm climate, land availability, and potential for profits to attract new growers from cold-weather locales. One 1893 pamphlet, titled "Land of Sunshine," read like a landholding company prospectus from the Isle, complete with pictures of southern California's lush landscapes and touting the area's desirable climate and promise of wealth.[16] Much like advertisements that promoted town centers on the Isle, domestic citrus promoters touted California as a place where American life could be perfected. Historian Matt Garcia argues that "writers often projected the image of the yeoman farmer as the ideal citrus rancher and the foundation for a new and improved society in the far West."[17] Isle promoters' campaigns were consistent with those of Florida and California. They not only appropriated much of the same rhetoric and promotional points but also claimed that domestic citrus land was closed off to further settlement, suggesting the Isle as the next citrus frontier.

Citrus had been a marginal industry on the Isle before Americans arrived. According to one report, the Isle hardly even had any citrus trees before U.S. settlement.[18] But U.S. entrepreneurs identified citrus, particularly grapefruit, as well suited for the Isle because its soil was deep and well drained. Geographer Morton D. Winsberg argued that entrepreneurs also chose grapefruit because it was getting a high price in U.S. markets and was durable enough to withstand shipping back to

[16] Douglas Cazaux Sackman, *Orange Empire: California and the Fruits of Eden* (Berkeley: University of California Press, 2005), 36. See also Catherine Cocks, *Tropical Whites: The Rise of the Tourist South in the Americas* (Philadelphia: University of Pennsylvania Press, 2013), 32–40.

[17] Matt Garcia, *A World of Its Own: Race, Labor, and Citrus in the Making of Greater Los Angeles, 1900–1970* (Chapel Hill: University of North Carolina Press, 2001), 19. See also Henry Knight, *Tropic of Hopes: California, Florida, and the Selling of American Paradise, 1869–1929* (Gainesville: University Press of Florida, 2013), 81–116.

[18] Exports of Grapefruit and Vegetables, June 14, 1923, Nueva Gerona – Isle of Pines, Cuba, Vol. 33, Correspondence, 1923 – Part III, Record Group 84, NARA.

the United States.[19] This turn-of-the-century interest came at a time when the U.S. citrus industry was enjoying substantial growth. Produce that had once been primarily imported from the Mediterranean and the West Indies was being grown more commonly by domestic farmers.[20] Settlers hoping to capitalize on this interest imported citrus trees from Florida to jumpstart commercial growing on the Isle. Produce included grapefruits, oranges, lemons, limes, and tangerines, as well as pineapples. As the Isle's citrus industry took root, it made significant inroads into U.S. markets. Eighty-four percent of U.S. grapefruit imports in 1914 were from Cuba, up from just 11.5 percent in 1906; produce from the Isle made up four-fifths of those shipments.[21] Isle fruit's journey from tree to table was a cumbersome process, however. Local packers sent the fruit to the ports at Nueva Gerona and Jucaro in preparation for a steamship to Batabanó. From there, fruit went by truck or train to Havana before being shipped to the United States – most often New York – and then to local markets.

The Isle's major competitive advantage over domestic U.S. producers was its longer growing season. At the turn of the century, Florida was still reeling from the "great freeze" of 1894–5 that destroyed much of that season's citrus crop and spurred growers to move further south.[22] This climatic consideration also explained growers' interest in the Isle, where the weather was warmer and ran no risk of frost. Fruit typically came into bearing six to eight weeks before Florida, giving Isle growers a window in which they had virtually no competition in U.S. markets. During that time, citrus prices reached their peak and business grew to its most active. Grapefruit crates, which usually weighed seventy pounds, sold for upwards of $4 apiece. This price gave growers an average net return of fifty cents a box after expenses such as picking, packing, and shipping.[23] But when Florida and California fruit entered the market, prices dropped,

[19] Morton D. Winsberg, "Costs, Tariffs, Prices and Nationalization: The Rise and Decline of the American Grapefruit Industry on the Isle of Pines, Cuba," *American Journal of Economics and Sociology* 20 (October 1961): 544.

[20] Louis W. Ziegler and Herbert S. Wolfe, *Citrus Growing in Florida*, Revised Edition (Gainesville: University Press of Florida, 1975), 6.

[21] Carmen Diana Deere, "Here Come the Yankees! The Rise and Decline of United States Colonies in Cuba, 1898–1930," *Hispanic American Historical Review* 78 (November 1998): 758.

[22] Ziegler and Wolfe, *Citrus Growing in Florida*, 6; Mark Derr, *Some Kind of Paradise: A Chronicle of Man and the Land in Florida* (Gainesville: University Press of Florida, 1998), 84.

[23] Estimates derived from Irene A. Wright, *Isle of Pines* (Beverly, MA: Beverly Printing Company, 1910), 73.

FIGURE 3.1. Grapefruit pickers at the grove of R. I. Wall, one of the most prominent American businessmen on the Isle. U.S. entrepreneurs identified citrus fruit as the surest way to wealth on the Isle because the soil was deep and well drained, the produce was durable enough to withstand shipping back to the United States, and citrus was a rapidly growing industry in U.S. markets.
Source: The Isle of Pines (1913).

making it cost-prohibitive for Isle producers to continue shipping to the United States. When domestic U.S. production hit full bloom, Isle growers could not compete. In the 1922–3 season, for example, Isle producers shipped some 230,000 crates of grapefruit to the United States, the highest on record at the time. In Florida alone, however, growers produced an estimated 6 million crates.[24]

Nevertheless, landholding companies consistently promised high returns on investment for those engaged in citrus production – and at rates higher than could be found doing similar work in the United States. The Isle of Pines Company maintained that, "If you are willing to work

---

[24] The Grapefruit Industry, September 3, 1923, Nueva Gerona – Isle of Pines, Cuba, Vol. 33, Correspondence, 1923 – Part III, Record Group 84, NARA. To further illustrate the disparity, grapefruit exports to the United States averaged 170,000 boxes from 1921–5. During that same period, domestic U.S. production was 8.7 million boxes. Deere, "Here Come the Yankees!" 758–9.

half as hard [on the Isle], as you do in the States, you can make money faster than you ever could in this country."[25] It suggested that pioneers could earn anywhere from $300 to $1,000 an acre for their produce. Inspired by such promises of wealth, settlers may have harbored unrealistic expectations about how easy it would be to start a citrus grove. Dan Smith, who lived on the Isle for more than forty years, recalled that many small growers had dollar signs in their eyes. "Just plant you a little tree and sit back on the porch and go out and pick the money off the trees," he said about settlers' expectations about the ease of citrus growing. "Except it didn't work out that way."[26]

In fairness, promotional literature did offer caveats about who should take advantage of commercial opportunities on the Isle. In its 1901 prospectus, the Isle of Pines Company cautioned that, "A man with no means at all should not go to the Isle of Pines … but any intelligent person, with sufficient means … to pay necessary living expenses until a crop can be raised cannot make a mistake in emigrating to the Isle of Pines."[27] The Tropical Development Company–owned newspaper, the *McKinley Herald*, was even more precise as to who would not be suited for life on the Isle. One article from September 1905 maintained that, "A person in moderate circumstances – say with only a hundred dollars or so ahead, inexperienced in agricultural work – will rarely make a desirable colonist.… [T]hose who have good paying positions here [in the United States] should not hasten to give them up for the purpose of settling on their property at McKinley *unless* they have capital enough to draw on."[28] Years later, U.S. consuls on the Isle issued similar warnings to those inquiring about starting business ventures. In 1921, for example, Charles Forman wrote, "It is generally thought that only men of some means should attempt citrus fruit growing: men with a capital of at least $10,000. Much money has been lost in this business owing to lack of judgement [*sic*] and insufficient capital on the part of investors."[29] Over time, it became evident that a great deal of capital – often outside the range of the farmers and middle-class investors to whom most

[25] Isle of Pines Company, "McKinley, Isle of Pines: A City of Orange Groves in the American District of Cuba" (New York, 1911), 59.
[26] Irma and Dan Smith oral history interview with Frederick Swetland Jr., May 28, 1969, tape 11, 3, SFA.
[27] Isle of Pines Company, "Isle of Pines," 14.
[28] "Suggestions for Intending Settlers," *McKinley Herald*, September 1905.
[29] Charles Forman to W. M. Avent, January 27, 1921, Nueva Gerona – Isle of Pines, Cuba, Vol. 24, Correspondence, 1921 – Part I, Record Group 84, NARA.

advertisements were targeted – was required to make a successful go of it on the Isle.

Many of these warnings, though, went unheeded. Indeed, starting up even a small grove proved an expensive enterprise for most settlers. Journalist Irene A. Wright estimated it cost roughly $2,500 to start a ten-acre grove and that a farmer had to be prepared to spend at least $5,000 over five or six years until groves came into profitable bearing.[30] As a result, many of the first growers had difficulty making ends meet during the non-bearing years. Not surprisingly, the first commercial shipment of grapefruit from the Isle in 1907 elicited a great deal of local fanfare – and perhaps some relief. "This is the thing the American settlers of the Isle of Pines have been working for, striving for, knowing and believing and trying to convince others of for four years," the *McKinley Herald* exclaimed.[31] The first crop sold from $5–7 per crate in New York markets, a development that the newspaper called the biggest thing to happen to the Isle since the USS *Maine* sank in February 1898 and set the stage for U.S. intervention in Cuba.

As groves started to bear fruit, U.S. newspapers printed stories about small growers that offered narratives of struggle, hard work, and ultimately success. The *New York Sun* recounted the experience of one small, anonymous grower who began his tale with a caveat: "You must understand that [the Isle] is no place for a poor man; that is, a man without some capital." The grower claimed to have bought ten acres for $500 sight unseen from an agent in Cleveland. He was led to believe his tract was just a few miles from one of the Isle's ports along accessible roads. Accessibility was not what he found. The roads were but "rough trails winding in and around the palms and pines … [and] we were unable to distinguish our land from the rest of the woods." Worse, the house on the land was a one-room shack with a leaky roof. He would have returned to the United States, but he "had burned my financial bridges, and so I stayed." The grower spent more than $2,000 in start-up costs, not including living expenses. But when his groves and vegetable garden came into bearing five years later, he claimed gross sales of $2,100 selling exclusively on the Isle, mostly to visitors at a local hotel. "A man with a

---

[30] Wright, *Isle of Pines*, 69. Wright's estimate included $350 to purchase ten acres; $270 to clear the land; $50 for fencing; $500 to purchase trees; and $1,200 to care for the grove for three years, including fertilizer and labor. Her estimate presumed the landlord would outsource the work. Expenses would be reduced if the landowner did most of the work.

[31] "ISLE OF PINES EARLY GRAPEFRUIT SELLS AT RECORD-BREAKING PRICES," *McKinley Herald*, December 1907.

young grove on his hands has his work cut out for him every day in the week, 10 hours a day, too," he said. "But when the results begin to come in you can't help feeling it's worth the labor."[32]

For the small grower who experienced success, the good times were brief. World War I started the small growers' decline. Although neither the United States nor Cuba was an active combatant at the war's outset, the United States commercially supported the Allied Powers. This support diverted a great deal of shipping to Europe. As a result, Isle growers saw fewer opportunities and increased shipping costs to U.S. markets at a time when new groves were coming into bearing. Moreover, the cost of fertilizer skyrocketed from $30 to $95 a ton during the war years. The situation worsened after the United States and Cuba formally entered the conflict in April 1917. The U.S. War Trade Board restricted the import of many non-essentials, including most fruits and vegetables, to free up cargo space for war materiel. Isle growers, led by the local chamber of commerce, protested the move. But their lobbying efforts met with little success. To add further injury, the Isle experienced a devastating hurricane in September 1917 that wiped out a number of groves and caused annual grapefruit exports to drop by nearly two-thirds.[33] The cumulative effect took a heavy toll on small growers who could no longer sustain their enterprises. Smith recalled that, "Most of those early [groves] had been abandoned about 1915 or so. The owners didn't live there and after five or six years of putting money in they quit."[34] Not coincidentally, estimates of the settler population also show that the U.S. presence began to decline during this period.

The fact that large-scale growers, typically those with forty acres of land or more, tended to fare better financially than their smaller counterparts was not unique or remarkable. After all, these growers had the benefit of more capital at their disposal to absorb start-up costs, make necessary repairs in the event of hurricane damage, and grow more produce that would yield greater returns. But their ventures were helped, in part, by the small growers' failures. Smith noted that many large growers expanded their businesses by adding abandoned groves to their holdings.[35] Like the small grower, large growers also had high expectations that

---

[32] Article reprinted in "Pioneering in the Isle of Pines," *Idaho Statesman*, February 2, 1915.

[33] In 1917, growers exported 97,324 crates of grapefruit. The following year, grapefruit exports plummeted to 33,194 crates. Citrus Fruit Culture on the Isle of Pines, undated, Nueva Gerona – Isle of Pines, Cuba, Vol. 55, Correspondence, 1943 (File No. 812–891), 1944 (File No. 000-123), Record Group 84, NARA.

[34] Irma and Dan Smith oral history, May 28, 1969, tape 11, 2, SFA.

[35] Ibid.

citrus production would be a self-sustaining enterprise that would fund their ventures on the Isle. Growers such as August C. Kopf, Westervelt D. Middleton, and John A. Miller, who all owned more than 100 acres of citrus each, enjoyed success for decades from their citrus ventures.

But even large growers faced each season with anxiety. The Miller family, for example, was not immune to such apprehension. Bill Miller, grandson of John A. Miller, recalled that selling grapefruit under the Treasure Island brand had provided his family with a "good living" despite perpetual concerns: constant upkeep of the groves; continuous need for fertilizer; market prices for produce; and fear of hurricanes.[36] The Swetland family also struggled despite cultivating hundreds of acres in San Francisco de las Piedras. Between 1908 and 1914, the family divided citrus production among six companies – Pineland, Highland, Upland, Riverside, Valley, and Camaraca – and even opened their own packinghouse. As one internal report in 1916 indicated, however, their citrus production encountered a variety of problems. A fungal outgrowth in the Pineland section necessitated a significant replanting. At Highland, about fifteen acres of oranges produced "unsatisfactory fruit" and required a rebudding that would take two years to catch up with the rest of the section. Growth and production at Upland and Riverside remained stunted because of the "incompetence or indifference of its superintendent."[37] Such difficulties were common among citrus growers both large and small. The Swetlands were fortunate, however, that the company's and the family's well-being were not solely tied to the health and production of the groves. Not all settlers were so fortunate.

When it became clear that citrus might not produce the immediate returns most settlers had hoped for, some turned to vegetables as a complementary export industry. Commercial growing did not begin in earnest until the early 1910s. Smith claimed that his father, a tobacco farmer from North Carolina, was the first grower to ship vegetables from his family's farm in Columbia to the United States. Once the harvest reached full bearing, "it was almost a guaranteed income" – an estimated $500 to $1,000 a season, he said.[38] Unlike the citrus industry, which concentrated its exports within August and September, Isle growers sold vegetables mostly between November and May. Available data show that vegetable

---

[36] Bill Miller interview with author, August 9, 2014.
[37] "Report of Special Committee, authorized by the Directors of The Swetland Packing Company," June 19, 1916, SFA.
[38] Irma and Dan Smith oral history, May 28, 1969, tape 10, 3, SFA.

FIGURE 3.2. A young citrus grove in San Francisco de las Piedras. Promotions typically showed such groves in development to entice potential settlers with the potential for the Isle's growth. Settlers who engaged in citrus farming, however, often struggled to make a profit.
Source: The Isle of Pines (1913).

exports, though significantly less than citrus, followed the same general trends as fruit during the 1920s and 1930s. Exports nearly tripled from the early- to mid-1920s, before declining sharply as a result of the October 1926 hurricane. But they steadily increased again over the next five years until finally suffering the devastating effects of the Great Depression.[39]

Tourism

In addition to exports, turn-of-the-century U.S. entrepreneurs envisioned tourism as an industry that would financially sustain the American colony. Boosters in Florida, California, and the Caribbean – as well as government officials and entrepreneurs in mainland Cuba – were involved

[39] Between 1921 and 1931, Isle producers exported an average of 95,982 crates per season, reaching a peak of 162,668 crates in 1925–6. Vegetable crates averaged thirty-six pounds per crate. "1930–1931 Crop Year Shows Another Big Gain in Volume," *Isle of Pines Post*, August 25, 1931, 2.

in similar projects at the same time as the lure of tropical locales began to take hold in the American imagination.[40] The idea of the Isle as a tourist resort, though, was not new. During the colonial era, wealthy Spaniards and Cubans went there to enjoy its medicinal springs. Winsberg argued, however, that the Isle's stigma as a former pirate hideout and penal colony undermined its reputation and thus deterred nineteenth-century tourists.[41] U.S. landholding companies sought to change that status. Some predicted that American clients would eagerly flock to a newly developed locale. "The reputation of the island as a health resort is spreading in the United States," the *McKinley Herald* wrote in 1905. "It is safe to predict that the Isle of Pines will far outstrip Florida as a winter resort in the not far distant future, not only because of its more salubrious climate, but also because of its picturesque and diversified scenery, beautiful drives and abundant mineral waters."[42] Settlers echoed that idea. Samuel B. Wellington touted the Isle as a tourist destination, calling it "a place for wealthy Americans to go to at any time in the year, winter or summer.... They are somewhat sick of Bermuda and Nassau. The Hawaiian Islands are too far away, the mainland of Cuba is too much Spanish and is not suitable for Americans."[43] By implication, the Isle of Pines offered just the right mix of the exotic and the familiar that would appeal to American tourists.

Although no available data indicate precisely the industry's financial impact, the Isle drew American tourists during the early twentieth century. Many of the first tourists were men of means who went not just to enjoy a warm-weather resort, but also to scout land for purchase. An eleven-person party from West Duluth, Minnesota, in 1904 may have been among the first Americans to travel to the Isle expressly as tourists. But the trip was somewhat of an investor's junket as the group was also looking to inspect the land.[44] A decade later, George Stetson of Portland,

---

[40] Knight, *Tropic of Hopes*, 45–80; Cocks, *Tropical Whites*, 73–95; Christine Skwiot, *The Purposes of Paradise: U.S. Tourism and Empire in Cuba and Hawai'i* (Philadelphia: University of Pennsylvania Press, 2010), 87–128.

[41] Morton D. Winsberg, "The Isle of Pines, Cuba: A Geographic Interpretation," (PhD diss., University of Florida, 1958), 54.

[42] "McKinley, Isle of Pines, as a Health Resort," *McKinley Herald*, June 1905.

[43] Samuel B. Wellington to U.S. Realty and Improvement Company, November 4, 1911, 1910–29 Central Decimal File, General Records of the Department of State Relating to the Internal Affairs of Cuba, NARA Microcopy 488, Roll 27, File 837.014P/100.

[44] "Many Going to Isle of Pines," *Duluth News-Tribune*, November 13, 1904. There is no record of the party's leader, J. J. Frey, purchasing land or any follow-up reports about his experience on the Isle.

Oregon, spent six weeks on the Isle. He gave his hometown newspaper a favorable report about the Isle's mineral springs, comfortable climate, and burgeoning sport-fishing. "If the same amount of development is made in the next five years as in the past five it will be one of the greatest tourist resorts on the Western hemisphere," he said.[45] Such stories burnished the idea of the Isle as a desirable destination for Americans to go and experience something foreign.

A handful of American-owned hotels helped facilitate this nascent industry. McKinley's Orchid in the Pines was one of the first. Built by R. W. Dunning, the hotel opened in March 1906. It had twelve bedrooms and could accommodate up to twenty-four guests. The hotel often played host to Tropical Development Company executives.[46] A few years later, the West McKinley Inn opened with three floors and a forty-person capacity. The Isle of Pines Company, which built the hotel, claimed it was the first on the Isle "equipped for the convenience of tourists, health and pleasure seekers."[47] Amenities included a refrigerator, indoor plumbing, and a natural swimming pool on the premises. Both hotels, however, did not stay open for long, undermined by a drop in luxury travel during World War I and the ensuing postwar recession. By 1923, the U.S. consul reported only three American-owned hotels on the Isle – in Nueva Gerona, Santa Fe, and Santa Barbara – with no mention of the inns in McKinley and West McKinley.[48]

Despite landholding companies' glittering promotions to the contrary, the Isle had limited appeal as a tourist destination. The trip's expense restricted accessibility for those of average means. Other factors tarnished its allure. Most of the first tourists went for health or business purposes. After that, there was little else for the tourist to do. In the 1920s, U.S. consuls lamented the lack of recreational activities. One wrote: "Other than the climate which is excellent from January to March, inclusive, there are very few attractions for the tourist; there are no facilities provided for such sports as golf and tennis, and unsatisfactory arrangements for sea fishing may be affected only with difficulty."[49] Although the Isle had

[45] "Isle of Pines Is Seen," *The Oregonian*, July 3, 1914.
[46] Tropical Development Company, *McKinley in the Making* (Buffalo, NY, 1906), 20–1.
[47] Isle of Pines Company, "McKinley, Isle of Pines," 44.
[48] Charles Forman to Secretary of State, January 9, 1923, Nueva Gerona – Isle of Pines, Cuba, Vol. 31, Correspondence, 1923 – Part I, Record Group 84, NARA. These hotels, respectively, were the Hotel San Jose, Santa Rita Springs Hotel, and the Santa Barbara Inn. The hurricane of October 1926 destroyed the latter.
[49] Review of Commerce and Industries, January 14, 1927, Nueva Gerona – Isle of Pines, Cuba, Vol. 45, Correspondence, 1927 – Part II, Record Group 84, NARA. U.S. consul

FIGURE 3.3. The Santa Barbara Inn was one of a handful of American-owned and operated hotels during the early twentieth century that catered to American tourists. But undermined by a drop in luxury travel during World War I and the ensuing postwar recession, most such hotels shuttered by the early 1920s. The Santa Barbara Inn remained in operation until it was destroyed in the October 1926 hurricane.
Source: The Isle of Pines (1913).

plenty of beachfront property, bathhouses were rare. Likewise, movie theaters were sparse. In the early 1920s, one film was shown per week on Sunday nights in Nueva Gerona. But according to U.S. consul Charles Forman, "the films are said to be poor. There is no other public entertainment except cock fights."[50] Another U.S. consul doubted that tourism would ever become a significant industry without entrepreneurs first investing in more advertising, transportation improvements, better

---

Sheridan Talbott told one inquirer that the Isle once had golf courses, but that they had "fallen into disuse in recent years and the number of persons here who might be interested in this sport is not sufficiently great to justify the anticipation of its renewal under existing conditions." It is not clear what entities operated the courses. Talbott to Stumpp & Walter Company, June 17, 1926, Nueva Gerona – Isle of Pines, Cuba, Vol. 44, Correspondence, 1926 – Part V, Record Group 84, NARA.

[50] Consular Post Report, January 15, 1921, Nueva Gerona – Isle of Pines, Cuba, Vol. 24, Correspondence, 1921 – Part I, Record Group 84, NARA.

accommodations, and recreation.[51] Indeed, tourism remained a stunted industry until the 1950s.

Entrepreneurial Ventures

Although many settlers engaged in citrus and vegetable farming, a few maintained enterprises in service of the local economy. Their activity underscored U.S. capital's dominance during the early twentieth century. These entrepreneurs were generally well-to-do and operated key commercial institutions such as banks, shipping, and general stores. Their businesses catered to all Isle residents, or at least those who could afford such services. Results, however, were mixed, subject to the same forces that affected the citrus, vegetable, and tourist industries.

The history of banks on the Isle before U.S. settlers' arrival is unclear. But as the American presence increased, some of the wealthiest entrepreneurs banded together in 1905 to form the Isle of Pines Bank.[52] T. J. Keenan, the Pittsburgh publisher and ardent annexationist, became the bank's first president. Its directors included many prominent investors, including James A. Hill of the Isle of Pines Company and Horace Hayes of the Tropical Development Company. Benito Ortíz, a substantial landowner during the colonial era who later became the Isle's *alcalde*, also was among the bank's directors. His inclusion in this and other ventures illustrated two important realities that belied promoters' rhetoric and depiction of conditions on the Isle. First, that Americans relied on local participation to ensure the success of their enterprises and could not operate strictly among or on behalf of fellow nationals. Second, that a certain class existed among the local population who possessed financial clout that matched – and in some cases surpassed – that of settlers; elite status was not solely an American birthright. While U.S. capital was undoubtedly the prominent feature of this particular enterprise, Ortíz's presence showed that the lines sometimes blurred between "American," "Cuban," or "Spanish" businesses, a blending that would become an even more common feature later in the century.

Despite its impressive array of backers, the Isle of Pines Bank failed in October 1915, reportedly only the second bank failure in all of Cuba

---

[51] Review of Commerce and Industries, January 11, 1926, Nueva Gerona – Isle of Pines, Cuba, Vol. 42, Correspondence, 1926 – Part II, Record Group 84, NARA.

[52] For a history of the bank, see María Marta Hernández, et al., *Isla de Pinos y las Compañías Norteamericanas* (La Habana: Comisión de la Escuela de Historia de la Universidad de la Habana, 1970), 14–32.

since independence.[53] The specific reasons for its demise are unclear, but it was presumably linked to the commercial decline groves suffered during World War I. Another American-run bank, however, withstood the struggling economy. The National Bank & Trust Company opened in 1912, led by other landholding company executives. This group included Robert I. Wall as president, John A. Miller as vice president, and Louis C. Giltner as cashier, all of whom were also large landowners. For a time, it was the only bank on the Isle and it remained in operation until 1934.[54]

The Isle of Pines Steamship Company was another critical American-led enterprise. Some of the company's officers also had links to the Isle of Pines Bank, including Keenan and Hill, who each served as company president, and William J. Mills, the longtime company manager. Although it was neither the first shipping company to operate between the Isle and Cuba nor the only American-operated line, the Isle of Pines Steamship Company proved the most popular after its 1906 founding. Many settlers traveled to the Isle on one of its three steamships – the *Cristobal Colon* (the oldest), the *Pinero*, or the *Cuba* – an experience that left indelible memories for some.[55] Citrus growers often used the Isle of Pines Steamship Company to transport their produce. One estimate suggested that its three ships could carry as many as 150,000 boxes of grapefruit a month.[56] First-class fares, which included a train between Havana and Batabanó, cost $7.60 in 1910; second-class fares $4.25.[57] The company employed many foreign nationals among its workforce of about thirty. It remained in American hands until July 1, 1958, when it was sold to a group of Cuban investors.[58]

[53] Isle of Pines Bank Failure, March 31, 1916, Nueva Gerona – Isle of Pines, Cuba, Vol. 4, Miscellaneous record book – August 5, 1910, to August 28, 1919, 163, Record Group 84, NARA.

[54] Commercial and Economic Conditions on the Isle of Pines, November 10, 1920, Nueva Gerona – Isle of Pines, Cuba, Vol. 21, Correspondence, 1920 – Part II, Record Group 84, NARA; The Isle of Pines, Cuba, report by LaRue Lutkins, May 14, 1944, Nueva Gerona – Isle of Pines, Cuba, Vol. 55, Correspondence, 1943 (File No. 812–891), 1944 (File No. 000-123), Record Group 84, NARA.

[55] For examples, see Frederick Swetland Jr., *Isle of Pines*, 1, and Philip Bullock, "This Is My Life," (2006), unpublished autobiography. The hull of the *Pinero* sits near the port of Nueva Gerona as a monument.

[56] "Isle of Pines Steamship Company Important Factor to Growth," *Isle of Pines Post*, November 26, 1931.

[57] Wright, *Isle of Pines*, 89. Round-trip rates to and from Havana reached $12 in 1924. See advertisement in *Isle of Pines Appeal*, March 29, 1924.

[58] Adolph B. Kelm to Benjamin Bird, June 30, 1958, Fondo: A. B. Kelm, Legajo 1, Expediente 2-2, Papeles de la Logia, AHM; Kelm to Ada Wynn Patten, April 5, 1959,

FIGURE 3.4. The S.S. *Cristobal Colon* was the oldest of the Isle of Pines Steamship Company's three ferries. The American-owned company, founded in 1906, proved the most popular carrier of settlers and goods to and from mainland Cuba during the republican era.
Source: The Isle of Pines (1913).

Some Americans also opened retail stores to cater to their fellow settlers. These stores provided goods that settlers prized, including certain foods, clothes, and tools that were almost all imported from the United States. According to a 1914 estimate, there were twenty-eight "American stores" on the Isle, presumably those owned by U.S. citizens that sold goods from the United States.[59] One U.S. consul noted that "most of the better stores" were American-owned and "patronized by all; American goods being liked and preferred by everybody to all others."[60] The biggest stores – such as the ones run by Ralph B. Heeren, Charles F. Fetter, and Aaron Koritzky – were located in Nueva Gerona. But most of the

Fondo: A. B. Kelm, Legajo 1, Expediente 8, Papeles de la Logia, AHM; Hernández, et al., *Isla de Pinos y las Compañías Norteamericanas*, 19–21, 36–48.

[59] Vervie Sutherland to James L. Rodgers, June 1, 1914, Nueva Gerona – Isle of Pines, Cuba, Vol. 12, Correspondence, 1913–14, Record Group 84, NARA.

[60] Annual Report on Commerce and Industries for 1918, report by William Bardel, April 22, 1919, Nueva Gerona – Isle of Pines, Cuba, Vol. 18, Correspondence, 1919 – Part I, Record Group 84, NARA.

U.S.-founded towns had American general stores as well. For example, landholding companies operated stores in McKinley and Columbia; Heeren and Fetter opened branches of their businesses in Santa Barbara, which had the largest concentration of Americans. Not coincidentally, many of these stores shuttered in the mid-1920s as settlers began returning to the United States.

Labor

Settlers who opened their own farms or businesses often could not do all the work by themselves. Consequently, they hired laborers, primarily unskilled workers, to support their enterprises. American laborers were fairly uncommon, mostly because they commanded high wages. Instead, most of the labor was drawn from the local population, including *pineros* and foreign nationals from the British West Indies. This dynamic reinforced a hierarchical social structure that featured Americans on top as employers and *pineros* and Caribbean islanders below as workers who relied on settlers for wages. It also revealed that U.S.-led enterprises needed local labor to support their ventures. This connection illustrated that a mutual dependence between Americans and *pineros* indeed existed, yet it was an arrangement that U.S. promoters and annexationists often ignored in their arguments and one that Cubans seemed loathe to admit.

The extent to which *pineros* engaged in wage labor during the Spanish colonial era is unclear. Anecdotal evidence suggests that *pineros* were mostly subsistence farmers. Winsberg, for example, maintains that the majority of Cubans who migrated to the Isle during the first half of the nineteenth century, when the Isle's population grew from roughly 100 people to nearly 1,000, were poor and either squatted or bought small parcels of land. Rather than engage in livestock raising that was common among *hacendados*, most of these newcomers farmed for themselves.[61] Despite the Isle's lingering reputation as a backwater with sparse commercial opportunities, its population continued to grow during the second half of the century. The desire to escape mainland Cuba during a chaotic era of independence movements certainly was a factor in this increase. The 1899 Cuban census indicates that nearly one-third of the Isle's men worked as domestic or personal servants.[62] Many would engage in similar work for American employers.

---

[61] Winsberg, "Isle of Pines, Cuba," 52.

[62] *Report on the Census of Cuba, 1899* (Washington, DC: Government Printing Office, 1900), 406. Specifically, 614 men and thirty-three women worked in "domestic and

Migrants from the British West Indies represented the other significant group in the Isle's labor pool. Their presence was part of a broader trend of West Indian labor migration at the turn of the century. Hundreds of thousands of people from British-controlled islands traveled throughout the Caribbean region in search of work. Many worked for Americans as farmhands in private enterprises like the United Fruit Company in Central America or as unskilled workers for the U.S. government in the construction and maintenance of the Panama Canal.[63] In Cuba, while most of the roughly 300,000 migrants from the West Indies went there primarily to work on sugar plantations, they also represented a sizeable portion of the support personnel at the Guantánamo Bay Naval Base.[64] Their inclusion illustrated that foreign-born workers were essential to U.S. imperial efforts, however unrecognized or unacknowledged they may have been. The Isle colonial project was no different as a small segment of these migrants went there as well. Those who arrived in the late nineteenth century tended to live on the sparsely habited South Coast, clustered in the town of Jacksonville, and engaged in fishing. But as Americans began establishing groves and gardens at the turn of the twentieth century, even more Cayman Islanders and Jamaicans – more than 700, according to one estimate – arrived to work on these new farms.[65]

Many U.S. farmers and business owners favored West Indian migrants because they spoke English. Most of the first U.S. settlers did not speak Spanish, and showed little inclination to learn because many assumed the United States would eventually annex the Isle. With English-speaking foreign nationals working for them, there was even less incentive. This dynamic was particularly the case with domestic workers. As one U.S. consul noted, women from the Cayman Islands were the most sought-after household workers because they labored for "relatively low

personal service," the largest occupational category among the Isle's population. The next-largest occupation was "agriculture, fisheries, and mining" with 403 men. Some 536 men were considered "without gainful occupation."

[63] Jason M. Colby, *The Business of Empire: United Fruit, Race, and U.S. Expansion in Central America* (Ithaca, NY: Cornell University Press, 2011); Michael E. Donoghue, *Borderland on the Isthmus: Race, Culture, and the Struggle for the Canal Zone* (Durham, NC: Duke University Press, 2014); Julie Greene, *The Canal Builders: Making America's Empire at the Panama Canal* (New York: Penguin Press, 2009); Michael L. Conniff, *Black Labor on a White Canal: Panama, 1904–1981* (Pittsburgh: University of Pittsburgh Press, 1985).

[64] Jana K. Lipman, *Guantánamo: A Working-Class History between Empire and Revolution* (Berkeley: University of California Press, 2009).

[65] Juan Colina la Rosa, *Caimaneros y Jamaicanos en Isla de Pinos* (Nueva Gerona: Ediciones El Abra, 2006), 12–25.

wages and solve the difficulty which might otherwise be encountered in obtaining servants who are able to speak the English language."[66] Cayman Island men, meanwhile, more often worked as farm hands on American properties in places such as Santa Barbara, San Francisco de las Piedras, and McKinley. There was a rich irony – often lost on settlers – that the white colony they were purportedly trying to establish was so dependent on black labor. But employers ignored that juxtaposition in large part because West Indian workers had developed a reputation elsewhere in the Caribbean as competent, dependable laborers.[67] This label surely would have been known to those on the Isle.

For their part, English-speaking foreign nationals recognized they had an advantage in finding work with American employers and enjoyed more than merely wages. A native of Jamaica, Sylvia Adina Baker Forrest migrated to the Isle via the Cayman Islands in 1929 looking for a job. Through friends, she met Harriet Wheeler, a staunch annexationist in the mid-1920s, and began working for her. Over the next fifteen years, Forrest happily took care of Wheeler's domestic chores. "I couldn't find a better home," Forrest recalled. "She called me daughter and made no distinction with her own."[68] Even after Wheeler died, Forrest said she and the other domestic workers remained in the house until the 1960s. Similarly, Rulle Ebanks's parents migrated from the Cayman Islands and later began farming for an unnamed American around 1930. The family enjoyed a close relationship with their employer to the extent that after the American died, they moved into the house and took over the farm.[69]

Such friendly experiences contrasted sharply with the discrimination, abuse, and safety hazards that West Indian workers often endured while working on U.S.-owned plantations and projects elsewhere in the Caribbean. Compared to corporations such as the United Fruit Company, Isle grove owners were not as systemically predatory toward workers. They were operating on much smaller scales and in closer confines with employees. This dynamic helps explain the better treatment that workers generally enjoyed and why employees did not tend to engage in the kind

[66] Commerce and Industries of the Isle of Pines, Cuba, for the Calendar Year 1925, report by Sheridan Talbott, June 23, 1926, Nueva Gerona – Isle of Pines, Cuba, Vol. 42, Correspondence, 1926 – Part II, Record Group 84, NARA.

[67] Colby, *Business of Empire*, 8.

[68] Quoted in Jane McManus, *Cuba's Island of Dreams: Voices from the Isle of Pines and Youth* (Gainesville: University Press of Florida, 2000), 53.

[69] Ibid., 54–5.

of resistance (e.g., strikes, unionism) that characterized labor relations elsewhere in the Caribbean region.

That is not to suggest, however, that working for Americans was free from conflict. Competition for jobs led to friction between *pineros* and *caimaneros*, especially during times of economic stress. Such tensions also were evident in mainland Cuba, where Cuban workers saw their Afro-Caribbean counterparts as competition, taking jobs and depressing wages.[70] In the midst of an early-1920s recession, for example, Forman noted that farm wages on the Isle had declined. In one of the few instances of labor mobilization, some *pinero* workers refused to work for less pay.[71] But their tactic to push for higher wages was thwarted when "a good many men from the Cayman Islands have arrived here to work on the fruit groves. This has caused some resentment in the ranks of local labor."[72] Although no violence erupted, the episode revealed deep divisions. According to one Cuban study, many *pineros* considered *caimaneros* on the bottom rung of the Isle's social ladder, and *pineros* often accused *caimaneros* of various crimes, primarily theft.[73] This division between two of the Isle's largest working groups gave employers, many of whom were Americans, an upper hand in setting labor costs and conditions.

In some instances, Americans recruited laborers to come to the Isle to work for them. The Tropical Development Company placed advertisements in Havana newspapers looking for workmen to clear some of its tract in McKinley for orange groves. In the summer of 1905, the company president, Horace P. Hayes, hired twenty-six men in Havana and another twelve in the port city of Batabanó, paying for their passage to Nueva Gerona.[74] Three years later, when the company finished clearing and planting the last of its 500-acre orange and grapefruit grove that consisted of a purported 45,000 trees, it hired another fifty workers from Havana to supplement its existing labor force.[75] Such hiring practices

[70] Lipman, *Guantánamo*, 44–53; Marc McLeod, "Undesirable Aliens: Haitians and British West Indian Immigrant Workers in Cuba, 1898 to 1940" (PhD diss., University of Texas, 2000); Robert B. Hoernel, "Sugar and Social Change in Oriente, Cuba, 1898–1946," *Journal of Latin American Studies* 8 (November 1976): 215–49.

[71] Wiltse Peña Hijuelos, et al., *Con Todo Derecho: Isla de la Juventud* (Havana, 1986), 55.

[72] Report on "Unemployment, Public Order, and Health Conditions," August 26, 1921, Nueva Gerona – Isle of Pines – Cuba, Vol. 25, Correspondence, 1921 – Part II, Record Group 84, NARA.

[73] Academia de Ciencias de Cuba, "Serie Isla de Pinos No. 27: Situación social en Isla de Pines antes de la Revolución," Salvador Morales, et al., eds. (La Habana, 1969), 11.

[74] "Work on Manigua Orange Groves," *McKinley Herald*, July 1905.

[75] "500-ACRE ORANGE AND GRAPEFRUIT GROVES ARE ENTIRELY PLANTED," *McKinley Herald*, July 1908.

suggest that local labor was either insufficient or unreliable during the first years of U.S. settlement.

U.S. citizens – at least white ones – were largely discouraged from coming to the Isle as unskilled laborers for two reasons. First was the pay scale. "There is no shortage of unskilled labor at reasonably low wages, but dependable skilled labor is scarce and inadequate to the limited demands of the Island," one U.S. consul reported. "However, American workmen would doubtless be dissatisfied with the existing wage level."[76] The other rationale was that a white unskilled worker would have to "work alongside of Jamaica negroes and Cubans of the laboring class and would have to be strong to keep up and you would not make much."[77] Such work would be beneath a white worker and thus risk his social status.

Some American laborers ignored the warnings and went to the Isle anyway. Eighteen-year-old Ernest Gruppe took his chances in 1908 when he left his home in Milwaukee, Wisconsin. Gruppe had been a farmer, mostly raising vegetables, but he made a living on the Isle performing odd jobs. He worked on various construction and farming projects and also for store owners Koritzky and Fetter; he served as a manager for the latter. Gruppe made a modest living, but did well enough to purchase a thirty-three-and-a-half-acre plot in Santa Ana that he retained after returning to the United States in 1925.[78] Dorothy Anderson's parents also were among the working class. Her family came to the Isle from Philadelphia in 1921 in the hope that a warmer climate would help ease her mother's unspecified illness. Anderson's father had agreed to swap houses with another Isle resident sight unseen. He was a carpenter whose work included construction on the home of Westervelt D. Middleton, one of the Isle's largest grove owners. Anderson's mother, meanwhile, was well enough to teach at private schools in Santa Fe, Nueva Gerona, and later at the American Central School. For reasons unclear, the family left the Isle and returned to the United States in 1929.[79] Although both anecdotes may not have been typical of all settlers, they do show that some Americans made modest livings even if they were not grove or business owners.

---

[76] Commerce and Industries Quarterly Report, October 9, 1926, Nueva Gerona – Isle of Pines, Cuba, Vol. 42, Correspondence, 1926 – Part II, Record Group 84, NARA.

[77] Charles Forman to Arthur Oakes, December 14, 1923, Nueva Gerona – Isle of Pines, Cuba, Vol. 31, Correspondence, 1923 – Part I, Record Group 84, NARA.

[78] Ernest Gruppe oral history interview with Frederick Swetland Jr., June 27, 1971, tape 17, 1–2, 4; tape 19, 1, SFA.

[79] Dorothy Anderson oral history interview with Frederick Swetland Jr., June 21, 1971, tape 22, 1–4, SFA.

During the first two decades of the twentieth century, wages for unskilled work typically ranged from $1 to $1.50 a day. Americans tended to get the higher end while *pineros* and foreign nationals were paid less. One reason was the perception, common among settlers, that American laborers "work harder and accomplish more than Cubans will."[80] One U.S. military report suggested that local workers accepted the discrepancy because it represented a better wage than they had been accustomed to earning. "From all appearances the Cuban laborer likes the American very much, one very strong reason is that now he draws double pay when compared to the Spanish regime, and is treated as a workingman and not a serf," Lt. Robert Tittoni wrote.[81] The wage scale remained consistent for some time except for after World War I, when the Isle experienced a significant labor shortage and wages increased by some fifty cents a day across the board.[82] The postwar labor shortage affected all of Cuba, particularly because of the rapid expansion of the sugar industry. This phenomenon peaked with the so-called Dance of the Millions in 1920 when sugar prices – which ranged between three and four cents a pound during the war years – reached an all-time high of 22.5 cents a pound before plunging back to 3.8 cents before the end of the year.[83] Consequently, wages across Cuba – including the Isle – retreated to their prewar levels.

As was typically the case in both the United States and Cuba, female wage workers were paid significantly less than their male counterparts, particularly in domestic service. According to a 1922 U.S. consul estimate, women domestic workers earned $8 to $15 a month, with American women presumably paid on the higher end. In contrast, the going rate for male domestic workers was $30 to $40 a month.[84] Women also commonly worked as citrus or vegetable packers at packinghouses. Females were preferred because the work did "not require great strength."[85] But it was one job in which a woman could earn more than an unskilled male

[80] Wright, *Isle of Pines*, 85.
[81] Tittoni to Charles Magoon, October 21, 1906, Provisional Government of Cuba, "Confidential" Correspondence, 1906–1909, Box 1, Folder 003, Record Group 199, NARA.
[82] William Bardel to J. Herbert Parker, March 8, 1919, Nueva Gerona – Isle of Pines, Cuba, Vol. 18, Correspondence, 1919 – Part I, Record Group 84, NARA.
[83] Louis A. Pérez Jr., *Cuba: Between Reform and Revolution*, 4th ed. (New York: Oxford University Press, 2011), 169–72.
[84] Charles Forman to Secretary of State, February 21, 1922, Nueva Gerona – Isle of Pines, Cuba, Vol. 28, Correspondence, 1922 – Part I, Record Group 84, NARA.
[85] Labor and Wages, report by Charles Forman, June 11, 1924, Nueva Gerona – Isle of Pines, Cuba, Vol. 35, Correspondence, 1924 – Part III, Record Group 84, NARA.

laborer, depending on her productivity. Female workers earned five cents a crate and would pack anywhere between sixty and eighty crates a day. But this work was limited to the height of the export season, generally August and September.

Workers with grievances against employers used the local courts to find redress, particularly before the Municipal Court and the Judge of the First Instance. Most of the dozens of suits involving U.S. employers and businesses were brought up by foreign nationals, rather than *pineros*. In most instances, plaintiffs took their employers to court to win full payment of promised wages – some had written contracts – or compensation for injuries suffered on the job. Cases typically involved $40 to $100. Contrary to American complaints, the courts found for the employers seemingly as often as they did for workers. For example, Albert H. Swetland, son of Truman Swetland and manager of the family's estate at San Francisco de las Piedras, was named in four cases before the Municipal Court between 1910 and 1913. In two of the cases, the judge found for the workers who were seeking full payment of wages for work performed on the Swetlands' property; in the other two cases, Swetland won.[86] This trend held in most local court cases involving Americans and illustrated that despite settlers' claims to the contrary, Isle judges found in their favor more often than they maintained. The volume of cases also suggests that workers generally had enough confidence in the Isle's court system to seek resolution of their disputes there.

Despite the occasional tensions and promotional pretenses to the contrary, U.S. entrepreneurs needed local labor to see their groves and businesses come to fruition. Given the vast amount of work necessary to clear the land, plant trees, pack fruit, and ship produce off the Isle, the burgeoning commercial citrus industry – an American creation – depended on the participation of Cuban and West Indian workers. At the same time, these workers relied on newly arriving Americans for wage work in place of the Spanish colonial-era *hacendados*. Moreover, these new enterprises were invigorating the local economy and commercially developing an area widely viewed for centuries as a backwater.

---

[86] For examples of the court finding for the plaintiffs, see Juzgado Municipal de la Isla de Pinos, 1901–1958, *Daniel Ferrir v. A. H. Swetland*, Legajo 11, Expediente 181, and *Jacob Sandowsky v. A. H. Swetland*, Legajo 12, Expediente 216, AHM. For examples of the court finding for the defendant, see Juzgado Municipal de la Isla de Pinos, 1901–1958, *Alejandro Martinez Puente v. A. H. Swetland*, Legajo 11, Expediente 184, and *Bruce Lafton v. A. H. Swetland*, Legajo 12, Expediente 205, AHM.

In a trenchant reflection on American–*pinero* relations in the 1910s and 1920s, U.S. consul LaRue Lutkins argued that relations were superficially cordial because the penetration of U.S. capital made it expedient for *pineros* to welcome Americans. Below the surface, though, each group viewed the other warily. He maintained that Americans regarded Cubans as "an inferior people" but kept up a friendly disposition "only so long as the Cubans were willing to recognize American superiority and accept a subordinate position." Lutkins continued that *pineros* tolerated such chauvinism "partly out of sheer expediency and partly because they recognized that American energy and progressiveness had benefited the island in many ways. But while remaining more or less acquiescent and friendly, the Cubans naturally continue to resent the Americans' bland assumption of superiority."[87] His assessment cogently captured not only the tension between Americans and *pineros* during the first quarter of the twentieth century, but, more important, their mutual dependence. While settlers relied on local labor to support their business ventures, *pineros* also needed Americans for jobs and recognized that U.S. capital was helping to develop commercially a place generally ignored under Spain. For leaders of the new Cuban republic, this influx of U.S. capital was certainly welcome, if not the new settlers' presumptions of superiority and push for annexation that often came with it.

U.S. settlers on the Isle of Pines in the early twentieth century had a variety of reasons to relocate: adventurism, leisure, patriotism, health, and rejuvenation. But the chief motivation for the majority of Americans was the opportunity to improve their standard of living, or at least to live comfortably enough to sustain their new homes. To this end, promoters and settlers commonly maintained that the most effective way to achieve that goal was through the commercial development of the Isle's natural resources, specifically citrus. As a result, the exportation of grapefruit – primarily to the United States – became the primary driver of the Isle's economy for decades. The conceit was that industrious and hard-working Americans willing to sacrifice and struggle could accomplish something that languid Spaniards and Cubans were unable to do for centuries – make the Isle commercially viable. In reality, however, local labor was essential to that endeavor. Settlers could not do all the

[87] "The Isle of Pines, Cuba," report by LaRue Lutkins, May 14, 1944, Nueva Gerona – Isle of Pines, Cuba, Vol. 55, Correspondence, 1943 (File No. 812–891), 1944 (File No. 000-123), Record Group 84, NARA.

work to remake the landscape into profitable groves and gardens without help. *Pineros* and other foreign nationals were indispensable partners in this transformation.

While the first few years of these efforts were not easy, the optimism for success remained strong, particularly during the first decade of U.S. settlement. To ensure that their efforts would pay off in the long term, many settlers figured that only the Isle's annexation to the United States would secure their investments. To spur annexation, settlers and investors made a determined effort to Americanize the Isle. Not only would such efforts help ease settlers' transition to a new land, but it would also support the case for annexation. A flourishing, organized colony of Americans abroad would surely demand the U.S. government's consideration. Annexation could rid settlers of ineffective Cuban rule while also eliminating tariffs on goods and produce that they sold back to U.S. markets. Such a prospect would also enhance property values and fulfill the Isle's economic promise. By the time of U.S. entry into World War I, U.S. citizens continued to migrate to the Isle and built up their homes, groves, businesses, and institutions to form distinctly American communities.

4

Creating Community

More than most Americans, Samuel B. Wellington of New York could appreciate how much the Isle of Pines had changed during the early twentieth century. In 1897, he first ventured there to drink of its mineral waters and soak up the warm sunshine in hopes of improving his failing health. Although Wellington admired the Isle's natural surroundings, accommodations were scarce. Steamship travel was infrequent, only a few stores were open, and infrastructure was virtually nonexistent. Nevertheless, he recognized that the Isle had potential for growth. "At that time, it appeared to my mind what a beautiful spot the place would be if it could be Americanized," he wrote.[1]

By 1911, Wellington's vision of an Americanized Isle of Pines was becoming a reality. Since his first visit, thousands of fellow U.S. citizens had settled and invested there. The changes they initiated were clearly evident: miles of new roads; bridges; thousands of acres under cultivation for citrus fruit and vegetables; a wireless telegraph system; regular transportation to and from mainland Cuba; hotels; stores; schools; churches; newspapers; and a bank. Americans owned or operated most of the farms, businesses, and institutions of note. But more than just bricks and mortar, settlers also made a cultural and stylistic impression. English was commonly spoken throughout the Isle. The U.S. dollar served as the primary currency. And the architecture of settlers' houses – often with two

[1] Samuel B. Wellington to U.S. Realty and Improvement Company, November 4, 1911, 1910–29 Central Decimal File, General Records of the Department of State Relating to the Internal Affairs of Cuba, NARA Microcopy 488, Roll 27, File 837.014P/100. Wellington's background and extent of his property holdings on the Isle are not clear.

stories, running water, and indoor fireplaces – was unlike anything *pine-ros* had seen before.

Settlers made Americanizing the Isle a top priority, one that had both personal and practical benefits. The replication of life in the United States – complete with familiar institutions, customs, and modern conveniences – offered a way to help ease settlers' transition to living in a foreign land. It also helped them to protect their investments in groves, businesses, and property. Settlers looked to create distinctly American hallmarks as a way to bolster their argument for U.S. annexation, which promised to be a boon to property values and commercial activity. At the very least, settlers hoped their Americanization would convince U.S. policymakers to eliminate tariffs on goods they were exporting back to the United States. Since tariffs were designed, in part, to protect domestic producers, settlers wanted to display their American-ness to show that they should not be subject to such duties simply because they were operating outside the United States.

This American-ness illustrated, as historian Brooke Blower has argued, that America was not just rooted in physical geography but also in social and cultural institutions.[2] In the case of the Isle, this dynamic involved many values and customs that distinguished settlers from *pineros* and other foreign nationals. These features included whiteness, Protestant spirituality, export-oriented capitalism, technology, efficiency, and the English language. Many settlers presumed that Spanish and Cuban myopia had prevented the Isle from flourishing during the colonial era, a time when most large landholders operated cattle ranches and small farmers did little more than grow for themselves. These activities, settlers maintained, failed to exploit effectively the Isle's abundant natural resources. This ideology suggested that Americans and their more advanced culture could generate prosperity and a modern society in a place that had been heretofore mismanaged.

The creation of towns stood at the center of settlers' efforts to Americanize the Isle. These towns revealed a sense of utopianism among settlers and town planners who did not want merely to replicate American life but rather to perfect it by creating a more ideal society. Their emphases on cooperation and an agriculture-based economy revealed anxieties about changes taking place in contemporary American society. Landholding companies were the primary catalysts, designating certain

[2] Brooke L. Blower, *Becoming Americans in Paris: Transatlantic Politics and Culture between the World Wars* (New York: Oxford University Press, 2011).

spaces in their tracts for centralized settlement and commercial activity in ways that bore some resemblance to the Garden City movements in the United States and England. These spaces allowed for the formation of institutions such as schools, churches, and social clubs that supported demonstrations of American-ness. Planners gave these towns colloquial names, such as McKinley, Westport, and Columbia (the feminine personification of the United States). Some of these towns endured for a generation or more. Others, like La Siguanea, barely got past the planning stages and served as a cautionary tale of over-ambition and unfulfilled promise. None, however, rivaled the Isle's long-established towns, Nueva Gerona and Santa Fe, in size and scope.

Cubans from all walks reacted to settlers' community building with ambivalence. In 1903, Manuel Sanguily introduced a bill in the Cuban Senate that would have both prohibited selling land to foreigners and required congressional authorization to establish a town.[3] Policymakers in Havana, though, generally tolerated American settlement if it meant they would help grow the local economy. Cuban historian Eduardo Lens credited Americans for ushering a sense of sophistication and cosmopolitanism on the Isle. He referred to U.S. communities as "beautiful little towns" (*"los bellos pueblecitos"*) and lauded settlers for the distinctive architecture of their houses.[4] *Pineros*, meanwhile, mostly seemed to accept the U.S. presence. They worked on the farms and houses of U.S. landowners and enjoyed cordial relations with settlers. But politicians and private citizens drew the line at U.S. annexation. They accepted the introduction and proliferation of American styles, customs, and institutions, but made clear their belief that the Isle of Pines remained sovereign Cuban territory.

American communities during the first generation of U.S. settlement tried to form in isolation, apart from *pineros* and other foreign nationals. In reality, since locals were essential participants in activities ranging from land clearing and grove planting to construction and business patronage, settlers were indeed part of the broader Isle community. Nevertheless, some areas on the Isle seemed like U.S. territory. The American-run Nueva Gerona Board of Trade boasted on its letterhead: "The Isle of Pines is the Largest American Colony in the World Outside of the United

---

[3] Carmen Diana Deere, "Here Come the Yankees! The Rise and Decline of United States Colonies in Cuba, 1898–1930," *Hispanic American Historical Review* 78 (November 1998): 741.

[4] Eduardo Lens, *La Isla Olvidada: Estudio Físico, Económico y Humano de la Isla de Pinos*, (La Habana, 1942), 17.

States."[5] For settlers in the early 1910s, lifestyles were said to be similar to what they found in the United States, which became a selling point for landholding companies. One promotion claimed that settlers need not adapt to Cuban customs because the "communal life is that of the United States. It is not necessary to speak Spanish. The schools are American, the social life is American, and the people are good, stout, whole-souled, hospitable Americans."[6]

The trend did not last. By the mid-1920s, commercial prospects foundered and the U.S. Senate finally resolved the sovereignty question by ratifying the Hay-Quesada treaty. As a result, the U.S. population dwindled and American communities began to die out.

The Growing American Community

When U.S. troops reoccupied Cuba in September 1906, they found an American community on the Isle still in its nascent stages. U.S. authorities conducted a rough census that found nearly 200 American men living there – far fewer than the inflated numbers that landholding companies and annexationists claimed.[7] Maj. Frederick Foltz reported in November that settlers were still laying the groundwork for their communal and commercial enterprises – literally, in most cases. Foltz did not find established American neighborhoods, per se, but rather areas in which settlers tended to gravitate. "They do not live in towns, but their orchards cluster around four distinct centers [Santa Fe, Columbia, McKinley, and Los Indios]."[8] Institutions and modern amenities were still in relatively short supply.

Socioeconomically, the Isle did not quite resemble the middle-class haven landholding companies portrayed it as. Foltz's report revealed that most of the first settlers were much more well-to-do. Their cash reserves enabled

[5] Nueva Gerona Board of Trade to William Jennings Bryan, April 24, 1915, 1910–29 Central Decimal File, General Records of the Department of State Relating to the Internal Affairs of Cuba, NARA Microcopy 488, Roll 27, 837.014P/131.

[6] Santa Fe Land Company and Isle of Pines United Land Companies, "Marvelous Isle of Pines: 'That Magnificent Land of Sunshine, Health, and Wealth'" (Chicago, 1914), 38.

[7] American Men on Isle of Pines, undated, Provisional Government of Cuba, "Confidential" Correspondence, 1906–1909, Box 1, Folder 003, Record Group 199, NARA. By town, the breakdown was: Santa Fe (eighty), Nueva Gerona (forty-two), Los Indios (twenty-eight), Columbia (twenty-seven), and McKinley (twenty). Women and children were not enumerated in this report.

[8] Foltz to Charles Magoon, November 12, 1906, Provisional Government of Cuba, "Confidential" Correspondence, 1906–1909, Box 1, Folder 003, Record Group 199, NARA.

them more easily to absorb start-up costs for their groves, businesses, and homes. "I must report these colonists as of an unusually high class, well educated and intelligent, having come to the Island with sufficient funds to buy their farms, plant them in oranges, grape fruit and lemons, and have sufficient funds in reserve to support themselves for the four years during which they must wait before they can expect a return in money."[9] By the end of the U.S.-run provisional government in January 1909, however, as groves and gardens began to flourish and businesses got off the ground, more middle-class Americans made their way to the Isle. One travel writer observed: "The great majority are men of moderate means who have come here for health, to escape the Northern winters and who must make their living out of the soil."[10] Journalist Irene A. Wright recognized a shift in class dynamics among settlers. "Some of them are people of means, to whom the groves are pastimes pleasant during the winter season. Others are kept awake nights by the imperative necessity of holding both ends together."[11] This stark division of means within the American community would stand out during the remainder of the U.S. presence.

Despite socioeconomic differences, settlers promoted cooperation based on common interests and a shared identity as Americans. Such a communitarian vision suggested that the Isle could be the place in which to create a more perfect American society. The Santa Fe Land Company, for example, used the idea as a selling point. "So many 'American colonies' in foreign countries think too much of the 'individual' to ever reach the pinnacle of 'success for the whole.' The Americans in the Isle of Pines appear to be 'pulling together' for the prosperity of their colony, instead of every man for himself."[12] Millie Giltner, the daughter of one of the first settlers and the wife of a prominent U.S. businessman, recalled that settlers supported each other's ventures. In her opinion, it made for a more intimate community. "I think on the whole we had really a very wonderful community life on the island," she said. "If the Methodists were having something everybody went to the school. If the Catholics had something down at the central park everybody went down to help out. It's community and you don't have that up here [in the United States]."[13]

[9] Ibid.

[10] Frederic J. Haskin, "The Republic of Cuba: An American Colony in the Tropics," *The State (Columbia, SC)*, January 21, 1909.

[11] Irene A. Wright, *Isle of Pines* (Beverly, MA: Beverly Printing Company, 1910), 9.

[12] Santa Fe Land Company, "Marvelous Isle of Pines," 35.

[13] Millie Giltner oral history interview with Frederick Swetland Jr., March 13, 1969, 14, SFA.

Her remarks not only rejected the idea of the rugged individual so deeply engrained in frontier mythology, but also rebuked the urbanization and social isolation that was a growing feature of early twentieth-century U.S. society. As historian Steven Conn notes about that era, "Americans of many stripes looked at the dizzying growth of industrial cities and saw loss: the loss of intimate social relations replaced by anonymity, and of nurturing communities replaced by alienation. They were convinced that 'community' could not be achieved in the modern city."[14] The Santa Fe Land Company's promotion and Giltner's comments reflected those concerns while suggesting that an idealized, agrarian-centered, Jeffersonian community could be replicated on the Isle of Pines.

Some observers, however, disputed the notion of a cooperative community. These reports suggested rivalries sprang up *between* American settlements. George B. Tracy, a U.S. vice consul in Nueva Gerona, was one who held a jaundiced view. "Cooperation has not been developed to any great extent, but the people are coming to it gradually," he wrote in 1920.[15] Wright argued that settlers worked together often, but offered one caveat to her portrayal. "Jealousy, there is; but it is between communities, rather than persons.... The rivalry, before mentioned, which exists between towns (a frontier condition which makes for improvement and growth) does not enter into private or social affairs."[16] Commercial concerns became the main source of friction between settlements. One 1907 U.S. military report noted that Americans in Nueva Gerona and Santa Fe were in constant competition with one another trying to attract new residents who would buy land and start businesses.[17]

Indisputable, though, was the proliferation of construction projects, institutions, and products that bore a distinctly American imprint. These efforts were designed, in part, to attract more settlers and ease the anxieties of living in a foreign land. For those who could not wait for improvements and conveniences, they brought them themselves. One settler stated that having her old household items helped to smooth the transition to domestic life on the Isle. "I made up my mind before coming down that if

---

[14] Steven Conn, *Americans against the City: Anti-urbanism in the Twentieth Century* (New York: Oxford University Press, 2014), 6.

[15] Tracy to Richard J. Biggs Jr., September 23, 1920, Nueva Gerona – Isle of Pines, Cuba, Vol. 22, Correspondence, 1920 – Part III, Record Group 84, NARA.

[16] Wright, *Isle of Pines*, 92, 94.

[17] Tittoni to Charles Magoon, January 19, 1907, Provisional Government of Cuba, "Confidential" Correspondence, 1906–1909, Box 1, Folder 003, Record Group 199, NARA.

we were to make the Isle our home we must have the home surroundings to be happy and contented. I am not sorry that, with very few exceptions, we brought everything we had, including cats, dog, and a bird."[18] As more settlers established themselves and demand for U.S. goods grew stronger, modern conveniences – at least according to American norms – grew increasingly evident. General stores, most of which were run by settlers, began carrying familiar products such as ice-cream sodas, cured hams, and chewing gum.[19]

The pace of change seemed to surprise even some settlers. According to his hometown newspaper in 1911, George W. Upham of Marshfield, Wisconsin, was impressed by the "marked prosperity in the island and great growth and improvement since his previous visit six years ago.... The towns are modern and sanitary and all improvements [are] of a permanent nature."[20] Similarly, William Schultz noted the vast improvements in transportation. Paved roads had proliferated thanks largely to projects initiated under the provisional government, although their upkeep – or lack thereof – remained a source of contention between settlers and Havana officials. In addition, Schultz stated that he could make it back to his hometown of Fond du Lac, Wisconsin, in only four days – much faster than previous trips.[21] Reports about improvements in transportation and availability of familiar goods strongly suggested the Isle's proximity to the United States, literally and figuratively. Such stories surely were meant to appeal to potential settlers considering an investment in the Isle of Pines.

Institutionalizing Americanization

Another important element that appealed to settlers was the growth of American-style institutions. This development illustrated four important points about the U.S. presence: the increasing numbers of settlers; improved collaboration among Americans; their desires to attract additional settlers; and their intention to live indefinitely on the Isle. These institutions – which included schools, churches, social clubs, and newspapers – offered settlers the opportunity to replicate, perform, and

---

[18] Undated letter of Gertrude E. Christy quoted in Wright, *Isle of Pines*, 98.
[19] William D. Boyce, *United States Colonies and Dependencies* (Chicago: Rand McNally, 1914), 527.
[20] "A Visit to the Isle of Pines," *Marshfield Times*, March 15, 1911. Upham operated a furniture store in Marshfield and owned at least twenty acres in the San Juan tract.
[21] "Time Reduced to the Isle of Pines," *Fond du Lac Commonwealth*, June 25, 1912.

improve American ways, ideas, and customs. They also served as venues wherein settlers could socialize with like-minded, like-identified people who were experiencing similar challenges in establishing a new home in an alien land.

Schools

American-run schools represented the most significant American-style institution on the Isle. Fed up with a Cuban public school system they considered ineffective, settlers circumvented it by opening private, English-language schools for children of U.S. citizens. During the first two decades of the century, schools opened in U.S. settlements across the Isle. These schools allowed American children to continue their education under American auspices, following familiar curricula in their native language. They also helped to preserve American styles and customs among youths. Furthermore, these schools gave nuclear families more incentive to move to the Isle together, secure in knowing that American education was available. As a result, families with children were more common among settlers than the lone frontiersman. Of the nearly 200 U.S. households registered with the U.S. consulate in Nueva Gerona between 1913 and 1917, approximately 120 had children.[22]

Although privately run and dependent on local donations, these schools were not able to cut all ties with the Cuban government. They relied on the government for financial assistance to supplement teacher salaries and to supply necessities such as desks and books. When such assistance did not come, settlers grew upset. For example, in May 1910, a trio claiming to represent the "American Board of Education of the Isle of Pines" lodged a protest with U.S. Minister to Cuba John B. Jackson. According to their complaint, the Cuban government had reduced monthly stipends to eight American primary schools from $62.50 to $50, then cut them altogether prior to the 1909–10 school year. Although Jackson's predecessor, Edwin Morgan, had successfully lobbied the Cuban government to restore aid to four of the schools, it only offered $44 a month. The trio wanted Jackson to persuade Havana officials to restore aid to $50 a month to nine American schools, arguing that settlers were the largest taxpayers on the Isle.[23] In response, Jackson defended the

[22] Nueva Gerona – Isle of Pines, Cuba, Vol. 58, Isle of Pines Certificates of Registration, 1913–1917, Record Group 84, NARA.
[23] J. F. Redmond, L. G. Bell, L. W. Giltner to Jackson, May 4, 1910, 1910–29 Central Decimal File, General Records of the Department of State Relating to the Internal Affairs of Cuba, NARA Microcopy 488, Roll 27, File 837.014P/80.

Cuban government. He pointed out that funding for English-language teachers had been one of the first budget cuts because it would cause the least disadvantage to Cuban students, the government's top priority, because it was "under no legal obligation to provide special schools for English-speaking children." Jackson reminded the group that "you are asking for <u>favors</u>, and not <u>rights</u>, and that in making a <u>demand</u> you may run a risk of losing what has already been obtained and of being told that the Americans must be content with the same schools provided for the Cubans."[24] In any event, Cuban funding for American schools continued, but at more modest rates.

A few American-run schools, primarily those that included high school, were sustained through parochial ties. One of the first was St. Joseph's Academy in Nueva Gerona, established in 1912 by Benedictine nuns from the United States. For reasons unclear, the archdiocese of Havana took control of the school in 1926 and renamed it Colegio San José.[25] Rev. M. M. Steward, a U.S. missionary, founded another parochial institution in Nueva Gerona, the American Academy. Classes were conducted in the Methodist church.[26] At about the same time, Rev. William Decker, an Episcopalian missionary, founded the Santa Fe Academy. This school, in the Isle's other major town center, opened with thirty-seven students in 1914.[27]

By the early 1910s, the presence of American schools emerged as a selling point for landholding companies. "The children of these American homes attend American schools taught by American teachers, while parents and children are able to attend the Sunday School and the church of their choice as was their wont in the states," the San Juan Heights Land Company boasted.[28] In reality, these schools may have been less effective than portrayed. James F. Tracy, George Tracy's son, attended the first and second grades in the early 1920s. His school was housed in a three-room wooden building – one room for grammar school, one for high school, and a meeting room. Throughout first grade, James and his twin brother, William, spent most of their time in the meeting room "making paper

[24] Jackson to Redmond, Bell, Giltner, May 16, 1910, 1910–29 Central Decimal File, General Records of the Department of State Relating to the Internal Affairs of Cuba, NARA Microcopy 488, Roll 27, File 837.014P/80. Emphasis in original.

[25] Wiltse Peña Hijuelos, et al., *Con Todo Derecho: Isla de la Juventud* (La Habana, 1986), 78.

[26] "Weekly Budget from the Isle of Pines," *Cuba News*, September 12, 1914.

[27] "Isle of Pines News Notes," *Cuba News*, September 26, 1914.

[28] San Juan Heights Land Company, "The Isle of Pines: The Garden Spot of the World" (Cleveland, 1914), 19.

chains and houses and coloring pictures with crayons, etc. We really did not learn anything."[29] To Tracy's surprise, he and his brother failed and had to retake first grade. The second go-round was much more productive than the first. With two additional classmates and a new teacher who followed Ohio's state curriculum, he recalled many pleasant school days studying outdoors during his second run through first grade.

Most of these schools did not endure for long, owing mostly to the decline of the American population that began after World War I. By the early 1920s, only four American schools remained – in McKinley, Santa Barbara, Santa Fe, and Columbia – none of which offered classes in high school, suggesting that the academies begun by Stewart and Decker did not survive.[30] As a result, settlers who wanted to maintain American schools were compelled to consolidate their efforts. This set the stage for the American Central School, which opened in 1925 and soon flourished not only as a key institution for retaining American customs and curricula, but also as a space that facilitated greater cooperation and collaboration among Americans and *pineros*, who eventually made up a majority of the student body.

Churches

Places of worship also proved important markers of the U.S. presence. Thanks to 400 years of Spanish influence, Catholicism remained the dominant religion in Cuba. But as historian Louis A. Pérez Jr. has shown, the Church's presence was fairly weak outside of Havana.[31] Protestant missionaries from the United States poured into Cuba at the turn of the century to steer Cuban Catholics away from what one missionary called "an uncultured intellect, a perverted conscience, and a corrupt life."[32]

On the Isle, U.S. missionaries became particularly active. Rev. A. R. Archibald, one of the first to arrive, began conducting services in Columbia in July 1902 from the porch of one of the first American homes. The service was significant not just for its spiritual expression, but also for its socializing aspects. Services were both rituals and anchors for

---

[29] Jim Tracy, "Random Thoughts on Growing Up" (2005), unpublished memoir, courtesy of April Jean Tracy.

[30] Consular Post Report, January 15, 1921, Nueva Gerona – Isle of Pines, Cuba, Vol. 24, Correspondence, 1921 – Part I, Record Group 84, NARA.

[31] Louis A. Pérez Jr., *Cuba and the United States: Ties of Singular Intimacy*, 2nd ed. (Athens: University of Georgia Press, 1997), 130–1.

[32] J. Milton Greene, a U.S. missionary in 1910, quoted in Pérez, *Cuba and the United States*, 130.

full-day gatherings. Some worshippers brought picnic baskets to services, which became a tradition in later years.[33] By 1912, missionaries from at least five Protestant denominations had established churches: Methodist, Lutheran, Episcopal, Union, and Seventh-Day Adventist.

Methodism ranked as the largest, most influential Protestant denomination thanks to U.S. missionaries. During those formative years at the turn of the century, J. T. Redmon was perhaps the most active. A native of Tennessee, Redmon came to the Isle in 1907 to replace another minister. His mission emphasized cooperation among the denominations, rather than promoting one church over another. According to one chronicler, Redmon traveled as many as 250 miles a month by horseback to preach to settlers, an estimated 35 percent of whom regularly attended services.[34] Like other ministers, Redmon celebrated several weddings, mostly involving settlers. But Redmon and other ministers also presided over marriages in the Methodist church involving Jamaican citizens.[35] The phenomenon illustrated how Methodist missionaries' reach extended beyond U.S. settlers, whom they were initially meant to support.

At least one missionary, Hester Anna Greer, sought to appeal to foreign nationals. Born in 1880 and raised Methodist in her native Indiana, Greer joined the Church of God and was ordained as a minister in 1913. In 1931, she began her foreign missionary work, first going to Jamaica and the Cayman Islands before settling in Cuba. In 1935, she was sent with her daughter, Gretchen, to the Isle, where she became the first missionary for her denomination. As an African-American woman, Greer was somewhat of a rarity among missionaries and especially among settlers. Greer, however, made no mention in her writings of any difficulties living on the Isle because of race or of her relationships with other Americans. Given her previous work among Jamaicans and Cayman Islanders, it is likely that her missionary work targeted that audience. Although Greer never mentioned the size of her congregation, it apparently endured even after she returned to the United States in the early 1940s. Her church/meeting house that was destroyed in the hurricane of 1944 and rebuilt by Gretchen and Gretchen's husband two years later remained standing as late as 1980.[36]

[33] "Church Privileges Early Established," *Isle of Pines Appeal*, April 30, 1921.

[34] Sterling Augustus Neblett, *Methodism's First Fifty Years in Cuba* (Wilmore, KY: Asbury Press, 1976), 70.

[35] For examples, see Colección Iglesias: Expedientes de Matrimonios, 1901–1918, AHM. Foreign nationals, mostly from the Cayman Islands or Jamaica, were married by U.S. pastors in Lutheran and Episcopal churches as well.

[36] Hester Anna Greer Papers, Box 1, Folder 3, Correspondence – 1940–1942, IHS.

Social Clubs

Since the majority of settlers lived on farms outside of town centers, opportunities to socialize through day-to-day activity were infrequent. Social clubs helped to fill the void. These clubs brought settlers together and reinforced common customs and a common national identity. Social associations proliferated across the Isle during the first decade of U.S. settlement. Some clubs were specific to particular towns; others had a broader reach, aimed at catering to all settlers. They appealed to varying segments of Americans on the Isle – men, women, children, families, farmers, businessmen – and were distinct markers of the U.S. presence.

These clubs also exemplified settlers' efforts to retain and display their American-ness. The Nueva Gerona–based American Club was one of the largest. At its peak, the club boasted more than 100 members. The clubhouse was stocked with newspapers and magazines (presumably from the United States), a piano and dance floor, as well as an in-house cook to prepare meals for members. "The Club is in short the general rendezvous and social centre of the island," Wright wrote.[37]

Social clubs also reflected settlers' concerns. For example, in 1918, a group of U.S. businessmen formed the Isle of Pines Chamber of Commerce. Truman Swetland was named the organization's first president.[38] Designed to promote commercial activity, the Chamber coalesced in the wake of a devastating hurricane in 1917 that destroyed many settlers' farms and groves and briefly crippled the Isle's export production. Some settlers even began returning to the United States. In one of its advertisements seeking members for $5 a year, the Chamber wrote that, "About three years ago it was realized that the affairs of the Isle of Pines had reached a crisis and that it was necessary for the people to organize and pull together or give up in despair." It also listed five qualities required from its members: "Co-Operation, Stick-to-it-ness, Smiles, Friendship, and Common Sense."[39] The Chamber of Commerce was just one of numerous business associations comprised mostly of settlers.

Social clubs also provided an important space for women to interact and exert their influence outside the home. Their activities paralleled those of Progressive-era women reformers back in the United States who were becoming more directly involved in civil society. Most female settlers came to the Isle with their husbands or fathers and were expected to

---

[37] Wright, *Isle of Pines*, 95.
[38] "Body of Swetland Will Be Sent Home," *Miami Herald*, February 16, 1928.
[39] Isle of Pines Chamber of Commerce advertisement, *Isle of Pines Appeal*, April 30, 1921.

maintain the domestic sphere. Millie Giltner intimated that Isle life was rather boring for women at first, especially since men were focused on building houses and starting citrus groves while they were relegated to a subordinate status as caregivers in the home. She said, "The wives just put up with all this nonsense.... Mother always said the women didn't like the Isle of Pines as much as the men did."[40] Frederick Swetland Jr. made a similar observation. He told one fellow settler that "the women generally didn't like the place, the men did.... I don't know how many women really liked the Isle of Pines or who stayed because they had to."[41]

But women became active participants in improving the Isle's sociability, primarily by organizing public gatherings and social clubs. "You will observe that Isle of Pines 'society' has a feminine tone," said Helen Rodman Jones, who along with her husband, Harry, cultivated "Jones's Jungle," an arboretum and tourist attraction that continued into the twenty-first century. "In fact the men here when they do appear at a social affair have a decidedly 'dragged out' appearance – 'dragged out' by their wives.... Any eavesdropper who slipped up unnoticed to learn the topics of their earnest conversation would overhear dissertations on 'orange culture,' 'fertilizer,' 'transportation,' and little more. The women have to furnish the gayety [*sic*]."[42]

To that end, women formed the first social club for settlers, the ladies-only Hibiscus Club in February 1905. Based in Santa Fe, the Hibiscus Club originally had twelve members. Within a decade, the club had a waiting list for new members and eventually grew to as many as seventy-five women. The group organized a variety of gatherings, dances, and fundraisers on behalf of other American-run institutions, most often schools. It also founded a library that accumulated more than 2,000 volumes by the early 1920s.

The Hibiscus Club inspired the creation of similar groups. The Pioneer Club was perhaps the largest women's group – designed for women in Nueva Gerona and Columbia and meeting every two weeks, often in the form of day-long gatherings to which families also were invited. Other women's groups emphasized more than just sociability. The Women's Economic Club of Santa Barbara attempted to recreate high society.

---

[40] Millie Giltner oral history interview with Frederick Swetland Jr., March 13, 1969, tape 1, 13–14, 26, SFA.

[41] Betty Barothy oral history interview with Frederick Swetland Jr., March 13, 1969, tape 5, 6, SFA.

[42] Quoted in Wright, *Isle of Pines*, 95.

Comprised of "some of the most prominent ladies of the Santa Barbara colonies and an associate membership of gentlemen from all parts of the island who are prominent financially," the group threw a reception on New Year's Eve 1912 to celebrate the opening of its $3,000 clubhouse. The event reportedly stood as "the most splendid social affair that Americans on the Isle of Pines have ever seen. It was ... a magnificent demonstration of what all of the Americans in the Isle of Pines can do in the way of a social event when they get together."[43] By the mid-1920s, however, as settlers' fortunes sagged, women's groups looked to ease the collective burden. For example, in November 1924, Millie Giltner and Emily Middleton founded the Women's Exchange in Nueva Gerona. This mini-enterprise brought women together to buy, sell, or trade clothes and goods among themselves. The exchange illustrated settlers' efforts to help one another and sustain the U.S. community during difficult times. It further showed the crucial responsibilities women had assumed in helping to sustain the struggling American colony.

Newspapers

English-language newspapers served a critical function for settlers as a medium in which to exchange news, ideas, and opinions. It also was a useful tool in informing Americans in the United States about how settlers were faring. While its emphasis was on local news and developments, newspapers also carried reports from the United States, often about the state of the citrus industry. American-run newspapers reported about the comings and goings of settlers and various social engagements, but also offered windows into popular perceptions about the state of the U.S. community and attitudes toward Cuban neighbors and authorities.

The *Isle of Pines Appeal* became the most popular and longest-running American-run publication. Founded in April 1904 by Arthur E. Willis, the weekly *Appeal* for a time was also the only newspaper produced on the Isle. Circulation at its peak was approximately 1,500 subscribers, more than half of whom were in the United States. The *Appeal* was designed, in part, to support settlers' interests and to promote American groves and businesses. Like other newspapers, the *Appeal* depended on advertisers. U.S. entrepreneurs were frequent supporters. Nevertheless, U.S. consul Charles Forman reported that "Advertisers are not very positive in their opinion of its effectiveness.... They advertise partly as they feel that the

---

[43] "Brilliant Affair Was Club Opening," *Isle of Pines Appeal*, January 4, 1913.

paper should be supported in the interest of the island."[44] That support helped to keep the *Appeal* in circulation until 1926.

Although the *Appeal* remained a fervent supporter of U.S. annexation, editorials were largely cordial to *pinero* authorities. Even after Willis was arrested and jailed in 1918 following an argument with a member of the Rural Guard, the U.S. consul remarked that such behavior was out of character. "I have never heard him utter a word of dissatisfaction toward the Cuban Government," William Bardel wrote. "In fact I know he has as many friends among the Cubans as he has among the Americans on this island."[45]

The same could not be said for the *Appeal*'s editor, E. L. Slevin. A former Rough Rider, Slevin stayed in Cuba after the War of 1898 and worked for English-language newspapers in Havana. According to one Cuban government report, Slevin developed an anti-Cuban reputation and was referred to as "the only radical American journalist in the country."[46] He continued this acerbic approach after becoming editor of the *Appeal* in 1922. Not coincidentally, the newspaper's editorials became increasingly critical of Cuban authority, especially as the U.S. Senate renewed consideration of the Hay-Quesada treaty. These editorials drew the ire of Cuban authorities. In June 1923, Slevin was charged with libel against Carlos Manuel Valdes Montiel, the Isle's Judge of the First Instance. Slevin remained jailed for nearly three weeks as he awaited trial and was eventually fined $60. U.S. vice consul George Tracy commented that the Slevin case cast settlers in a negative light. "The general attitude of the Havana press, and especially the present attitude towards Mr. Slevin, is very offensive and obnoxious to all Americans on the Isle of Pines. It creates an unfavorable impression on visitors and retards the progress of the island."[47]

---

[44] Department of Commerce Individual Periodical Report, prepared by Charles Forman, American Consul, June 5, 1922, Nueva Gerona – Isle of Pines, Cuba, Vol. 29, Correspondence, 1922 – Part II, Record Group 84, NARA.

[45] Bardel to William Gonzales, November 6, 1918, Nueva Gerona – Isle of Pines, Cuba, Vol. 16, Correspondence, 1918 – Part II, Record Group 84, NARA.

[46] The report blamed Slevin's belligerence on his propensity to drink excessively. It also noted Slevin's exclusion from the American Club in Havana, suggesting the American community there shunned him. R. Muñoz, Jefe de la Policía Judicial, to Secretaria de la Presidencia, July 4, 1923, Donativos y Remisiones, Legajo 70, Expediente 47, Alfredo Zayas y Alfonso – Book I, 14, ANC. One study, however, argued that Slevin was well-respected among Americans and *pineros*. Julio Antonio Avello, "The Isle of Pines as a Factor in United States–Cuban Relations" (MA thesis, Southern Illinois University, 1969), 58–9.

[47] Tracy to C. B. Hurst, November 23, 1923, Nueva Gerona – Isle of Pines, Cuba, Vol. 31, Correspondence, 1923 – Part I, Record Group 84, NARA.

The Slevin case, though, underscored rising tensions between settlers and *pineros* in the mid-1920s as well as the catalytic role the *Appeal* played in fanning the flames.

Although the *Appeal*'s successor, the *Isle of Pines Post*, operated in less contentious times, its content reflected settlers' growing anxieties. Published twice monthly by the American Legion beginning in November 1927, the *Post* was less politically charged than the *Appeal*, owing much to the fact that the sovereignty question already had been resolved. Instead, the *Post* primarily emphasized social gatherings among settlers (including comings and goings), cultivating support for U.S. institutions like the American Central School, and keeping close tabs on the state of the citrus industry in the United States. All three issues were paramount to the future of U.S. settlement. Much like its impact on settlers, economic realities, particularly the onset of the Great Depression, also crippled the *Post*. By 1932, the newspaper informed readers who could not afford the $2 yearly subscription that it could barter with goods and produce, or delay payment indefinitely.[48] Such appeals did not help. The *Post* ceased operations by the end of the year, by which time the U.S. population numbered fewer than 300.

U.S. Consulate

The consulate stood as the most conspicuous sign of official U.S. presence. Based mostly in Nueva Gerona, but for a short time in Santa Fe, the consulate both supported and undermined settlers. On one hand, the consulate recognized the significant presence of U.S. citizens and offered them a direct link to the U.S. government. Over the years, many settlers turned to the consulate in search of protection and assistance. On the other hand, the consulate also signified that the U.S. government considered the Isle foreign territory, thus undercutting annexationists' argument. Foltz may have been the first to suggest the idea, recommending one in November 1906 to help alleviate the "friction" between settlers and Cuban authorities.[49] As late as February 1910, the State Department argued that conditions on the Isle did not "justify" a consulate.[50] But

---

[48] "Notice Subscribers," *Isle of Pines Post*, June 25, 1932.
[49] Foltz to Charles Magoon, November 12, 1906, Provisional Government of Cuba, "Confidential" Correspondence, 1906–1909, Box 1, Folder 003, Record Group 199, NARA.
[50] Huntington Wilson to Sen. Knute Nelson, February 25, 1910, 1910–29 Central Decimal File, General Records of the Department of State Relating to the Internal Affairs of Cuba, NARA Microcopy 488, Roll 27, File 837.014P/76.

it evidently had a change of heart because on August 1, 1910, Vervie Sutherland took the oath of office as U.S. consul and set up in Nueva Gerona.[51] Befitting the low priority the State Department placed on the post, Sutherland was not a professional diplomat as was becoming more commonplace at the turn of the century. Rather, he owned a real estate agency on the Isle; his work at the rank of vice consul was simply a side job. U.S. officials in Havana approved of the arrangement provided he opened the consulate every day. After Sutherland resigned in October 1916, the State Department employed full-time, professional diplomats.

The consulate essentially served three functions. The first was to register U.S. citizens, primarily those who lived on the Isle year-round. Those who resided only part of the year generally were not enumerated, which made accurate counts of settlers at any given time difficult. Nevertheless, the consulate's work at least provided a base from which to gauge estimates of the U.S. population. Between 1913 and 1929, the consulate registered 262 heads of households totaling 659 U.S. citizens.[52] The second function was to promote commercial opportunities. Domestic U.S. businesses and prospective investors frequently inquired with the consul about market conditions and prospects. For the most part, consuls preached caution – a stark contrast from landholding companies' booster promotions. "Living is high," Sutherland told one inquirer. "I would not advise anyone to come here with the intention of doing extensive development work without a fair amount of capital to start with as I should judge that it would take $5,000 or $10,000 to plant a five or ten acre citrus fruit grove and bring it into bearing. I would not advise one to purchase land here without first seeing it."[53] But he also advised that if one could afford to live on the Isle, the rewards were plentiful. "If a man has a good position as a mechanic in an American city he is a great deal better off than a poor man here without sufficient means to raise a citrus fruit grove. While on the other hand if he has sufficient means, I believe him better off here than he would be in the north."[54]

[51] Nueva Gerona – Isle of Pines, Cuba, Vol. 4, Miscellaneous Record Book –August 5, 1910 to August 28, 1919, 1-1, Record Group 84, NARA.

[52] Nueva Gerona – Isle of Pines, Cuba, Vol. 59, Isle of Pines Registration Applications, 1913–1929, Record Group 84, NARA.

[53] Sutherland to William J. Mills, February 11, 1912, Nueva Gerona – Isle of Pines, Cuba, Vol. 10, Correspondence, 1912, 267, Record Group 84, NARA.

[54] Sutherland to C. M. Reaber, July 20, 1913, Nueva Gerona – Isle of Pines, Cuba, Vol. 11, Correspondence, 1913–1914, 70, Record Group 84, NARA.

The consulate's third function was to serve as a resource for settlers looking for U.S. government assistance. Settlers often requested the consul's help in navigating Cuban bureaucracy, particularly when it came to registering property. Consuls, at times, were called upon to lobby *pinero* officials, especially as settlers tried to ward off squatters and petty thieves. The consul also was one of the first resources to whom settlers turned when they ran afoul of Cuban authorities. Americans who faced fines or jail time frequently contacted the consul to get U.S. diplomatic support for their defense. In some instances, settlers asked the consul to call in the U.S. military for protection. For example, in June 1912, as Cuban authorities violently suppressed Afro-Cuban protests for political participation, settlers feared a similar uprising on the Isle. Specifically, they expected either a guerrilla insurgency or an invasion of Afro-Cubans from Pinar del Rio and asked Sutherland to call in the U.S. Army.[55] Settlers made a similar request in 1925 in advance of the U.S. Senate vote on the Hay-Quesada treaty out of concern that its failure might spark a violent backlash among *pineros*.[56] The U.S. military was not deployed in either case, but it illustrated settlers' faith in the consulate to defend them.

Consuls, however, seemed largely disillusioned about the effectiveness of their work and life on the Isle. William Bardel, the first career diplomat assigned to the consulate, was particularly disenchanted with his assignment. "This post is far from agreeable to me," he wrote. "Leaving aside living conditions, which are next to unbearable here, I find after a total elimination of the question of annexation, the work of this post entirely too unimportant for a Consul of 18 yrs experience."[57] Another note from Bardel revealed his boredom. "While in this 'one-horse post' the official business is sadly lacking in importance, our good friends, the many Americans here, take good care not to allow me to be idle by keeping me busy with unofficial affairs."[58] One of his successors concurred that the Nueva Gerona post did not require much attention because of the Isle's economic condition. In a response to a State Department inquiry

[55] Sutherland to Arthur M. Beaupre, June 8, 1912, Nueva Gerona – Isle of Pines, Cuba, Vol. 10, Correspondence, 1912, Record Group 84, NARA.

[56] W. H. Shutan, Military Attaché, to U.S. Embassy, Havana, February 3, 1925, 1910–29 Central Decimal File, General Records of the Department of State Relating to the Internal Affairs of Cuba, NARA Microcopy 488, Roll 29, File 837.014P/359.

[57] Bardel to Wilbur Carr, December 5, 1918, 1910–29 Central Decimal File, General Records of the Department of State Relating to the Internal Affairs of Cuba, NARA Microcopy 488, Roll 27, File 837.014P/153.

[58] Bardel to Heaton W. Harris, December 5, 1918, Nueva Gerona – Isle of Pines, Cuba, Vol. 16, Correspondence, 1918 – Part II, Record Group 84, NARA.

about the disadvantages of his post, Charles Forman wrote: "Lack of commercial importance, making it difficult to do commercial work that counts. The office is classed as a consulate. In my opinion it should be a vice consulate."[59] Nevertheless, Forman maintained some optimism, particularly about living on the Isle: "As a place to live it is not so bad; it is healthy, not extremely hot, and there is a good deal of American society. As a beginner's post I should rank it as fairly good provided one can afford to keep a Ford automobile."[60]

As the American community began to dwindle in the 1920s, State Department officials saw less of a need for a consulate. It closed in June 1929 to much protest from the remaining settlers. They now had to address their U.S. government business with the consulate in Havana, which was still an expensive and time-consuming trip. Although the consulate in Nueva Gerona reopened from 1942–4, its main emphasis was to keep tabs on German and Japanese nationals who lived or were incarcerated on the Isle, rather than to administer to settlers, who by then numbered only a few hundred. Nevertheless, the consulate ranked as an essential signifier of the U.S. presence and its records offer valuable insight into the U.S. community.

American Towns

In addition to institutions, American-founded towns offered another significant appeal to the potential settler. These communities promised familiar surroundings in a foreign land. Landholding companies not only designated certain sections of their tracts as community centers, they also were instrumental in the planning, construction, development, and promotion of these towns. While these towns afforded settlers the opportunity to replicate American life, they also gave them a chance to perfect it according to a more cooperative ethic. Although individual initiative was said to be critical to ensuring the long-term prospects of one's home or farm, these communities suggested that such efforts did not have to be pursued in isolation. Town founders and settlers promoted their communities as centers of cooperation, especially evident in the variety of social clubs and mutual aid societies in each location.

---

[59] Forman to State Department, June 12, 1923, Nueva Gerona – Isle of Pines, Cuba, Vol. 32, Correspondence, 1923 – Part II, Record Group 84, NARA.
[60] Forman to Charles Hosmer, July 15, 1923, Nueva Gerona – Isle of Pines, Cuba, Vol. 31, Correspondence, 1923 – Part I, Record Group 84, NARA.

The first of these American towns was Columbia, located on the northeastern side of the Isle, two miles from the port of Jucaro. The Isle of Pines Land and Development Company, led by C. M. Johnson and Ira Brown, founded the town in 1902 within the 15,000-acre Santa Rosalia tract. The first residents were a group of Iowa farmers whose journey had garnered attention in U.S. newspapers.[61] Most of the settlers grew citrus fruit and winter vegetables for export. Millie Giltner, Brown's daughter, recalled that amenities were few and far between for the first settlers, who had to travel ten miles on dirt trails to Nueva Gerona to buy essentials.[62] At its height in the early 1910s, Columbia boasted about 100 residents and had a school, general store, post office, and church. It also had a variety of clubs, including the Ladies Aid Society as well as a group for unmarried residents called the Columbia Social Club.[63]

Although the Isle of Pines Land and Development Company ceased operations in 1910, the town endured. Its most notable feature was the American Cemetery. Established in August 1907 after company representative Louis C. Giltner, Millie's future husband, petitioned the *ayuntamiento* for permission, the cemetery was privately maintained by the American-run Cemetery Association.[64] One Cuban study claims that settlers established the cemetery because of unease with sanitary practices at the Isle's main cemetery in Nueva Gerona as well as religious reasons.[65] Archival evidence, however, does not reveal any mention of religion in correspondence about the cemetery. It nevertheless became the final resting place for many U.S. citizens.

The Isle featured nearly a dozen U.S.-settled towns. Populations varied from a few dozen to a few hundred. Some towns, like McKinley, endured for a generation or more. Others, like La Siguanea, barely survived the planning stages. The development of each offers insight into settlers' hopes and desires, the elements of American-ness they privileged, and the challenges they faced in trying to realize their dreams.

---

[61] Detail taken from Charles Forman, "Personal Notes of Americans Interested in the Isle of Pines," October 11, 1923, 1910–29 Central Decimal File, General Records of the Department of State Relating to the Internal Affairs of Cuba, NARA Microcopy 488, Roll 28, File 837.014P/219; Frederick A. Fernald, "Americans Busy on Isle of Pines," *Fort Worth Star-Telegram*, November 20, 1905.

[62] Millie Giltner oral history, March 13, 1969, 3, SFA.

[63] Wright, *Isle of Pines*, 46–7, 95.

[64] Wright, *Isle of Pines*, 47; Secretaría de Gobernación, Legajo 18, Expediente 406, August 14, 1907, ANC.

[65] Hijuelos, et al., *Con Todo Derecho*, 75.

Case Study: McKinley

The town of McKinley demonstrated important elements of American-
ness that landholding companies and settlers privileged. The Tropical
Development Company founded the town on January 1, 1905, within
a 5,200-acre tract in Santa Barbara that it had purchased from the Isle
of Pines Company. The company sold bonds in its enterprise that gave
investors the right to buy land. Investors had to purchase one bond for
every ten acres; bonds went for $76.50 each and land was sold for $35
an acre, $40 if along a riverfront. The company's name, in honor of slain
U.S. President William McKinley, was telling, considering annexationists frequently claimed (on specious grounds) that McKinley intended to
make the Isle a U.S. territory. The Tropical Development Company, which
superimposed McKinley's face on a picture of the Isle in its prospectus,
accomplished two goals by associating itself with the late president: it
drew a connection to the annexationist argument and demonstrated its
patriotism as a way to deflect charges of speculation.

Efforts to develop the town reveal much about settlers and investors'
motivations as well as the expectations and desires they projected onto
the Isle. "We are helping to develop a fertile and charming island into a
progressive agricultural section, instinct with the life of twentieth century
America," the Tropical Development Company–run *McKinley Herald*
wrote. "The curtain has been rung down upon the old Spanish regime!
Citizens of McKinley, you may well feel that you are on the firing line of a
new civilization."[66] The *Herald* drew explicit comparisons to nineteenth-
century pioneering that spread U.S. and Anglo-Saxon culture across the
North American continent. "Many of our settlers are descendants of
those who developed the resources of the Niagara frontier and all of them
have in their veins that love of conquest, that bulldog tenacity of purpose
which has ever been characteristic of the Anglo-Saxon race."[67] Much like
its efforts to associate itself with William McKinley, by establishing a link
of continuity with previous pioneering the company could argue that its
entrepreneurial efforts were not merely self-interested or speculative, but
also for the greater good of the United States and its citizens.

Promotions to buy land and live in McKinley also were infused with a
sense of latter-day Puritanism. Depictions of the Isle conjured echoes of
John Winthrop's celebrated "City upon a Hill" reference in 1630 about
the potential a new world offered to form a more perfect society and

---

[66] "Sec'y Comstock Visits McKinley," *McKinley Herald*, January 1907.
[67] "The First Year's Work at McKinley," *McKinley Herald*, December 1905.

serve as an example for others to follow. They also reflected Progressive-era sensibilities about the ideal community, which historian David Noble described as one in which "the individual would not have to sacrifice any of his autonomy and independence through participation in group endeavor."[68] The organizers of McKinley tried to find that balance.

More important, promoters suggested that the Isle of Pines offered settlers the opportunity to perfect American ways. Some of the *Herald*'s articles revealed dissatisfaction with the direction of American life and suggested that the Isle offered a place in which settlers could reverse unsettling trends. "At home, industrial conditions are becoming more and more unsatisfactory and the avenues of opportunity more and more restricted," the *Herald* wrote. "The spirit of the age breathes CO-OPERATION, BROTHERHOOD and EQUAL PRIVILEGES, while the economic bands of a worn-out System only serve to distort into ugly forms the tendencies of the times which they cannot control."[69] By extension, the Isle in general and McKinley in particular promised a place where settlers could renew the American way of life. "What wonder, then, if the MAKERS of McKINLEY are pioneers, no less in a new country than in a new thought?" the *Herald* asked.

What wonder if the old ideas of COMPETITION are left behind, if the old SUPERSTITIONS and BELIEFS in the limitations of SENSE and SELF are abandoned ere the journey is begun and if, with the Southern Cross to guide them, these ISLE OF PINES AMERICANS are blazing for themselves and their children a newer, broader and fairer highway than man has ever trod before – the HIGHWAY OF TRUTH![70]

In essence, the company suggested that McKinley could become an exemplar by renewing American society based more on cooperation than individualism, privileging agricultural rather than industrial work, and with more opportunity to improve one's standard of living through hard work. It also reflected a Populist sensibility that criticized oligarchs and corporations for stifling farmers and middle-class Americans. The Isle offered settlers a chance to see what they could make for themselves without interference from the wealthy interests limiting the benefits Americans of average means could enjoy. Ironically, it was indeed wealthy men who were most involved in landholding companies and stood to benefit the most when settlers bought land from them.

---

[68] David W. Noble, *The Progressive Mind, 1890–1917* (Chicago: Rand McNally, 1970), ix.
[69] "The Isle of Pines," *McKinley Herald*, December 1907.
[70] Ibid.

Although their promotional efforts aimed to appeal to farmers and middle-class Americans, the Tropical Development Company made clear that a life in McKinley, particularly in its early stages of development, was not suitable for everyone. One company director in 1905 cautioned potential settlers that living in McKinley would not be easy. Albert B. Young wrote that the town, with virtually no infrastructure or amenities yet, was "in a crude state, and that one must be prepared for the inconveniences incident to a pioneer undertaking."[71] Other articles in the *Herald*, which was designed for McKinley residents and Tropical Development Company bondholders, frequently warned that sufficient capital was necessary to clear and plant groves, purchase supplies, and tide one over until groves came into bearing. The newspaper warned that it might be some time before settlers saw a return on their investments and suggested that those who disputed the Isle's promise lacked the patience and fortitude for such challenging work. Floyd C. Payne, a native of Kansas who lived in McKinley through at least 1917, supported that idea. "There are some who have come down here to settle who have not liked it here, and probably when they get back to the States will circulate bad reports concerning conditions here, but these people have expected too much and were not prepared to put up with conditions to be found in any new country," he wrote. "We do not want these kind of people here."[72]

Finding adequate shelter was the biggest challenge for McKinley's first residents. Some settlers embraced the sense of adventurism. For example, W. E. Poor and Samuel Corbin of Buffalo shared quarters in one tract while they helped clear each other's land. "We are living in tents, cooking over a camp fire, and thoroughly enjoying the novelty of the arrangement," Poor wrote.[73] The first permanent dwellings varied in size, but also underscored the disparity of means among settlers. On the modest end, Rev. George W. West claimed to have built a twelve-by-twenty-foot house in eleven days for only $58. The *Herald* lauded West as an example of "what a man can do single-handed and alone with little or no previous experience in farm work and at a very small outlay of capital."[74] In contrast, former Buffalo Mayor Erastus Knight, a Tropical Development Company director, built a much more ostentatious home. For roughly

[71] Young, "An Appreciative Visitor," *McKinley Herald*, April 1905.
[72] F. C. Payne to H. S. Gillette, November 30, 1905, quoted in "A Letter from McKinley," *McKinley Herald*, February 1906.
[73] Poor to F. A. Fernald, Tropical Development Company treasurer, February 20, 1905, quoted in "Correspondence from McKinley," *McKinley Herald*, April 1905.
[74] "A Letter from Rev. Geo. W. West," *McKinley Herald*, March 1906.

$1,800 his house had indoor plumbing, including a bathroom (rather than an outhouse), a laundry room, and perhaps most impressively, running water – features that the *Herald* wrote were "indispensable in the States and were regarded by Mr. Knight as equally indispensable at McKinley."[75]

Other construction projects proliferated in McKinley during its first few years. The Tropical Development Company built an on-site head-quarters that stood two stories. It featured living quarters that included fifteen bedrooms, a dining room, and kitchen. A general store was attached to the building as well. The company also erected a sawmill that supplied the raw material for town structures. But the company was not alone in commissioning construction projects. R. W. Dunning and his wife built the town's first hotel, The Orchid in the Pines. Measuring forty-by-ninety-six feet, the hotel boasted an eight-foot-wide veranda, twelve bedrooms, a reception hall, and a dining room. The bathroom featured a 3,000-gallon water tank fed from a nearby well. The hotel had indoor lighting thanks to a carbide generator. Rates were $3 a day with two persons to a room, $18 for a week.[76]

Institutions were slower to develop in McKinley than groves and dwellings. That delay was due in large part to the Tropical Development Company's call to residents to focus on clearing and improving their land first. The company's promotional efforts reinforced this dictum by showing numerous pictures of cleared plots in its advertisements.[77] In putting American industriousness on display, the company also implicitly supported annexationists' claim that settlers were making better use of the land than Spaniards or *pineros* ever did or could. Another reason for the institutional lag was that many residents, at least those who could afford to, lived in McKinley only during the winter months. This trend put a drag on the population.[78] But as residents finished clearing their land,

[75] "Mr. Knight's New House in East McKinley," *McKinley Herald*, November 1907.

[76] Details taken from Tropical Development Company, *McKinley in the Making* (Buffalo, NY, 1906), 8–9, 20–3.

[77] Ibid., 30–4.

[78] As addressed in Chapter 2, population figures for settlers are imprecise, at best. The situation at McKinley provides an illustrative case in point. The *Herald* in August 1905 claimed that McKinley had 147 residents, and expected that number to rise to 400 by the end of the year. But in September 1906, the U.S. military conducted a rough census of settlers and counted only twenty men in McKinley. The wide discrepancy can be attributed to the fact that official U.S. figures usually only counted year-round residents, whereas estimates from landholding companies and annexationists typically factored in part-timers as well as, presumably, people who bought land but never relocated.

built their dwellings, and waited for their groves to bloom, institutions proliferated.

Aside from roads and infrastructure, settlers and town planners considered a school one of the most important development projects. In its company prospectus, the Tropical Development Company promised to build a schoolhouse if the school-age population in McKinley reached fifty, so long as the residents furnished a teacher.[79] Although the school-age population at the time is unclear, the company erected a schoolhouse in 1908, a development that gave McKinley residents the "full assurance that their children will have the same advantage as those who live in any American village."[80] The school relied heavily, but not exclusively, on resident donations. The Cuban government also supported the endeavor, providing desks and books as well as the teacher's salary in keeping with its pledge to U.S. officials that it would support schools on the Isle. In the next few years, however, as additional private schools opened in McKinley, only one continued to receive modest government assistance – $10 to offset rent and $5 more for janitorial services.[81]

As schools proliferated, so too did other institutions. Another of the Tropical Development Company's pledges was to construct a church and give the deed to the denomination with the largest number of followers once the town reached a population of 300.[82] It followed through in 1907 after it established a partnership with Rev. A. W. Knight of the Episcopal Church in Cuba. The company donated the land to Knight, who provided $500 for building materials and furnishings and promised to make the church available for any other denomination to use as well. The company and Knight asked McKinley residents to help with the construction.[83] Settlers also established a public library as another common-use institution. The first opened in 1907 with eighty-nine volumes.[84]

[79] Tropical Development Company, "McKinley, Isle of Pines," 57.
[80] "Progress and Prosperity at McKinley," *McKinley Herald*, November 1908.
[81] J. L. Pearcy to Vervie P. Sutherland, September 5, 1912, Nueva Gerona – Isle of Pines, Cuba, Vol. 10, Correspondence, 1912, Record Group 84, NARA. It is unclear why Cuban officials did not financially support the other schools in McKinley or precisely how many were there.
[82] Tropical Development Company, "McKinley, Isle of Pines," 57. The company also claimed it would build a second church if the town's population reached 1,000, but that project apparently never came to fruition.
[83] "The New Episcopal Church," *McKinley Herald*, September 1907.
[84] "Free Circulating Library for McKinley," *McKinley Herald*, February 1907. According to one Cuban study, the first public library for *pineros* did not open until 1951 in Santa Fe. Hijuelos, et al., *Con Todo Derecho*, 70.

By 1910, settlers had founded a host of clubs that illustrated the elements of social and commercial life McKinley residents deemed important. The Carnation Club, established in 1906, was the most notable. Named for President McKinley's favorite flower, this women's club marked one of the first of its kind on the Isle. According to its constitution, the club's object was to assist in the "mutual improvement of its members in a social and literary way."[85] Members, who paid $1 a year in dues, primarily organized fundraisers for various town benefits, most often for schools.

Commercially, McKinley had two major organizations, the McKinley Fruit Growers Association and the McKinley Chamber of Commerce. The former dealt mainly with issues involving citrus culture, but the latter was more far-reaching and ambitious. For example, in August 1912, the McKinley Chamber of Commerce proposed an annual tax of twenty-five cents per acre on all property owners. The money collected would be used to support improvement projects on behalf of the town's schools and roads.[86] It is not clear, however, how residents responded to the Chamber's proposed plan.

McKinley's time as a thriving U.S. settlement was brief. During World War I, an estimated seventy-five settlers lived there year-round.[87] But shortly after the war, like populations in other U.S. settlements, McKinley's population began to decline, owing mostly to commercial failures. One longtime resident of the Isle, Adolph B. Kelm, recalled that when he first came to McKinley in 1916, it "was a very busy colony." But by 1950 he counted only one English-speaking family who still lived in town – and they were Canadian.[88] Even while the Isle experienced a resurgence in commercial activity in the mid-1950s, investors had scant interest in McKinley. Unimproved land prices there remained depressed at about $10 an acre, nearly $30 an acre less than at its peak a half-century earlier.[89]

Case Study: La Siguanea
Although McKinley experienced a slow, steady decline from its brief height, the town could at least boast a period of interest and activity.

---

[85] Woman's Carnation Club, Constitution and By-Laws, Fondo: Papelería de Extranjeros Residentes en Isla de Pinos, 1910–1975, Folder 2, AHM.

[86] McKinley Chamber of Commerce circular, August 1, 1912, Nueva Gerona – Isle of Pines, Cuba, Vol. 10, Correspondence, 1912, 290, Record Group 84, NARA.

[87] Americans Living on the Isle of Pines, August 23, 1915, Nueva Gerona – Isle of Pines, Cuba, Vol. 14, Correspondence, 1915, 231, Record Group 84, NARA.

[88] Kelm to Julia Larson, May 30, 1950, Fondo: A. B. Kelm, Legajo 4, Expediente 36, AHM.

[89] Adolph B. Kelm to Julia Larson, March 27, 1955, Fondo: A. B. Kelm, Legajo 4, Expediente 36, AHM.

La Siguanea had far less of either. But the efforts that went into form-ing this town reveal much about how U.S. investors and entrepreneurs considered another type of an ideal community, one that would appeal to certain Americans and yield significant returns.

La Siguanea formed the centerpiece of the Andorra Realty Company's 7,800-acre tract on the Isle's southwest coast. Developers considered the location attractive because they thought Siguanea Bay could – with sig-nificant dredging and development – be the site of a deep-water port that would provide direct transportation to and from the United States. The U.S. military first raised the idea in 1901, but officials determined that such efforts were not feasible.[90] Private U.S. developers, however, were not deterred. A similar project was under way in Los Indios, a few miles north of Andorra's property, where a few dozen settlers lived in relative isolation because of the Isle's poor roads. Los Indios eventually developed its own institutions, including a school, church, general store, post office, and hotel. Planners for La Siguanea tried to do the same, but their designs were more ambitious.

Unlike most other U.S. settlements that were advertised with farm-ers and the middle-class investor in mind, La Siguanea was expressly designed to appeal to wealthier Americans. It was less rhetorically uto-pian than McKinley, but more exclusive. "We are trying to make it the policy to have this town site unique and different from the various other settlements on the Isle of Pines," one town planner wrote. "If we can get the first people who build to put up attractive bungalows the idea is that the property will become valuable more quickly than the prop-erty on other parts of the Island."[91] Irene A. Wright wrote that the New Jersey–based Andorra Realty Company envisioned La Siguanea as "the great winter resort of the Isle of Pines and to accomplish that purpose no expense will be spared."[92] To that end, designers carefully considered the town's aesthetics. These factors included emphasis on a particular architectural style and unique features such as wide avenues in the town center, open spaces for playgrounds and parking areas, and a private dock for yachts. For help, the company turned to Olmsted Brothers, a

---

[90] Frank McCoy to Adjutant-General, Havana, March 12, 1901, in *Isle of Pines: Papers Relating to the Adjustment of Title to the Ownership of the Isle of Pines*, 68th Cong., 2d sess., 1924, S. Doc. 166, 174.

[91] James Frederick Dawson to H. A. Diller, September 26, 1910, Job File 3606, Folder 2 – January–October 1910, Reel 214, Olmsted Associates Records, Manuscript Division, LOC.

[92] Wright, *Isle of Pines*, 55.

Boston-based landscape architectural firm founded by Frederick Olmsted Jr. and John C. Olmsted. They were the sons of Frederick Law Olmsted, who famously had worked on New York's Central Park and the National Mall in Washington, DC. Olmsted Brothers drew up most of the plans and designs for La Siguanea at the directive of Andorra executives.

William Warner Harper, president of the Andorra Realty Company, had big, if somewhat vague, ideas for La Siguanea. "I am desirous that it should be a model city with pretty squares," he wrote. "I would also like to locate a number of Churches. The Catholic, Presbyterian, Methodist, and Episcopal denominations are quite prominent there, and these people should be given some of the best locations, locating nearer the public parks."[93] Harper left it to James Frederick Dawson and his team at Olmsted Brothers to work out the details. Olmsted Brothers estimated that it would cost some $275,000 to plan and develop La Siguanea. But it expected Andorra to yield a return of nearly $690,000 from the sale of land. Residential lots made up about 60 percent of the town's area; most of the rest would be dedicated to parks or squares it described as "breathing spaces." It recommended dividing the town into three districts: business, residential, and suburban. The latter would be reserved for larger tracts. The business district would house the proposed dock, as well as a wharf and a warehouse. Olmsted Brothers estimated that La Siguanea could sustain up to 4,500 residents – ambitious considering the entire Isle's population was officially 3,276 residents as of 1907.[94]

Olmsted Brothers' design bore hallmarks of the Garden City movement taking place in the early twentieth century. Towns in this vein were conceived as more open, ordered, and environmentally conscious alternatives to the rapid and seemingly haphazard urbanization taking place in the United States and England. One of the other fundamental aspects of such garden cities, historian Stanley Buder has argued, was their "promise to redefine and strengthen community in a modern world that challenged and reduced community significance."[95] These concepts were evident in

[93] Harper to James Frederick Dawson, December 31, 1908, Job File 3606, Folder 1 – 1908–1909, Reel 214, Olmsted Associates Records, LOC.
[94] Estimates and designs taken from Dawson to W. W. Harper, August 13, 1909, Job File 3606, Folder 1 – 1908–1909, Reel 214, Olmsted Associates Records, LOC; Cost of Town of Siguanea, January 29, 1910, Job File 3606, Folder 1 – 1908–1909, Reel 214, Olmsted Associates Records, LOC; "Andorra Realty Company, Isle of Pines, Town of Siguanea, Cuba," Olmsted Brothers report, February 1, 1910, Job File 3606, Folder 2 – January–October 1910, Reel 214, Olmsted Associates Records, LOC.
[95] Stanley Buder, *Visionaries and Planners: The Garden City Movement and the Modern Community* (New York: Oxford University Press, 1990), ix.

the planning for La Siguanea. Garden cities also were often associated with utopian movements and Progressive-era social reformers. Frederick Olmsted Jr., though, was more interested in Garden City planning as a more efficient form of municipal management and so wanted to divorce garden cities from reform movements.[96] Not surprisingly, correspondence relative to the planning of La Siguanea is absent of any explicitly reformist language.

In terms of La Siguanea's architectural style, Dawson's consideration varied markedly from other U.S. settlements. In contrast to other U.S. towns like McKinley that looked to replicate American designs, Dawson argued that La Siguanea should be in keeping with the "Spanish style." As historian Catherine Cocks has noted, such an approach was common among architects of new upscale neighborhoods in Florida and California to evoke warm climates and bright sunshine.[97] This style applied both to homes, which Dawson maintained should be single-story bungalows, as well as to public buildings such as schools, churches, and municipal sites. Correspondence suggests it was rather a hard sell for Dawson, who explained his idea to one settler. "I am trying to get the management of the Andorra Company to erect office buildings and a hotel, etc. in the near future on the Spanish style; that is with a tile roof and some sort of concrete plaster sides," he wrote. "I hope you will seriously consider building your bungalow in some good simple Spanish style and not try to Americanize it to such an extent that it will look entirely out of place."[98] In a follow-up note, Dawson insisted that the "Spanish style" was not inferior, but rather it was practical and aesthetically in keeping with the Isle. "There should be no prejudice against it on your part because it is used by the natives, but, instead, that should be a point in its favor because the methods of construction used there have been tested for a long time and we certainly feel that to adopt any style of building either in construction or in appearance like what is used in New England would be a mistake both from the useful standpoint and from the artistic."[99] Based on the town plans Olmsted Brothers revealed in 1910, it appears that Dawson's argument won out.

---

[96] Ibid., 161–2.

[97] Catherine Cocks, *Tropical Whites: The Rise of the Tourist South in the Americas* (Philadelphia: University of Pennsylvania Press, 2013), 92–3.

[98] Dawson to H. A. Diller, September 26, 1910, Job File 3606, Folder 2 – January–October 1910, Reel 214, Olmsted Associates Records, LOC.

[99] Dawson to H. A. Diller, October 20, 1910, Job File 3606, Folder 2 – January–October 1910, Reel 214, Olmsted Associates Records, LOC.

Promotion of the "Spanish style" in La Siguanea was not limited solely to the architecture. Others involved in the project took it up when it came to giving names to town sites and streets. C. L. Gaines, an engineer at work on the town, tried to impress upon Andorra executives that La Siguanea was a more appropriate name than those that others were considering because "La Siguanea is much more 'spanish' than Siguanea City, which is rather a funny combination and mix-up."[100] Gaines also lobbied to have street names reflect figures in the Isle's history. These included streets or parks named for Christopher Columbus, the first European on the Isle; Hernando Pedroso, who received title to the Isle from the Spanish crown in 1630; as well as some of the prominent landowning families from the late eighteenth century. He also suggested naming a few streets after saints, following Spanish custom.[101] Another member of the Olmsted team reminded town planners to use proper grammar when writing terms in Spanish. "Don't omit the accents," he urged.[102] When Olmsted Brothers unveiled the town plan in December 1910, it featured many of Gaines's suggestions, illustrating designers' quest to hearken to the Isle's Spanish heritage.

Despite Olmsted's victory in the debate over La Siguanea's style, other evident tensions appeared between it and Andorra. Primarily, Harper put pressure on Dawson to hurry the town's design so construction could begin in earnest. For the sake of expediency, Harper wrote, "I wish that you would give your heart and soul to the development of the town site rather than the planning of the dock."[103] Dawson, however, insisted that more careful consideration be given to the dock, which he argued was the lynchpin of the town project since it could provide a direct link to the United States, something no port on the Isle could sustain.[104] Although it is not clear in the final design who won out, the debate underscored Harper's quest to move forward quickly on the project and to begin selling plots to potential settlers – so much so that he was apparently willing

[100] Gaines to Olmsted Brothers, April 29, 1910, Job File 3606, Folder 2 – January–October 1910, Reel 214, Olmsted Associates Records, LOC.
[101] Gaines to Olmsted Brothers, October 1, 1910, Job File 3606, Folder 2 – January–October 1910, Reel 214, Olmsted Associates Records, LOC.
[102] Frederick Blossom memo, undated, Job File 3606, Folder 2 – January–October 1910, Reel 214, Olmsted Associates Records, LOC.
[103] Harper to Dawson, December 22, 1909, Job File 3606, Folder 1 – 1908–1909, Reel 214, Olmsted Associates Records, LOC.
[104] Dawson to Harper, December 24, 1909, Job File 3606, Folder 1 – 1908–1909, Reel 214, Olmsted Associates Records, LOC.

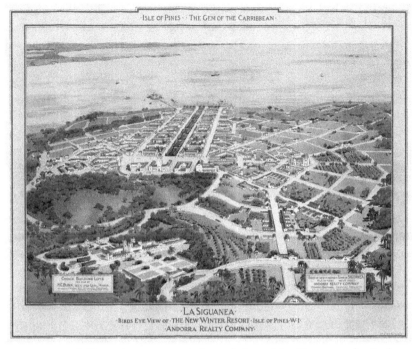

FIGURE 4.1. A December 1910 artist's rendering of La Siguanea, the Andorra Realty Company's proposed town on Siguanea Bay on the Isle's southwest coast. Designed by Olmsted Brothers to appeal to wealthier settlers, the town never got past the planning stages.
Source: Records of the Olmsted Associates, Box OV7, Job File 3606, Manuscript Division, Library of Congress. Reproduction courtesy of the Library of Congress.

to gloss over a critical piece of the project that was central to the town's appeal.

Harper's desire for expediency also revealed the Andorra Realty Company's precarious financial position as it sought to earn back the money it had spent to acquire its tract. In October 1909, Harper admitted as much, telling Olmsted Brothers his company was strapped for cash and requesting the company only develop plans adequate enough to show potential settlers. The money from those sales, Harper wrote, would then be reinvested in Olmsted Brothers for more detailed plans. At the time, Andorra did not have the money to follow through with all its plans, including the dock. "We must creep before we walk in this matter," Harper told Olmsted Brothers. "We can only do a little each year for some time to come and for that reason, cannot you give us something that is not too elaborate and expensive for the present?"[105] The answer, apparently, was "no." Dawson replied that plans could not be done piecemeal but rather in total. Moreover, Dawson enclosed a copy of the contract for services in which Olmsted agreed to work for Andorra for $5,000 plus expenses until July 1912.[106]

Even after Olmsted Brothers finished the town plan, financial tensions persisted.[107] Months after the work contract expired Andorra still had not paid Olmsted Brothers. In sending a past due notice of $7,774.22, John C. Olmsted added a scornful note to Harper: "It seems to me it is very unjust, arbitrary and unkind, when we have done our best to carry our part of an agreement, that the other party to the agreement should fail to make adequate arrangements for paying the amount due us.... I know I should not treat an architect who had made plans for a house for me so unjustly."[108] Harper did not deny his company was in arrears nor did he promise payment was forthcoming. Rather, he expressed regret for entering into such a costly undertaking. "It was the greatest error in my career that I allowed the company to go into this expenditure, when our finances were so limited. I explained all this to Mr. Dawson at the time, but he was so enthusiastic over the proposition we did not use good judgment.... [I]t was bad business to have a lot of professional work done when we were not in a position to do the physical work to the grounds."[109] Andorra continued to lag in its payments into 1913, to the extent that to cover some of its debts, it deeded some land in its tract to Olmsted Brothers. But the full balance remained unpaid over the next few years.

Andorra's problem reflected a stagnating real estate market on the Isle, particularly in the southwest. Settlers there not only had to take

[105] Harper to Olmsted Brothers, October 9, 1909, Job File 3606, Folder 1 – 1908–1909, Reel 214, Olmsted Associates Records, LOC.
[106] Dawson to Harper, October 12, 1909, Job File 3606, Folder 1 – 1908–1909, Reel 214, Olmsted Associates Records, LOC.
[107] By this time, the Andorra Realty Company had been bought by Hammond, Hammond and Baker of Columbus, Ohio. The company also owned the San Pedro Development Company and controlled the San Pedro/Ohio tracts. María Marta Hernández, et al., *Isla de Pinos y las Compañías Norteamericanas* (La Habana: Comisión de la Escuela de Historia de la Universidad de la Habana, 1970), 23. The exact nature of the Andorra–Olmsted arrangement after the transaction is unclear, but Andorra apparently remained in debt to Olmsted Brothers.
[108] Olmsted to Harper, October 31, 1912, Job File 3606, Folder 4 – 1912–1921, 1945, Reel 214, Olmsted Associates Records, LOC.
[109] Harper to Olmsted, November 6, 1912, Job File 3606, Folder 4 – 1912–1921, 1945, Reel 214, Olmsted Associates Records, LOC.

a cumbersome route to get to the Isle but also had to cross overland to an area with few navigable roads. The area was thus largely isolated. Attempts to create an oceangoing port in which large ships could sail directly to and from the Isle never came to fruition; the best developers could manage was a small port at Los Indios that could accommodate ships that operated in at least seventeen feet of water.[110] Much of the Andorra Realty Company's land went unsold or undeveloped. As a result, Andorra struggled to repay its debts to Olmsted. "For a long time I have been much annoyed and embarrassed by the account owed you by the Andorra Realty Company," Harper wrote to Dawson in October 1914. "It has been most difficult to sell land and is more so at this time. Everything is improved very much on the Isle of Pines since last year, but it is difficult to turn things into real cash."[111] Despite developers' vision and efforts, La Siguanea never materialized in reality as it did on paper. It served as a cautionary tale about landholding companies' ambition, as well as a warning that the Isle of Pines may not fulfill the utopian promise U.S. entrepreneurs and settlers had projected onto it.

For a short while during the early twentieth century, optimism about the Isle's potential remained evident. Settlers' efforts at community building made a favorable impression on Americans elsewhere in Cuba. In February 1915, the English-language, Havana-based *Cuba News* ran an editorial praising the work settlers had done to modernize the Isle and argued that it served as a model for the rest of Cuba to follow, akin to a city upon a hill:

President [Mario] Menocal and other government officials have visited the great American settlement, the Isle of Pines, and they have seen demonstrated there what American enterprise, resourcefulness, and industry, backed by some capital can do in a place which has had no advantages other than admirable climate, an adaptable soil and the isolation from troublesome or jealous neighbors. The settlers and developers of the Isle of Pines ... are making it the most prosperous community of its size in the republic. Let [Menocal] cast his eye over the island of Cuba today and see if he can pick out a section of country of the same size of the Isle of Pines where there is greater prosperity, greater average intelligence, greater industry shown, greater preparations for the future, and more steadfastness of purpose. There is none in Cuba.[112]

[110] Sutherland to Eberhardt, January 26, 1915, Nueva Gerona – Isle of Pines, Cuba, Vol. 13, Correspondence, 1914–15, 123, Record Group 84, NARA.

[111] Harper to Dawson, October 16, 1914, Job File 3606, Folder 4 – 1912–1921, 1945, Reel 214, Olmsted Associates Records, LOC. Harper also enclosed a check for $1,000 to go toward the debt.

[112] "The Right Kind of Developers," *Cuba News*, February 20, 1915.

At the time of the editorial, the U.S. community on the Isle had reached its peak. With an estimated 2,000 U.S. citizens having established at least part-time residences as well as schools, churches, social clubs, newspapers, and towns, life for Americans there in many ways resembled life in the United States.

Indeed, during the first two decades of the twentieth century, settlers on the Isle successfully recreated in many ways the life they had – or would have liked to have had – in the United States. Through the proliferation of American-style institutions, settlers not only developed familiar features to ease the transition to living in a foreign land but also demonstrated their American-ness. The first generation of settlers considered themselves pioneers laying the groundwork for further U.S. settlement. More important, the communities they established were not merely carbon-copy reproductions of what they had in the United States. Rather, they were to be improvements to the ideal American society.

But these prominent displays of American-ness and community building had political and commercial motives, as well. They were designed primarily to compel the U.S. government to annex the Isle. Its formal incorporation into the Union was considered the lynchpin to the long-term sustainability of American settlement and investment. Most settlers and promoters presumed that if Cuban sovereignty was upheld, U.S. interest in developing the Isle would wither. But if it could be affirmed as U.S. territory, either through purchase or diplomatic negotiation, then turn-of-the-century settlers and promoters figured they were sitting on a veritable treasure trove of untapped wealth that would redeem their sacrifices and struggles. The key would be convincing the U.S. government while neutralizing *pineros* who welcomed American capital but not necessarily the American flag.

5

The Sword of Damocles

It was a cool, spring day on April 2, 1924, when T. J. Keenan and seven others met with President Calvin Coolidge to argue in favor of the United States acquiring the Isle of Pines. Keenan had done this at the White House before. In November 1902, he was part of a four-man delegation that had lobbied President Theodore Roosevelt for the Isle's annexation. But officials in the Roosevelt administration saw little strategic or commercial utility to it and so the group's plea fell on deaf ears. More than twenty years later, Keenan was at it again.

Keenan's experience and social standing made him a natural for the 1924 group. A prominent businessman who had once owned the *Pittsburgh Press*, Keenan ran the Isle of Pines Bank and held significant landholdings, including a home reputedly costing $50,000. For nearly a quarter-century, Keenan was one of the most vocal advocates of annexation. He had made numerous appeals before a variety of newspapers and U.S. officials, often framing his case in equal terms of opportunity, patriotism, and fear of Cuban mismanagement. His primary goal in 1924 was to convince the U.S. Senate to reject the odious Hay-Quesada treaty, the 1904 agreement that recognized Cuban sovereignty on the Isle of Pines. Settlers' persistent lobbying had successfully kept the treaty tabled and unratified in the Senate for two decades while Cuba maintained administrative authority. Technically, though, the Isle remained in diplomatic limbo and the treaty, Keenan had argued, hung "like the Sword of Damocles over the heads of the unfortunate Americans on the Isle of Pines."[1]

---

[1] T. J. Keenan to Philander Knox, January 30, 1913, 1910–29 Central Decimal File, General Records of the Department of State Relating to the Internal Affairs of Cuba, NARA Microcopy 488, Roll 29, File 837.014P/106.

The 1924 delegation was different from the 1902 version in one significant respect – it included women. The new group featured Harriet Wheeler, Marguerite Fetter, Minnie Hall, and Florence Tichenor. Their inclusion reflected the reality that women were full participants in the political process thanks to the recent passage of the 19th Amendment. But their presence was also meant to appeal to policymakers' sympathies. As traditional keepers of the domestic sphere, the women were a shrewd choice to represent settlers who, annexationists argued, would be deprived of their homes should the treaty be ratified. It was also consistent with contemporary notions of civic housekeeping, that women's domestic duties prepared them for promoting community and political stability – and that, in turn, community and political stability could help women with domestic duties. The *Isle of Pines Appeal* lauded what it called "noble American women [who] are fighting for their homes, and the homes of all of us."[2]

The group meeting with Coolidge did not only represent the roughly 700 U.S. settlers still living on the Isle or the nearly 10,000 who owned property there. Its members carried with them a petition bearing 110,000 signatures as well. In a letter accompanying the petition, the group maintained that "the American settlers have been subject to an unlawful, most humiliating and unbearable de facto Cuban Government for over 20 years. Many have lost faith and left; some died in despair, and a great majority are holding on to their property in the firm belief and faith that our Government will live up to its representations that the 'Isle of Pines is United States Territory.'"[3] Their eleven-page letter, appended with supporting correspondence, laid out a well-worn case annexationists had argued since 1898: Spain had ceded the Isle in the Treaty of Paris; President William McKinley and the Department of War had informed U.S. citizens to that effect; based on such information, thousands of Americans went to the Isle and invested their time, talent, and treasure to make what had been a backwater into a commercially viable locale; and the Cuban government's mismanagement threatened the long-term viability of those investments. Moreover, the group contended that because the United States had spent some $1 billion in support of Cuban independence – factoring the cost of the War of 1898, subsequent occupations, and pensions to military veterans – Cuba owed the United States

---

[2] *Isle of Pines Appeal*, December 6, 1924.

[3] T. J. Keenan, et al., "Isle of Pines: Historical and Political Status," April 2, 1924, Manuscript Division, LOC.

FIGURE 5.1. Members of the delegation who met with President Calvin Coolidge at the White House on April 2, 1924, bearing a petition with a purported 110,000 signatures in support of U.S. annexation of the Isle of Pines. Their visit intensified the debate over the Isle's sovereignty.
Courtesy of the Library of Congress, Prints and Photographs Division, LC-DIG-npcc-11009.

something in return. The intimation was that title to the Isle of Pines represented a good start. The letter concluded that U.S. annexation would "do justice to the American settlers and property owners on this Isle who have been shamefully neglected by our Government for over 20 years" and that should the Hay-Quesada treaty be ratified, it "would be a blot on our American History."[4]

Cubans vehemently differed. While many *pineros* seemed to welcome U.S. capital and had good working relationships with American employers, most rejected the prospect of annexation. In fact, the debate over sovereignty was the primary source of tension between settlers and *pineros* during the first quarter of the twentieth century. Every few years, annexationists would renew their efforts – some more serious and coordinated than others – only to be met with opposition from *pineros*, Havana

---

[4] Ibid.

officials, and policymakers in Washington. In times when the annexation drive was on the metaphorical back-burner, though, settler–*pinero* relations appeared quite cordial. This ebb-and-flow began almost from the initial arrivals of Americans. When the first rumors of U.S. annexation started circulating at the turn of the century, one Havana-based newspaper, *La Discusión*, wrote that "such a rapacious robbery would be brutal aggression."[5] That it took more than twenty years for the United States to ratify the treaty offended many Cubans even years after the fact. Cuban scholar Rolando Álvarez Estévez, writing in the politically charged revolutionary era, argued that the sovereignty issue and the lengthy delay in the treaty's ratification brought "untold humiliation and disrespect to our national sovereignty."[6]

Although annexationist arguments had little political, legal, or even popular support in the United States, most Cubans surely were aware of Americans' historical track record of acquiring territory on specious claims. In the 1820s, the Mexican government invited Anglo-Americans to settle its sparsely populated province of Texas in the hopes of commercially developing the area and whitening the population. A decade later, those settlers – angered by what they considered an ineffective Mexican government and a tariff policy that inhibited their ability to trade abroad – rose up in rebellion, won Texan independence, and eventually secured annexation to the United States.[7] More contemporary to the Hay-Quesada debate, U.S. citizens in Hawai'i – who made up just 2 percent of the population – had compelled the U.S. government in 1898 to annex the islands. Throughout their decades-long campaign, annexationists often portrayed local Hawaiian leaders as inefficient or corrupt.[8] U.S. settlers on the Isle of Pines leveled similar charges on Cuban officials. Given that recent history, Cuban concerns about the prospect of losing the Isle to the United States were certainly understandable despite Cuba's strong legal claim and Washington's general lack of interest.

The sovereignty question, though, remained the central issue for settlers during the first quarter of the twentieth century, underlying all other considerations. American annexation promised to reward settlers'

---

[5] Quoted in "Gomez Answers Wood," *Hartford Courant*, November 29, 1900.

[6] Rolando Álvarez Estévez, *Isla de Pinos y el Tratado Hay-Quesada* (La Habana: Instituto Cubano del Libro, 1973), 21.

[7] Timothy J. Henderson, *A Glorious Defeat: Mexico and Its War with the United States* (New York: Hill and Wang, 2007), 24–101.

[8] Tom Coffman, *A Nation Within: The Story of America's Annexation of the Nation of Hawai'i* (Kane'ohe, HI: Epicenter Press, 1998), 68, 259–60.

investments by tearing down prohibitive tariff walls, opening the Isle to further commercial exploitation, and vastly increasing their property values. It also would rid them of ineffective Cuban rule and return them under the Stars and Stripes, with which they still strongly identified. Their ultimate failure to bring it about not only shattered their hopes, it also definitively illustrated that an era of American expansion – that of acquiring territory for settlement – was over.

Quest for Annexation

U.S. settlers' desire to annex a part of Cuba was part of a long tradition. Prominent U.S. policymakers such as Thomas Jefferson, John Quincy Adams, and William Seward had advocated acquiring the entire Cuban archipelago. Americans' zeal for obtaining Cuba, however, cooled considerably with the War of 1898. Western business interests involved in beet sugar production worried that the inclusion of Cuba and its vast cane sugar industry would flood the domestic market and undermine their enterprises; better to keep Cuban sugar behind the U.S. tariff wall. Hence, Colorado Sen. Henry Teller's amendment to the U.S. war resolution against Spain that disavowed designs on Cuba's annexation. More important, however, after the war more Americans recognized that Cuba had a significant mixed-race population, a legacy of centuries of slavery that ended only in the 1880s. This factor fed concerns about annexation's effect on the U.S. body politic. Pointedly, political cartoons that had depicted Cuba as a white female to solicit support for U.S. intervention in Cuba's War of Independence later portrayed the country as a rambunctious black child after the conflict.[9]

U.S. interest in the Isle of Pines was not evident until the War of Independence. The U.S. Naval War College in 1895 may have been the first body to suggest annexing it. In preliminary plans it sent to the Navy Department in the event the United States went to war with Spain, the College proposed that the United States acquire the Isle as compensation for securing Cuban independence. As war came closer to reality, however, refined plans made no mention of annexing the Isle.[10]

But discussion about the Isle's annexation revived in 1899. Americans interested in commercial opportunities in newly acquired lands from

[9] John J. Johnson, *Latin America in Caricature* (Austin: University of Texas Press, 1980), 80–95, 122–35, 142–3, 166–71.
[10] David F. Trask, *The War with Spain in 1898* (New York: Macmillan, 1981), 74, 78.

Spain thought that included the Isle. To them, the Isle was separate from "Cuba" and by virtue of Article II of the Treaty of Paris, it rightfully belonged to the United States. Its status, however, was unclear even to officials in the Department of War, which was in charge of administering the military occupation of Cuba. In particular, Assistant Secretary George D. Meiklejohn and Assistant Adjutant General John J. Pershing, both of whom fielded citizen inquiries on the matter, hedged on a definitive answer. Usually, they stated that the matter awaited action from Congress. In August 1899, however, Pershing wrote that the Isle did indeed belong to the United States. "I am directed by the Assistant Secretary of War [Meiklejohn] to advise you that this Island was ceded by Spain to the United States and is, therefore, a part of our territory, although it is attached at present to the Division of Cuba for governmental purposes."[11] Meiklejohn repeated this assertion the following year. In a response to another citizen inquiry, he wrote, "In reply I beg to advise you that the Isle of Pines was ceded to the United States by Spain, and is therefore a part of our territory, although it is at present attached to the Division of Cuba for governmental purposes."[12] There is no further indication as to the grounds on which Meiklejohn and Pershing made their contentions. Private correspondence, however, reveals that the duo had made their claims without the approval of their superior, Secretary of War Elihu Root, who would later make clear his difference of opinion.[13]

Amid this haze, correspondence from private citizens at the turn of the century shifted from inquiries about annexation to full-fledged lobbying

---

[11] Pershing to George Bridges, August 14, 1899, General Records, General Classified Files: 1898–1945, Box 72, Record 377, Record Group 350, NARA.

[12] George D. Meiklejohn to A. C. Goff, January 15, 1900, General Records, General Classified Files: 1898–1945, Box 72, Record 377, Record Group 350, NARA.

[13] Root to Sen. Thomas C. Platt, December 18, 1903, in *Isle of Pines: Papers Relating to the Adjustment of Title to the Ownership of the Isle of Pines*, 68th Cong., 2d sess., 1924, S. Doc. 166, 284. Private correspondence among U.S. officials suggests that Root and Meiklejohn were not always on the same page. Gen. Leonard Wood, military governor of Cuba during the U.S. occupation, wrote, "I am a little embarrassed by the numerous telegrams that I receive from Mr. Meiklejohn. A good many of them show that he is entirely ignorant of what you are doing at certain instances." Wood to Root, May 12, 1900, Leonard Wood Papers, Box 28, General Correspondence – 1900, Manuscript Division, LOC. Sen. Orville Platt, chairman of the Senate Committee on Relations with Cuba, disapproved of Meiklejohn's assertion that the Isle was U.S. territory. "It is most unfortunate that a letter was written by a subordinate of the war department, without the knowledge of the secretary of war, saying that the title was in the United States. Even the secretary of war could not have given such information, but in fact, he knew nothing whatever about the letter." Platt to A. Kellogg, January 4, 1904, Orville Platt Papers, Box 2, Official Correspondence: 1900–1905 – Various Subjects – Vol. 1, 204, CSL.

for it. As the U.S. military occupation of Cuba wound down, some settlers expressed concern about the prospect of living under a civilian Cuban government. In January 1902, Keenan and Charles Raynard sent a petition to Root with eighty-two signatures asking for the Isle's formal incorporation into the United States. The crux of their argument lay in the presumption that transitioning from a military to a civilian administration would bring about "a period of unrest and uncertainty," and thereby put their property and safety at risk.[14] Later that year, Keenan, Samuel H. Pearcy, and J. H. H. Randall made a similar plea to Secretary of State John Hay around the time they were in Washington to meet with President Roosevelt. The trio represented some 300 petitioners who viewed Cuba's governance since its May 1902 independence as "insufficient, vexatious, oppressive, and every way unsatisfactory."[15]

The Hay-Quesada Treaty

Settlers' faith that the Isle was to be the next U.S. frontier was shattered on July 2, 1903. U.S. Minister to Cuba Herbert G. Squiers and Cuba's Acting Foreign Minister José M. García Montes negotiated a treaty that relinquished U.S. claims to the Isle in recognition of a separate agreement in which Cuba leased Guantánamo Bay and Bahía Honda to the United States. Although the Cuban Senate ratified the Squiers–García agreement two weeks later, the treaty was nullified when the U.S. Senate failed to consider it within the stipulated seven-month timeframe. Hay and Cuban Minister to the United States Gonzalo de Quesada signed a new treaty on March 2, 1904, on the same terms but with no time limit for ratification. In the interim, Cuba's government would administer the island as if it were sovereign Cuban territory.

For Cuban officials, the Hay-Quesada treaty marked the culmination of nearly three years of diplomatic efforts. The Cuban Senate argued that the decision to place the Isle in limbo via Article VI of the Platt Amendment had come under duress. It stated that Cuba had no choice but to accept the stipulation, along with the other seven amendments, if it wanted to end the U.S. occupation and attain independence.[16] The

---

[14] Keenan and Raynard to Root, January 25, 1902, General Records, General Classified Files: 1898–1945, Box 72, Record 377, Record Group 350, NARA.

[15] Keenan, Pearcy, and Randall to Hay, November 8, 1902, General Records, General Classified Files: 1898–1945, Box 72, Record 377, Record Group 350, NARA.

[16] El Senado de la Republica de Cuba al Presidente de la Republica, January 31, 1923, Donativos y Remisiones, Alfredo Zayas y Alfonso – Libro I, Legajo 70, Expediente 47, ANC.

Cuban Constitutional Convention had offered counterproposals to Article VI, but Root rejected them, insisting that all articles of the Platt Amendment be accepted without revision.[17] Tomás Estrada Palma, who had dual U.S.-Cuban citizenship before becoming Cuba's first president, believed that the Isle was and always had been Cuban territory. In private correspondence shortly after the Platt Amendment passed, Estrada Palma wrote that he wanted the United States to recognize Cuba's right to the Isle. But if the "Great Republic" insisted on taking it, Cuba should demand "concessions" in return.[18] In the first year of Estrada Palma's presidency, his administration pressed Squiers to sign a formal treaty that recognized Cuba's sovereignty. Its pleas were too emotional for Squiers's liking. "I was surprised to find [Estrada Palma] so deeply interested – sentimentally – in the Island of Pines question – even aggressively so," Squiers wrote to Hay.[19] Despite Squiers's protests, the conditions Estrada Palma presented eventually became the framework for the Hay-Quesada treaty, which the Cuban Senate ratified on June 8, 1904.

U.S. officials determined that the Isle was worth relinquishing. Root, a renowned corporate lawyer before President William McKinley tapped him to join the Cabinet, maintained that the United States had no legal basis to claim the Isle. He pointed out that during the Spanish colonial era, it had been considered among the hundreds of islands surrounding the coast of mainland Cuba and had been administered as part of the province of Havana. The Isle "was as much a part of Cuba as Nantucket is a part of Massachusetts," he wrote.[20] Meeting with settlers in March 1903, Squiers was lukewarm about the prospects of long-term commercial success. "It is difficult to believe that the advantages are as great as they are claimed to be by our people," he asserted. "The island has remained so long dormant and shows but few signs of former cultivation or occupation."[21] More important, military surveys found that the waters

---

[17] Memorandum of May 18, 1901 (author unknown); M. Morua Delgado to Constitutional Convention, May 21, 1901; and Diego Tomayo, et al., to Constitutional Convention, May 24, 1901, Donativos y Remisiones, Legajo 84, Expediente 112, ANC.

[18] Estrada Palma to Maj. Gen. Juan Rius Rivera, September 7, 1901, in Cosme de la Torriente, *Mi Misión En Washington: La Soberanía de La Isla de Pinos, 1923–1925* (La Habana: Imprenta de la Universidad de la Habana, 1952), 115–16.

[19] Squiers to Hay, April 14, 1903, John Hay Papers, Reel 17 – Correspondence, 1903, Manuscript Division, LOC.

[20] Root to Sen. Thomas C. Platt, December 18, 1903, in *Isle of Pines*, 68th Cong., 2d sess., 1924, S. Doc. 166, 284.

[21] Squiers to Hay, March 18, 1903, *Isle of Pines*, 68th Cong., 2d sess., 1924, S. Doc. 166, 187. Squiers was persona non grata among U.S. citizens on the Isle after his July 1903 agreement with García. "Squiers in Disfavor in Isle of Pines," *Trenton Times*, November 30, 1903.

around the Isle were too shallow to sustain a naval base; Guantánamo Bay had a much better deep-water harbor in a better location near the Windward Passage.[22] Gen. Leonard Wood, military governor of Cuba during the U.S. occupation, cogently articulated the U.S. position in a note to Root: "The Isle of Pines I think we can afford to drop if necessary. There is no good harbor on the island except on the west coast and this has only eighteen feet of water on the bar and it would be immensely expensive to improve."[23] As long as the Cuban government respected the property rights of Americans – in other words, so long as Havana kept an open door to commercial opportunity – the Roosevelt administration had no qualms with Cuba retaining sovereignty.

In the months before Hay-Quesada's signing, settlers and investors intensified their lobbying. Their pleas, however, were largely ignored. Squiers dismissed most of the lobbyists, telling Sen. Shelby Cullom, chairman of the Senate Foreign Relations Committee, that those "who are complaining most are the land speculators. The people who actually own the land, I think, are quite well satisfied."[24] Annexationists, though, found an ally in John T. Morgan. The Alabama senator was a powerful voice on the Senate Foreign Relations Committee, which largely supported ratifying Hay-Quesada. But Morgan dissented, claiming it would hurt U.S. citizens on the Isle, many of whom went there based on prior government assurances that it was or would become U.S. territory.[25] He successfully kept the treaty in committee, where it would languish for more than twenty years.

The delay in ratification made Cuban officials uneasy. Quesada remained concerned that the longer the treaty was left unratified, the more time annexationists had to sway senators against the agreement. He took his concerns to Roosevelt and Root, who each expressed support

---

[22] Stephen Irving Max Schwab, *Guantánamo, USA: The Untold History of America's Cuban Outpost* (Lawrence: University Press of Kansas, 2009); Jana Lipman, *Guantánamo: A Working-Class History between Empire and Revolution* (Berkeley: University of California Press, 2009).

[23] Wood to Root, April 4, 1901, Elihu Root Papers, Box 169, Special Correspondence: Leonard Wood, Manuscript Division, LOC. Annexationists disputed the military's findings about the Isle's shallow water, arguing that larger ships drawing between twenty and twenty-five feet of water could, in fact, reach it. Charles Raynard to John Hay, May 27, 1902, General Records, General Classified Files, 1898–1945, Box 72, Record 377, Record Group 350, NARA.

[24] Squiers to Cullom, December 2, 1903, in *Isle of Pines*, 68th Cong., 2d sess., 1924, S. Doc. 166, 213.

[25] Sen. John T. Morgan and Sen. William A. Clark, "Views of the Minority," in *Isle of Pines*, 68th Cong., 2d sess., 1924, S. Doc. 166, 223–303.

for Quesada's position but stated they would not force the Senate's hand on the issue.[26] Recent history certainly informed Havana's anxieties. Privately, Estrada Palma noted that annexationists' activities reminded him of how Americans had acquired Hawai'i just a few years earlier and he was eager to see that the Isle of Pines did not suffer a similar fate. In a March 1905 letter to Quesada, the Cuban president maintained that losing the Isle would be an "injustice" that would torpedo good U.S.–Cuban relations.[27]

If the Estrada Palma administration believed that U.S. popular sentiment supported the annexationists, those fears were probably unfounded. Editorials across the United States supported the Hay-Quesada treaty. The *New York Times* argued that relinquishing the Isle would be good for U.S. relations with Cuba and Latin America.[28] The *St. Louis Globe Democrat* commented that Hay-Quesada illustrated the United States' magnanimity toward Cuba and "will gratify the pride of that country and will be another proof of the good will of the United States."[29] Even the *Fond du Lac Commonwealth*, hometown newspaper of many settlers, supported the treaty. "[T]he fact that the sovereignty of the Isle of Pines is finally settled is worth a good deal. The government, maintained by Cuba, will be stable and all property interests will be well protected."[30]

Newspapers that served rural areas tended to support the treaty, but mostly out of local concerns. Some publications in Wisconsin, for example, doubted the Isle's potential, fearing that it was a money pit for investors. They argued that migrations could cause a worker shortage and settlers risked racial degeneration by living among tropical people. The *Marshfield Times* commented: "Northern people degenerate in the tropics. The third generation will see them with their hair sticking out of the top of their hats, astride a barebacked mule with a rooster under each arm going to a cock fight on a Sunday. There is no necessity for sending a dollar outside this state for investment in foreign enterprises where there is such a demand for industries at home."[31] The *Eau-Claire*

---

[26] Gonzalo de Quesada to Carlos E. Ortiz Coffigny, January 18, 1905, in Gonzalo de Quesada, *Documentos Históricos* (La Habana: Editorial de la Universidad de La Habana, 1965), 49–54.

[27] Estrada Palma to Gonzalo de Quesada, March 21, 1905, in ibid., 55–6.

[28] "The Isle of Pines," *New York Times*, December 5, 1903.

[29] Reprinted in "The Isle of Pines," *San Jose Mercury News*, July 19, 1903.

[30] *Fond du Lac Commonwealth*, July 3, 1903. The newspaper later turned against the treaty, writing the following year that it was a "manifest injustice." *Fond du Lac Commonwealth*, February 26, 1904.

[31] "Stick to Wisconsin," *Marshfield Times*, February 12, 1904.

Leader wrote: "If the money that is sent annually out of this state to build up foreign states was kept at home and invested in needed industries it would soon make Wisconsin one of the wealthiest states in the union."[32]

Despite support for Hay-Quesada in the United States, settlers on the Isle – at least the most vocal ones – remained vehemently opposed. In addition to Article II of the Treaty of Paris and Article VI of the Platt Amendment, their arguments generally addressed at least one of four themes. The first was the idea that Cuba owed the United States for its efforts in securing Cuban independence. That Cubans did not express such gratitude – by such a gesture as ceding the Isle to the United States – appalled settlers.[33] One letter to Morgan read: "The Cubans as a class are the most ungrateful people one ever met; they do not consider that they owe the United States anything for the millions we spent and the lives sacrificed to set them free. Ten such islands would not recompense us for our sacrifices."[34] Another writer, H. A. Cole of Chicago, who claimed to own 260 acres on the Isle, wanted to convince the Roosevelt administration of the "appalling ingratitude of the Cuban people to America and Americans. Americans are hated to-day in Cuba worse than the Spaniards ever were."[35]

Cole's argument drew on a second theme: a desire for security. Settlers called on the U.S. government to help protect their property and investments because they did not trust Cuban authorities to do so. Cole wrote that Cuban officials "take every opportunity to make life a burden to any American enterprise that has to pass through their hands. That is why we demand the protection of the American Government."[36] Although he did not apparently own property on the Isle, Charles Reed of Cincinnati supported annexationists on principle. He argued to new Secretary of War William Howard Taft that because many Americans went to the Isle believing it to be U.S. territory, the U.S. government owed them protection of their interests.[37]

---

[32] Quoted in "Stay at Home," *Marshfield Times*, February 26, 1904.

[33] U.S. policymakers also cited notions of gratitude to justify policies toward Cuba. Louis A. Pérez Jr., "Incurring a Debt of Gratitude: 1898 and the Moral Sources of United States Hegemony in Cuba," *American Historical Review* 104 (April 1999): 356–98.

[34] William Durham to Morgan, January 25, 1903, in *Isle of Pines*, 68th Cong., 2d sess., 1924, S. Doc. 166, 292.

[35] H. A. Cole to John T. Morgan, January 13, 1906, in *Isle of Pines*, 68th Cong., 2d sess., 1924, S. Doc. 166, 314.

[36] Ibid.

[37] Reed to Taft, October 20, 1905, General Records, General Classified Files, 1898–1945, Box 72, Record 377, Record Group 350, NARA.

Settlers also advocated annexation because a Cuban Isle of Pines was bad for business. Correspondence between the Pearcy brothers illustrated this third theme. In a February 1906 letter, Samuel Pearcy lamented the Senate Foreign Relations Committee's majority report advocating Hay-Quesada's ratification. Its effects could already be felt on the Isle's business, he wrote. "[It] killed the sale of land, and for the first time since the Americans bought (land) in the island, started the price downward and made things dull. The people are down in the mouth and some who have been improving their little homes … are anxious to sell for enough to get back to the States."[38]

Finally, settlers worried Americanization might be for naught if the island ultimately became subject to the rule of non-Anglo-Saxons and not part of the United States. The concept of the Isle as safe for whites had been one of the landholding companies' key sales pitches. Their claims included "The Only White Man's Country and All American Colony Possible in the West Indies" and "This is an American's country and a white man's country in every sense of the word."[39] Cole wrote that settlers had changed "the entire atmosphere of the island, making it strictly American, with American churches, Sunday schools, free schools in every community on the island, and paying for same out of our own pockets. We just want to stay American citizens. We want our children to be American citizens; that's all."[40] There was a palpable fear among settlers that their work in modernizing the Isle would be ruined if left to Cubans.

A Declaration of Independence

Given U.S. officials' apparent lack of interest in acquiring the Isle, annexationists tried to force the issue. Throughout the first decade of the twentieth century, scattered reports suggested imminent armed American uprisings. In January 1903, some settlers protested the Cuban government's tax collection and threatened to revolt.[41] Violence never came, however. Meanwhile, some annexationists feared that *pineros* and

[38] S. H. Pearcy to J. L. Pearcy, February 21, 1906, in *Isle of Pines*, 68th Cong., 2d sess., 1924, S. Doc. 166, 17.

[39] The Isle of Pines Investment Company, "The Pineland Bulletin" (Cleveland, 1908); San Juan Heights Land Company, "The Isle of Pines: The Garden Spot of the World" (Cleveland, 1914), 23.

[40] Cole to John T. Morgan, January 13, 1906, in *Isle of Pines*, 68th Cong., 2d sess., 1924, S. Doc. 166, 313.

[41] "Will Not Pay Taxes," *Hartford Courant*, January 21, 1903; "The Isle of Pines," *Fond du Lac Daily Commonwealth*, January 22, 1903.

former Spanish officers would stage a rebellion of their own to make the Isle independent. At least that is what they told Wood in the waning days of the U.S. occupation. "It is rumored that they have a new flag, different from that of Cuba, and are going to make a demonstration in favor of an independent republic," Samuel H. Pearcy said.[42] No other sources, however, referenced any such rumors. More likely, Pearcy was trying to convince Wood to leave some soldiers on the Isle to protect U.S. citizens after Cuba became independent.

The most serious potential for violence came in November 1905. On the heels of disputed elections in Cuba and fearing political unrest, the American Club announced it was forming a committee to spur the Isle's annexation to the United States. It elected representatives, including a secretary of state and a delegate to the U.S. Congress. T. B. Anderson, named the group's secretary of state, told Roosevelt that after waiting three years for the U.S. government to annex the Isle, settlers were seizing the initiative. He argued that this step was "the most effective way to receive justice and equity from our national lawmaking body," presumably by forcing U.S. policymakers to consider the issue.[43] Although none of the annexationists referenced it directly, their actions drew unmistakable parallels to the Hawaiian Revolution of 1893 in which U.S. business interests toppled the long-reigning monarchy to set the stage for U.S. annexation.[44]

The club's actions triggered a wave of protest in Cuba. Editorials in Havana newspapers, which tended to ignore the Isle, sharply criticized what they viewed as an attack on Cuban sovereignty. One newspaper called the potential loss of the Isle a "tremendous calamity" to the Cuban nation and referred to Americans as "modern pirates."[45] Another publication warned its readers that settlers were following the same playbook that resulted in the United States obtaining Texas and Hawai'i. It argued that Cuba needed to reassert its sovereignty over the Isle – by force, if necessary.[46] According to one report, some 300 *pineros* took that suggestion to heart. Armed with machetes and guns, they gathered in support of *alcalde* Juan M. Sánchez and the *ayuntamiento* to demonstrate against

[42] Pearcy to Wood, May 8, 1902, in *Isle of Pines*, 68th Cong., 2d sess., 1924, S. Doc. 166, 175.

[43] Quoted in "Isle of Pines in Secession," *Janesville Daily Gazette*, November 15, 1905.

[44] Stephen Kinzer, *Overthrow: America's Century of Regime Change from Hawaii to Iraq* (New York: Times Books, 2006), 9–30.

[45] "Nuestras 'Posesions de Ultramar,'" *La Discusion*, November 26, 1905.

[46] "Fin del Año," *La Lucha*, November 15, 1905.

the American Club's action. Sánchez, however, denied the story, saying the specter of 300 *pineros* making an armed demonstration stemmed from a hypothetical question he had been asked about what *would* happen if settlers launched an uprising.[47]

Cuban officials made various public objections. The *ayuntamiento* on November 17 issued a formal protest, pinning the unrest squarely on landholding companies. The town council argued that these companies wanted the Isle to become U.S. territory based on the assumption that it would boost property values.[48] From Havana, the Estrada Palma administration sent the gunship *Araña* to keep the peace, though by the time it arrived off the Isle's coast, the crisis had subsided. Last, some 1,500 *pineros* signed a petition to Roosevelt protesting the American Club's actions. The petition pledged a desire to remain part of Cuba and contained a paean to the president: "Not that we are ungrateful to the blessings bestowed upon us by the American intervention, but because we feel perfectly satisfied with our Cuban Government ... We trust that, faithful to the Treaty of Paris, the American Congress will do justice to our country and we specially trust in your honorable self, the best friend of Cuba."[49] The petition subtly rejected two annexationist pillars – Cuba's ingratitude and Article II of the Treaty of Paris – while pledging a firm trust in Roosevelt to do right by Cuba.

From the start, the Roosevelt administration disavowed the American Club's efforts. The *New York Times* reported: "The claim made by the colonists is repudiated in toto and the Government will take no steps under the pretext of protecting American citizens to aid the miniature revolution that is said to have been set up against the Republic of Cuba."[50] Yet that repudiation did not deter the American Club, which sent its territorial representative, Edward Ryan, to Washington to lobby for annexation. Those efforts came to a halt on November 27 when Secretary of State Root, who had assumed the office after Hay's death earlier that year, wrote a stern letter to Charles Raynard, president of the American Club. In response to Raynard's inquiry about how the American Club could go about forming a territorial government, Root wrote that it legally could

---

[47] "Actitud de los Cubanos," *La Lucha*, November 27, 1905; "Isle of Pines," *La Lucha*, November 27, 1905.

[48] Reprinted in "La Situación Política en Isla de Pinos," *La Lucha*, November 21, 1905.

[49] English translation reprinted in *La Lucha*, November 19, 1905.

[50] "President Frowns on Isle of Pines Revolt," *New York Times*, November 16, 1905.

FIGURE 5.2. Secretary of State Elihu Root, a former corporate lawyer, argued that the United States had no legal basis on which to claim sovereignty over the Isle of Pines. His public rebuke of the American Club's efforts for annexation in 1905 would earn him the enmity of U.S. settlers for years to come.
Courtesy of the Library of Congress, Prints and Photographs Division, LC-USZ62-92819.

not because they were in sovereign Cuban territory. He went on to state the administration's position on the Isle in no uncertain terms:

In my judgment the United States has no substantial claim to the Isle of Pines. The [Hay-Quesada] treaty merely accords to Cuba what is hers in accordance with international law and justice.

At the time of the treaty of peace which ended the war between the United States and Spain the Isle of Pines was and had been for several centuries, a part of Cuba. I have no doubt whatever that it continues to be a part of Cuba, and that it is not and never has been territory of the United States.... You may be quite sure that Cuba will never consent to give up the Isle of Pines and that the United States will never try to compel her to give it up against her will.[51]

[51] Root to Raynard, November 27, 1905, in *Isle of Pines*, 68th Cong., 2d sess., 1924, S. Doc. 166, 4. In private comments to his biographer years later, Root revealed a deep

Root's letter dealt a crippling blow to the annexationist movement. Not surprising, settlers' animus toward Root ran deep. "After that decision in the Isle of Pines case it is needless for Secretary Root to look for support in Marinette, Fond du Lac or Watertown," one Wisconsin newspaper wrote.[52] Others argued that Root, who had worked closely with corporations during his career in private practice, was beholden to domestic tobacco interests that feared competition from Isle growers. Samuel H. Pearcy wrote: "We have conclusive evidence that certain people high in official authority in the United States, who are in position to prevent the Isle of Pines being recognized as United States territory, are at present holders of interests in large tobacco plantations in Cuba, and we believe in addition to that that these same people are largely interested in the tobacco trusts in a professional capacity."[53] Settlers' grudge against Root extended for years. In an editorial against U.S. tariff policy in 1929, the *Isle of Pines Post* recalled Root's betrayal: "A former Secretary of State used his prestige and office to alienate this Island ... in the service of Tobacco Interests who saw it as a serious menace to their monopoly of the Cuban industry if American residents were allowed to carry out their development of tobacco growing to ship the product into the States duty free."[54]

In a public response, Raynard refuted Root's arguments. He insisted that the Isle legally belonged to the United States and that annexation was in the nation's best interests. Raynard's appeal was patriotic and personal. "[T]o our astonishment and deep regret we find you arrayed on the side of our enemies. And even more deeply do we regret the appearance, for the first time in the history of our country, of [an] American Secretary of State who is not only willing but anxious to abandon a portion of American territory and a large number of American citizens to an alien and lawless Government, for no consideration and for motives which he seems unwilling to disclose."[55] Raynard's letter reflected a distrust of Root, who was

---

mistrust of annexationists' motivations. He recalled "the intense activity of the islanders in favor of Annexation and their wide propaganda in the U.S. describing the island as an Eden and swindling many farmers especially through Iowa and adjoining states." Philip C. Jessup Papers, Box I, Folder 210, Cuba, undated, Manuscript Division, LOC.

[52] *Wausaw Record* editorial reprinted in "Tough on Root," *Janesville Daily Gazette*, December 9, 1905.

[53] S. H. Pearcy to Joseph L. Pearcy, February 21, 1906, in *Isle of Pines*, 68th Cong., 2d sess., 1924, S. Doc. 166, 19.

[54] *Isle of Pines Post*, June 1, 1929.

[55] Raynard to Root, December 14, 1905, in *Isle of Pines*, 68th Cong., 2d sess., 1924, S. Doc. 166, 47. In a separate letter to the Associated Press, Raynard stated that annexationists had $200,000, munitions, and 6,000 men at the ready if they ever used force to defend the "rights of Americans" on the Isle. Cuba's Secretary of the Interior, Freyre Andrade,

widely viewed as too close to corporate interests to support effectively the average U.S. citizen. Raynard suggested settlers' "enemies" were tobacco interests in the United States leery of potential rivals on the Isle. Moreover, settlers like Raynard condemned Root for not adhering to the path of territorial acquisition that had long been a hallmark of U.S. policy. Raynard portrayed Root as eager to surrender territory, suggesting that Root was cravenly denying U.S. citizens an opportunity on the frontier that previous officials had actively supported. Even more insulting, Root's rejection of annexation left U.S. citizens "to an alien and lawless Government" that presumably would not administer to their needs.

By contrast, Cubans enthusiastically supported Root. Havana newspapers printed Spanish translations of Root's letter to Raynard and praised Root for defending Cuban sovereignty. One headline referred to Root and Squiers, who had negotiated the original treaty, as "Our Everlasting Friends."[56] Twenty years later, when Hay-Quesada finally came before the U.S. Senate for ratification, supporters of Cuban sovereignty cited Root's letter in their argument that the Isle rightfully belonged to Cuba.[57]

Meanwhile, U.S. newspapers expressed skepticism about annexationists' motives. Many outlets blamed land speculators for stirring up trouble. The *New York Times* credited Root for discouraging "those absurd boomers of the Isle of Pines."[58] The *Hartford Courant* argued that settlers embodied the worst traditions of expansionism. "It is filibusterism, pure

---

was said to be unimpressed, believing the U.S. government would thwart any settler rebellion. "Isle of Pines Army and $200,000 Promised," *New York Times*, December 17, 1905.

[56] "Nuestros Amigos de Siempre," *La Discusión*, November 30, 1905. Praise for Squiers in the Cuban press was at odds with reports in the United States about Squiers's sudden resignation on November 29 as U.S. minister to Cuba. U.S. newspapers reported that he had encouraged the annexationists on the Isle and may have harbored aims for the United States to annex the entire country. Such views put him at loggerheads with Root as well as the Estrada Palma administration. But the idea of Squiers supporting annexationists does not square with the historical record, particularly his correspondence with Hay two years earlier that the Isle was worth relinquishing. Indeed, the *New York Times* later reported that Squiers's comments in an interview with another newspaper in which he suggested that Marines should keep the peace on the Isle may have been misconstrued as support for the annexationists. "Minister Squiers Out; Morgan Goes to Cuba," *New York Times*, November 30, 1905; "Envoy Called Down, Quits," *Chicago Daily Tribune*, November 30, 1905; "H.G. Squiers Returns; Won't Say Why He Quit," *New York Times*, December 6, 1905.

[57] Carlos A. Vasseur, *El Derecho de Soberanía Sobre la Isla de Pinos* (Panama: Star and Herald, 1925); Cuban House of Representatives declaration, Donativos y Remisiones, Alfredo Zayas y Alfonso, Book II, 44, undated, Legajo 70, Expediente 48, ANC.

[58] "The Isle of Pines," *New York Times*, November 30, 1905.

and simple, that is on exhibition today in the Isle of Pines – petty, silly filibusterism, fortunately unstained as yet by the bloodshed that turned [William] Walker's raid on Nicaragua into a tragedy. The Cuban authorities have shown a praiseworthy forbearance thus far, under impudent provocation."[59] In aligning itself against the annexationists, the *Grand Forks Herald* tweaked settlers by turning stereotypes of tropical peoples against them. "We often talk of the excitable Latin races, and explain their proneness to revolution on the score of blood. The experience of the gentlemen who bought estate on Cuba's little island seems to show that the race question is not entirely responsible for people making fools of themselves. Climate seems to have something to do with it."[60]

Pressing the Case

When the United States reoccupied Cuba in September 1906, annexationists held out hope again that the Isle might become part of the United States. But Taft, who briefly served as provisional governor of Cuba, quickly quashed those dreams by stating that the Roosevelt administration had no interest. It had "never been taken possession of by America, and I don't know why anybody should be misled with respect to the attitude of the Executive Department.... Mr. Hay's attitude and Mr. Roosevelt's have never been in doubt."[61] Taft's successor as provisional governor, Charles Magoon, likewise had argued that the Isle belonged to Cuba. During his time as a legal advisor in the Department of War, Magoon offered a hypothetical to reinforce his contention that the United States had no claim to the Isle: "Let us suppose that Spain had announced its intention of [relinquishing Cuba] and had withdrawn from the mainland of Cuba and adjacent keys but insisted on maintaining sovereignty over the Isle of Pines. Would such action have been considered full compliance with the demand of the United States?"[62]

After annexationists failed to drum up support in the executive branch, they turned to the judiciary. Looking to force the government's hand, Edward J. Pearcy, Samuel's son, refused in September 1903 to pay duties on 2,000 cigars he had imported from the Isle. He claimed his goods were

---

[59] "Today at Nueva Gerona," *Hartford Courant*, November 25, 1905.

[60] *Grand Forks Herald*, December 9, 1905.

[61] Taft to Charles Reed, October 23, 1905, General Records, General Classified Files, 1898–1945, Box 72, Record 377, Record Group 350, NARA.

[62] Magoon to Alvey Adee, December 12, 1903, General Records, General Classified Files, 1898–1945, Box 72, Record 377, Record Group 350, NARA.

not subject to the Dingley tariff because they came from domestic U.S. territory. Nevada N. Stranahan, duty collector for the port of New York, confiscated the cigars, spurring Pearcy to file suit in U.S. District Court against the federal government in Stranahan's name. The court found for the government, but Pearcy appealed to the Supreme Court. In April 1907, the Court unanimously ruled for the government in the case of *Pearcy v. Stranahan*.[63] It agreed that the Isle of Pines was part of Cuba, which, as a "foreign country" was subject to the Dingley tariff. Chief Justice Melville Fuller ruled that in light of the Spanish government's colonial administration of the Isle as part of the geopolitical designation of "Cuba" – as evidenced by budgets and censuses – "it seems clear that the Isle of Pines was not supposed to be one of the 'other islands' ceded by article II [of the Treaty of Paris]."[64] In essence, the Court upheld Root's view of the Isle and the drive for annexation suffered another devastating blow.

Not every American on the Isle pushed for annexation. Some were quite content with Cuban rule, grew weary of annexationists, and said as much to U.S. officials. A. Dudley Sr., who owned a tool-manufacturing plant in Michigan and a ten-acre grove on the Isle, claimed that the Americans he met were all "fully satisfied with the conditions existing" there. He continued that many settlers looked askance on men such as Pearcy and Raynard for being "entirely too aggressive" in their annexationist efforts. Dudley maintained that their arguments were "not warranted by actual conditions nor [reflected] the sentiment of the people of the island."[65] Dudley's position echoed the findings of U.S. Army Capt. J. A. Ryan. In a January 1907 report, Ryan asserted that most of the settlers he met "are quite contented and that there are at present no abuses being committed against them. Those I met are a very high class of Americans, they talked freely and did not mention any grievances."[66] He concluded that previous tensions stemmed more from settlers' ignorance of the Spanish language and Cuban law rather than any innate political, economic, or cultural conflict with *pineros*.

Nevertheless, determined annexationists continued to press their case with Roosevelt's successor, Taft. In the waning days of the Taft

---

[63] Justice William Henry Moody abstained.

[64] *Pearcy v. Stranahan*, 205 U.S. 257, 266, (1907).

[65] A. Dudley Sr. to Charles E. Magoon, January 29, 1907, Provisional Government of Cuba, "Confidential" Correspondence, 1906–1909, Box 1, Folder 003, Record Group 199, NARA.

[66] Ryan to Maj. Frederick S. Foltz, January 31, 1907, Provisional Government of Cuba, "Confidential" Correspondence, 1906–1909, Box 1, Folder 003, Record Group 199, NARA.

administration (1909–13), Keenan played up the racial angle by arguing that annexing the Isle would be a unique opportunity for the United
States because it already contained "within the tropics an actual colony
of the Caucasian race. Every other desirable Southern land has been pre-
empted by an undesirable population."[67] Such line of reasoning reflected
early twentieth-century racial ideology that presumed tropical areas
inhabited mostly by non-whites were simply too hot to sustain republican governments and industrious behavior. Keenan suggested that the Isle
was a notable exception.

Annexationists were encouraged by the inauguration of a new,
Democratic administration in 1913. In February, President-elect Woodrow
Wilson's Secretary of State designate, William Jennings Bryan, visited the
Isle. His trip came in the wake of rumors that the Cuban government
planned to open a prison in Nueva Gerona for Afro-Cuban inmates captured during the confrontation with the Independent Party of Color (PIC)
in 1912.[68] Bryan, though, insisted that the Cuban government had no
such intentions. He also gave no assurances as to the Wilson's administration's approach toward the Isle. Hoping to sway an apparently indecisive
president-elect, supporters of annexation flooded the White House with
petitions.[69] The petitions spurred some newspapers to suggest buying the
Isle.[70] But like his Republican predecessors, Wilson showed little interest. Such restraint was somewhat at odds with Wilson's aggressive policy
toward the Caribbean region, where he initiated military interventions in
Mexico, Hispaniola, and mainland Cuba. But Wilson was not looking to
extend U.S. settlement in those instances and neither was he willing to do
so on the Isle of Pines.

[67] Keenan to Philander Knox, January 30, 1913, 1910–29 Central Decimal File, General
Records of the Department of State Relating to the Internal Affairs of Cuba, NARA
Microcopy 488, Roll 27, File 837.014P/106.

[68] Julio Antonio Avello, "The Isle of Pines as a Factor in United States–Cuban Relations"
(MA thesis, Southern Illinois University, 1969), 49–50.

[69] E. J. Shover to William Howard Taft, February 6, 1913, 1910–29 Central Decimal File,
General Records of the Department of State Relating to the Internal Affairs of Cuba,
NARA Microcopy 488, Roll 27, File 837.014P/106; George W. Paulson to Taft, February
18, 1913, 1910–29 Central Decimal File, General Records of the Department of State
Relating to the Internal Affairs of Cuba, NARA Microcopy 488, Roll 27, File 837.014P/
106; H.L. Shepherd to Bryan, June 20, 1913, 1910–29 Central Decimal File, General
Records of the Department of State Relating to the Internal Affairs of Cuba, NARA
Microcopy 488, Roll 27, File 837.014P/106.

[70] "Once More the Isle of Pines," *Philadelphia Inquirer*, March 12, 1913; "Better Let Him Buy
It," *Miami Herald*, March 14, 1913; "Making the Isle of Pines American Territory," *San Jose
Mercury News*, April 9, 1913. At least one outlet, however, expressed exasperation about
this prolonged issue: "Whose Isle of Pines Are You?" *Charlotte Observer*, March 22, 1913.

FIGURE 5.3. President-elect Woodrow Wilson's Secretary of State designate, William Jennings Bryan, seen at center holding his hat, visited the Isle in February 1913. His visit came at a time when settlers hoped a new Democratic administration might take a different view toward the Hay-Quesada treaty than its Republican predecessors. Wilson and Bryan, however, showed little interest in the issue.
Source: The Isle of Pines (1913).

The persistent lobbying, however, bothered Cuban officials such as Secretary of State Manuel Sanguily. Writing to U.S. Minister to Cuba John B. Jackson in February 1911, Sanguily maintained that the Isle's unresolved status was "a continual source of annoying difficulties to both Governments and of constant friction between the North American subjects who have settled there and Cuban authorities in that territory."[71] Two years later, Sanguily made the case again to Jackson's successor, Arthur Beaupre. He was concerned that annexationists might provoke a violent incident and found their protests "offensive to our people."[72]

[71] Sanguily to Jackson, February 8, 1911, U.S. Department of State, *Foreign Relations of the United States, 1911* (Washington, DC: Government Printing Office, 1918), 136.
[72] Sanguily to Beaupre, March 17, 1913, 1910–29 Central Decimal File, General Records of the Department of State Relating to the Internal Affairs of Cuba, NARA Microcopy 488, Roll 27, File 837.014P/110.

Beaupre was already wise to such views. Days earlier, he had informed Bryan that annexationists were arousing the ire of Cuban officials and press. "It is reported," Beaupre wrote, "that Cuban Government takes the ground that this propaganda constitutes conspiracy against Cuban sovereignty and will act accordingly."[73]

Aside from a brief renewal of efforts in 1916 following the U.S. purchase of the Danish West Indies (now U.S. Virgin Islands), calls for the Isle's annexation remained relatively muted for the duration of Wilson's administration.[74] During that time, there were even some subtle signs of a détente between annexationists and *pineros*. The *Isle of Pines Appeal*, which for years referred to its location as "Isle of Pines, W.I." in a conspicuous snub of Cuban sovereignty, began listing "Isle of Pines, Cuba" on its masthead instead.[75] It even printed stories that praised local officials, including *alcalde* Ramon Llorca Soto ("an exemplary citizen"), Judge Carlos Manuel Valdes Montiel ("a popular official"), and Rural Guard Commander Lt. Vicente Pino ("regarded very highly"). "It is safe to say," an editorial stated, "that in no other colony in the world do the native population and foreign settlers get along so congenially, as on the Isle of Pines."[76] Although the *Appeal*'s sentiment came at a time of tranquility between Americans and *pineros*, expressions of satisfaction with Cuban officials reflected a desire to encourage settlers to remain on the Isle at a time when many were returning to the United States.

Beneath the surface, however, discontent with Cuban governance lingered. The declining fortunes – and numbers – of the American community stemming from struggling businesses, property damage from tropical storms, and persistent transportation and infrastructure issues factored into this uneasiness. Since these maladies were occurring under Cuba's watch, its authority represented an easy scapegoat for settlers who presumed that U.S. annexation – still a remote possibility while Hay-Quesada remained unratified – would remedy their myriad of problems. Not only was Cuba's government ineffective and hence a significant source of settlers' angst, but these annexationists argued that officials also harbored

---

[73] Beaupre to Bryan, March 13, 1913, 1910–29 Central Decimal File, General Records of the Department of State Relating to the Internal Affairs of Cuba, NARA Microcopy 488, Roll 27, File 837.014P/109.

[74] "The Unhappy Isle," *New York Times*, August 17, 1916; "Would Annex Isle of Pines," *New York Times*, August 18, 1916.

[75] For example, see issue of May 15, 1920. In 1924, as the push intensified for Hay-Quesada's ratification, the paper listed its location as "Isle of Pines AND Cuba" before reverting back to "Isle of Pines, W.I." See editions of March 29 and June 21, 1924.

[76] "The American Atmosphere of the Isle of Pines," *Isle of Pines Appeal*, April 30, 1921.

ill will toward U.S. citizens. As former U.S. vice consul George B. Tracy opined, "We are handicapped in every way by an inferior government which is full of graft and corruption and hatred for everything and everybody American."[77]

The ascension of Calvin Coolidge to the Oval Office following the August 1923 death of Warren G. Harding brought about renewed calls for annexation. Proponents played a variety of angles. One line of argument suggested that the Isle of Pines was a legitimate spoil of war from the conflict with Spain. Veterans across the country expressed their support for the Isle's annexation. One 1898 veteran claimed that ceding the Isle to Cuba would be a mistake if "for no other reason than to gratify a lust for more land on the part of that government and without any corresponding advantage to the United States."[78] Longtime settler Frank S. Hervey appealed to racial concerns. "Why have we been subjected to the most malicious mongrel race, who everyone in the United States realize are not capable of self government?"[79] Isle resident George A. Evans proposed a racist and paternalist explanation for *pineros'* arbitrary and ineffective authority. "There seems to be no laws other than the declarations of the judges, who are often of colored blood with minds of ten year old boys," he alleged.[80] A letter from Marguerite Gardner Seig underscored a gendered component to the annexationist argument. She told Coolidge that "we have helped with our husbands to develop this island from a penal colony of Spain to a place of beauty and should be able

---

[77] Tracy to Secretary of War John W. Weeks, January 7, 1924, 1910–29 Central Decimal File, General Records of the Department of State Relating to the Internal Affairs of Cuba, NARA Microcopy 488, Roll 28, File 837.014P/237.

[78] Francis H. Knauff to Coolidge, November 28, 1924, 1910–29 Central Decimal File, General Records of the Department of State Relating to the Internal Affairs of Cuba, NARA Microcopy 488, Roll 28, File 837.014P/300. See also J. St. Clair Favrot to Coolidge, December 1, 1924, 1910–29 Central Decimal File, General Records of the Department of State Relating to the Internal Affairs of Cuba, NARA Microcopy 488, Roll 28, File 837.014P/304; Charles S. Wragg to Coolidge, December 26, 1924, 1910–29 Central Decimal File, General Records of the Department of State Relating to the Internal Affairs of Cuba, NARA Microcopy 488, Roll 29, File 837.014P/321. For an exception, see William J. O'Donnell, on behalf of United Spanish War Veterans of the District of Columbia, to Sen. William Borah, December 21, 1924, in Torriente, *Mi Misión En Washington*, 249–50.

[79] Hervey to Charles Evans Hughes, September 27, 1923, 1910–29 Central Decimal File, General Records of the Department of State Relating to the Internal Affairs of Cuba, NARA Microcopy 488, Roll 28, File 837.014P/216.

[80] Evans to Charles Evans Hughes, February 27, 1925, 1910–29 Central Decimal File, General Records of the Department of State Relating to the Internal Affairs of Cuba, NARA Microcopy 488, Roll 29, File 837.014P/374

to say happiness, but can not because of the daily terror we live under because of these Cuban officials; we are no longer safe, they threaten us with what they will do when they own the Island."[81] Her contention suggested two sides of the same gendered coin. On one hand, Seig pointed out that women worked alongside men in developing the Isle into a productive locale. On the other, her reasoning also illustrated that women still needed protection – in this case, from a Cuban menace – that only a paternal U.S. government could provide.

One common theme that threaded through annexationists' mid-1920s campaign was the fear of what would transpire on the Isle if and when Cuban sovereignty was affirmed. Tracy warned that, "If the Isle of Pines is given to Cuba, we should all be compelled to depart, abandoning our property and homes; and the Isle of Pines would again become a pasture as before the American Occupation."[82] His argument revealed two important assumptions among annexationists. First, stating that the Isle might be "given" away presumed that it was part of the United States already and that Cuba had no rightful claim to it. Second, Tracy expressed the connection that settlers' developments and investments on the Isle over the last quarter-century would wash away with the tide of unquestioned Cuban sovereignty. Or, as T. B. Anderson maintained, the Isle would "revert back to the bats and owls."[83] Such a viewpoint, though, ignored not only the fact that the Cuban government had been administering the Isle while these developments and investments were taking place, but also that Americans by the mid-1920s were already leaving the Isle well before Hay-Quesada's formal resolution.

Ratification

When the U.S. Senate finally agreed to consider the Hay-Quesada treaty, the impetus had less to do with conditions on the Isle and more with growing anti-American sentiment across Cuba. The country was in the midst of an economic crisis brought on by the crash of sugar prices

---

[81] Seig to Coolidge, December 25, 1923, 1910–29 Central Decimal File, General Records of the Department of State Relating to the Internal Affairs of Cuba, NARA Microcopy 488, Roll 28, File 837.014P/219.

[82] Tracy to Charles Evans Hughes, February 9, 1924, 1910–29 Central Decimal File, General Records of the Department of State Relating to the Internal Affairs of Cuba, NARA Microcopy 488, Roll 28, File 837.014P/237.

[83] Anderson to Secretary of State Bainbridge Colby, July 30, 1920, 1910–29 Central Decimal File, General Records of the Department of State Relating to the Internal Affairs of Cuba, NARA Microcopy 488, Roll 27, File 837.014P/157.

following the "Dance of the Millions." Discontented Cubans increasingly protested their country's dependence on U.S. markets as well as their limited political independence under the Platt Amendment.[84] The grievances awakened a nationalist fervor. As a consequence, a backlash erupted against U.S. colonies in Cuba, including those on the Isle, which drew attention to the treaty that the U.S. Senate had ignored for two decades. Cuban politics also were at play. President Alfredo Zayas, battered by charges of corruption, was looking for a foreign policy victory to resuscitate his image.

To that end, Zayas in October 1923 appointed noted lawyer, diplomat, and War of Independence veteran Cosme de la Torriente as ambassador to the United States. His chief objective – laid out by Cuban Secretary of State Carlos Manuel de Céspedes – was to lobby U.S. senators to ratify the Hay-Quesada treaty. Céspedes suggested that the most effective way to accomplish this aim was to work through Washington's "smart set." This group included not just the U.S. senators who would vote on ratification, but also congressmen, military officers, and other people of influence who could, in turn, drum up sympathy for Cuban sovereignty.[85] As part of his self-described "mission in Washington," Torriente worked the diplomatic social scene. In particular, he credited Ida Grant, daughter-in-law of former President Ulysses S. Grant, for helping him gain entrée into Washington high society and informally meet with a variety of politicians and diplomats to whom he could pitch Cuba's case.[86]

Torriente's argument on Cuba's behalf was grounded on two premises. The first was that Spain had never considered the Isle of Pines separate from Cuba and therefore it was not part of the "other islands" ceded to the United States under the Treaty of Paris. As evidence, Torriente cited an affidavit from Wenceslao Ramírez de Villa-Urrutia, a member of Spain's negotiating team in 1898, who stated that Spain never intended to separate the Isle from Cuba.[87] The second pillar supporting Cuba's case was *pineros'* self-identification. "Who were the inhabitants of the Isle of Pines?" Torriente asked. "Cubans. The inhabitants of the Isle of Pines have always been considered to be, racially and juridically, Cubans,

[84] Louis A. Pérez Jr., *Cuba under the Platt Amendment, 1902–1934* (Pittsburgh: University of Pittsburgh Press, 1986).

[85] Céspedes to Torriente, October 31, 1923, Donativos y Remisiones, Alfredo Zayas y Alfonso – Libro I, Legajo 70, Expediente 47, 29–38, ANC.

[86] Torriente, *Mi Misión En Washington*, 95–6.

[87] Villa-Urrutia to Mario García Kohly, May 6, 1924, in Torriente, *Mi Misión En Washington*, 212–13.

and were enumerated as such in the Census of 1899, as in all censuses of Cuba taken by Spain."[88]

Torriente found support among many U.S. officials. His warning that the Isle's questionable sovereignty bred Cuban resentment of the United States registered with Secretary of State Charles Evans Hughes.[89] Hughes hoped Hay-Quesada's ratification would engender goodwill toward the United States not only in Cuba, but in Latin America more broadly, where a variety of military interventions in the Caribbean region during the first quarter of the twentieth century had earned the United States the moniker "Colossus of the North" from critics. Similarly, Coolidge feared that keeping the Isle might lead to charges of "Yankee Imperialism" and viewed the treaty as a good-faith token that would help the United States' standing in the Western Hemisphere.[90]

Some officials who had prior experience on the Isle simply did not think that it was worth the trouble. William Bardel, who served as U.S. consul in Nueva Gerona in 1918–19, reported to the Department of State years later that the Isle's annexation would be "a most undesirable proposition" because its potential for profitability had been overstated. While he conceded that Hay-Quesada's ratification "may hurt some Americans who were unwise enough to settle there, my loyalty to our Government dictates to me that I should do my best to prevent this mistake from being made."[91] Col. H. J. Slocum, who had reported from the Isle numerous times during the military occupation of 1899–1902, told Sen. David A. Reed that the Isle's value to the United States was "nil" and that it was "not worthy of our great Government." Furthermore, he anticipated that if the Isle was annexed, it would be a source of "constant friction" with Cuba.[92]

Other private groups with power and influence supported the treaty. Businessmen with ties to Cuba wanted the issue resolved in Cuba's favor, not out of concern for competition from the Isle as many annexationists posited, but rather to maintain a favorable commercial climate. One historian has argued that Americans with interests in mainland Cuba supported the treaty out of fear that its rejection would spur a nationalistic

---

[88] Torriente to Charles Evans Hughes, November 29, 1924, 1910–29 Central Decimal File, General Records of the Department of State Relating to the Internal Affairs of Cuba, NARA Microcopy 488, Roll 28, File 837.014P/294.

[89] Torriente, *Mi Misión En Washington*, 57.

[90] "Coolidge Would Let Isle of Pines Go," *New York Times*, January 21, 1925.

[91] Bardel to Assistant Secretary of State Wilbur Carr, December 23, 1924, 1910–29 Central Decimal File, General Records of the Department of State Relating to the Internal Affairs of Cuba, NARA Microcopy 488, Roll 29, File 837.014P/323.

[92] Slocum to Reed, May 26, 1924, in Torriente, *Mi Misión En Washington*, 225–7.

backlash against their businesses.[93] Clarence J. Owens, president of the Southern Commercial Congress, called Hay-Quesada "a vital issue, affecting the amity of a Hemisphere" and urged its ratification.[94]

As was the case when the treaty was signed, U.S. newspapers in the mid-1920s generally supported ratification too, on the basis that its defeat would seriously undermine the country's standing in the hemisphere. The *New York Times* argued that "the honor of the United States is at stake, together with its reputation for fair dealing with the Latin-American republics."[95] The *Washington Post* maintained that if the United States annexed the Isle, it "would stand before Latin America as a trickster seeking to acquire neighboring territory while pretending to be the protector of all American republics against foreign aggression."[96] Such arguments illustrated that support for Hay-Quesada's annexation ran deep in the United States.

Nevertheless, annexationists and opponents mobilized intense campaigns to sway the debate. In November 1923, *pineros* organized La Columna de Defensa Nacional de Isla de Pinos in favor of the treaty. Local lawyer and retired teacher Enrique Bayo Soto was named chairman of the group, which also featured a number of Isle officials, including *alcalde* Ramon Llorca Soto and municipal judge Antonio Vignier.[97] Their efforts did not endear them to settlers. U.S. consul Charles Forman branded Bayo a troublemaker for his public support of the treaty and for antagonizing settlers. In a particularly galling display of insolence, Bayo reportedly insulted *Isle of Pines Appeal* editor E. L. Slevin by using the informal "tú" form of Spanish when speaking with him.[98]

The Isle's *ayuntamiento* added its voice to the debate. In a January 1925 resolution, the council insisted that *pineros* wanted to remain a part of Cuba. It refuted annexationists' charges that Cubans were not

[93] Robert F. Smith, *The United States and Cuba: Business and Diplomacy, 1917–1960* (New Haven, CT: College and University Press, 1960), 107–11.

[94] Owens to unknown, December 4, 1924, 1910–29 Central Decimal File, General Records of the Department of State Relating to the Internal Affairs of Cuba, NARA Microcopy 488, Roll 29, File 837.014P/331.

[95] "Isle of Pines Treaty," *New York Times*, January 24, 1925.

[96] "The Isle of Pines," reprinted in *Hartford Courant*, January 27, 1925.

[97] Roberto Únger Pérez, et al., *Americanos en la Isla* (Nueva Gerona: Ediciones El Abra, 2004), 36; Diego Rodríguez Molina, et al., *El Verdadero Descubrimiento* (1996), 37; Wiltse Peña Hijuelos, et al., *Con Todo Derecho: Isla de la Juventud* (La Habana, 1986), 48; Álvarez Estévez, *Isla de Pinos y el Tratado Hay-Quesada*, 60.

[98] Racial Relations as Affected by the Hay-Quesada Treaty, April 15, 1925, 1910–29 Central Decimal File, General Records of the Department of State Relating to the Internal Affairs of Cuba, NARA Microcopy 488, Roll 29, File 837.014P/390.

sufficiently "grateful" to the United States and asserted that *pineros* did not want to be "slaves to another nation," no matter how friendly. While the council decried annexationists' "campaign of defamation and agitation," it also recognized that a distinct minority of Americans on the Isle was carrying out such activities.[99] By minimizing the extent of the annexationist sentiment, the *ayuntamiento* not only suggested its unpopularity even among settlers, but it also made sure not to use broad pejorative brush strokes in which to paint all Americans, who still played an enormous role in the local economy.

In mainland Cuba, popular efforts in support of Hay-Quesada's ratification took place as well. The Havana-based El Comité Patriótico Pro Isla de Pinos organized many of the activities, which included holding public rallies and distributing Cuban flags to teachers on the Isle.[100] It served as an umbrella group in which other organizations, including La Columna on the Isle and the Anti-Imperialist League of the Americas (led by Cuban Communist Party founder Julio Antonio Mella), could work together to raise awareness about the Hay-Quesada treaty.[101] Spurred by El Comité, demonstrations erupted across Cuba. Students and local officials from Matanzas to Cienfuegos to Antilla pressed their case directly to U.S. diplomats in the hopes of convincing U.S. officials to support the treaty.[102] Cuban businessmen, including those in the National Federation

---

[99] Acuerdo del Ayuntamiento de la Isla de Pinos, January 6, 1925, in Torriente, *Mi Misión En Washington*, 289–90. For English translation, see Torriente to Hughes, January 18, 1925, 1910–29 Central Decimal File, General Records of the Department of State Relating to the Internal Affairs of Cuba, NARA Microcopy 488, Roll 29, File 837.014P/334.

[100] Osvaldo Valdés de la Paz to Cosme de la Torriente, March 12, 1924, in Torriente, *Mi Misión En Washington*, 91–4. Honorary members included politicians such as Zayas, Céspedes, Torriente, *alcalde* Ramon Llorca Soto, and former *alcalde* Juan M. Sánchez.

[101] Jane McManus, *Cuba's Island of Dreams: Voices from the Isle of Pines and Youth* (Gainesville: University Press of Florida, 2000), 38–9; Molina, et al., *El Verdadero Descubrimiento*, 38; Pérez, et al., *Americanos en la Isla*, 36; Hijuelos, et al., *Con Todo Derecho*, 48–9; Álvarez Estévez, *Isla de Pinos y el Tratado Hay-Quesada*, 60–2.

[102] Enrique Hernandez Cartaya to Charles Evans Hughes, January 23, 1925, 1910–29 Central Decimal File, General Records of the Department of State Relating to the Internal Affairs of Cuba, NARA Microcopy 488, Roll 29, File 837.014P/339; Frank Bohr, U.S. consul Cienfuegos to U.S. Department of State, January 29, 1925, 1910–29 Central Decimal File, General Records of the Department of State Relating to the Internal Affairs of Cuba, NARA Microcopy 488, Roll 29, File 837.014P/358; Horace J. Dickinson, U.S. consul Antilla, to Hughes, February 25, 1925, 1910–29 Central Decimal File, General Records of the Department of State Relating to the Internal Affairs of Cuba, NARA Microcopy 488, Roll 29, File 837.014P/370; Alcalde de Matanzas to Frank Kellogg, March 9, 1925, 1910–29 Central Decimal File, General Records of the Department of State Relating to the Internal Affairs of Cuba, NARA

of Economic Corporations of Cuba, also petitioned U.S. officials.[103] All these efforts suggested that the Isle had become a *cause célèbre* for Cuban nationalism.

For the most part, Cuban elites recognized that the Isle of Pines held little tangible, economic value to Cuba. The attachment was more emotional and symbolic; maintaining sovereignty was a matter of national integrity and respect. Critics increasingly saw non-recognition of Cuba's right to the Isle as offensive. One writer in 1924 stated that the "delay of ratification has led to a spirit of anti-Americanism in Cuba."[104] Osvaldo Valdés de la Paz, the president of El Comité Patriótico Pro Isla de Pinos, stated that while Cuba should be thankful for U.S. political, economic, and military help through the years, such gratitude should not come at the expense of Cuba's dignity and honor.[105] Cuban historian Emilio Roig de Leuchsenring recast the honor argument. He maintained that the United States would lose face if it did not formally recognize what rightfully belonged to Cuba.[106]

Cuban supporters of Hay-Quesada used reports of settler abuse of *pinero* authority to support their position. In May 1924, a group of Americans, including Slevin and *Appeal* publisher Arthur E. Willis, allegedly attacked the Isle's chief of sanitation after he had cited an American business owner for failing to properly clean and disinfect his establishment. Forman reported that the incident had been greatly exaggerated and that no physical attack had taken place. Nevertheless, the story ran with great fanfare in the Havana press as an example of settler misconduct. "Obviously the effect of such false reports is to create prejudice against the Americans living in the Isle of Pines and to injure them in the estimation of the outside world," Forman wrote.[107]

That same month, the Havana press stirred up a controversy among settlers. *El Heraldo* published a story that sharply criticized settlers for defying local authority. It called them "habitual drunkards and other

Microcopy 488, Roll 29, File 837.014P/377; Álvarez Estévez, *Isla de Pinos y el Tratado Hay-Quesada*, 63.

[103] Crowder to Hughes, January 13, 1925, 1910–29 Central Decimal File, General Records of the Department of State Relating to the Internal Affairs of Cuba, NARA Microcopy 488, Roll 29, File 837.014P/332; "Demand the Isle of Pines," *New York Times*, January 17, 1925.

[104] Fernando Ortíz quoted in Álvarez Estévez, *Isla de Pinos y el Tratado Hay-Quesada*, 71.

[105] Ibid., 62.

[106] Ibid., 71.

[107] Forman to C. B. Hurst, May 8, 1924, Nueva Gerona – Isle of Pines, Cuba, Vol. 36, Correspondence, 1924 – Part IV, Record Group 84, NARA.

conscienceless fanatics [who] have made on the Isle of Pines a campaign of defamation against our authorities there." But the newspaper claimed that this distinction did not apply to all Americans. There were some who "assure us that the Cuban authorities on the Isle of Pines have always conducted themselves with exquisite correctness and nobility and that the campaign that is made against them is [self-]interested." It cited two settlers in particular, Santa Barbara residents R. C. Sanborn and J. F. Stair, who expressed satisfaction with Cuban authority on the Isle and emphasized that not all Americans "follow the inspirations of the small annexationist group captained by Slevin."[108] Slevin and the *Appeal* quickly rebutted, claiming that *El Heraldo* had fabricated the quotes attributed to Sanborn and Stair. The *Appeal* argued that sentiments attributed to the duo were surely manufactured because otherwise, "Had Mr. Sanborn or Mr. Stair said the things attributed to them it would have been quite impossible for them ever again to live comfortably among their fellow countrymen on the Isle of Pines."[109] The *Appeal*'s contention suggested that settlers who did not adhere to the annexationist line or were sympathetic to *pinero* authorities would be ostracized from the American community.

As the debate intensified in 1924 and early 1925, some settlers feared the rising tensions on the Isle would turn violent. At their behest, Forman made an appeal to the U.S. Embassy in Havana that Marines be sent to keep the peace. Subsequent investigations found Forman's depiction of conditions exaggerated and the embassy denied his request. W. H. Shutan, a military attaché, made a personal inspection of the Isle in February 1925 and concluded "most emphatically that no valid reason existed to justify the fear of violence against Americans ... With the exception of a small group of Americans on one side, and a very small group of Cubans on the other, all Americans and natives on the Isle of Pines live on friendly terms and in harmony." Most *pineros* bore no grudge against settlers, he reasoned, save for the editorial board of the *Isle of Pines Appeal* for inflaming the debate.[110] Shutan's findings – and tone – suggested exasperation among U.S. officials toward settlers and the annexation issue.

---

[108] "The Authorities of the Isle [of] Pines Behave Themselves Well," *El Heraldo*, May 17, 1924, reprinted in *Isle of Pines Appeal*, May 24, 1924.

[109] "Will Sanborn Prosecute El Heraldo?" *Isle of Pines Appeal*, May 24, 1924.

[110] W. H. Shutan to U.S. Embassy, Havana, February 3, 1925, 1910–29 Central Decimal File, General Records of the Department of State Relating to the Internal Affairs of Cuba, NARA Microcopy 488, Roll 29, File 837.014P/359.

Only the U.S. Senate, though, could end the debate. The Foreign Relations Committee had taken the first step by recommending Hay-Quesada's approval. In fact, it had happened on three occasions – February 1906, December 1922, and February 1924 – yet the treaty never came before the full Senate. During the lame-duck session of the 68th Congress, the Coolidge administration pressed senators to resolve the matter.

Opponents did just enough to stall a vote. Sen. William Borah, chairman of the Senate Foreign Relations Committee, resisted calls to present the treaty for consideration before the close of the session. He was helped by Sen. Royal Copeland, an unabashed annexationist who wanted to "take immediate steps to negotiate with Cuba a new and proper treaty, which will attach the Isle of Pines to the United States, giving us honorable and unquestioned possession."[111] In January 1925, Borah and Copeland claimed the original treaty was missing and said that the Senate could not consider the measure without it. Two days later, it was found by a clerk in the Senate library, "stained and dusty, but intact."[112] Other annexationist senators, perhaps realizing the tide of sentiment against them, began hedging their bets and introduced resolutions to ensure the rights of U.S. citizens living on the Isle. Sen. Kenneth McKellar called for a separate, provisional government on the Isle, one that would eliminate tariffs on trade and provide a bill of rights to American residents in the Cuban constitution. The Senate rejected the resolution.[113]

Such measures only forestalled the inevitable. Because the vast majority of senators had taken office long after the treaty's signing – only four remained in the Senate since 1904 – most of them regardless of party affiliation seemed to follow the lead of the Coolidge administration, which wanted ratification. Perhaps swayed by the weight of domestic and international pressure, Borah consented to discussing the treaty among the full Senate during a special session of the 69th Congress in March 1925. Opponents, though, continued to battle against the treaty. On March 12, Copeland conducted an eight-hour filibuster that may have been counterproductive. One writer argued that it "disgusted the majority of the senators ... [and] enabled those favoring ratification to have a definitive date set for taking a vote on the treaty."[114] When a vote was

---

[111] Quoted in "The Isle of Pines Treaty," *New York Times*, January 24, 1925.
[112] "Coolidge Presses for Pines Treaty," *New York Times*, January 25, 1925; "Missing Isle of Pines Treaty Found Under Dome of Capitol," *New York Times*, January 27, 1925.
[113] Avello, "The Isle of Pines as a Factor in United States–Cuban Relations," 81–2.
[114] Clarence Eugene Oswald, "The Adjustment of Title to the Ownership of the Isle of Pines," (MA thesis, University of California, 1935), 62. See also, "Isle of Pines Treaty

set for the following day, Copeland introduced a resolution to postpone consideration until a Senate committee investigation could be completed. That proposal was rejected. So too was Sen. Frank Willis's resolution, akin to McKellar's from two months earlier, calling for U.S. citizens to have a bill of rights in the Cuban constitution.

Ultimately, the U.S. Senate voted 63–14 (with nineteen abstentions) to ratify the treaty, easily passing the two-thirds threshold. The Senate attached two reservations that the Cuban government ultimately accepted. One was from Borah and ensured all present and future U.S. treaties with Cuba also applied to the Isle of Pines. The other, introduced by Sen. James Reed, clarified that the word "foreigners" in the treaty would mean "foreigners who receive the most favorable treatment under the Government of Cuba." Both measures looked to maximize the rights and privileges of U.S. citizens on the Isle yet were of little consolation to annexationists.

Celebrations erupted across Cuba after the treaty's ratification. On the Isle, *alcalde* Ramon Llorca Soto said, "At last for the Pineros the restlessness in which we lived has ceased. The Isle of Pines, Cuban by nature and Cuban by sentiment, will not be separated from the Cuban state."[115] In Havana, an estimated crowd of 20,000 revelers gathered in a parade attended by U.S. Ambassador to Cuba Enoch Crowder.[116] In Cienfuegos, government agencies closed their offices and townspeople threw a parade that featured schoolchildren, local officials, and remarks from the U.S. consul.[117] One Cuban newspaper editorial conveyed a sense of relief as well as optimism for future U.S.–Latin American relations. *La Prensa* opined that Hay-Quesada's ratification "will without doubt help to diminish the bad feeling which, it is useless to deny, certain Latin American countries harbor towards the policy of the United States in the Caribbean Sea."[118]

Comes to Vote Today," *New York Times*, March 13, 1925; Avello, "The Isle of Pines as a Factor in United States–Cuban Relations," 84–6.

[115] Quoted in "Treaty Brings Joy to Cuban Officials," *New York Times*, March 16, 1925.

[116] Enoch Crowder to Frank Kellogg, March 26, 1925, 1910–29 Central Decimal File, General Records of the Department of State Relating to the Internal Affairs of Cuba, NARA Microcopy 488, Roll 29, File 837.014P/385.

[117] Frank Bohr to Frank Kellogg, March 19, 1925, 1910–29 Central Decimal File, General Records of the Department of State Relating to the Internal Affairs of Cuba, NARA Microcopy 488, Roll 29, File 837.014P/386.

[118] "The Solving of the Isle of Pines Question," *La Prensa*, March 15, 1925, translation in 1910–29 Central Decimal File, General Records of the Department of State Relating to the Internal Affairs of Cuba, NARA Microcopy 488, Roll 29, File 837.014P/386.

To settlers, word of ratification was devastating. Frederick Swetland Jr. remembered that when he heard the news at his house, "There was silence all around the table.... [T]he sword had at last fallen."[119] Other settlers were put off by the celebrations enjoyed by their island neighbors. Millie Giltner said that when she heard the news and went to Nueva Gerona, she "saw these Cubans with the American flags out in the street throwing them on the ground and spitting on them. Those people on the Isle of Pines had more than they ever would have had if we hadn't have gone there."[120] Similarly, Ernest Gruppe asserted that the Isle had meant little to Cuba until Americans began developing it. "Cuba had no interest in the Isle of Pines," he said. "It meant nothing to them at that time. It was just a penal colony. But to us it meant everything. Even the [*pinero*] people, at that time, had no particular feeling for Cuba because they were not really a part of Cuba.... The Isle of Pines was always a stepchild of Cuba."[121]

Some settlers looked for scapegoats. Chief among them was Elihu Root. His rejection of the annexationist case nearly twenty years earlier still stuck in settlers' craw because it set a precedent that other U.S. officials followed. The *Appeal* called him "the Isle of Pines' worst enemy."[122] Frederick Swetland Sr. wrote that, "every time I think of the Cubans and former Secretary of War Root attempting to utterly disregard the rights of United States citizens and the wishes of President McKinley and the Paris Peace Commissioners, I get hot all over."[123] Women in the delegation that met with Coolidge in April 1924 also received some blame. As longtime settler Edith Sundstrom recalled: "The men said that if they had sent a male delegation, everything would have been different.... But how could those men blame Harriet Wheeler?"[124]

A few Americans refused to give up the fight. One month after ratification, Frederick Swetland Sr. tried to convince the U.S. Senate to purchase the Isle from Cuba, using the country's debt to the United States as leverage. Swetland figured his biggest obstacle would be U.S.-based

[119] Frederick L. Swetland Jr., *Isle of Pines*, 27–8.
[120] Millie Giltner oral history interview with Frederick Swetland Jr., March 13, 1969, tape 1, 8, SFA.
[121] Ernest Gruppe oral history interview with Frederick Swetland Jr., June 21, 1971, tape 18, 4, SFA.
[122] "Pan-American Union Bulletin on Treaty," *Isle of Pines Appeal*, October 25, 1924.
[123] Swetland to L. J. Tabor, December 20, 1924, Folder: Southern Fruit Co. – Stockholders; Isle of Pines Treaty, SFA.
[124] Quoted in McManus, *Cuba's Island of Dreams*, 40.

tobacco companies that might object to potential competition from the Isle (even though the Isle's tobacco industry was negligible).[125] His idea found at least one sympathetic figure in Frank Willis. The Republican senator from Ohio, from where the Swetland family hailed, proposed that if the Cuban government could not repay the cost of the second U.S. military intervention from 1906–9, the United States would accept the Isle instead.[126] The idea, however, went nowhere. There was no more disputing who owned the Isle of Pines.

On one level, the U.S. Senate's ratification of the Hay-Quesada treaty merely kept the status quo. The Cuban government had been administering the Isle since independence in May 1902. That arrangement remained the same after the Squiers–García agreement in July 1903, the Hay-Quesada treaty's signing in March 1904, and the treaty's ratification in March 1925.

On another level, however, the resolution of the sovereignty question had much broader implications. Affirming Cuban sovereignty over the Isle of Pines marked the end of U.S. territorial expansion for the sake of settlement. Although the United States would continue to acquire additional territory after 1898 – including Wake Island, American Samoa, the U.S. Virgin Islands, and the Northern Mariana Islands – those lands were obtained for geostrategic purposes, not to extend the frontier. Had the spirit of Manifest Destiny continued to linger in the twentieth century, the Isle of Pines seemed perfectly suited to further American landed expansion. And while a vocal coterie of annexationists remained, their nineteenth-century ideology no longer had a place in a twentieth-century world in which an open door to commercial opportunity was seen as more important to the national interest.

Among Cubans, popular demonstrations supporting Hay-Quesada drew attention to the neocolonial relationship between the United States and Cuba in the early twentieth century. One group of students at the University of Havana made the connection explicit. Although they favored the sentiments of Hay-Quesada, they did not celebrate its ratification. These students maintained that "The Isle of Pines belongs to Cuba, but Cuba is not free.... [T]he Washington Government with the Platt Amendment and the abuse of its forces, has converted the Island

---

[125] Swetland to C. A. Dyer, April 7, 1925, Folder: Southern Fruit Co. – Stockholders; Isle of Pines Treaty, SFA.

[126] Avello, "The Isle of Pines as a Factor in United States–Cuban Relations," 91.

into a Colony."[127] By connecting the sovereignty question to the broader issue of U.S.–Cuban relations, successful demonstrations in favor of Hay-Quesada's ratification also helped to set the stage for the end of the thoroughly unpopular Platt Amendment that governed U.S.–Cuban relations and limited Cuban independence. Within a decade, it would be abrogated.

Hay-Quesada's ratification was momentous for U.S. settlers as well. It definitively crushed their faith that the Isle's status would change, a belief on which many staked not only their investments but their livelihoods. Nearly twenty-five years of lobbying had ended in failure. Frederick Swetland Jr. wrote that, "From 1904 until 1925 the sword of Damocles hung over the Americans on the Isle of Pines.... Few believed that the sword would fall."[128] But when it did, the American colony – already in decline for reasons addressed in Chapter 6 – was pushed further to the brink.

With the sovereignty question settled, so too was the primary issue that shaped the lives of those on the Isle of Pines during the first quarter of the twentieth century. Its open-endedness had compelled many Americans to move there. Their ensuing activities transformed the political, economic, social, cultural, and physical landscape. The sovereignty question also affected the tenor of local relations. Although Americans and *pineros* cooperated in entrepreneurial endeavors and enjoyed cordial relations, the idea of the Isle's annexation to the United States remained deeply divisive.

That bitterness would linger among the dwindling American colony for years to come. Many of those who remained did so simply because they could not afford to return to the United States. Their hardscrabble lives would produce resentment, not just toward their *pinero* neighbors, but also toward the U.S. government. These self-proclaimed pioneers felt abandoned by their representatives and their country. Their struggles would mark the next twenty-five years of the American presence on the Isle of Pines.

---

[127] The University Students Against the Yankee Imperialism and the Servile Attitude of the Cuban Government, contained in Enoch Crowder to Secretary of State Frank Kellogg, March 26, 1925, 1910–29 Central Decimal File, General Records of the Department of State Relating to the Internal Affairs of Cuba, NARA Microcopy 488, Roll 29, File 837.014P/385. See also Avello, "The Isle of Pines as a Factor in United States–Cuban Relations," 109–11.

[128] Swetland, *Isle of Pines*, 27.

PART TWO

BECOMING GOOD NEIGHBORS

6

A Time of Struggle

Like most other Americans who had gone to the Isle of Pines during the early twentieth century, Frederick Swetland Jr. in the 1940s was enthusiastic about the prospect of making a fortune there. His family had engaged in a variety of business ventures on the Isle over the years. Shortly after purchasing some 10,000 acres in San Francisco de las Piedras in 1908, the Swetlands started the Isle of Pines Investment Company to sell land in their tract. They operated the Southern Fruit Company that grew grapefruit and oranges for commercial export. The family also engaged in cattle ranching and opened part of their home as an inn for tourists. Swetland had visited the Isle frequently as a child, recalling it as "the place where he had longed to be."[1] As an adult, Swetland was eager to take the reins of the family business, confident that the Isle offered the opportunity where an enterprising individual could become wealthy.

But his father, Frederick Swetland Sr., threw cold water on the idea. Although the family had long enjoyed the Isle as a winter resort, their enterprises had failed to turn a profit. Frederick Sr. reminded his son of the family's dismal business history: "I have, as you may recall, repeatedly told you that I thought you were wasting your productive years by any attempted Island operation and that you should as soon as possible, and decidedly for your own good, give up your ideas for development of the Island property and make yourself a place in this country."[2] By the

---

[1] Frederick L. Swetland Jr., *Isle of Pines*, 4. In this passage, Swetland referred to his childhood self in the third person.

[2] Frederick Swetland Sr. to Frederick Swetland Jr., July 7, 1947, SFA. Senior's letter had been prompted by a letter from Junior, who criticized his father and uncles for no longer

1940s, the family had shut down the Southern Fruit Company and was considering closing the Isle of Pines Investment Company, which had sold only about 3,000 acres. Four decades of commercial struggles were more than enough to convince Frederick Sr. that nothing his son did could turn the family's fortunes.

Frederick Swetland Sr.'s remarks reflected the popular notion that American efforts on the Isle of Pines were a failure after the U.S. Senate's ratification of the Hay-Quesada treaty. In reality, the American colony had been in retreat for nearly a decade by that point. A myriad of problems festering since the mid-1910s had contributed to this decline: property damage from tropical storms; questionable business practices; prohibitive tariffs; poor-performing enterprises; stunted transportation and infrastructure improvements that continued to make getting to, from, and around the Isle timely and expensive. While annexation got more attention from settlers than these other critical issues, proponents saw attachment to the United States as the panacea for the colony's ills.

In the years following Hay-Quesada's ratification, the community of Americans on the Isle of Pines was reduced to a pale shadow of what it had once been. From a peak of some 2,000 settlers in the mid-1910s, the U.S. population dwindled to fewer than 300 by the 1930s. Sydney A. Clark painted a bleak picture in his 1936 travel narrative. The Isle's most notable American-owned hotels had closed. Mineral springs, one of the main attractions, were little used. The port of Jucaro on the Isle's northeast coast, often frequented by Americans, lay virtually abandoned. And towns such as Columbia "once eager and flourishing, are now like the ghost towns of California's Mother Lode."[3] Such descriptions bear an unmistakable resemblance to another failed Americanizing project contemporary to the one on the Isle: Henry Ford's rubber plantation, Fordlandia, deep in the Brazilian rain forest.[4] Like settlers on the Isle, Ford – somewhat naïvely – was looking to bring about prosperity abroad through the exploitation of an unfamiliar land on the strength of technology, innovation, and free-market capitalism. But while Ford's U.S. workers could return home after the plantation was sold off, many Americans on the Isle remained because they had no choice. Those who could not afford to leave struggled to eke out a living. Some settlers

using the family's property for commercial purposes. Frederick Swetland Jr. to Isle of Pines Investment Company, June 29, 1947, SFA.

[3] Sydney A. Clark, *Cuban Tapestry* (New York: National Travel Club, 1936), 146.

[4] Greg Grandin, *Fordlandia: The Rise and Fall of Henry Ford's Forgotten Jungle City* (New York: Picador, 2009).

died virtually destitute. Others harbored deep resentments: toward the U.S. government for not supporting annexation; toward landholding companies for selling them false promises; and toward the Cuban government for not doing more to improve the Isle's infrastructure and commercial prospects.

This next phase of the American presence on the Isle of Pines took place as broader U.S. relations with Cuba and the rest of Latin America were shifting during the 1920s and 1930s. While the United States maintained its commercial and geostrategic interests in the region, it had to adapt to the economic realities of the Great Depression and resistance from critics who resented the numerous military interventions in the Caribbean region undertaken by the "Colossus of the North." To that end, the U.S. government made token gestures of good will. In Cuba, these measures included ratifying the Hay-Quesada treaty in 1925 and abrogating the Platt Amendment in 1934. The most notable shift – which was more in style than of substance – was the adaptation of the Good Neighbor Policy. First articulated by President Herbert Hoover, his successor, Franklin Delano Roosevelt, expanded on this idea by pledging not to interfere in the internal affairs of other Latin American countries. Ostensibly, this policy meant that the United States would take a hands-off, military-less approach to the region. In effect, though, it often produced cozier relationships with elites and authoritarians who shared U.S. interests.[5] Nevertheless, the veneer of the Good Neighbor paid off in an era of strong hemispheric solidarity, particularly during World War II.

Such a good neighborly approach was evident in relationships between Americans, Cubans, and the multinational population of the Isle. With the annexation question resolved, few public flare-ups of anti-American sentiment occurred during the second quarter of the twentieth century. The U.S. citizens who remained were less conspicuous than they were during the Hay-Quesada era and many lived in hardscrabble conditions. Yet they remained prominent. Their influence was sustained, in part, by aligning more closely with English-speaking European migrants with whom they shared linguistic, racial, and cultural similarities. Over time, such alliances would extend to other groups outside this cadre, but would have to wait for the next generation to come during mid-century.

[5] David F. Schmitz, *Thank God They're on Our Side: The United States and Right-Wing Dictatorships, 1921–1965* (Chapel Hill: University of North Carolina Press, 1999), 46–84.

Hurricanes

The success of settlers' enterprises – or, more accurately, the *optimism* for success – sustained the U.S. community during the early twentieth century. When they faltered, so too did the American community. Of all the reasons for commercial and community failures, tropical storms may have been the most significant. Not only did they cause the greatest damage to settlers' businesses and property, but these storms also spurred Americans' exodus from the Isle. Settlers rarely expressed concern about hurricanes, perhaps because landholding companies' promotions barely made any mention of such storms. But hurricanes ravaged the Isle every few years, including at least seven instances during the nineteenth century.[6] During the early twentieth century, the Isle experienced strong storms in 1906 and 1910, but none quite as physically and emotionally damaging as the hurricanes of 1917 and 1926.

Already beset by economic difficulties as a result of World War I – when the prices for fertilizers skyrocketed and shipping was curtailed – settlers' challenges were compounded by a major hurricane on September 25, 1917. The storm destroyed buildings, uprooted trees, and ravaged infrastructure. "Quite a number of poorly built houses were completely demolished," the *Isle of Pines Appeal* reported.[7] Grace Hart Crane, mother of poet Hart Crane, heard the news from her property's caretaker. "Our place, with the exception of the house alone, is in total ruin," she wrote her son. "The house is some damaged and was almost blown off the foundation – Many families are destitute…. All trees vines shrubs, etc are laid flat on the ground."[8] The damage also affected public spaces. The roof of the Methodist church in Columbia was blown off and the port at Los Indios remained closed for more than a year.[9] The storm took a huge toll on the Isle's biggest industry as well. According to one estimate,

---

[6] The U.S. Division of Insular Affairs claimed the Isle suffered through major hurricanes in 1844, 1846, 1865, 1870, 1876, 1885, and 1894. "The Isle of Pines (Caribbean Sea): Its Situation, Physical Features, Inhabitants, Resources, and Industries" (Washington, DC: Government Printing Office, 1902), 15.

[7] The newspaper's description continued, however, that "the island is better off as many of them were eyesores and uninhabitable." "Island Is Gradually Recovering from Storm," *Isle of Pines Appeal*, July 27, 1918.

[8] Grace Hart Crane to Hart Crane, October 3, 1917, in *Letters of Hart Crane and His Family*, Thomas S. W. Lewis, ed. (New York: Columbia University Press, 1974), 76.

[9] Sterling Augustus Neblett, *Methodism's First Fifty Years in Cuba* (Wilmore, KY: Asbury Press, 1976), 107; William Bardel to William E. Gonzales, U.S. Minister to Cuba, December 16, 1918, Nueva Gerona – Isle of Pines, Cuba, Vol. 16, Correspondence, 1918 – Part II, Record Group 84, NARA.

half of the Isle's grapefruit was wiped out.[10] The Swetland family alone estimated it lost 50,000 crates worth of grapefruit amid the damage.[11]

The 1917 hurricane signaled the high tide of U.S. settlement. The destruction took more than just a physical and financial toll on settlers – it took a psychological one as well. Frederick Swetland Jr. wrote that the storm "blew away more than [settlers'] houses. It also blew away their illusions and their hopes, which even before that had begun to ebb. The inward tide of immigration which had begun in 1902 had long since arrested; after 1917 the tide turned."[12] Indeed, for those who had been losing money on their settlements or businesses, the storm was the last straw. "So much money sunk in that place, and now no hope of ever getting a cent out of it," Grace Hart Crane wrote. "This is all very discouraging in a financial way to me, as I had thought that by getting the place in good shape we might be able to sell it perhaps this winter even at a sacrifice – It looks now that one couldn't give it away."[13] Many other settlers did give their property away or abandoned it to return to the United States. Post-hurricane estimates of settlers declined sharply, from some 2,000 around the start of World War I to about 700 in 1918.

Three years later, the hurricane still cast a pall over the dwindling American community. Among those who remained – mostly large landowners or smaller ones who could not afford to return to the United States – a public discourse of resolve permeated. This rhetoric suggested that the remaining settlers were the strongest of the lot and encouraged them to rebuild. The *Isle of Pines Appeal* noted in 1920 that "Many of the 'old timers' who weathered the discouragement of the storm are still with us, and every Isle of Pines man or woman can point them out with pride as the ones to whom the island owes her present and fast growing prosperity."[14]

If citrus production is any indication, the Isle's commercial prospects did recover. Grapefruit exports increased from 33,000 crates in 1918 to almost 288,000 in 1926.[15] Swetland attributed the turnaround to "those

---

[10] Annual Report on Commerce and Industries for 1918, report by William Bardel, April 22, 1919, Nueva Gerona – Isle of Pines, Cuba, Vol. 18, Correspondence, 1919 – Part I, Record Group 84, NARA.

[11] Frederick Swetland Sr. to Gale V. Smith, March 22, 1924, SFA.

[12] Swetland, *Isle of Pines*, 32.

[13] Grace Hart Crane to Hart Crane, October 3, 1917, in *Letters of Hart Crane and His Family*, 76–7.

[14] "The Faculty of 'Coming Back,'" *Isle of Pines Appeal*, December 4, 1920.

[15] LaRue Lutkins to Paul Minnemum, March 9, 1943, Nueva Gerona – Isle of Pines, Cuba, Vol. 55, Correspondence, 1943 (File No. 812–891), 1944 (File No. 000-123), Record Group 84, NARA.

who stayed [after the 1917 hurricane who] were better adapted to survive; either better capitalized, better schooled for the life, possessors of stronger backs and sharper minds or just plain luckier. They had endurance and toughness, badly needed for the blows ahead."[16] Indeed, that endurance and toughness would be needed again after another, more devastating hurricane that added further injury to settlers still reeling from Hay-Quesada's ratification.

Dorothy Anderson recalled the night of October 19–20, 1926. As wind howled around her one-story wood house in Columbia, Anderson's family members gathered in the kitchen where they huddled under the table for safety. Shortly after midnight, the house succumbed to the powerful winds and fell down. "It sounded like a cannon," she said. "I remember Mother was knocked out." Her youngest brother was pinned down in the collapse and it took her father hours to free him. Meanwhile, Anderson, her mother, and another brother sought cover in the grove, holding on to trees for dear life amid the torrential rains and punishing winds in the predawn darkness. In the chaos, Anderson suffered a significant injury of her own – a piece of wood embedded in her arm; it took more than a year to pull out all the splinters. In the morning, she saw the extent of the devastation: furniture, clothing, and uprooted trees strewn about the property. "Nothing else in Columbia was blown down but everything around our place was gone, nothing was standing," she said. "No trees – nothing. Every tree in the grove was uprooted.... My mother's chickens had the feathers blown out of them like they were plucked."[17]

Anderson's tale was indicative of the devastation wrought by the October 1926 hurricane, one that by all accounts was far more destructive and costly than the 1917 storm. One settler stated that the Isle's only wind gauge broke at 150 miles an hour.[18] Three Americans were among the seventeen dead; an additional sixty-six people were seriously injured, including four Americans. U.S. consul Sheridan Talbott estimated that one-fourth of the Isle's trees were uprooted; flooding was rampant; roads were impassable; and outside communication limited because of a

[16] Swetland, *Isle of Pines*, 37.
[17] Dorothy Anderson interview with Frederick Swetland Jr., June 21, 1971, tape 22, 1–2, SFA. Additional detail from Elizabeth Bullock to Drusilla Bullock, October 27, 1926, in "Mrs. Bullock Pictures Horrors and Ravages of Tornado on Isle of Pines," *Penn-Yan Chronicle-Express*, November 18, 1926, courtesy of Paul Bullock.
[18] Elizabeth Bullock to Drusilla Bullock, October 27, 1926, in "Mrs. Bullock Pictures Horrors and Ravages of Tornado on Isle of Pines," *Penn-Yan Chronicle-Express*, November 18, 1926, courtesy of Paul Bullock.

FIGURE 6.1. The hurricane of October 1926 caused significant damage through-out the Isle. Three U.S. citizens were among the seventeen dead following the storm that crippled the American community still reeling from the ratification of the Hay-Quesada treaty a year earlier. Of the nearly 100 homes occupied by U.S. citizens, nearly half were considered destroyed or damaged beyond repair. Courtesy of Archivo Histórico Municipal de la Isla de la Juventud.

downed telegraph station. Of the nearly 100 homes occupied by settlers, about half were considered destroyed or damaged beyond repair. Talbott estimated that the Isle sustained roughly $1.5 million worth of damage.[19]

The storm came at a particularly inopportune time for the Isle's export economy. Grapefruit production had been steadily increasing since the 1910s and forecasts were optimistic for 1927. But because of the storm, Isle growers only exported some 26,000 crates that year, the lowest on record. Not only did growers lose fruit off the trees, some lost a significant portion in transit as well. Frederick Swetland Jr. estimated that his family lost 10,000 crates in the storm when a cargo ship sank in Havana harbor.[20] As for the Isle's vegetable production, forecasts had predicted 1927 would be the strongest year on record. After shipping some 150,000 boxes of vegetables in 1926 – almost all before the storm – growers expected to produce double or triple that number the following

[19] Report of Hurricane of October 19–20, 1926, November 19, 1926, Nueva Gerona – Isle of Pines, Cuba, Vol. 41, Storm, 1926 – Part I, Record Group 84, NARA.
[20] Swetland, *Isle of Pines*, 30–1. The family's packinghouse also sustained severe damage in the storm as two walls of brick and cement "exploded" from the force of the wind.

year.[21] But as a result of the hurricane, Isle growers sent only 110,000 crates to the United States in 1927, a crushing letdown in light of the preseason forecasts.[22] "This proved to be the dark hour before the dawn," the *Isle of Pines Post* wrote in 1931. "Optimism was very unpopular and 'Better catch the next boat back' became almost a slogan."[23] Many settlers took that mantra to heart. As a result of the property damage and consequent business failures, the U.S. population numbered just a few hundred by the close of the 1920s.

Business Failures

Most Americans' commercial enterprises, especially those engaged in citrus, did not enjoy much long-term success. Small growers' failures were evident by World War I. As longtime resident Millie Giltner recalled, "I bet no more than five or six people ever made any money."[24] Large growers – those who cultivated forty acres or more – were not immune to disappointment, either. The Swetland family, for example, planted six 100-acre groves, each set up as a separate company: Upland, Highland, Pineland, Riverside, Camaraco, and Valley. The latter three never came to fruition, mostly owing to the poor soil in those locations.[25] The family eventually consolidated the remaining holdings into The Southern Fruit Company. But this collective enterprise fared no better. Poor irrigation limited the groves' bearings. By the 1930s, Frederick Swetland Sr. estimated that despite financial support from the family's other business interests, The Southern Fruit Company's losses ran into the "hundreds of thousands of dollars."[26] With the Great Depression closing markets and limiting additional financial support, the family ceased commercial fruit growing in 1937. The Swetlands were not the only large growers to see their enterprises fail. By World War II, only some thirty American companies or individuals continued to grow citrus, eight of which had more than twenty acres.[27]

[21] Report of Hurricane of October 19–20, 1926, November 19, 1926, Nueva Gerona – Isle of Pines, Cuba, Vol. 41, Storm, 1926 – Part I, Record Group 84, NARA.

[22] Basic Report on Vegetable Production in the Isle of Pines, February 2, 1928, Nueva Gerona – Isle of Pines, Cuba, Vol. 51, Correspondence, 1928 – Part III, Record Group 84, NARA.

[23] "Story of Isle of Pines," *Isle of Pines Post*, May 25, 1931.

[24] Millie Giltner interview with Frederick Swetland Jr., March 13, 1969, 16, SFA.

[25] Swetland, *Isle of Pines*, 92–3.

[26] Swetland to A. E. Wolfgram, November 13, 1931, SFA.

[27] Citrus Fruit Growers, Isle of Pines, Cuba, February 26, 1944, Nueva Gerona – Isle of Pines, Cuba, Vol. 57, Correspondence, 1944 (File No. 813–892), Record Group 84,

Settlers blamed their business failures on a number of factors, including prohibitive U.S. tariffs, costly transportation, and damage from hurricanes. But the issues that undermined American entrepreneurial activities went deeper. Many business models had fundamental flaws that invariably set up enterprises for failure that, in turn, led to the erosion of the American community.

Tariffs

The chief complaint of settlers who sold export commodities back to the United States was the persistence of duties on their products. Tariffs were designed, in part, to protect domestic producers from foreign competition. It added a tax on foreign-made goods, thereby raising the price of the product that would, in theory, compel domestic consumers to purchase American-made or grown goods instead. In the case of Cuba, domestic U.S. producers of sugar and tobacco feared that unfettered access for Cuban goods would drive down prices. Hence, a tariff was put in place. But considering the depth of U.S. investment in Cuba's staple industries as well as a desire to open Cuba as a market for finished goods, the United States and Cuba signed a reciprocity treaty in 1903. The deal reduced U.S. duties on Cuban products by 20 percent in exchange for a 20 percent to 40 percent cut on Cuban duties of U.S. goods. U.S. entrepreneurs on the Isle, however, were not satisfied. Given its minimal market share compared to domestic U.S. producers of citrus and vegetables, tariffs undercut what little competitive advantage the Isle's longer growing season gave them. Moreover, since tariffs were designed to protect American business, U.S. entrepreneurs argued that they were being unfairly hurt by the tariff. The tariff issue was the primary reason entrepreneurial settlers wanted the United States to annex the Isle.

Although settlers had lobbied against duties since their arrival, tariffs were low compared to later years. During World War I, the tariff on grapefruit was between fourteen and twenty-eight cents a crate.[28]

NARA. According to the Isle of Pines Chamber of Commerce, the Isle's largest grower was British-owned Howard Brothers, which had 233 acres of citrus. The largest American grower was J. A. Miller & Sons with 135 acres of grapefruit. W. D. Middleton was the only other American with 100 acres – seventy-three in grapefruit, seventeen in oranges, and ten in limes. One study estimated that by 1945, citrus had declined to roughly a $100,000-a-year industry, about one-third of the Isle's agricultural production. Morton D. Winsberg, "Isle of Pines, Cuba: A Geographic Interpretation" (PhD diss., University of Florida, 1958), 113.

[28] Santa Fe Land Company and Isle of Pines United Land Companies, "Marvelous Isle of Pines: 'That Magnificent Land of Sunshine, Health, and Wealth'" (Chicago, 1914), 18.

In 1922, the Fordney-McCumber tariff increased duties to nearly sixty cents a box. Settlers cried foul. "These increased duties are felt as a severe handicap," U.S. consul Charles Forman wrote. "Although some of the colonists are doing well the island as a whole is not progressing as it should. It needs population and capital and is not getting them partly because the increase in the United States Tariff cuts off so much of the growers' profits."[29] Despite such complaints, citrus production continued to thrive throughout the 1920s, suggesting that some growers were still turning a profit. But that trend changed with the onset of the Great Depression and the adoption of the protectionist Smoot-Hawley tariff in 1930 that placed duties of up to eighty-four cents per box on grapefruit.[30] The following year, grapefruit production reached its all-time peak with exports of 301,442 crates before beginning a steady decline.[31] Along with declining prices and the increased cost of shipping, the new duties made doing business in the United States cost-prohibitive.

Isle growers blamed domestic producers for initiating the tariff increases. They suggested that domestic growers feared competition from the Isle and persuaded legislators to boost tariffs as a result. For example, in the midst of a nationwide recession in 1920, California Rep. Charles H. Randall unsuccessfully proposed a much stiffer tariff that would have increased citrus duties to nearly $1.20 a box. The *Isle of Pines Appeal* blamed it on "California interests" who along with their "Florida cousins" were attempting to "crush the competition of the Isle of Pines by unfair legislation." The *Appeal* rallied Isle growers to fight this proposed legislation "that will make those fellows up in Florida and California think they have jumped into a wildcat's nest."[32] The episode illustrated settlers' antipathy toward domestic U.S. growers, who Isle-based entrepreneurs argued were stifling their businesses. One citrus company executive on the Isle, while lobbying against the Fordney-McCumber tariff, insisted that Isle producers

[29] Annual Report on Commerce and Industries, March 2, 1925, Nueva Gerona – Isle of Pines, Cuba, Vol. 38, Correspondence, 1925 – Part II, Record Group 84, NARA.

[30] The Smoot-Hawley tariff placed duties on fruit from Cuba as follows: three-tenths of a cent per pound from August 1 to September 30; six-tenths of a cent during the month of October; and 1.2 cents from November 1 through July 31. See Morton D. Winsberg, "Costs, Tariffs, Prices and Nationalization: The Rise and Decline of the American Grapefruit Industry on the Isle of Pines, Cuba," *American Journal of Economics and Sociology* 20 (October 1961): 547. Most Isle growers made the bulk of their exports in August and September.

[31] Citrus Fruit Culture on the Isle of Pines, undated, Nueva Gerona – Isle of Pines, Cuba, Vol. 55, Correspondence, 1943 (File No. 812–891), 1944 (File No. 000-123), Record Group 84, NARA.

[32] "Death to the Isle of Pines," *Isle of Pines Appeal*, December 11, 1920.

posed no threat to domestic growers. Not only did the Isle's production pale in comparison to Florida's, he wrote, but higher tariffs would cripple the citrus industry, destroy the U.S. community, and eliminate revenue altogether from duties. "If the proposed increase in duty remains in the bill, it will mean the property values of some seven to eight thousand American citizens who have interests on the Isle-of-Pines, will be destroyed," F. C. Stevens wrote. "Our growers cannot take on this increased duty and continue to maintain our orchards.... If the duty be increased, the growers on the Isle-of-Pines, will, in my opinion, be driven out of business."[33] Although the Isle's citrus industry withstood the Fordney-McCumber tariff, the duties from Smoot-Hawley took a greater toll.

For a time, Isle growers shifted their focus to Great Britain as their major market. The trend had begun tentatively in 1922, with a shipment going to England via New York.[34] During the Isle's peak year of grapefruit exports in 1931, only about 75,000 crates went to the United States; most of the rest went to England for sale there or reshipment to other European markets.[35] But the British market's opening was short-lived. In 1932, British duties increased to forty cents a box.[36] From then on, grapefruit exports began a slow, steady decline, shipping more than 200,000 boxes only once more during Cuba's republican era.

The onset of depression brought significant changes to the vegetable industry, as well. In the 1920s, peppers were the predominant crop, making up nearly 70 percent of exports; eggplants and cucumbers represented the other significant products.[37] That dynamic changed in the 1930s beginning with the Smoot-Hawley tariff that placed duties of three cents per pound on winter vegetables. That meant a tax of roughly $1.15 per crate, which usually sold for about $5 in U.S. markets.[38] Combined with increased production and competition from mainland Cuba, pepper and eggplant exports declined sharply. Cucumbers, however, survived thanks to demand, and became the Isle's top vegetable industry. While vegetables remained a secondary export for American entrepreneurs, the

[33] Stevens to Sen. William Calder, April 7, 1922, SFA.

[34] Exports of Grapefruit and Vegetables, June 14, 1923, Nueva Gerona – Isle of Pines, Cuba, Vol. 33, Correspondence, 1923 – Part III, Record Group 84, NARA.

[35] "Fruit and Vegetable Summary for Crop Year 1931–1932 on Isle," *Isle of Pines Post*, August 10, 1932.

[36] "English Tariff Set Affects Isle's Fruit," *Isle of Pines Post*, January 25, 1932.

[37] Basic Report on Vegetable Production in the Isle of Pines by Sheridan Talbott, February 9, 1928, Nueva Gerona – Isle of Pines, Cuba, Vol. 51, Correspondence, 1928 – Part III, Record Group 84, NARA.

[38] "What the New Tariff Means on Isle Vegetables," *Isle of Pines Post*, July 1, 1930.

greater attention it received after World War I illustrated settlers' attempt to adapt to prevailing economic conditions and maintain a place on the Isle.

Transportation

Since their arrival, settlers lamented the poor condition of roads and ports. Improvements undertaken during the U.S.-run provisional government of 1906–9 fell into disrepair without sustained upkeep that Havana officials were slow to address – a factor that annexationists frequently cited in their argument. Frederick Swetland Jr. wrote that roads "were commonly in such bad shape, so wash-boarded, it was torture to drive them in the cars of that day."[39] At times, settlers took it upon themselves to make improvements. Swetland recalled that his family often collaborated with another U.S. family to maintain roads in the San Francisco tract. The Havana-based *Cuba News* in 1914 reported that "All the road work now being done on the Isle of Pines is by the American residents.... There have been many miles of roads built in the Isle of Pines this way, much more than the government has built, and certainly at much less expense than that the government paid for the roads it had built here."[40] This account suggested that settlers' repair work was of a higher caliber than anything the Cuban government could muster. Regardless of the quality of their work, their actions not only underscored settlers' emphasis on the importance of private initiative but also revealed an impatience to make improvements.

The quest for road repairs aligned Americans and *pineros*. The Isle's *ayuntamiento* typically had little money to undertake repairs and was dependent on Havana to pay for them. The *Isle of Pines Appeal* in 1924 recognized this common concern amid the din of the annexationist clamor: "That the natives (Pineros) are not absorbing the prejudices of certain Cuban officials is evidenced by their willingness to join with the Americans and aid in repairing the much neglected highways and bridges."[41] In the late 1920s, local administrators, including *alcalde* Ramon Llorca Soto, made numerous appeals to Havana. After nearly two years of lobbying by Llorca Soto, the Isle of Pines Chamber of Commerce, and women's social clubs, the Gerardo Machado administration approved

---

[39] Swetland, *Isle of Pines*, 43–4.
[40] "Shipping Fruit from Isle of Pines," *Cuba News*, August 29, 1914.
[41] "As 'Twas and Will be Again on Isle Unless," *Isle of Pines Appeal*, July 5, 1924.

substantial road repairs that mollified – temporarily, at least – Americans and *pineros*.[42]

Yet frustration remained for many Americans with the process of merely getting to the Isle. By the 1920s, little about the voyage from the United States had changed. Raymond H. Swetland had grown tired of it. "The Swetlands have given up going to the Isle of Pines simply because they will not subject themselves to the hardships of the sort of transportation available and many, many others have done likewise," he wrote in 1923. "If a boat or boats of ample capacity leaving and arriving at decent hours had been placed on the run, the Isle of Pines people would not find themselves in the position they are now in. You cannot build up a country until you first build up the means of getting to it."[43]

Settlers' frustration with the Isle's transportation networks was about more than just personal inconvenience. These issues put their enterprises at risk. Getting their produce to U.S. markets was a time-consuming and expensive process, made more difficult by shoddy roads and inconsistent shipping. They argued that given the public benefit provided by improved infrastructure and transportation, the Cuban government should have done more to ameliorate those concerns. But while Cuba's sovereignty was still an open diplomatic question and the slim chance remained that the United States might annex the Isle, the Cuban government had little incentive to bow to settlers' demands.

In terms of shipping, some private companies stepped in to fill the void but found little success. The Isle of Pines Transportation and Supply Company, known as the Isle Line, briefly operated a schooner between Nueva Gerona and Mobile, Alabama, beginning in 1909. But the enterprise did not last long, presumably because of minimal traffic. In August 1920, another company began the Tampa–Isle of Pines Line, ushering direct service to and from Florida. The line made two trips a month from Nueva Gerona, primarily for cargo. One report suggested that another company was looking to establish direct service to and from New York.[44] But the Tampa line did not last long and the New York line apparently foundered. Forman was vague as to the reasons for their failures. "The lack of success, in my opinion, has been chiefly due to the bad judgment or bad management of the American shipping concerns,"

[42] For letters of appeal to the Machado administration, see Secretaria de la Presidencia, 1902–1958, Legajo 39, Expediente 20, ANC.

[43] Raymond H. Swetland to Isle of Pines United Land Companies, September 26, 1923, SFA.

[44] Annual Report on Commerce and Industries for 1920, May 6, 1921, Nueva Gerona – Isle of Pines, Cuba, Vol. 25, Correspondence, 1921 – Part II, Record Group 84, NARA.

he wrote in 1924.⁴⁵ Whether he was referring to issues of traffic, costs, or other concerns is unclear. Albert Swetland had his own theory: too much competition among shipping lines minimized traffic that made it unprofitable to operate. The *Isle of Pines Appeal* reported in 1921 that Swetland had warned "against trying to get more than one outline line to stop here. He sighted [*sic*] our experience a few years ago when several lines were bidding for the business with the result that the shipments were so divided up that no one of them had business enough to make the stop pay, so we lost them all."⁴⁶ It apparently happened again in the early 1920s, when after a brief spike in traffic, the Tampa line suddenly stopped. As a result, settlers' frustrations with transportation continued.

Practices

Many settlers blamed external factors – tariffs, lack of assistance from the U.S. and Cuban governments, hurricanes – for undermining their enterprises. But a deeper examination reveals that many did themselves no favors, out of ignorance or arrogance, with the way they conducted their businesses. These other factors were just as significant, if not more so, than those settlers cited.

Despite settlers' reliance on agriculture as a commercial enterprise, many did not grow food for themselves. They were not self-sufficient and, as a result, they depended on imports for sustenance. Factoring in the cost of shipping for goods from the United States or mainland Cuba, this was an expensive lifestyle. Irene A. Wright recognized this trend early in American settlement. In 1910, she noted that settlers "devoted themselves to citrus fruit culture, to the very detrimental neglect of everything else.... In their enthusiasm over [citrus], the Americans have sometimes failed to provide themselves with food, or their draft animals with feed."⁴⁷ Moreover, many of the first settlers did not grow their own vegetables; it did not become a commercial phenomenon until the late 1910s. Wright was astonished at the "impractical spirit of some settlers in the Isle of Pines, who, with every natural condition inviting them to raise vegetables still import them, canned, at very heavy expense, for their own consumption; who, needing ready money, fail to see in vegetable gardens at least

⁴⁵ Trade Promotion Work at Nueva Gerona, Isle of Pines, Cuba, January 3, 1924, Nueva Gerona – Isle of Pines, Cuba, Vol. 34, Correspondence, 1924 – Part II, Record Group 84, NARA.

⁴⁶ "Atlantic Fruit Line Promises Direct Service," *Isle of Pines Appeal*, March 19, 1921.

⁴⁷ Irene A. Wright, *Isle of Pines* (Beverly, MA: Beverly Printing Company, 1910), 65.

a means of saving if not of actual gain."[48] By the end of the decade, little had changed as settlers continued to engage in monoculture. Farmers still narrowly focused on commercial growing rather than self-sufficiency and thus relied on imported foodstuffs. As U.S. consul William Bardel critically noted in 1919, "This necessitated the buying of many articles at high prices which they could have raised on their own farms for almost nothing. Some of the farmers here in this respect have become wiser, others will have to follow if they wish to live more comfortably."[49] Considering that many settlers were returning to the United States, it was a lesson that went largely unheeded.

Settlers' lack of cooperation and foresight also undermined the long-term viability of their enterprises. U.S. consuls were especially critical of settlers in this regard. Forman argued that U.S. settlements would have been strengthened if they were more concentrated, particularly near a suitable port, rather than diffused across the Isle. Centralization, he argued, would have strengthened institutions and put more pressure on the local government to maintain roads and infrastructure. Smaller U.S. settlements made it more difficult for businesses and communities to flourish, he wrote. Separation meant that "the cost of local transportation is increased, the opportunities for social life are diminished, and the settler is more liable to become dissatisfied and discouraged – the settler's wife especially so."[50] Forman continued that Isle businesses also suffered because of insufficient marketing, which he called the "chief defect" in the Isle's economy. Until Isle businesses could promote their products collectively like those from Florida and California, their profit margins would continue to shrink in comparison. Forman's observations implied that the social and business community of settlers lacked cohesion.

Like Forman, Sheridan Talbott maintained that the devastation wrought by the 1926 hurricane presented settlers an opportunity to operate more cooperatively. He was especially critical of "prominent individuals ... who are apparently unwilling to sacrifice self-interest in any degree for the general good of the community but engage in continuous wrangling and destructive criticism of any suggestion of cooperation or plan for the betterment of the whole people."[51] Although Talbott did

[48] Ibid., 80.

[49] Annual Report on Commerce and Industries for 1918, April 22, 1919, Nueva Gerona – Isle of Pines, Cuba, Vol. 18, Correspondence, 1919 – Part I, Record Group 84, NARA.

[50] Economic Conditions in the Isle of Pines, March 19, 1923, Nueva Gerona – Isle of Pines, Cuba, Vol. 32, Correspondence, 1923 – Part II, Record Group 84, NARA.

[51] Talbott Report of Hurricane of October 19–20, 1926, November 19, 1926, Nueva Gerona – Isle of Pines, Cuba, Vol. 41, Storm, 1926 – Part I, Record Group 84, NARA.

not offer specific examples of failed cooperation, his comments suggest that settlers were foolishly following the ethos of the rugged individual. Instead of working in concert with one another – in terms of coordinating settlements, lobbying the Cuban government to improve the Isle's infrastructure, or patronizing one direct carrier to the United States – most entrepreneurs operated independently. Perhaps not coincidentally, many of their businesses failed. This development also suggests that settlers did not heed to a significant extent the cooperative mantra espoused in landholding company promotions.

When it came to citrus, many growers failed due to sheer ignorance. Although many settlers were farmers by trade, others came from professional backgrounds and had done little farming before coming to the Isle. Few had experience in growing citrus, particularly among the first generation of settlers who mostly hailed from the U.S. Northeast and Midwest where subtropical crops were not grown. Many of them, Dan Smith said, "had been in some other business in the States and they believed they could make money on their citrus fruit but they didn't know the first thing about it."[52] Edith Sundstrom recalled that her father, Carl Larson, was one such settler. She said he had failed to grow cucumbers and eggplants on a commercial scale before he later managed to make a living as a citrus grove manager – though not without hard work. "My father was convinced he would make his fortune and spend his time sitting on the porch smoking big, fat cigars," she said. "First, he knew nothing about farming. And then he bought a pig in a poke."[53] Forman concurred with such observations. Among settlers who had been middle-class professionals or men of means, he wrote, "quite probably the majority were not adapted for the life of a farmer."[54] Instead, many of the wealthy large grove owners contracted out the work. Many more, however, tried and failed to become citrus farmers because they thought it was the fastest way to wealth. Frederick Swetland Jr. surmised that these failed citrus growers fell victim to ignorance of citrus and unrealistic expectations. He conceded that landholding companies deserved some of the blame for inflating expectations, but insisted that "it wasn't misrepresented maliciously, it was misrepresented simply for lack of understanding."[55]

---

[52] Irma and Dan Smith interview with Frederick Swetland Jr., May 28, 1969, tape 11, 3, SFA.

[53] Quoted in Elinor Burkett, "The Last American," *Miami Herald*, September 4, 1988.

[54] Economic Conditions in the Isle of Pines, March 19, 1923, Nueva Gerona – Isle of Pines, Cuba, Vol. 32, Correspondence, 1923 – Part II, Record Group 84, NARA.

[55] Frederick Swetland Jr. in Ernest Gruppe interview, June 21, 1971, tape 20, 3, SFA.

Not every settler saw it that way. Some believed that landholding company executives took advantage of them by overpromising what the Isle had to offer, and they argued so in the U.S. press. One anonymous writer in the *New York Times* compared land deals on the Isle to similar practices in Florida whereby "Americans of small means and less discretion have been sadly swindled."[56] A. J. Craig wrote to *The Oregonian* to blame "land speculators" for dishonestly promoting the Isle as a tropical paradise that compelled Americans to buy land sight unseen. "Hundreds of American families have been ruined, both financially and physically by going to the island," he lamented.[57]

Landholding companies struggled as well. Although they had bought up virtually every large tract during the first decade of the twentieth century, by the 1940s they had only resold an estimated 60 percent of their holdings.[58] The Isle of Pines Investment Company and the Andorra Realty Company, for example, struggled to cover their initial investments. In fact, the Swetland-run Isle of Pines Investment Company ceased keeping detailed financial records for more than twenty years simply because it "was not doing any business."[59] No sources precisely indicate how the others fared, though one example suggests all did not go well. Executives in the early 1920s considered consolidating their large holdings under one umbrella corporation – mostly as a power play against the Cuban government and to compel annexation to the United States – but those negotiations proved fruitless.[60] Within two decades, most of the U.S.-based landholding companies had shuttered. The Isle of Pines Company was one of the last when it closed in 1950 after Edward J. Pearcy sold the company's remaining property to Cuban buyers for between $1 and $5 an acre.[61] That price was roughly the market rate for undeveloped property on the Isle – a far cry from the $40 to $50 that companies charged almost a half-century earlier.

---

[56] A Recent Visitor to Cuba, "Status of the Isle of Pines," *New York Times*, August 20, 1916.

[57] "Place Not Fit for White Men," *The Oregonian*, June 19, 1914.

[58] The Isle of Pines, Cuba, report by LaRue Lutkins, May 14, 1944, Nueva Gerona – Isle of Pines, Cuba, Vol. 55, Correspondence, 1943 (File No. 812–891), 1944 (File No. 000-123), Record Group 84, NARA.

[59] Raymond H. Swetland to David Swetland, October 15, 1948, SFA.

[60] Clement J. Wall to Robert I. Wall, July 24, 1922, SFA. Negotiations among landholding company executives, including the Swetland family, continued for more than a year and a half before apparently falling through around February 1924 when correspondence suddenly ended.

[61] A. B. Kelm to R. S. Alfonso, U.S. vice consul, Havana, February 11, 1950, Fondo: A. B. Kelm, Legajo 4, Expediente 34, AHM.

Renewing Old Practices

The flight of U.S. capital in the 1920s and 1930s compelled Cubans to reengage in activities with which the Isle had been associated under Spain. One of these was the creation of a new prison: the Presidio Modelo. Construction of this panopticon-style facility a few miles east of Nueva Gerona began in February 1926. Its design was inspired by the ideas of English philosopher Jeremy Bentham and modeled after the Stateville Correctional Center near Joliet, Illinois. The prison was run by the Cuban government and relied on inmate labor for construction, maintenance, and sustenance (prisoners kept a farm for meat, poultry, food, and vegetables). When it was completed in October 1931, the prison had a capacity of 5,000 inmates.

Although the Presidio Modelo was designed to spur the local economy, some Cuban intellectuals maintained that it had the opposite effect. In a 1949 essay, Waldo Medina blamed the prison's construction for further discouraging already reluctant foreign investors and stymieing attempts to turn the Isle into a tourist haven.[62] Antonio Núñez Jiménez argued that the prison gave the Isle a bad name by reinforcing its colonial-era reputation as a haven for pirates and prisoners while stoking fear among *pineros*.[63] According to Bill Miller, an American citizen whose family lived on the Isle for three generations, the remaining U.S. settlers were convinced that the Cuban government built the prison as retribution against the American colony for their opposition to the Hay-Quesada treaty. Settlers, he said, "always felt that the reason they chose the island for the prison was to get even with the Americans."[64] While there is no evidence to suggest vengeance as a factor in the prison's construction, the Presidio Modelo would come to make a significant imprint on the Isle. During World War II, part of it was used to house Japanese, German, and Italian nationals in internment camps similar to those in the United States. In the mid-1950s, the prison would hold Fidel and Raúl Castro after their failed attack on the Moncada Barracks. It closed in 1967 yet remains standing – somewhat ironically – as a tourist attraction.[65]

---

[62] Waldo Medina, "Isla Profanada," in *Aquí, Isla de Pinos* (La Habana: Instituto Nacional de la Reforma Agraria, 1961), 65–6.

[63] Antonio Núñez Jiménez, *Autobiografía de Isla de Pinos* (La Habana: 1949), 22.

[64] Bill Miller interview with author, August 9, 2014.

[65] Jane McManus, *Cuba's Island of Dreams: Voices from the Isle of Pines and Youth* (Gainesville: University Press of Florida, 2000), 50–1; Juan Colina la Rosa, et al. *Síntesis Histórica Municipal: Isla de la Juventud* (La Habana: El Abra, 2011), 100; "Cuba's Presidio Modelo," report by LaRue R. Lutkins, March 20, 1944, Nueva

Another way in which the Isle's denizens coped with the decline of the citrus industry was by reviving cattle-raising, which had been a staple during Spanish colonialism. During the colonial era, Spanish and Cuban *hacendados* commonly engaged in cattle-raising, reaching a peak of some 8,800 head in the late eighteenth century.[66] This work provided beef and dairy for themselves and for local markets. As suggested by landholding companies' depictions of this activity, though, Americans' attitudes remained ambivalent. On one hand, they portrayed cattle-raising as an ineffective use of the Isle's resources, suggesting that American ingenuity would maximize the Isle's untapped potential as an export-based economy. As the Isle of Pines Company asserted, cattle-raising was a key industry primarily because *pineros* had "a natural disinclination to do the necessary work incident to the cultivation of crops."[67] Not coincidentally, the cattle industry significantly declined during the first years of the U.S. presence.[68] On the other hand, when trying to assure American audiences that they would encounter a friendly and palatable local population, companies portrayed cattle-raising *hacendados* as exemplars of *pinero* society and pictures of gentility. The Cañada Land & Fruit Company claimed that the typical *pinero* "is very much of a gentleman and prefers not to do much manual labor, but enjoys riding around on horseback to look after his stock."[69]

By the early 1920s as U.S. settlers were fleeing in larger numbers, cattle-raising was making a comeback. Gregorio "Goyo" Hernández, a Cuban landowner from Nueva Gerona, had an estimated 400–500 head of cattle, said to be the largest collection on the Isle. Wealthy U.S. settlers who remained followed suit. Edward J. Pearcy had one of the largest herds, some 300 head of cattle in 1923.[70] Pearcy's activity, along with that of others including the Swetlands, portended a revival of the industry. The practice came back into vogue as a sign of one's wealth and gentility. One study estimated that by 1957 American and Cuban ranchers

---

Gerona – Isle of Pines, Cuba, Vol. 57, Correspondence, 1944 (File No. 813–892), Record Group 84, NARA.

[66] Wright, *Isle of Pines*, 26.

[67] Isle of Pines Company, "The Isle of Pines: Uncle Sam's Latest Acquisition of Territory" (New York, 1901), 13.

[68] Wright, *Isle of Pines*, 26. According to Wright, the number of cattle on the Isle plummeted to 4,018 in 1908, the lowest on record.

[69] Cañada Land & Fruit Company, "Isle of Pines: Land of Fruit and Flowers" (Marinette, WI, 1903), 20–1.

[70] "Cattle Raising," report by Charles Forman, July 30, 1923, Nueva Gerona – Isle of Pines, Cuba, Vol. 33, Correspondence, 1923 – Part III, Record Group 84, NARA.

owned 20,000 head of cattle between them, making livestock raising the Isle's third-largest industry behind citrus and vegetables.[71]

Hardscrabble Lives

After periods of trauma, such as the hurricanes of 1917 and 1926, Isle entrepreneurs enjoyed surges of productivity. Taking the Isle's main industry as a key indicator, grapefruit exports equaled or surpassed pre-hurricane levels within two or three years. But this recovery was mostly limited to the large landowners. Year-round settlers who depended on their small groves or businesses to live on the Isle did not experience the same resurgence. They faced tremendous financial difficulty when their enterprises failed. Many of these settlers had sold their possessions in the United States to pay for travel and start-up costs. By the mid-1920s, it became clear for most of them that their commercial endeavors would not pay off. Most settlers returned to the United States, willing to sell their land at a loss or abandon it altogether. Others could not even do that. With the onset of the Great Depression, land prices diminished and interest all but vanished. Frederick Swetland Jr. said these settlers "had no place to go and clung on, more weather-beaten each year."[72] Many of them died on the Isle, virtually destitute.

Impoverished settlers were evident well before the 1917 hurricane. Some were experiencing financial hardship even during the peak of U.S. settlement. For example, one unidentified family in Santa Barbara requested help from the American community to pay for passage back to the United States. According to U.S. consul Vervie P. Sutherland, this family of nine was so poor that the local Ladies Economic Club had taken to making clothes for them because "the whole family are practically nude."[73] The father was a piano-tuner by trade and wanted to return to the United States to find work. Settlers petitioned the consulate on the family's behalf and raised $50 to pay for their return trip to the United States. The family secured passage at half price – $4.90 each for a second-class ticket to Tampa – thanks to the U.S. consulate. The episode revealed the difficult conditions for some settlers. Motivations for the U.S. community's assistance, however, are unclear. Some settlers may have wanted to remove a poor, working-class family from the community's midst. Others

[71] Winsberg, "Isle of Pines, Cuba," 135–6.

[72] Swetland, *Isle of Pines*, 37.

[73] Sutherland to Hugh S. Gibson, U.S. Charge d'Affaires, Havana, September 3, 1912, Nueva Gerona – Isle of Pines – Cuba, Vol. 10, Correspondence, 1912, Record Group 84, NARA.

may have simply been sympathetic to the family's plight. Regardless, it would not be the last such instance.

Settlers' exodus began in earnest shortly after the September 1917 hurricane. As the population declined, William Bardel surmised that "more than 90% would be only too glad to [leave] if they could, they eking out a scant living and having mostly to assume vocations unknown to them, many of which are below their stations in life." His remark is telling in light of his description of most settlers as "middle class, fairly well educated, intelligent and respectable." It suggests that these settlers found farming beneath them, perhaps made clear when its physical toll became so evident. Additionally, their failing enterprises took them below a standard of living that they expected to enjoy. Bardel predicted that "when the opportunity offers itself, most of these Americans will sell out their holdings and follow those who returned to the Unites States before them."[74]

That prospect, however, was not easy in light of plunging land values. Landholding companies sold real estate for up to $50 an acre during the first decade of the twentieth century, when most settlers made their purchases. By the mid-1920s, undeveloped land was going for less than half that price; in the 1940s, it dropped to $5 an acre.[75] This decline put settlers in a financial bind, unable to recoup their investments. As a result, many of them simply could not afford to return to the United States.

The predicament posed a dilemma to some naturalized U.S. citizens who risked losing their American citizenship because of their lengthy absences from the United States. In a 1921 affidavit to explain his protracted foreign residence, Friedrich W. Stiegele, a native of Germany who lived in Akron, Ohio, before settling in McKinley in 1907, said that "Property here has decreased in value since I bought and could not be sold except at a sacrifice. I am not a rich man, and cannot afford to stand the loss of selling and moving to the United States."[76] Another German native and naturalized U.S. citizen, Henry Windeler, explained that he faced a similar dilemma. He went to Santa Barbara in 1909 from Brooklyn, New York, with his wife and five children and "invested all my money in

[74] Bardel to Wilbur Carr, December 5, 1918, 1910–29 Central Decimal File, General Records of the Department of State Relating to the Internal Affairs of Cuba, NARA Microcopy 488, Roll 27, File 837.014P/153.

[75] Talbott to Herbert Underwood, February 3, 1926, Nueva Gerona – Isle of Pines, Cuba, Vol. 44, Correspondence, 1926 – Part V, Record Group 84, NARA; LaRue Lutkins to Emma Smith, April 26, 1943, Nueva Gerona – Isle of Pines, Cuba, Vol. 55, Correspondence, 1943 (File No. 812-891), 1944 (File No. 000-123), Record Group 84, NARA.

[76] Affidavit of Fred W. Stiegele, Nueva Gerona – Isle of Pines, Cuba, Vol. 24, Correspondence, 1921 – Part I, Record Group 84, NARA.

land here." As of 1925, he said, "the value of my property is $6,000 but it cannot be sold under present conditions except at a great sacrifice. I have no income except from my property here."[77] Other naturalized citizens in the same situation cited financial hardship or health issues to explain their absences. Most were allowed to keep their U.S. citizenship, including Stiegele, who died on the Isle in 1934 and was buried at the American Cemetery in Columbia.

Axel Gunnar Sundstrom, Edith's brother-in-law, was in a similar quandary in the 1930s. His tale encapsulated the promise and pitfalls of making a living on the Isle of Pines. A native of Sweden, Sundstrom lived in Fitchburg, Massachusetts, for nine years working at a local steel mill. After suffering an eye injury on the job, he soon thereafter contracted pneumonia and moved to the Isle in 1917 hoping to improve his health. Once there, he began growing his own vegetables for export while working in local citrus groves to make ends meet. But physical ailments limited such work. He later helped his son, Axel Sundstrom Jr., operate a general store and gas station in Nueva Gerona. Business, however, remained slow as Americans left the Isle and the Great Depression took hold. Despite numerous attempts to find work back in the United States, Sundstrom seemed resigned to staying on the Isle.[78] After World War II, the Sundstroms sold their nearly bankrupt gas station to Ramon Llorca Soto, the former *alcalde*, who had worked as an accountant for them.[79]

Settlers of advanced age had the most difficulty adjusting to declining financial fortunes. Hart Crane took a particular interest in the plight of Harry and Helen Jones. The elderly couple, who since 1902 had operated an arboretum and tourist attraction called "Jones' Jungle," found themselves in dire financial straits by the mid-1920s. According to Crane, the couple risked losing their property to the Cuban government – he did not explain why – and would get no more than $5 an acre for it. "Furthermore, they are both quite penniless, and live entirely on what he can gather as a taxi-driver and the little fee they charge for visiting the jungle," Crane wrote. "But Jones is no worse off than others – in many ways. He is only too old to ever hope to take hold anywhere else again."[80]

[77] Affidavit of Henry Windeler, Nueva Gerona – Isle of Pines, Cuba, Vol. 37, Correspondence, 1925 – Part I, Record Group 84, NARA.

[78] A. B. Kelm to George F. Scherer, American Vice Consul, Havana, April 5, 1938, Fondo: A. B. Kelm, Legajo 10, Expediente 91, AHM.

[79] Saul Llorca, e-mail message to author, August 23, 2014.

[80] Hart Crane to Grace Hart Crane, May 14, 1926, *The Letters of Hart Crane, 1916–1932*, Brom Weber ed., (New York: Hermitage House, 1952), 253.

The Joneses managed to get by over the next few years until Harry died of "senility" at age seventy-nine in 1938. Helen then sold some of the couple's property and lived off roughly $25 a month until she died at age eighty-five in a 1960 house fire.[81]

Some settlers were determined not to suffer the same fate as the Joneses. Ernest Gruppe, who lived in Santa Fe with his wife and two children, sold his belongings in 1925 shortly after the U.S. Senate ratified the Hay-Quesada treaty and moved to Florida to start anew. "I remember my remark to [*Isle of Pines Appeal* publisher A. E.] Willis was that as far as the Isle of Pines was concerned I would rather get out when I was 40 years old and start over than wait until it was impossible or impractical," he said.[82] Many other settlers at the time left for Florida as well. According to U.S. consul Charles Forman, Florida was a popular destination for Americans on the Isle because it was "reported to be making rapid strides in population and wealth" in much the same way the Isle had been depicted some twenty years earlier.[83] Much like the Isle, though, Florida's land boom also experienced a bust as its real estate industry infamously collapsed in the mid-1920s as a result of overspeculation and fraud.[84]

Many small landowners who could not afford to leave depended on financial assistance from family members in the United States or from their fellow settlers. Adolph B. Kelm, one of the increasingly few Americans who could afford to live comfortably thanks to his steady work with the Isle of Pines Steamship Company, said that many of the struggling settlers were reluctant to ask for help. "These old folks are of the pioneer type who prefer to suffer hardships rather than ask for direct help," he wrote. "How some of them get along is more than I can explain."[85] Some settlers

[81] Report on Death of Harry Jones, April 13, 1938, Fondo: A. B. Kelm, Legajo 8, Expediente 79, AHM; Kelm to George Moore, August 13, 1946, Fondo: A. B. Kelm, Legajo 8, Expediente 79, AHM; Report of Death of Helen Rodman Jones, February 19, 1960, Fondo: A. B. Kelm, Legajo 8, Expediente 79, AHM. The circumstances of the fire that killed Helen Jones were not resolved. Some residents suspected foul play by Presidio Modelo escapees in search of money.

[82] Ernest Gruppe interview, June 21, 1971, tape 19, 1, SFA.

[83] Forman to Rumsey Pump Company, May 7, 1925, Nueva Gerona – Isle of Pines, Cuba, Vol. 40, Correspondence, 1925 – Part IV, Record Group 84, NARA.

[84] Homer B. Vanderblue, "The Florida Land Boom," *Journal of Land and Public Utility Economics* 3 (May 1927): 113–31; Samuel Proctor, "Prelude to the New Florida, 1877–1919" in *The New History of Florida*, Michael Gannon ed. (Gainesville: University Press of Florida, 1996), 266–86.

[85] Kelm to George Moore, Anglo-American Association, Havana, March 26, 1936, Fondo: A. B. Kelm, Legajo 8, Expediente 70, AHM.

simply could not get by – or chose not to. In one of the few documented cases of suicide, William Henry Gregg was found in his home in McKinley in April 1921 dead from a self-inflicted gunshot wound. A seventy-four-year-old widower, Gregg had no family on the Isle, where he had lived for nearly a decade. He owned roughly thirty acres in two tracts and had just $37 in his personal bank account when he died.[86] Although there was no sign of a suicide note, the circumstances suggest his financial difficulties, perhaps his loneliness, contributed to the decision to take his own life.

For many of the settlers who remained on the Isle, circumstances improved little. After the U.S. consulate in Nueva Gerona closed, Kelm was left with the grim task of updating the U.S. embassy in Havana about the state of the American community, including settlers' deaths. A sample of these bulletins reveals that many of them faced significant financial hardships in their last years:

- Frank Ludlum, 80: "During his last few years he was in exceedingly poor financial circumstances and was practically supported by the kindness of his friends and neighbors."[87]
- August Swanson, 71: Left no estate and "was entirely alone in the world."[88]
- George Ward, 92: Died "entirely destitute. Burial arrangements were taken care of by old friends and neighbors."[89]
- Emma Rose Westow, 79: Left small estate that "will barely cover the actual funeral costs."[90]
- Geraldine Lillian Blauvelt, 38: At time of death from tuberculosis, "was destitute."[91]
- Milton Pennock, 87: "He lived in very humble circumstances and was destitute at the time of his passing."[92]

---

[86] Report of Death of American Citizen, April 5, 1921, Nueva Gerona – Isle of Pines, Cuba, Vol. 25, Correspondence, 1921 – Part II, Record Group 84, NARA.

[87] Report on Death of Frank Ludlum, July 29, 1936, Fondo: A. B. Kelm, Legajo 8, Expediente 68, AHM.

[88] Report on Death of August Swanson, November 13, 1938, Fondo: A. B. Kelm, Legajo 8, Expediente 76, AHM.

[89] Report on Death of George Ward, February 14, 1939, Fondo: A. B. Kelm, Legajo 8, Expediente 73, AHM.

[90] Report on Death of Emma Rose Westow, February 21, 1939, Fondo: A. B. Kelm, Legajo 8, Expediente 75, AHM.

[91] Report on Death of Geraldine Lillian Blauvelt, February 2, 1940, Fondo: A. B. Kelm, Legajo 8, Expediente 76, AHM.

[92] Report on Death of Milton Pennock, October 2, 1942, Fondo: A. B. Kelm, Legajo 8, Expediente 77, AHM.

- Louis Whiting, 89: Made the Isle his permanent home in 1917 "with ample finances, and for many years lived in comfortable circumstances. [After Hay-Quesada's ratification], his business and agricultural interests in this island took a turn for the worse and he gradually lost all of his capital until at the time of his passing he was almost entirely dependent upon others."[93]
- Sarah Helen Simpson, 87: "Deceased died destitute.... With the relinquishment of American interest in the island and the gradual decline of our investments, and advancing years, she lost everything."[94]
- Richard Schmidt, 87: "Died almost destitute" and could not afford to return to the United States.[95]

Kelm's reports not only illustrated the dire conditions in which many U.S. citizens found themselves, particularly among the elderly, but also underscored three important assumptions within the American community. First, his accounts frequently referred to deceased settlers as "pioneers." This reference revealed that the colonizing ethos that had inspired many U.S. citizens to come to the Isle remained in settlers' collective consciousness long after the Isle's sovereignty had been verified. Furthermore, the term "pioneer" validated the hardscrabble living conditions of the deceased. It suggested that they were the ones who had laid the foundations for the homes, farms, and institutions that remaining settlers enjoyed. Moreover, the term gave value and meaning to the poverty they endured, crediting them as important pillars of the American community.

Most reports of deceased U.S. citizens mentioned their burial in the American Cemetery in Columbia. In many cases, other settlers paid to bury the deceased who either did not have any other family on the Isle or were too poor to afford the expense out of their meager estates. Although this was not always an instance of charity – Kelm noted that settlers who paid for the burials attempted to get reimbursed from the family of the dead – it does illustrate that settlers deemed it important that Americans be buried with other Americans, rather than in public Cuban gravesites. This imperative suggests that national identity, of which race and class were intimately linked, continued as a powerful marker among Americans of

---

[93] Report on Death of Louis B. Whiting, February 9, 1951, Fondo: A. B. Kelm, Legajo 8, Expediente 74, AHM.

[94] Report on Death of Sarah Helen Simpson, May 28, 1951, Fondo: A. B. Kelm, Legajo 8, Expediente 81, AHM.

[95] Notice of Death of U.S. Citizen, September 18, 1957, Fondo: A. B. Kelm, Legajo 9, Expediente 83, AHM.

the 1930s and 1940s, a time when their numbers dwindled. Their resistance to sharing cemeteries with *pineros* implied that Americans of this era – many of whom were among the first generation of settlers – still were not comfortable with the idea of fully integrating with the native population.

Last, Kelm's reports reveal a lingering antipathy to the Hay-Quesada treaty years after its ratification. Kelm often referred to the treaty's approval as the turning point in settlers' fortunes, even though the treaty merely affirmed existing conditions. Settlers, however, felt abandoned by the U.S. government. Some expressed a sense of betrayal that their efforts to carry the flag abroad were not supported by policymakers back home.

They apparently took their disappointment out on the closest government representative they could find, the U.S. consul. L. J. Keena, the U.S. consul general in Havana, recommended to the State Department in January 1928 that the consulate in Nueva Gerona be closed because the "local American Colony is composed of people ... who feel that their interests were much jeopardized by the signing of the treaty, and they take a certain satisfaction in venting their spite on the resident American official."[96] The consulate ceased operations on June 30, 1929.[97]

The closing of the U.S. consulate was just one of many signs of Americans' waning presence. American communities also declined and nearly disappeared during the 1930s and 1940s. Towns that once had large concentrations of settlers, including Santa Barbara, Columbia, McKinley, and Los Indios, bore little resemblance to their peaks decades earlier. As one U.S. consul wrote, these "formerly thriving towns boasting an established community life of their own, are now no more than small settlements with one or two English-speaking families living in the vicinity.... [D]istricts where American colonization projects once flourished, are now virtually deserted sites."[98] After World War II, large landowners began leaving as well. Edward J. Pearcy in 1950 not only sold off the Isle of Pines Company's remaining land, but he also disposed of his home and some 1,000 acres of personal property for a reported

---

[96] Keena to Secretary of State, January 4, 1928, Nueva Gerona – Isle of Pines, Cuba, Vol. 49, Correspondence, 1928 – Part I, Record Group 84, NARA.

[97] The consulate reopened from 1942 to 1944. Its primary purpose was to keep tabs on Japanese and German nationals.

[98] Isle of Pines, Cuba, report by LaRue Lutkins, May 14, 1944, Nueva Gerona – Isle of Pines, Cuba, Vol. 55, Correspondence, 1943 (File No. 812–891), 1944 (File No. 000-123), Record Group 84, NARA.

$20,000 and moved back to the United States.[99] A year earlier, another large landowner, August C. Kopf, sold his property to Cuban investors. Since 1910, he had been a fixture on the Isle as one of the few successful citrus exporters. But he, too, returned north. As Kelm noted, "another one of the better American plantations will be taken out of the American column. I am sorry to say that slowly but surely the American colony is declining."[100]

In an attempt to maintain their familiar customs in this post–Hay-Quesada era, U.S. settlers made outreach to other foreign nationals, particularly white, English-speaking migrants from Canada and Europe to join the community of Americans. The *Isle of Pines Post* opined that Canadians and Europeans, in particular, were considered among the "American" community because "they speak our language and 'belong.'"[101] Their inclusion was assumed, as evident in one advertisement for a dance: "Don't forget that all white English Speaking Colonists of the Isle of Pines are automatically invited to the Armistice Dance on the evening of November 10th.... Invitations will only be sent to Cuban Officials and members of the Cuban Colony so if you are a 'Limey,' 'Yank,' 'Squarehead,' 'Jerry,' or 'Canuck' don't be formal – Crank up 'Lizzie' and bring the family, and that's that."[102] By mid-century, the term "American" often was used to refer to any white English speaker, regardless of national origin. For example, one of the Isle's most notable foreign-born residents in the post–Hay-Quesada era, Margaret "Peggy" Rice, was known locally as "*la americana*" – even though she was a native of England who had come to the Isle via Canada in 1931.[103]

This expansion of the term "American" illustrated three important dynamics. First, it showed the persistence of U.S. influence, at least as a brand, even after most settlers returned to the United States. Second, it

---

[99] A. B. Kelm to Julia Larson, May 30, 1950, Fondo: A. B. Kelm, Legajo 4, Expediente 36, AHM.

[100] A. B. Kelm to Julia Larson, November 11, 1949, Fondo: A. B. Kelm, Legajo 4, Expediente 35, AHM.

[101] "New Census Gives Isle of Pines a Population of 9,454," *Isle of Pines Post*, November 26, 1931.

[102] "An Invitation," *Isle of Pines Post*, November 1, 1928. The slang terms referred to people from Britain, the United States, Scandinavia, Germany, and Canada, respectively.

[103] "Peggy, 'la americana,'" Guillermo Maquintoche Vázquez in Margaret Peggy Rice, *Mi Vida Hasta Aquí: Las Memorias del Margaret Peggy Rice*, translated by Guillermo Maquintoche (Nueva Gerona: Ediciones El Abra, 2009), i–vi; McManus, *Cuba's Island of Dreams*, 60–1.

illustrated the malleability of identity particularly as political, economic, and social conditions in the 1930s and 1940s allowed for other foreign nationals to be considered "Americans" when that would not have been the case in the early twentieth century. Third, it demonstrated U.S. settlers' resolve to maintain a foothold on the Isle even after it became clear that annexation was no longer an option.

The steady decline of the American community was not the denouement U.S. settlers envisaged when they came to the Isle of Pines at the dawn of the twentieth century. Many had assumed that as long as they could effectively exploit the Isle's natural resources, they would be able to afford a comfortable lifestyle in their new surroundings. Although immediate success was not likely, with a little patience and hard work, groves would come into bearing and the profits would accumulate. In time, their commercial success would allow them to retire to a life of leisure. This plan, however, overlooked many important factors. It presumed a deep knowledge of citrus farming, sufficient start-up capital, public infrastructure improvements, the elimination of tariffs, and safety from natural disasters. These factors ended up overwhelming most Americans' commercial endeavors, which, in turn, eroded the U.S. community.

The decline of American commercial activity also had a deep impact on local workers. One study has argued that the departure of settlers led to a period of economic stagnation on the Isle, particularly when it came to agricultural production.[104] *Pineros* and foreign nationals had come to depend on American farm and business owners for employment. When settlers left, they lost their jobs. But the American exodus produced one benefit: many locals took over lands settlers had abandoned. In some cases, they assumed control over the property of their former employers who had died.[105] In other instances, locals used land on which Americans had either never lived, paid taxes, or acquired title from the Cuban government. Regardless of the circumstance, the phenomenon of abandoned property allowed for many *pineros* and *caimaneros* to make their own living off the land. By 1945, an estimated 40 percent of farms were run by squatters.[106]

---

[104] Academia de Ciencias de Cuba, "Serie Isla de Pinos No. 23: Latifundismo y Especulación," Delfín Rodríguez, et al., eds. (La Habana, 1968), 9.

[105] McManus chronicles two of these examples in *Cuba's Island of Dreams*, 52–5.

[106] Winsberg, "Isle of Pines, Cuba," 105–6.

The presence of Americans on the Isle of Pines, however, endured. The few studies that address U.S. settlement generally presume that the U.S. community effectively disappeared after the Hay-Quesada treaty's ratification and the hurricane of October 1926.[107] Indeed, records show that fewer than 300 Americans remained on the Isle during the 1930s and probably even fewer during the 1940s. But the Isle would enjoy a revival in the 1950s, spearheaded by large investors in Cuba and the United States who looked once again to tap its potential as a resort location. This development spurred a new generation of Americans to come to the Isle, many of whom made it their home. Unlike the turn-of-the-century settlers who explicitly sought to maintain their American way of life, settlers of mid-century demonstrated a greater willingness to integrate with the Isle's multiethnic and multinational population. The 1950s saw a great deal more cooperation among Americans and *pineros* in commercial and social institutions. This interaction had such an effect that by the time of the Cuban Revolution in 1959, many Americans considered themselves *pineros* as well.

---

[107] Carmen Diana Deere, "Here Come the Yankees! The Rise and Decline of United States Colonies in Cuba, 1898–1930," *Hispanic American Historical Review* 78 (November 1998): 757; Louis A. Pérez Jr., *Cuba and the United States: Ties of Singular Intimacy*, 2nd ed. (Athens: University of Georgia Press, 1997), 126; Julio Antonio Avello, "The Isle of Pines as a Factor in United States–Cuban Relations" (MA thesis, Southern Illinois University, 1969), 94.

7

"A Happy Society"

On any given Saturday during the mid-twentieth century, hundreds – if not thousands – of residents on the Isle of Pines came together in Nueva Gerona. It was a day for running errands, picking up supplies, and socializing. Travel writer Sydney A. Clark in 1936 described a typical Saturday in Nueva Gerona as a "strange paradoxical picture of Tennessee-in-Cuba" with a bustle of vendors, activities, and personalities.[1] William Stimson, living on the Isle with his mother and siblings as a young boy in the late 1950s, reflected that on Saturdays he encountered "the most wondrous array of aromas and smells and sounds.... Vendors with little roadside carts were sizzling and cooking and frying things and selling them. In every doorway there was a store or a cafe. The array of goods for sale was nothing short of incredible. It was a delight to the senses."[2] Little League baseball was also a fixture of these weekly gatherings. Eli Swetland, son of Frederick Swetland Jr., would often play in front of local spectators while his parents took care of errands. He recalled the competition of mostly Spanish-speaking Cuban peers as "fierce" but enjoyable.[3]

Most remarkable about these mid-century Saturday gatherings, at least in comparison to social life in the early twentieth century, was their broad, multinational participation. In addition to Cubans and Americans was a plethora of other foreign nationals, including migrants from the Cayman Islands, Jamaica, England, Canada, Germany, Hungary, Sweden,

[1] Sydney A. Clark, *Cuban Tapestry* (New York: National Travel Club, 1936), 148–9.
[2] William Stimson, "The Isle of Pines, Cuba – Thirty-Five Years Later," *Tropic* (Sunday Magazine of the *Miami Herald*), August 3, 1997. www.billstimson.com/writing/the_isle_of_pines_cuba.htm (accessed May 11, 2016).
[3] Eli Swetland interview with author, July 10, 2009.

Japan, and China. With the annexation question long since resolved and most settlers having already returned to the United States, Americans were no longer the Isle's most conspicuous foreign presence, just one of many. Nor were they as self-isolated as they were a half-century earlier. This era saw U.S. citizens, albeit a smaller population than they had been before, much more deeply integrated into the broader Isle community. Such an ethos was evident in the Little League games. In previous decades, sporting competitions would usually pit Americans and Cubans *against* each other with national bragging rights on the line.[4] In the 1950s, they tended to play on the same team. "It was just such a wonderful life that we had," Irma Smith, who spent much of her life on the Isle, said. "You associated with everybody. We were all friends. It didn't matter what relation you were, what your financial means were or what your background was in any way."[5]

This transition took place as a new generation of Americans arrived. In contrast to the pioneers of the turn of the century, these more recent arrivals – who came as tourists, missionaries, retirees, and teachers – showed a greater willingness and desire to engage *pineros* in ways beyond the hierarchical structure of employer and employee. Many of them were bilingual and more likely than their early-century predecessors to interact with the local population as classmates, patrons, and friends. This change was not sudden or universal among all Americans and there were limitations to this accommodating ethic. Nevertheless, the tenor of relations among the Isle's inhabitants had clearly changed between the start of the century and the close of the 1950s.

This détente between Americans and *pineros* reveals important nuances to U.S. influence in Cuba in the years before the Cuban Revolution. Although indeed pervasive, U.S. capital and cultural norms were not all-encompassing. The U.S. presence was not preponderant, nor totally unwelcome. In fact, Cuban policymakers and entrepreneurs cultivated U.S. capital by encouraging Americans to come back to the Isle as tourists and investors. To that end, Cuban President Fulgencio Batista in 1955 made the Isle a free port (*zona franca*) that eliminated duties on imports there. Culturally, *pineros* valued certain U.S. lifestyles, as evidenced by

---

[4] For examples of various sporting competitions, see "McKinley Items," *McKinley Herald*, November 1908; "Yankee Basket Ball Team Beats Cubans," *Isle of Pines Appeal*, August 30, 1924; "American Central School Defeats Cuban Stars, 8–6," *Isle of Pines Post*, April 5, 1929.
[5] Irma and Dan Smith interview with Frederick Swetland Jr., May 28, 1969, tape 11, 5, SFA.

the fact that they increasingly sent their children to the American Central School. The U.S. community, which had struggled for years to keep the school open, depended on this influx of Cuban students who would come to constitute the majority of those enrolled. The school, then, was an important space that reflected changing social conditions. Meanwhile, institutions once dominated by Americans, like the Santa Fe Chapter of the Royal Arch Masons, became more multinational with members from the United States, Cuba, and European countries.[6] By the same token, it was more common to see Cuban clubs like the Sociedad Popular Pinera host Americans as guests, rather than the other way around as it had been a half-century earlier. By the late 1950s, relations between Americans and *pineros* displayed little overt animosity.

This friendly mood stood in stark contrast to the growing sense of anti-Americanism in mainland Cuba, particularly in Havana. U.S. government support of the repressive and unpopular Batista regime as well as the proliferation of vice that catered to tourists sparked a popular backlash against the United States that Fidel Castro exploited in his rise to power. Historian Dennis Merrill has argued that by mid-century, "tourists had replaced the Platt Amendment as the most noxious U.S. presence in the everyday lives of Habaneros."[7] That discouraging sentiment, though, was seldom evident on the Isle. Two factors account for *habaneros'* and *pineros'* disparity in attitudes toward Americans. First, by virtue of geography, the Isle was relatively isolated from the political turmoil in Cuba. Batista's forces did not clash with Castro's 26th of July Movement there. The relative tranquility on the Isle went a long way toward fostering a more cooperative ethic among its denizens. Second, Americans had far less of a presence on the Isle than in Havana and the rest of mainland Cuba. By the end of the 1950s, only about 200 Americans lived on the Isle out of a total population of 11,000.[8] Out of the nearly 350,000 U.S. travelers who came to Cuba at the peak of the tourism boom, only a small fraction made their way to the Isle.[9] The U.S. presence, then, while still significant in terms of cultural and commercial influence, was a far

---

[6] For a list of members from 1915–50, see Libro Registro de Masones de la Logia Evangelista de Isla de Pinos, Compañías, Sociedades, y Establecimientos de Isla de Pinos, 1905-1970, Legajo 1, Libro 25, AHM.

[7] Dennis Merrill, *Negotiating Paradise: U.S. Tourism and Empire in Twentieth-Century Latin America* (Chapel Hill: University of North Carolina Press, 2009), 135.

[8] "Only 37 Remain," *Hartford Courant*, February 13, 1961; Julián y Oro, *Isla de Pinos: 10 Años de Trabajo* (Guantánamo: Juan Marinello, 1978), 16–17.

[9] Louis A. Pérez Jr., *On Becoming Cuban: Identity, Nationality, and Culture* (Chapel Hill: University of North Carolina Press, 1999), 167.

cry from what it had been at the turn of the century. Presumably, this decreased presence – and the fact that the sovereignty question had long since been resolved – made Americans more palatable to *pineros* and helps explain why the Isle was generally free of anti-American sentiment at the time of the Cuban Revolution.

U.S. Interest Revived

As the 1920s exodus of settlers made clear, the U.S. community on the Isle of Pines suffered significant decline from its early-century height. The Great Depression and World War II compounded this effect and put the U.S. presence on the verge of extinction. A 1931 Cuban census counted just 276 U.S. citizens out of a total population of 6,791 people on the Isle, though the *Isle of Pines Post* insisted that Americans were under-counted.[10] The number of settlers dwindled still further in the ensuing years. When the U.S. consulate reopened in Nueva Gerona in 1942, primarily to keep track of activity among Axis sympathizers, it registered only 166 U.S. citizens.[11]

Despite this decline, signs of U.S. influence remained evident. Diplomatically, the United States and Cuba remained close during World War II. Shortly after Japan's attack on Pearl Harbor in December 1941, Cuba affirmed its solidarity with the United States by declaring war on Japan, Germany, and Italy. In support of U.S. concerns about Axis spies, the Cuban government placed many Japanese, German, and Italian foreign nationals in internment camps similar to those in the United States. Many of these suspects were sent to the Presidio Modelo, which housed an estimated 350 Japanese, fifty Germans, and twenty-five Italians during the war years.[12] In addition, the Cuban government allowed the U.S. military to open a naval air base near Santa Fe to look for German U-boats in the Caribbean.[13]

---

[10] "New Census of Isle's Population Shows Big Increase Lately," *Isle of Pines Post*, December 25, 1931.

[11] Citizens of the United States Residing in the Isle of Pines, July 8, 1942, Nueva Gerona – Isle of Pines, Cuba, Vol. 53, Correspondence, 1942 (Sept. 1–Dec. 31), 1943 (Through File No. 123), Record Group 84, NARA.

[12] Jane McManus, *Cuba's Island of Dreams: Voices from the Isle of Pines and Youth* (Gainesville: University Press of Florida, 2000), 70–3; Wiltse Peña Hijuelos, et al., *Con Todo Derecho: Isla de la Juventud* (La Habana, 1986), 60–1; Academia de Ciencias de Cuba, "Serie Isla de Pinos No. 27: Situación social en Isla de Pinos antes de la Revolución," Salvador Morales, et al., eds. (La Habana, 1969), 15; "Cuba Chooses Alien Camp," *New York Times*, April 9, 1942.

[13] Hijuelos, et al., *Con Todo Derecho*, 60; McManus, *Cuba's Island of Dreams*, 74–8.

Wartime diplomatic harmony, however, belied contentious personal relations. U.S. consul LaRue Lutkins in 1944 incisively described the state of relations between the two groups as well as the grievances each side harbored.

A steady deterioration of relations between the two groups has been apparent from about 1923 to the present day. The Americans have made no secret of their conviction that American customs, ideas, and governmental methods are superior to those of Cuba. Few of the Americans mix with Cubans except on a business basis, and many refuse even to allow any Cuban to enter their homes. In the case of community social events such as beach picnics, it is rarely that any Cubans are invited. Naturally, the Cubans have been resentful of such treatment and have in many instances retaliated by inflicting petty nuisances and difficulties upon the foreigners who have displayed contempt for them and their country. There are still a few local government officials who are quite friendly to the Americans, but the latter claim that for the most part any of them having to deal with the government authorities are met by red tape, prevarication, and only slightly-veiled hostility.[14]

Lutkins's assessment suggested that the intense lobbying on both sides over the Hay-Quesada treaty's ratification had left a deep divide between Americans and *pineros*. And despite their decline in numbers, settlers continued to give off an air of cultural superiority, much to *pineros'* resentment. The depiction also intimated that U.S.–*pinero* relations had hardly changed from the first days of U.S. settlement when settlers often clashed with authorities, depended on local wage labor, and remained socially self-isolated.

But during the 1950s, Americans began returning to the Isle, albeit on a much smaller scale than at the turn of the century. This next generation of Americans was a diverse bunch. They came as part of a wave of private postwar American outreach that was occurring elsewhere in the region and around the world. In contrast to the holdover settlers who had lived on the Isle for decades, the newer arrivals were much more likely to engage socially and commercially with *pineros* and other foreign nationals. These Americans did not carry with them the emotional scars from the annexationist dispute. Local businessmen and the Cuban government encouraged this influx. They not only promoted the Isle as a tropical paradise but also initiated infrastructure improvements and lobbied to make the Isle a free port to eliminate tariffs. These efforts brought a spike

---

[14] "The Isle of Pines, Cuba," report by LaRue Lutkins, May 14, 1944, Nueva Gerona – Isle of Pines, Cuba, Vol. 55, Correspondence, 1943 (File No. 812–891), 1944 (File No. 000-123), Record Group 84, NARA.

in the real estate market and revived the U.S. presence, though in a far less domineering form than at the turn of the century.

Christian missionaries were one such example. Although they were a minor but distinct presence during the early twentieth-century heyday of U.S. settlement, they retained a place even at mid-century. The influx of students from Asbury College, a nondenominational school in Kentucky, revived their influence. Jack Stowell and Ellsworth Culver, who were recent graduates of Asbury in 1948, were the first of this group. The two not only did missionary work and served as pastors at American congregations, but taught at the American Central School as well. In 1949, the duo returned with their wives to continue their work as teachers and pastors. Their success paved the way for a continuous presence by Asbury missionaries on the Isle and at the school throughout the 1950s.

Some Asbury missionaries reported living conditions to be very much like what the first U.S. settlers had found a half-century earlier. Their reports also revealed a waning, yet still evident, U.S. influence. For example, over the course of two weeks in 1949 in Santa Barbara, where one group worked with the Methodist church in town, missionaries reported that "most of the stations are only crude thatched huts with crude benches and kerosene lamps."[15] They cited dangers from large spiders and scorpions as well as sleeping in huts or tents. But the group's work also illustrated that missionaries' efforts were less focused on Americans and more on *pineros* and foreign nationals. The group conducted Bible study in Spanish in Santa Barbara, a town once dominated by Americans but now comprising mostly *pineros*. In Santa Fe, the group also did missionary work among Jamaicans and Cayman Islanders. Although churches featured far fewer U.S. citizens among their congregations, Americans still held positions of leadership in these Protestant churches that increasingly featured non-Americans.

In addition to missionary work, Americans of the 1950s were looking for a tropical paradise that they could call home. Most of the new settlers, however, did not go to the Isle in search of fortune. Instead, they sought a modestly priced winter home where they could live in leisure. "There are many Americans arriving for short visits and they all want to buy land," longtime settler Adolph B. Kelm wrote in 1955. "Not land in the interior of the island, but lands along a sweet water stream, or close to Santa Fé or Nueva Gerona."[16] Ralph Finn was one of those buyers. In 1954, he left

---

[15] "Gospel Team Cites Cuban Adventures," *Asbury Collegian*, November 5, 1949.
[16] Kelm to Julia E. Larson, March 27, 1955, Fondo: A. B. Kelm, Legajo 4, Expediente 36, AHM.

Key West, Florida, after hearing about the Isle from other Americans. He bought forty acres from a *pinero* broker overlooking the Río Mal País near Columbia. Although fellow Americans and modern amenities were few, Finn was attracted to "the tranquility, the natural beauty" of the Isle as well as its abundance of hunting and fishing.[17] For William Stimson, the Isle represented not leisure but adventure, a chance to live out a childhood fantasy. With the help of what he called a "sugar daddy," Stimson's mother secured sixteen acres on which his family lived after moving from Miami in July 1955. Based on the stories he had heard, the ten-year-old Stimson envisioned the Isle of Pines would be like the mythic Wild West. According to his mother, "people rode around on horses and (she embellished) the streets were just dirt streets and (she lied) the sidewalks were wooden, like in cowboy movies. I wanted to go West. I wanted to be part of the American dream."[18] Such sentiment could have just as easily been expressed by a turn-of-the-century settler.

Much of the revival in U.S. interest can be traced to Cuban efforts to spur tourism, which was designed to help diversify an economy largely dependent on sugar. Tourism had been a key industry for Cuba during the early twentieth century, but the disruption from World War II took a toll. According to one estimate, visitors to Cuba dropped from 127,000 in 1940 to just 12,000 three years later.[19] In Havana, tourism initiatives eventually spurred a backlash among Cubans who protested the proliferation of vice, crime, and corruption that came to be associated with the industry and U.S. visitors. Historian Christine Skwiot noted that "Habaneros came to agree with the M-26-7 [26th of July Movement] that tourism embodied much of what was wrong in Cuba."[20]

On the Isle, however, little of that sentiment emerged. For one, a new source of outside capital was needed to replace the declining citrus industry. By the 1950s, there were only about twenty commercial growers left, operating on roughly 800 total acres.[21] In addition, the new visitors

---

[17] Ralph Finn interview with Frederick Swetland Jr., March 15, 1969, tape 9, 1, SFA.

[18] William Stimson, e-mail message to author, May 17, 2011.

[19] Louis A. Pérez Jr., *Cuba: Between Reform and Revolution*, 4th ed. (New York: Oxford University Press, 2011), 215. See also Merrill, *Negotiating Paradise*, 110–14; Rosalie Schwartz, *Pleasure Island: Tourism and Temptation in Cuba* (Lincoln: University of Nebraska Press, 1997), 103–63.

[20] Christine Skwiot, *The Purposes of Paradise: U.S. Tourism and Empire in Cuba and Hawai'i* (Philadelphia: University of Pennsylvania Press, 2010), 197. See also Merrill, *Negotiating Paradise*, 103–40; Pérez, *On Becoming Cuban*, 166–98.

[21] Morton D. Winsberg, "The Isle of Pines, Cuba: A Geographic Interpretation" (PhD diss., University of Florida, 1958), 125.

and investors seemed to acquaint themselves well of the local culture, which went a long way toward maintaining relative social harmony. This development was similar to what was happening concurrently in Mexico, where tourists, retirees, and other private U.S. citizens were also flocking.[22] Historian Julio Moreno has argued that Mexicans cultivated an American commercial presence during the revolutionary era provided that such activities respected Mexican customs.[23] Such a dynamic was evident on the Isle as well. Furthermore, complaints about vice and crime were virtually nonexistent. Although the number of casinos is unclear, there were at least two brothels.[24] This number paled in comparison to Havana, where there were an estimated 270 bordellos as well as more prostitutes (11,500) than people on the Isle (11,000).[25] Elements of organized crime, which had deeply penetrated the Havana market, were said to be involved on the Isle, too, but their presence was less conspicuous. Two writers noted that reputed mobsters Lucky Luciano and Meyer Lansky had planned to buy land to start a resort hotel and casino, but no evidence survives of what became of that plan.[26]

While no precise figures exist of U.S. tourists on the Isle, they surely represented only a small fraction of those who went to Havana. The comparative dearth of traffic was not for a lack of promotion. Advertisements used much of the same discourse as U.S.-based landholding companies a half-century earlier. Promotions appropriated elements of exoticism, the Isle's legend as a pirate hideout, and its image as a tropical paradise to attract tourists during a time when travel abroad was becoming much more affordable thanks to improvements in air travel. For example, one 1958 report that described the Cuban government's tourism initiatives used images to reinforce its points. One picture harkened to the Isle's mythic past: a pirate standing in front of a ship and a treasure chest overflowing with booty. Another picture suggested the type of tourist whom officials were looking to attract: a well-dressed man (in a business suit and tie) and woman (in a dress and heels) coming off a plane with luggage in

[22] John Mason Hart, *Empire and Revolution: The Americans in Mexico since the Civil War* (Berkeley: University of California Press, 2002).

[23] Julio Moreno, *Yankee Don't Go Home!: Mexican Nationalism, American Business Culture, and the Shaping of Modern Mexico, 1920–1950* (Chapel Hill: University of North Carolina Press, 2003).

[24] Ron Williams interview with author, July 9, 2009.

[25] Pérez, *On Becoming Cuban*, 193.

[26] T. J. English, *Havana Nocturne: How the Mob Owned Cuba – and then Lost It to the Revolution* (New York: William Morrow, 2008), 33–4; Merrill, *Negotiating Paradise*, 126. See also Hijuelos, et al., *Con Todo Derecho*, 64–5.

hand.[27] This advertisement addressed a relatively new fixture in the Isle's development – commercial airline travel between Havana and Nueva Gerona. A Cuban carrier called Aerovia "Q" initiated regular service in 1948, part of a wave of transportation and infrastructure improvements designed to make the Isle more easily accessible and economically viable. Although instances occurred of airplanes taking produce directly to the United States, there was no commercial service for passengers.[28]

Travel articles in U.S. publications complemented Cuban promotional efforts by tapping into familiar tropes about the Isle. Some stories referred to it as a tropical paradise to connote its exoticism.[29] Many writers called it "Treasure Island," a common allusion at the turn of the century to the famed Robert Louis Stevenson novel that suggested a sense of adventurism in an otherwise placid locale.[30] But that tranquility also became a selling point. Writers idealized the Isle as a health resort because of its warm climate and medicinal springs.[31] One chronicler described the Isle as a "sleepy haunt [that] flaunts no luxury to lure the pampered traveler" but promised that those who made the trip would enjoy "both the stagnation and hope of the eerie, yet beautiful, Isle of Pines."[32] In promoting his family's sizable home as a vacation destination, Frederick Swetland Jr. touted its rustic charms. "[T]his is not the Hilton Caribe," he wrote, referring to the swanky resort in San Juan, Puerto Rico. "No electricity, we use carbide; no telephone, it's eight miles to the nearest town; no radio or television; nor do we have a bath for each room."[33] In a small advertisement he placed in the *Wall Street Journal*, Swetland noted that the family ranch, with rooms available for $20 a day per person, offered a "restful

[27] Nivio López Pellón, "Hablemos de Isla de Pinos y su régimen fiscal" (La Habana, 1958). This publication was a transcript of a radio broadcast conducted by López Pellón, a journalist.
[28] Winsberg, "Isle of Pines, Cuba," 186–9.
[29] "Tourists 'Discover' Cuba 462 Years after Columbus," *Hartford Courant*, January 2, 1955; Janeann and Arturo Gonzalez, "Tropical Paradise for Americans," *Coronet*, October 1957, 98.
[30] For examples, see Leonard Bourne, "Treasure Island Lies in Peaceful Caribbean," *Hartford Courant*, February 11, 1940; R. Hart Phillips, "Quiet Isle of Pines," *New York Times*, July 23, 1950; "Lovely Cuba has Varied Vacation Fun," *Hartford Courant*, June 3, 1951; "Romantic Cuba Small Island of Many Contrasts," *Hartford Courant*, February 26, 1956; June Wilcoxon Brown, "Isle of Pines," *American Mercury*, 1956, 134–6.
[31] Sydney Clark, "Island Idyll: Isle of Pines," *Travel*, 1953, 22; Brown, "Isle of Pines," 134; "Cuba Has Its Havana, Yes, But Other Attractions, Too," *Hartford Courant*, January 12, 1958.
[32] Euphemia Fosdick, "The Eerie Isle," *Senior Scholastic*, 1949, 19-T.
[33] Frederick Swetland Jr., undated letter, Isle of Pines Properties, 1955–56, SFA.

change of pace and scenery for bonetired executives and wives."[34] Unlike early twentieth-century depictions that chastised *pineros* for lacking the ingenuity and industry to exploit the land effectively, mid-century travel articles and advertisements were much more complimentary of locals' presumed pastoral approach and used that to appeal to sophisticated elites.

In addition to some of the well-worn selling points, travel articles highlighted other developments to pique Americans' interests. Hunting and fishing became major draws. The popular U.S. magazine *Field & Stream* in 1956 profiled the Isle's bounty of fish and fowl. The writer, Warren Page, claimed that the abundance of opportunity led to "one bothersome problem [that] exists at the Isle of Pines in August ... shoot or fish? ... The answer is always the same – plenty of both."[35] Page did most of his fishing through the camp run by Vic and Betty Barothy, which may have been the first of its kind on the Isle. The camp also drew noted fly-fishing enthusiast and baseball Hall of Famer Ted Williams, who called his visit "the greatest fishing trip I've ever been on" after catching a reported forty bonefish in one day.[36] Harvey Oppmann recalled that his parents, Paul and Catherine, visited the Isle from Ohio every January between 1950 and 1961 to take part in the bone fishing with light-tackle fly rods that Williams helped to popularize.[37]

While U.S. print media started to address the Isle of Pines once again, so too did entertainment. The Isle served as the backdrop for an episode of *Bold Venture*, a radio series starring Humphrey Bogart and Lauren Bacall that ran from 1951–2. Bogart played Slate Shannon, a Havana hotel owner who had a boat called *Bold Venture* that he chartered to various clients whose intrigues drove each episode. He was joined by Sailor Duval, Shannon's love interest played by Bogart's wife, Bacall. In the February 11, 1952, episode "Dentist's Gold," Shannon and Duval are

[34] Frederick Swetland Jr. to David Swetland, January 19, 1955, Island Letters, 1954–55, SFA; "Vacation Time Open," *Wall Street Journal*, November 3, 1955.

[35] Warren Page, "The Incredible Isle of Pines," *Field & Stream*, 1956, 80. Other articles that lauded the Isle's fishing opportunities include Joseph Cloyd, "Cuba's Isle of Pines," *American Magazine*, 1955, 90–2; "Sports-Minded Really Have Fun in Lively Cuba," *Hartford Courant*, December 1, 1957.

[36] Williams quoted in "Barothy Caribbean Lodge, Isle of Pines, Cuba," *Isle of Pines News*, September 1956. The monthly, bilingual *News* published two photos of Williams's excursion with Vic Barothy in its May edition. The newspaper also made a public appeal to American writer and Havana resident Ernest Hemingway to make a fishing trip to the Isle, but no evidence exists that he did. "Yesterday and Today," *Isle of Pines News*, June 2, 1956.

[37] Harvey Oppmann interview with author, August 16, 2014.

hired by Rhoda Gonzalez to take her to the Isle of Pines. Gonzalez's reasons for going to the Isle remain unclear and soon Shannon and Duval are wrapped up in a murder mystery involving a myriad of shady characters.

Much of the action during the roughly twenty-five-minute episode takes place on the boat but some dialogue reveals familiar attitudes toward the Isle. For example, at the start of the episode Duval sighs and takes in a deep breath. "What else is there to do on the Isle of Pines but sniff," she asks. At the end of the episode, the *Bold Venture* returns to the Isle, to which Duval says sarcastically, "Oh joy, oh joy, oh joy," before taking another deep breath. Then, echoing her comment at the beginning of the episode, Duval says to Shannon, "What did you bring me back to the Isle of Pines for? You know there's nothing else to do here but sniff." Shannon responds, "You come to one of the most beautiful islands in the Caribbean and you say fun is sniffing pine needles? Oh Sailor, you need therapy."[38]

The duo's comments reflected many early-century American notions about the Isle. Duval seems to appreciate the fresh air and natural surroundings, but her remarks – underscored by her tone – belie her boredom. Shannon, like the turn-of-the-century boomer-minded fortune hunters, recognizes that the Isle holds more intrigue and promise than just fresh air. Moreover, the Isle's lingering reputation for mystery and danger going back to the colonial era is evident. It is reflected in Gonzalez's murky reasons for going there and the shady cast of characters Shannon and Duval encounter. It seems a natural locale for a whodunit. On one hand, such a depiction would suggest that the Isle's perception among American audiences had not changed much in a half century. On the other hand, the fact that it was the setting for such a prominent radio program – featuring the star power of two of the most popular actors in Hollywood – reveals it was once again emerging into the popular U.S. consciousness.

Perhaps the most important development in the Isle's revival was its designation as a free port. Cuban President Fulgencio Batista in January 1955 issued Decree 2071 that exempted the Isle from taxes on merchandise, production, imports, and exports to stimulate trade and tourism. As a result, goods became more affordable, which appealed to tourists and retirees looking for an inexpensive winter home. At the time, the measure enjoyed widespread support. Frederick Swetland Jr. credited it

[38] *Bold Venture*, "Dentist's Gold," episode 47, February 11, 1952, https://archive.org/details/BoldVenture57Episodes (accessed May 11, 2016). My thanks to D. Tony Goins for finding this episode.

with stimulating tourism and winter home construction, making vegetables less expensive to grow and ship, and spurring more shops to open. "It was a BOOM, a Cuban boom, some forty years after the American boom," he wrote. "And nobody that I know of didn't like it."[39]

The measure proved popular among *pineros* as well. The Isle of Pines Improvement Association, which consisted mostly of *pinero* businessmen, had promoted the idea of a free port as far back as November 1949.[40] After the designation, one local Spanish-language publication called it a critical event that put the Isle on a path to "development and material progress."[41] As one *pinera* later recalled, the free-port designation evidently had its desired effect of spurring commercial activity. A teenager in the late 1950s, Elda Cepero Herrera worked during her school vacations at a local store that catered to tourists. She remembered the store did a booming business and that the "main streets on the Isle were filled with American tourists."[42]

Many Cuban businessmen took advantage of the Isle's tax-free status by buying land and creating housing developments and tourist resorts much like U.S. businessmen had done a half-century earlier. Some, like cattle rancher Gregorio "Goyo" Hernández, built up their holdings by buying at public auction small plots abandoned by Americans.[43] Others bought large tracts. Francisco Cajigas, a cattleman and merchant with ties to the Batista regime, was thought to be the Isle's largest landowner in the early 1950s after acquiring parcels such as San Juan, El Canal, and Los Almacigos that U.S. landholding companies once controlled. He even made an $80,000 cash offer to the Swetlands for San Francisco de las Piedras in 1952 that the family ultimately declined.[44]

Some of these Cuban entrepreneurs used the land to create suburban-style housing developments called *repartos*. Calling to mind the early twentieth-century activities of U.S. landholding companies, these businessmen parceled large tracts into smaller plots (roughly an acre) to appeal to the middle-class buyer regardless of nationality. One company included a map of its development as well as a sketch of a house interior

[39] Swetland, *Isle of Pines*, 69.
[40] Compañías, Sociedades, y Establecimientos de Isla de Pinos, 1905–1970, Libro de Actas de la Asociación Pro Mejoras de Isla de Pinos, 1949–1952, Libro 30, November 1, 1949, AHM.
[41] "La Zona Franca en Isla de Pinos," *Isla*, January 1956, 6.
[42] Elda Cepero Herrera interview with author, April 9, 2010.
[43] McManus, *Cuba's Island of Dreams*, 90.
[44] F. Diez Rivas to Frederick Swetland Jr., July 15, 1952, SFA.

in its advertisement in a Spanish-language publication. Its lots ranged from 3,000 to 5,000 square meters.[45] How well these houses sold is unclear. Kelm noted that *repartos* emerged in Nueva Gerona, Santa Fe, and Santa Barbara, but generally were not very popular because "the lot prices are excessive and I have noted that the prospective buyers are not satisfied with the condition of sale."[46] As a complement to those efforts, the Batista government approved infrastructure improvements across the Isle. This work included upgrades to roads, bridges, and the port of Nueva Gerona in anticipation of greater tourist traffic.

The arrival of Arthur Vining Davis fueled further speculation that the Isle would become the next great tourist destination of the Caribbean. Davis, the longtime chairman of the Aluminum Company of America (Alcoa) and one of the wealthiest men in the world, bought some 280,000 acres for roughly $2.6 million in the mid- to late 1950s with the aim of developing resort hotels.[47] Davis had ample experience in this field. In addition to his work at Alcoa, he owned resorts in Florida as well as several hotels and an airline. Isle business leaders anticipated that he would do the same there. As he wrote to one inquirer about his plans: "The Isle of Pines is quite a deserted area, but I am hoping to be able to put some life into the place in due course of time."[48] Davis's land purchases – done with the blessing and encouragement of Batista and Cajigas, with whom he later established a business partnership – inspired other Cuban investors to do likewise. These deals caused the Isle's real estate market to flourish briefly once again. Undeveloped land that had plummeted to less than $3 an acre during the 1940s spiked a decade later, usually between $40 and $75 an acre if it was located near water.[49]

But development along the South Coast, Bibijagua Beach, and the airfield near Nueva Gerona – the areas where Davis bought land – was slow in coming, which frustrated some businessmen and led others to question Davis's motivations. J. J. Brown, who managed Davis's holdings, argued that the heart attack the eighty-nine-year-old Davis suffered in

---

[45] "La Cotorra One-Acre Farms," *Isla*, January 1956, 34.

[46] Kelm to B. B. Robbins, September 24, 1957, Fondo: A. B. Kelm, Legajo 4, Expediente 37, AHM.

[47] Academia de Ciencias de Cuba, "Serie Isla de Pinos No. 23: Latifundismo y Especulación," Delfín Rodríguez, et al., eds. (La Habana, 1968), 11.

[48] Quoted in J. J. Brown, "Arthur Vining Davis and the Isle of Pines, 1955–1960," June 23, 1965, 17, SFA. Brown managed Davis's holdings on the Isle. He wrote this thirty-seven-page statement to show that Davis intended to develop commercially his vast landholdings and therefore should not be subject to expropriation by the Castro government.

[49] See "Davis, Ernest" in Fondo: A. B. Kelm, Legajo 2, Expediente 19, AHM.

October 1956 stunted development plans. This setback instigated criticism in the Havana press that Davis was not following through on the investment he promised.[50] Americans on the Isle also grew impatient with Davis when the expected development stalled and thus frustrated land values. "Mr. Arthur Vining Davis, who bought vast tracts of land here and who intended to improve his properties on a big scale has failed to do anything at all," Kelm wrote in April 1958. "His inactivity has acted as cold water to those people who bought for speculation."[51] Local businessmen, however, remained steadfast in their support. Leo C. Leone, editor of the bilingual *Isle of Pines News*, wrote an open letter to Davis in September 1956 defending him from critics and assuring him that he had locals' support.[52] It was no doubt a sound business strategy to stay in the good graces of a potential patron worth an estimated $350 million.[53] But it also revealed a willingness among Americans and Cubans – now long divorced from the antagonisms of the Hay-Quesada era – to work together in commercial projects. The same could be said about social and institutional endeavors as well.

The American Central School

By the 1950s, it was clear that the tenor of relations between Americans and *pineros* had significantly changed from their first encounters at the turn of the century. The acrimony from the Hay-Quesada treaty debate had subsided, the overwhelming U.S. presence had substantially dissipated, and newly arriving settlers were much more willing to engage the local population on terms beyond an employer–employee relationship.

---

[50] Brown, "Arthur Vining Davis and the Isle of Pines," 20, SFA.

[51] Kelm to Mrs. A. R. Towner, April 6, 1958, Fondo: A. B. Kelm, Legajo 4, Expediente 34, AHM. In an earlier letter, Kelm blamed Davis's land-buying spree for effectively overinflating the price of real estate, thus making it too expensive for the small investor. Kelm to Margaret Fish, March 11, 1957, Fondo: A. B. Kelm, Legajo 3, Expediente 24, AHM.

[52] Leone to Davis, September 4, 1956, printed in *Isle of Pines News*, September 1956. Leone had sold 2,600 acres to Davis and took credit for introducing the Alcoa chairman to the Isle of Pines. Brown, "Arthur Vining Davis and the Isle of Pines," 13, SFA; Leone, "Great Is Truth," *Isle of Pines News*, September 1956.

[53] Estimate taken from George Beebe, "Davis Buys Vast Tract Near Cuba," *Miami Herald*. Davis's Isle holdings, which the Castro government later seized, were valued at $4.2 million. "Estate of Industrialist Appraised at $86 Million," *New York Times*, May 9, 1964; U.S. Department of Justice, Foreign Claims Settlement Commission of the United States, Cuban Claims Program, Certified Claimant List, Claim CU-2620, www.justice.gov/fcsc/readingroom/ccp-listofclaims.pdf (accessed May 11, 2016).

Nowhere was this spirit – and its evolution – more evident than at the American Central School (ACS).

The ACS was a consolidation of the small, private American schools that had dotted the Isle during the early twentieth century. After spending a year in a rented house in Nueva Gerona, the school in 1926 moved into a permanent building in Santa Ana, a centralized location among the various U.S. settlements. U.S. entrepreneur John A. Miller, who ran a successful citrus grove and was an officer in the National Bank & Trust Company, donated the land. When the schoolhouse opened, approximately 100 students enrolled, two-thirds of whom were American.[54] Three American teachers were responsible for grades one through twelve. Courses followed the Florida state curriculum and were conducted in English with lessons emphasizing U.S. history and geography. Tuition cost $5 a month for one child, $8 for two children, and $10 for three. Administrators and supporters publicly portrayed the school as an institution designed for the children of U.S. citizens so they would not lose touch with their American roots. It also was a symbol of resolve among settlers that the U.S. community, reeling from commercial setbacks and a dwindling population, would endure. One writer's comment about the importance of American schools in Latin America also applied to the ACS: "The school is the hub around which turns the wheel of educational and social activities of an isolated North American colony in a foreign land."[55]

From its inception, however, the ACS depended much more on Cubans and the Cuban government than most school officials probably would have been willing to admit. As a private enterprise, the school relied on tuition, fundraisers, and donations to sustain it. But those funds proved insufficient. In its first years, the school looked to the Cuban government for up to one-fourth of its funding.[56] Even before the school's opening and just months after Hay-Quesada's ratification, a group of U.S. businessmen along with *alcalde* Ramon Llorca Soto appealed to Cuban President Gerardo Machado for financial support. The group claimed that the ACS would provide a good education not only for American children, but for young *pineros* as well.[57] The school also needed help from

[54] Hijuelos, et al., *Con Todo Derecho*, 78.

[55] Dean T. Fitzgerald, "The Role of American Schools in Latin America," *The School Review* 63 (May 1955): 296.

[56] "American Central School Starts Fifth Year October Seventh," *Isle of Pines Post*, September 15, 1929.

[57] La Comisión to Machado, June 8, 1925, Secretaria de la Presidencia, 1902–1958, Legajo 70, Expediente 65, ANC. The so-called *Comisión* consisted of four Americans and one

FIGURE 7.1. The American Central School as it stood in June 1960. Created in 1926 in the town of Santa Ana, the school was initially designed for children of U.S. citizens. In later years as American enrollments declined, school administrators embraced teaching U.S. customs to Cuban and other foreign national students. The school proved an important space in which the Isle's increasingly multinational community could come together. Courtesy of William Stimson.

local officials whenever roads fell into disrepair as they often did during the rainy season; it was a critical issue considering most students relied on bus transportation.

As the school struggled with its finances throughout the 1930s and 1940s – even teetering on the brink of bankruptcy – the enrollment of *pinero* and foreign national students became critical to its survival. By the early 1940s, Cuban students made up nearly one-third of the student body. Reflecting the Isle's broadening multinational makeup, the ACS also featured students from England, Canada, Sweden, Poland, and Hungary; later, it would also include students of Japanese and Chinese descent.[58] This trend continued into the next decade, when U.S. students comprised less than 20 percent of a student body that averaged around

pinero: Chamber of Commerce President H. P. MacCarthy, Chamber Secretary F. S. Harvey, *Isle of Pines Appeal* Publisher Arthur E. Willis, Isle of Pines Steamship Company representative Adolph B. Kelm, and Llorca Soto.

[58] Report made to the Coordinator's Committee by LaRue R. Lutkins, July 5, 1943, Nueva Gerona – Isle of Pines, Cuba, Vol. 54, Correspondence, 1943 (File No. 125–811.11), Record Group 84, NARA.

100 pupils. In the years preceding the Cuban Revolution, the American Central School enjoyed the highest enrollments in its history, thanks largely to the infusion of Cuban students who comprised a majority of the population.

Pineros supported the school for a variety of reasons. Much like Americans, Cubans in general also were dubious about their country's public school system. Historian Louis A. Pérez Jr. has argued that "public schools remained in disarray and disrepute through the early decades of the republic and by midcentury were generally discredited among Cubans of all classes.... Public schools were perceived as unable to prepare Cubans to meet the challenges of their time."[59] Cuban historian José Vega Suñol maintained that private schools, especially those operated by Americans, were highly valued throughout Cuba during its republican era.[60] Such institutions were associated with more effective education, which, in turn, was linked to opportunity and social mobility. Pérez has pointed out that Cubans dating back to the turn of the century held schools with English-language teaching in high regard given the "anticipated expansion of commercial and mercantile relations" between the United States and Cuba.[61]

This perspective was no different among *pineros* who supported the American Central School. One local writer, Sergio Montané y Soto, articulated this view in a 1941 article. Praising the ACS for its "modern methods" of teaching, he favorably compared classes there to spending seven hours a day in U.S. territory, talking with and learning from Americans. Recognizing the school's persistent financial difficulties, Montané argued that it would benefit *pineros* if the Cuban government subsidized the school to make American education available to more students. He also recommended that the Cuban Ministry of Education follow some of the examples set by the ACS, particularly in terms of supporting and providing instruction in English to Cuban students. "If we all agree that the English language is indispensable to a modern life, we should try to preserve and enhance a school at a place where English is taught as if it were on American soil," he wrote.[62]

---

[59] Pérez, *On Becoming Cuban*, 399–400.

[60] Suñol, *Norteamericanos en Cuba: Estudio Etnohistorico* (La Habana: Fundación Fernando Ortiz, 2004), 201–10.

[61] Louis A. Pérez Jr., *Cuba and the United States: Ties of Singular Intimacy*, 2nd ed. (Athens: University of Georgia Press, 1997), 128–9.

[62] Sergio Montané y Soto, "La American Central School: Una Escuela Interesante," *Pino Nuevo*, October 25, 1941, 4.

Montané's support of the American Central School had one notable qualification. He concluded that his embrace of U.S.-style education did not mean he was advocating for the Isle's Americanization. Rather, he embraced the idea that the Isle would be *"cubano hasta la muerte."*[63] Others similarly expressed such anxiety about U.S. education's impact on Cuban nationality. Pérez writes that "increasing numbers of Cubans worried about the effects of foreign schooling on children's capacity to develop ties to *patria*."[64] They worried that Cuban children who equated an American education and the English language with modernity and opportunity would view Cuba as deficient by comparison. Moreover, it could foster divided loyalties that might favor the United States at Cuba's expense. Nevertheless, *pineros* who could afford the tuition considered the ACS an attractive option.

Pinero students at the ACS generally were not fluent in English and often were not at the grade commensurate with their age had they lived in the United States. Many students who had gone through the Cuban primary school system would virtually start over again at the American Central School. Students in the high school were as old as twenty-three years of age. Eli Swetland recalled that as an eleven-year-old in fifth grade, he had classmates sixteen and seventeen years of age.[65] Elda Cepero Herrera, for instance, was sixteen years old when she started the fifth grade at the ACS. She had entered the school at the encouragement of her mother, a seamstress who believed that learning English at the ACS would better prepare her for the future. She took classes in a variety of subjects, including history and geography, which emphasized U.S. perspectives. Even outside of the classroom, Cepero's exposure to U.S. customs continued. At the school she experienced her first Thanksgiving, a celebration prepared by her favorite teacher, an American woman named Marie Holman.[66]

Not all Cuban students were Isle natives. Some came from mainland Cuba, drawn to the American Central School. Reina Acosta had come to the Isle with her two sisters in the mid-1950s after their father died. One of the reasons they moved in with their aunt and uncle on the Isle, Acosta's daughter Mary Anne Rutherford Kimsey said, was because they could afford to give the children an education at a place like the ACS.[67]

[63] Ibid. Roughly translated meaning "Cuban until the end."
[64] Pérez, *On Becoming Cuban*, 404.
[65] Eli Swetland interview with author, July 10, 2009.
[66] Elda Cepero Herrera interview with author, April 9, 2010.
[67] Mary Anne Rutherford Kimsey e-mail message to author, June 26, 2014.

Yolanda Diaz Hamby was a native of Havana when she came to the Isle in the late 1950s. It was supposed to be a short-term stay with her father, Armando Diaz, who owned a real estate office and served as a manager at a Nueva Gerona hotel. Soon after arriving, though, she enrolled in the ACS and decided she did not want to return to live with her mother and stepfather. "I fell in love with it," Hamby stated. "Everyone knew everyone else. We all got along."[68] The biggest benefit to studying at the American Central School, she said, was learning English because shortly after the Cuban Revolution, she moved to the United States.

Both the desire to learn English and the opportunity to go to an American school drew Nuri Anderson and her two sisters, Frances and Isis, back to the Isle in the mid-1950s. Anderson's family had deep roots on the Isle. Her mother's family could trace its heritage there to the Spanish colonial era. Her paternal grandfather, Frank Anderson, was a Chicago native who had owned a sugar mill in mainland Cuba before he moved to the Isle for health reasons during the early twentieth century. Although born on the Isle in 1943, Nuri Anderson and her family moved to Havana for a few years before they returned in 1955 in large part to learn English at the American Central School. Her fondest memories were of the social interactions with other students, including performing plays and going to parties. She counted the Millers as some of her family's closest friends. The school's yearly rotation of teachers, though, presented a slight challenge. "Sometimes we had different teachers from different parts of the United States," she said. "On the first day, it was hard to understand them because they had different pronunciations." Nevertheless, Anderson successfully learned the language and recalled that she and her sisters "had a very good time there."[69]

Among teachers, Cuban students' effort and dedication left a deep impression. "The kids just wanted to learn," Sarah Corson, a missionary from Asbury College who taught the seventh and eighth grades in the late 1950s, remembered. "We could send one class out under the mango tree to study physics or something else while we taught other classes in the classrooms. (We had a classroom each.) They would study very hard alone, and not even start talking except when one had a question and didn't understand and then the others would stop and explain it to him. We really loved those kids!"[70] Ron Williams, who took over the

[68] Yolanda Diaz Hamby e-mail message to author, November 2, 2012.
[69] Nuri Anderson interview with author, August 19, 2014.
[70] Sarah Corson, e-mail message to author, June 10, 2010.

seventh and eighth grades after Corson left, echoed those sentiments. A first-time teacher who spoke no Spanish, he dropped out of Williams College a semester before graduation to teach at the ACS. The students' zeal for learning made his job easier and helped overcome language barriers. "They were enthusiastic about getting an education," Williams said. "They were enthusiastic about school and they always wanted to do more."[71]

International friendships and relationships occurred frequently at the school. Cepero, for example, said that she got along very well with other teachers and students. Her best friend at the school was Derek Anderson, son of citrus exporter Thomas B. Anderson Jr. and his wife, Neri, a native *pinera*. Williams, who at twenty-two years of age was not much older than most of the students, also struck up many friendships. He joined a club volleyball team that featured ACS students and some locals. The team, in which he remained the lone American, often played during recess and once won a tournament at an American social club. He said he also struck up a relationship of sorts with a sixteen-year-old female student from another class. He intimated that the relationship was platonic as his encounters with the student were accompanied by a chaperone, usually her mother.[72]

Williams's account suggested a changing dynamic among Americans and Cubans. Stories of deep friendships or romantic relationships between the two national groups were virtually nonexistent during the early-twentieth century. It reflected the self-isolation of settlers as well as accepted social conventions, at least among Americans, that frowned upon consorting with *pineros*. As a young single man and recent arrival to the Isle, however, Williams carried none of those burdens with him in establishing a relationship with a Cuban student. Nevertheless, the power dynamics involved – namely, the authority and maturity he enjoyed – gave him pause. Nationality, however, apparently played no factor.

By mid-century, the U.S. government became an active supporter in fostering this genial relationship between Americans and *pineros* at the school. As a result, the ACS embraced a shift in emphasis, from keeping U.S. students in touch with the American way of life to introducing U.S. customs and history to non-American students. The transition was born out of financial desperation. With enrollment down and Cuban government funding slashed for reasons unclear, the school nearly closed in

[71] Ron Williams interview with author, July 9, 2009.
[72] Ibid.

1948. School administrators appealed to the U.S. Embassy in Havana for help. Officials put the ACS in touch with Roy Tasco Davis, who emerged as an important ally to the school. Davis was director of the Inter-American Schools Service (IASS), a bureau tasked by the U.S. Department of State during World War II to aid private American-run schools throughout Latin America. According to the IASS, there were 195 such schools in the region as of 1945, including twelve in Cuba. A decade later, there were an estimated 300 American schools in more than twenty countries in Latin America serving some 100,000 students annually.[73] Davis, a former diplomat to four Latin American countries, was particularly sympathetic to American schools' efforts to inculcate better relations between their host countries and the United States. The most significant impediment to that mission, he argued, was the often-difficult conditions in which teachers worked. "These schools have contributed significantly to the promotion of friendship between the people of our countries, in spite of the fact that in all but a few exceptional cases they are housed in inferior buildings and obliged to use unsatisfactory equipment, with underpaid and overworked instructors."[74] Davis helped the American Central School secure a grant of $1,376.89 in 1948, primarily for teachers' salaries. The award marked the start of steadily increasing aid from the IASS that would eventually reach $5,000 annually. With this aid, the school not only offered raises, but also hired additional teachers. By 1959, the school employed five full-time American teachers who each earned $200 a month. It also hired a Cuban Spanish-language instructor who taught all grades – but was paid only $140 a month.[75]

When the ACS reapplied for additional funding each school year, its reports explicitly linked the school's mission to broader U.S. interests, specifically fostering stronger U.S.–Cuban relations. This endeavor had resonance at a time when the United States sought to maintain hemispheric solidarity in a Cold War world. ACS correspondence during the 1950s featured less emphasis on providing for children of U.S. residents – since by this time they were a minority of the student population – and more

---

[73] Dean T. Fitzgerald, "The Significance of American Schools in Latin America," *Comparative Education Review* 1 (October 1957): 20; Fitzgerald, "The Role of American Schools in Latin America," 297.

[74] Roy Tasco Davis, "American Private Schools in Latin America," *National Association of Secondary-School Principals Bulletin* 29 (May 1945): 55.

[75] American Central School biannual report to Inter-American Schools Service, October 22, 1959, Records of American Sponsored Schools, Box 21, Cuba, Isle of Pines – American Central School, Record Group 59, NARA.

about the benefits the school offered to Cuban children. For example, Principal William Eddy in 1953 argued that the school served U.S. diplomatic interests by teaching Cuban students. "[I]t is very important to the United States to have 'good neighbors,' " he wrote. American-run schools like the ACS developed such neighbors, he argued, through education, which raised standards of living. He continued that the American Central School offered *pineros* "a chance to learn of America, what it stands for, and it has given them better opportunities to advance themselves through the learning of the English language.... From what I have been able to gather in talking with the parents and friends I believe this school has helped to cement better feelings between the two different races [i.e., nationalities]."[76] To support his contention, Eddy cited *pinero* students at the ACS who had gone on to careers in a variety of industries and with notable companies. He referenced former students who worked for Pan-American Airways and the Cuban Telephone Company, as well as others who went on to higher education in the United States after completing their studies at the ACS.

Eddy's comments shrewdly aligned the school's mission to prevailing U.S. policy and ideology. His report explicitly linked to nearly two decades of the United States' "Good Neighbor" approach in the hemisphere. In addition, Eddy's remarks illustrated that uplift ideology – that is, a sense of duty to improve perceived lesser peoples' standard of living – remained prominent. By arguing that the school benefited Cubans, Eddy also suggested that U.S. schools could make better neighbors by making them more like Americans. His emphasis on the importance of learning English revealed the presumption that it was the language of modernity. But above all, Eddy sought to impress upon the IASS that the ACS had become a shining example of enlightened self-interest, an enterprise that benefited both Americans and Cubans.

The school's efforts also elicited the attention of the U.S. Embassy in Havana, which was looking for ways to combat growing anti-Americanism in Cuba stemming from U.S. support of the unpopular Batista regime. Embassy correspondence during the early 1950s endorsed the school's mission in much the same vein as ACS administrators and recommended continued aid for it.[77] Public Affairs Officer Jacob Canter reported to the State Department in 1952 that supporting American-run

---

[76] William Eddy to U.S. Embassy, Havana, April 8, 1953, Records of American Sponsored Schools, Box 21, Cuba, Isle of Pines – American Central School, Record Group 59, NARA.

[77] Considering the embassy had put the ACS in touch with the IASS in the first place, it is possible that the embassy had a hand in shaping the school's reports.

schools was "one of the surest investments the United States Government can make in terms of creating a climate of favorable opinion toward the United States in the future." Instruction in English, lessons in U.S. history and literature, and shared cultural connections with American classmates developed among Cuban students "an attitude of friendship for the United States which no amount of adverse propaganda will be able to eradicate."[78] The following year, Canter again recommended that State Department grants continue. He argued that the ACS offered a unique, cost-effective way to foster better relations between the United States and Cuba at the grassroots level. "The American Central School on the Isle of Pines is similarly building pro-American attitudes.... Except for commercial motion pictures, perhaps the only direct American influence working on these pupils is that of their program of studies and their contact with their teachers," he wrote.[79] Canter's comments illustrated that programs like the American Central School were important projections of U.S. "soft power" – the reliance on attraction and subtle coercion – that would persuade the average Cuban to continue to support U.S. influence in their country.

School officials played up this role as well. In one of their last reports to the IASS, with the Batista regime on the verge of collapse in the late 1950s, school administrators argued that the ACS was more important than ever to maintaining good relations between the United States and Cuba. They noted that:

schools such as ours create a positive friendly feeling towards the U.S.A. and her democratic ideals. This strikes a lethal blow at diplomatic problems which may otherwise arise. An ounce of education is worth more than a pound of gun powder for it does not leave the bitterness of war. The best way to find a "Good Neighbor" is to be one: we kill the roots of diplomatic weeds before they get to the conference table; we spread our language and our customs to a foreign land making them more like us. This has value that no diplomat can bring in a brief case, a reciprocal value which pays tremendous dividends to our country.[80]

This description of the school's mission also illustrated a major attitudinal shift among Americans on the Isle. Whereas the first generation

---

[78] U.S. Embassy to Department of State, July 18, 1952, Records of American Sponsored Schools, Box 21, Cuba, Isle of Pines – American Central School, Record Group 59, NARA.

[79] U.S. Embassy to Department of State, March 26, 1953, Records of American Sponsored Schools, Box 21, Cuba, Havana – Ruston Academy, 1952–55, Record Group 59, NARA.

[80] American Central School biannual report to Inter-American Schools Service, September 30, 1958, Records of American Sponsored Schools, Box 21, Cuba, Isle of Pines – American Central School, Record Group 59, NARA.

of settlers generally remained self-isolated and largely uninterested in engaging *pineros*, settlers at mid-century – particularly those involved at the school – made inclusion of *pineros* a priority. At least one or two Cubans served on the school board. The Parent-Teacher Association, an organization once dominated by Anglo-Americans, began translating its monthly meetings into Spanish to encourage Cuban parents to take part. Evidently, *pineros* responded positively to these efforts. The school's yearly enrollment consistently numbered around 100 students with *pineros* a clear majority. By the late 1950s, the ACS was more popular and on sounder financial footing than at any point since its founding.

Contesting *Pineridad*

The American Central School illustrated that Americans on the Isle at mid-century were much more apt to engage their *pinero* neighbors than early-century settlers. Travel writer Sydney A. Clark, who had painted a bleak picture of U.S. settlements during the 1930s, returned in 1953 and observed that the social dynamics had changed considerably. "Since the Second World War an entirely new wave of Americans has started to roll quietly into the island," he wrote. "The wave of the present is significant, for it is integrated – fully and heartily – with the Cuban tide."[81] Indeed, while national identity remained central to U.S. citizens, many of them also claimed to feel a part of the larger Isle community. Frederick Swetland Jr. embraced that idea. In recalling the Isle's increased economic activity that resulted from its free port status, he wrote that "things were going our way, at last, we *Pineros* thought."[82] He also referred to the Isle community in familial terms. "*Pineros* of American descent were part of the great Island family. And a happy society," Swetland wrote.[83] Bill Miller also considered himself a *pinero*. Although his parents were U.S. citizens, he was born in Santa Ana in 1942 and spent the first eighteen years of his life on the Isle. Socially, his family engaged *pineros* more than other Americans. "I guess most of my better friends were the Cubans," he said. "I interacted more with the *pineros* – being a *pinero* myself."[84]

Some scholars have criticized such inclusive sentiments by Americans in foreign locales as examples of cynical platitudes to appropriate local identity for ulterior ends. Judy Rohrer, for example, has written about

[81] Clark, "Island Idyll," 24.
[82] Swetland, *Isle of Pines*, 69.
[83] Ibid, 66.
[84] Bill Miller interview with author, August 9, 2014.

whites in 1890s Hawai'i who claimed to be "Hawaiian at heart" while seeking U.S. annexation. She argues that while such claims may have been earnest ones by *haoles*, they nevertheless had the effect of erasing natives' culture and history by subsuming it into Americanization efforts.[85] One could make a similar argument for this phenomenon on the Isle of Pines. But sentiments like those Swetland and Miller expressed came long after the annexationist drive. There seemed little desire to erase the Isle's Cuban-ness or *pineridad*. Rather, their remembered sentiment, perhaps more fervent because of their exile years later, celebrated the Isle's multiculturalism.

Certainly, there were limits to this collegiality. Although Americans and *pineros* socialized to a much greater extent at mid-century, there were few examples of intermarriage. White settlers occasionally married European migrants and some of the few African Americans on the Isle married Jamaicans or Cayman Islanders, but rarely *pineros*. The only instance on local record of a U.S.–Cuban wedding came in November 1929 when Edith Sundstrom married her husband, Albert, a naturalized Cuban citizen originally from Sweden.[86] One child of naturalized U.S. citizens, William Koenig, married a *pinera* in January 1954. But Koenig was born in Santa Barbara and apparently never lived in the United States.[87] One of the few examples of a U.S.–Cuban marriage was between Holt Rutherford and Reina Acosta. The couple met in 1959 when Rutherford, a native of Miami who had recently finished college, taught at the American Central School where Acosta was a high school student in her early twenties. Rutherford and Acosta married in December 1960 and shortly thereafter moved to the United States.[88]

---

[85] Rohrer, *Haoles in Hawai'i: Race and Ethnicity in Hawai'i* (Honolulu: University of Hawai'i Press 2010), 43.

[86] Edith Sundstrom's parents, Carl and Astrid Larson, were also natives of Sweden but became naturalized U.S. citizens before they moved to the Isle from Connecticut in 1920. Juzgado Municipal de la Isla de Pinos, 1901–1958, Certificados de Matrimonio, 1901–1958, Legajo 21, Expediente 614, AHM; Elinor Burkett, "The Last American," *Miami Herald*, September 4, 1988.

[87] Juzgado Municipal de la Isla de Pinos, 1901–1958, Certificados de Matrimonio, 1901–1958, Legajo 25, Expediente 810, AHM. Koenig's parents, John and Hermine Koenig, were natives of Germany who moved to Cleveland, Ohio, before settling on the Isle in 1909. William was born shortly thereafter. William's older brother, Harry, was born in the United States and was thought to be the last U.S. citizen on the Isle when he died in 1995. McManus, *Cuba's Island of Dreams*, 27–8.

[88] Mary Anne Rutherford Kimsey e-mail messages to author, June 30, 2011, and June 26, 2014.

Despite the continued scarcity of marriages, attitudes toward international relationships between men and women were far different at mid-century than they were during the Hay-Quesada era. At the height of U.S. settlement, romantic relationships between Americans and *pineros* were virtually nonexistent or kept private. In part, this phenomenon – or lack thereof – was because many settlers arrived on the Isle as family units; the lone frontiersman was in the minority. Perhaps more important, given the tensions between Americans and *pineros* while the sovereignty question was still in play, open relationships would have challenged acceptable social conventions and resulted in scorn or sanction from their national group. Settlers of the 1920s decried perceived *pinero* advances on American women. U.S. consul Charles Forman relayed two such instances in May 1924 about "the disposition of some Cuban men to annoy American women." The first happened on a steamboat, in which a man looked into a room occupied by an American woman. In another, a Cuban man smiled and bowed to a woman who did not know him.[89] While each tale may seem innocuous, settlers' reactions to them revealed deep-seated fears about the erosion of American power, influence, and attractiveness at a time when the U.S. presence on the Isle was vulnerable.

Even at mid-century, not all U.S. citizens felt an affinity for *pineros*. Indeed, Frederick Swetland Jr. recognized a divide among Americans, particularly between those who had lived on the Isle for decades and those who arrived during the 1950s, many of whom were primarily winter residents. He identified a generational gap as younger Americans tended to be more sociable than older ones. "In the later days, say from 1955 to 1960, there were American members who fell into two categories," Swetland wrote. "Those lately come to the island as winter residents, and those native to the Island. Not many of the original pioneering Americans were left, and of them, few came to dances, but their sons and daughters attended."[90] Stimson acknowledged a divide among U.S. citizens as well. "The older waves of Americans sometimes looked down on and ridiculed the newer 'clueless' Americans," he recalled. Stimson continued that some Americans assumed superiority over Cubans by virtue of their U.S. citizenship, not necessarily because they were wealthier. "Also, although many of the Americans, or at least some of them, held themselves as an elite class above the Cubans, they were not anything special. Back

---

[89] Forman to Charles Evans Hughes, May 1, 1924, 1910–29 Central Decimal File, General Records of the Department of State Relating to the Internal Affairs of Cuba, NARA Microcopy 488, Roll 28, File 837.014P/273.

[90] Swetland, *Isle of Pines*, 66.

home in the U.S. they wouldn't be special at all, just ordinary people, even people from the fringe."[91] Ernest Gruppe was one American leery of forming a close-knit community with *pineros*. Although he claimed to be friendly with Cubans, he also insisted that they live separate lives. "We were always Americans. We never turned over to the Cuban idea," he said. "I had many friends in Cuba, still have, and mainly Cubans, but we always lived on the Isle of Pines as Americans and always looked on its features as American. We never got into the Cuban idea."[92]

Nonetheless, many *pineros* accepted the U.S. presence and even encouraged it. For example, local business leaders lobbied Arthur Vining Davis to continue his investment and development plans even after Fidel Castro's ascension to power. "We have long realized that the true treasures of the Isle of Pines have remained undeveloped and unexploited," one group wrote in February 1959. "We find that it is in our social and economic advancement that we not only welcome you here, but that we put our shoulders to the wheel in assisting you to put your plans and projects into operation."[93] The letter shows that local businessmen considered Davis a key ally and potential partner while the direction of the Castro revolution was still unclear. In retrospect, some *pineros* wistfully recalled an era of meaningful engagement and cultural exchange between the two national groups. "We celebrated the Fourth of July with them and they came to our dances and festivities," Santiago Blanco, a Cuban exile living in Miami, said in 1988. "Cubans bought the merchandise imported by the local stores and [Americans] began to eat native fruits, rice and black beans. We even got to the point that many *guajiros* – peasants – could speak English even though they could not read or write. We had a peaceful life. It was a place where you could sleep with your doors open. There were never any problems between the Americans and Cubans. We were all *pineros*."[94] Similarly, Lydia McPherson, born on the Isle to Jamaican parents, remembered a strong communal spirit among national groups, including U.S. citizens. "The Americans didn't discriminate," she recalled. "It was like a big family, and the Americans who lived here were like family with the other foreigners and with the Cubans."[95]

Even Cuban writers who criticized Americans for commercially exploiting the Isle credited them for helping to usher an enduring sense of

[91] William Stimson, e-mail message to author, May 16, 2011.
[92] Gruppe interview, June 27, 1971, 1, SFA.
[93] Quoted in Brown, "Arthur Vining Davis and the Isle of Pines," 35, SFA.
[94] Quoted in Burkett, "The Last American."
[95] Quoted in McManus, *Cuba's Island of Dreams*, 125.

cosmopolitanism. For example, one group who referred to the U.S. presence as the "neocolonial" era nevertheless credited American customs – as well as those of other foreign nationals – with enriching the Isle's social and cultural diversity.[96] Likewise, historian Eduardo Lens argued that Americans and foreign nationals who maintained their respective languages and heritages fostered a cosmopolitan sensibility among the Isle's inhabitants.[97] The multitude of national and ethnic influences became central to an emerging sense of *pinerismo* – a pride in the Isle's diversity that was central to its identity. Cuban writers were not the only ones who noticed and embraced this distinction. Stimson, who lived on the Isle from 1955 to 1960, recalled that the multiplicity of peoples and customs not only enriched his experience there but it also made the term *pinero* hard to define. "The island was like Noah's ark," he stated. "There were one or two of everything. Not so easy to categorize. It was a rich and wonderful place."[98]

Some writers, however, have resisted the idea of the Isle as a cohesive community. One of the few studies Cuban scholars have done about Americans living on the Isle has argued that *pineridad* resisted U.S. influence (including efforts at annexation) rather than accommodated it.[99] Cepero recalled that while Americans and *pineros* enjoyed warm relations, some separation remained. She said that residents from across the Isle tended to shop at the same stores and casually greeted one another. But she also noted that Americans "had a distinct lifestyle from ours" and that Cubans and Americans who visited the same clubs often self-segregated.[100]

A geniality among the Isle's multinational population was apparent to Sonia Martínez, though. A Cuban-American from Cienfuegos, she arrived in December 1958 with her mother, sister, and stepfather after going through a divorce. The family managed the American-owned hotel Casa Mañana in Nueva Gerona while Martínez worked as the personal secretary to the manager of the Hotel Colony on Siguanea Bay, the lone resort on the Isle to finish construction before the Cuban Revolution. Perhaps because she had a Cuban father and an American mother, Martínez could move seamlessly within both social circles. She

[96] Hijuelos, et al., *Con Todo Derecho*, 53–4.
[97] Eduardo Lens, *La Isla Olvidada: Estudio Físico, Económico y Humano de la Isla de Pinos* (La Habana, 1942), 10. See also Pérez, et al., *Americanos en la Isla*, 7.
[98] William Stimson, e-mail message to author, May 16, 2011.
[99] Pérez, et al., *Americanos en la Isla*, 6.
[100] Elda Cepero Herrera interview with author, April 9, 2010.

remembered a warm reception. "People were very friendly," she said. "Although we were newcomers to the island, we were accepted immediately by both the 'American colony' and the locals.... New Year's Day picnics at Bibijagua Beach were attended by the old guard (the American citizens that had lived there for a couple of generations) as well as the newer residents such as our family and others, and even some of the locals who moved in the same circles."[101]

Martínez's experience illustrated that divisions between national groups – particularly Americans and Cubans – had become more permeable by mid-century. This shift owed much to the fact that Americans had a much less domineering presence on the Isle than earlier in the century. At the time of the Cuban Revolution, roughly 200 Americans still lived on the Isle. They remained only a small fraction of the estimated 8,000 U.S. citizens who resided in Cuba, most of whom were in Havana.[102] Stimson recalled that the Isle was truly a multinational community. "It was a real melting pot," he stated. "The Americans were everywhere but there was no sense that they dominated the place."[103] Moreover, the new wave of Americans tended to be younger and more willing to engage their *pinero* neighbors. Although divisions remained, the relative tranquility on the Isle between Americans and *pineros* contrasted sharply with the tenor of diplomatic relations between the two countries after 1959.

As the 1950s drew to a close, it was clear that relations between Americans and Cubans on the Isle of Pines had significantly changed. Whereas turn-of-the-century U.S. settlers tended to be self-isolated and shunned social engagement with *pineros*, personal interactions were much more commonplace by mid-century. Both groups mutually sought improved relations. Many Cubans were motivated by a desire to learn English and attract U.S. capital. Meanwhile, the dwindling American colony needed Cuban participation to maintain institutions of influence such as the American Central School, which emerged as a key space to nurture such interactions. As a result, the 1950s saw a greater level of commercial

---

[101] Sonia Martínez, e-mail message to author, May 10, 2011.
[102] Estimate of the U.S. population in Cuba taken from Thomas G. Paterson, *Contesting Castro: The United States and the Triumph of the Cuban Revolution* (New York: Oxford University Press, 1994), 49. Estimates of the U.S. population on the Isle during the 1950s are scarce. A 1960 Anglo-American Directory lists 100 U.S. citizens on the Isle that year. By that time, however, many Americans had already returned to the United States. See http://cuban-exile.com/doc_201-225/doc0217.html (accessed May 11, 2016).
[103] William Stimson, e-mail message to author, May 16, 2011.

and social cooperation. Although relations seemed genuinely cordial, all members of the Isle community did not necessarily live together as one big happy family, figuratively or literally. While many of the Isle's inhabitants indeed considered themselves *pineros*, divisions among its peoples remained, though they were far less contentious.

Relations between Americans and *pineros* stood in stark contrast to events in mainland Cuba. The heavy American political, economic, and cultural presence produced a backlash among Cubans who opposed U.S. support of the Fulgencio Batista regime as well as the proliferation of vice that catered to U.S. tourists. Fidel Castro successfully tapped into that sentiment and drew support for his budding revolution that eventually froze diplomatic relations between the United States and Cuba. For a time, the Isle remained isolated from the Revolution's effects and the souring relations between the two countries. Many Americans on the Isle initially welcomed Castro's ascent to power. They were optimistic that the revolution would open political participation for their *pinero* friends and that many of Batista's economic policies – particularly the free port – would continue. For the better part of a year, they did. But by early 1960, as Castro consolidated his hold on power, he implemented sweeping reforms that changed the tenor of American–*pinero* relations and ushered the end of the U.S. presence on the Isle of Pines.

8

Revolution and the Last Exodus

As dusk approached on a rainy day in May 1960, a group of Americans waited anxiously at the Nueva Gerona airfield for their chartered plane. Unsettled by the changes taking place in Cuba since Fidel Castro had come to power in January 1959 – particularly the new government's expropriation of private property – four families surreptitiously arranged for a C-46 to fly in from Miami and pick up as many of their belongings as they could pack. These landowners feared that their possessions would be confiscated if they tried to leave the country with them. When the plane finally arrived just before evening, the Americans lit up the gravel runway with their car headlights. Hurriedly, they packed the plane with their valuables. Frederick Swetland Jr., who was among the group, loaded his family's fine china, dishes, and books. "All cargo was shoved in somehow, anyhow," he recalled. Within ten minutes the plane climbed back into the night sky. It was a fitting backdrop considering that the episode came just as the U.S. presence on the Isle of Pines was reaching its twilight after six decades.[1]

To U.S. settlers, the Castro reforms triggered a stunning turn of events that resulted in the demise of the American colony. Just months earlier, the Isle seemed in the midst of a revival. It had enjoyed a spike in commercial interest and activity unseen in decades, spurred by development projects and favorable tariff policies under the Fulgencio Batista regime. But Batista's fall and the sweeping changes the Cuban Revolution brought compelled Americans to return to the United States. The end did not come

---

[1] Details taken from Frederick L. Swetland Jr., *Isle of Pines*, 71–2; Eli Swetland interview with author, July 10, 2009.

immediately. Throughout 1959, many Americans remained sympathetic to the Revolution, holding out hope that it would provide more political freedoms and economic opportunities for their *pinero* neighbors. Indeed, at the outset, revolutionary leaders seemed to support the issues of most concern to settlers, including tourism, infrastructure improvements, and foreign ownership. But within a year, change came as Castro sought to integrate the Isle more closely with mainland Cuba. He revoked the Isle's free port (*zona franca*) status and initiated a program of agrarian reform that expropriated thousands of acres from the largest landowners.

Policy changes, in turn, affected attitudes and relationships between nationalities that grew fraught with tension yet again. Many settlers became embittered by the confiscation of their property and the change in attitude toward Americans. William Stimson, for example, had mostly fond memories of his time on the Isle as a boy. But he remembered one unnerving moment when a "little Cuban boy walked up to me and asked, in Spanish, 'Why are you an Imperialist?' ... I was outraged at the little boy's question."[2] Stimson's reaction revealed a deep sense of betrayal that many U.S. citizens seemed to share. Like other Americans at mid-century, he had supported and befriended *pineros* and felt integrated into the Isle's larger community. Although they remained a distinct group, Americans did not consider their presence dominating as the term "imperialist" implied. After the triumph of the Revolution, however, it was clear that the Isle was no longer immune from the escalating tensions between Washington and Havana.

While departing Americans were not shy in expressing their opinions about the changes taking place, local Cuban perspectives were somewhat muted. Some *pinero* business owners and entrepreneurs wanted Americans to stay. A few wrote to Alcoa chairman Arthur Vining Davis in February 1959 lobbying him to continue his efforts to develop the Isle's tourism industry.[3] The reactions of poor and working-class *pineros* – ostensibly the primary beneficiaries of Castro's reforms – were less clear. Those who could afford the tuition continued to send their children to the American Central School until it closed in 1961. Cuban publications, meanwhile, were almost universally supportive of Castro's policies concerning the Isle. For example, noted Cuban scholar Antonio Núñez Jiménez, who had fought on behalf of the Revolution, credited Castro for "liberating"

---

[2] William Stimson e-mail message to author, May 16, 2011.
[3] J. J. Brown, "Arthur Vining Davis and the Isle of Pines, 1955–1960," June 23, 1965, 35, SFA.

the Isle from large landowners – now mostly Cubans, but still including some Americans – who had controlled it since the Spanish colonial era.[4]

The changes in policy spurred the final exodus of Americans. Before the Revolution, roughly 200 Americans still lived there; many more visited annually as tourists. Those numbers, however, declined drastically after the triumph of Castro's 26th of July Movement. Although there were no explicit laws that deported Americans, many felt pressured to leave, even those who had not been to the United States in years. By May 1961, thirty-five U.S. citizens remained; a decade later, there were only seven.[5] Those who left the Isle expressed a range of emotions: a sense of loss for abandoning a place they considered home; anger toward the Castro government for taking their property; and regret that the Isle never fully lived up to the potential they had envisaged. Longtime settlers blamed the U.S. government for not annexing the Isle years earlier and for leaving it in incapable hands. Others maintained that Castro's policies undermined what was shaping up to be a tourist paradise. Regardless, the Cuban Revolution accomplished what years of hurricanes and commercial failures could not: effectively end the U.S. presence on the Isle of Pines.

¡Viva la Revolución!

When Fidel Castro arrived in Havana in January 1959, he encountered an outpouring of enthusiasm among Cubans overjoyed to see the end of Fulgencio Batista's regime. Historian Louis A. Pérez Jr. has argued that Batista's rule was a source of shame and embarrassment to the Cuban people since Batista had retaken formal political control via a *coup d'état* in March 1952.[6] As a result, many Cubans felt relieved to see him toppled. Some Americans on the Isle shared these feelings. "It was my country, and the fresh, bright heady feel of [Castro's] successful revolt against usurpation was one in which I shared," recalled Frederick Swetland Jr., who after years of numerous visits had moved his family to the Isle in 1957 to live year-round.[7] Adolph B. Kelm, who had lived on the Isle

---

[4] Waldo Medina, *Aquí, Isla de Pinos* (La Habana, 1961), 6. Núñez Jiménez wrote his comments in the prologue to this collection of essays by Medina.

[5] American citizens resident in the Isle of Pines, Cuba, May 17, 1961, Fondo: A.B. Kelm, Legajo 10, Expediente 96, AHM. Kelm kept an annual tally of U.S. citizens on the Isle until 1971.

[6] Louis A. Pérez Jr., *On Becoming Cuban: Identity, Nationality and Culture* (Chapel Hill: University of North Carolina Press, 1999), 446–8.

[7] Memorandum of Frederick Swetland Jr., March 7, 1961, 12, SFA.

for more than forty years at the time of the Revolution, also had high hopes that Castro's government would usher in more equitable political and economic reforms for Cubans: "I personally believe that Señor Fidel Castro is an honest man and holds out for his country the best of all things."[8] Their reactions mirrored the cautious optimism that some U.S. policymakers – including Vice President Richard M. Nixon and Sen. John F. Kennedy – initially held toward Castro, that he might be a leader with whom the United States could work.

During his first few months in power, Castro initiated a whirlwind of reforms. His ascent seemed to be a harbinger for a renewal of democracy and social justice, two things that had been in short supply given the political corruption and repression in Batista's Cuba. But Castro first sought to address the long-standing issue of income inequality by nationalizing key industries and utilities, introducing rent and price controls, and revitalizing education. Although he asserted that Cuba needed far-reaching change, he maintained during this early period that his platform was not communist, a source of great concern to the Cold War–era United States. In an appearance on *Meet the Press* in April 1959, Castro denied that his brother and key deputy, Raúl, was a communist. But as Castro's reforms took shape, it became clear that they were having an impact on the profit margins of entrepreneurs, both American and Cuban, who increasingly voiced their concerns to the upper reaches of the U.S. government. This resistance deepened fissures between the United States and Cuba that led to a break in relations, Castro's public embrace of socialism, and Cuba's alliance with the Soviet Union.[9]

These developments affected the Isle of Pines as well. Castro was no stranger to the place. After his initial uprising against Batista failed at the Moncada Barracks in July 1953, Castro was sentenced to fifteen years in the Presidio Modelo. He remained mostly in solitary confinement – officials feared his revolutionary rhetoric would inspire other prisoners – until he was released as part of a general amnesty in May 1955. From there, he went to Mexico to plan a new rebellion. After his triumph, Castro made numerous visits to the Isle, mostly using it as a vacation retreat. He frequently stayed in the Hotel Colony on Siguanea Bay. Sonia Martínez, a Cuban-American who moved to the Isle in 1958, worked

[8] Kelm to Margaret Fish, October 21, 1959, Fondo: A.B. Kelm, Legajo 3, Expediente 24, AHM.
[9] Aviva Chomsky, *A History of the Cuban Revolution* (Malden, MA: Wiley-Blackwell, 2011), 44–64; Louis A. Pérez Jr., *Cuba: Between Reform and Revolution*, 4th ed. (New York: Oxford University Press, 2011), 237–90.

at the hotel and recalled his visits. On one occasion in February 1960, Castro brought Soviet Minister Anastas Mikoyan during a formal state visit in which the Soviet Union was assessing Cuba as a potential ally. During another trip, Martínez arranged for a group of teachers and students from the American Central School to meet Castro. Ron Williams, a teacher at the ACS, was among the group. He recalled that Castro seemed particularly curious about the school's physical education program and dominated the conversation. "When you talked with Fidel you didn't do much in the way of talking," Williams said of the famously verbose Cuban leader. "You did more in the way of listening because he would never know when to stop. He kept going and going and going."[10]

Castro's involvement with the Isle was not merely for recreation. During his first visit as prime minister in June 1959, he announced a host of reforms pertaining to the Isle. Chief among these changes was revoking the Isle's status as a free port. Eliminating the special tax-free privileges on imports and goods that Isle residents, tourists, and businesses enjoyed, Castro claimed, would put *pineros* on equal footing with other Cubans and draw the Isle out of its historic isolation from mainland Cuba. That is not to say, however, that Castro sought to abolish tourism, one of the Isle's key industries. On the contrary, he pledged to support it. To this end, he promised additional highway construction, particularly to the South Coast; improvements to water, sewage, and communications systems; a reduction of air and sea fares; and more direct flights between the Isle and Florida.[11] Castro's measures were in keeping with his broader policy to revive tourism across the country in 1959. The new government allowed for gambling in tourist hotels, approved a $1 million loan to the newly opened Havana Hilton, and hosted the annual meeting of the American Society of Travel Agents. Such efforts would soon be undermined, however, by U.S. government antagonism and Castro's increasingly hostile rhetoric that scared off potential tourists.[12]

Some business and tourist activity continued, but it had clearly slowed from its pre-Revolution heights. One of the highlights was the filming of

[10] Ron Williams interview with author, July 9, 2009.

[11] Wiltse Peña Hijuelos, et al., *Con Todo Derecho: Isla de la Juventud* (La Habana, 1986), 82–3. With the exception of the latter pledge, Castro's government followed through on improvements throughout the 1960s, largely supported by youth volunteers. But the measures were designed to sustain and grow the Isle's agricultural output, rather than tourism. See Jane McManus, *Cuba's Island of Dreams: Voices from the Isle of Pines and Youth* (Gainesville: University Press of Florida, 2000), 99–110.

[12] Dennis Merrill, *Negotiating Paradise: U.S. Tourism and Empire in Twentieth-Century Latin America* (Chapel Hill: University of North Carolina Press, 2009), 153–76.

Rebellion in Cuba, a fictional story starring Lon Chaney Jr. and boxer Jake LaMotta about a group of Americans who aim to overthrow Castro. Although the movie was released to little popular or critical acclaim, the filming created some excitement among the locals. But this event was more the exception than the norm as businesses shuttered and hotel construction came to a halt. Local businessmen lobbied Arthur Vining Davis to continue his plans for development, but to no avail. According to Davis's manager, J. J. Brown, the Castro government showed little interest in working with Davis to continue to develop the Isle as a resort location. Brown recalled a disastrous October 1959 meeting with some of Castro's representatives. He found them "quite obstinate" in negotiations and concluded that he "could see no reason whatsoever for Mr. Davis continuing to attempt developing properties on the Island."[13] Brown, however, offered no details about the negotiations or conditions discussed in the meeting.

In addition to the free-port revocation, the Agrarian Reform Law was another major policy change that affected life not just on the Isle, but in all of Cuba as well. Announced in May 1959, the new law expropriated abandoned land and limited real estate holdings to 1,000 acres, or 3,333 acres (100 *caballerías*) if the land was being used to grow sugar, rice, or livestock. Land above that limit was nationalized into state-run cooperatives or given in sixty-seven-acre parcels to individuals – including squatters, renters, and sharecroppers – who were already using it. Owners were to be compensated with twenty-year bonds at 4.5 percent annual interest based on the tax-assessed value of the land. Although the new law only affected about 10 percent of the farms in Cuba, corporate interests, large landowners, and middle-class property owners resisted. Seeing little recourse for protest given Castro's popularity, many landowners fled to the United States. More than 60,000 Cubans migrated north each year from 1960 to 1962.[14]

On the Isle, the new agrarian reform policies affected only a minority of U.S. landowners, but it nevertheless made Americans apprehensive.

---

[13] Brown, "Arthur Vining Davis and the Isle of Pines," 36–7, SFA.

[14] Problems with compensation emerged at the start. According to one report, bonds were not to be converted into U.S. dollars. "U.S. Warns Cuba on Land Reform," *New York Times*, June 12, 1959. By the end of the year, the bonds had yet to be printed nor had a specific value of the expropriated land been calculated. "Economy of Cuba Shaken by Change," *New York Times*, December 19, 1959. For a synopsis of this policy and its consequences in Cuba, see Pérez, *Cuba*, 243–55; Hugh Thomas, *Cuba, or the Pursuit of Freedom*, updated edition (New York: Da Capo, 1998), 1215–33.

Kelm, whose landholdings were below the threshold for expropriation, argued that Castro's reforms, though well-intentioned, were too far-reaching because they jeopardized foreign investment. "His agrarian reform law is a good thing for the country people but here again it is impossible to rush so fast to prevent a serious stumble along the way," he wrote in October 1959. "To expropriate the large estates of American citizens, to my mind is a real serious error."[15] Swetland, whose real estate holdings were well over the expropriation threshold, sympathized with Castro's aim of redistributing land. But he deemed the agrarian reform law an ineffective approach. As Swetland put it, "in his anxiety to get rid of the rats, Fidel burned down the barn."[16]

Despite Americans' concerns, the Agrarian Reform Institute (INRA) that oversaw the process of redistribution apparently made no immediate move to seize U.S.-owned property. Swetland claimed that the Isle's *alcalde*, Mariano Rives, and other *pineros* made a personal plea to Castro to refrain from expropriating land on the Isle since only twelve to fifteen properties qualified. "With a wave of his hand," Swetland wrote, "[Castro] said they would not be bothered."[17] Feeling assured that his property was safe from expropriation, Swetland went about his normal routine during the summer and fall of 1959. In addition to his regular planting and plowing, he added fifty cows to his considerable stable, bought a sawmill, and received a government permit to cut pine on his property. In another sign that suggested agrarian reform would proceed differently on the Isle, the Cuban government in October 1959 announced that foreigners would be allowed to purchase up to forty acres of land for recreational purposes.[18] The announcement signaled a shift in policy from the agrarian reform law that specified only Cuban nationals could buy land.

Castro subsequently had a change of heart when it came to expropriating foreign-owned land on the Isle. Swetland claimed to know why. During one of his Isle retreats in January 1960, Castro flew by helicopter over San Francisco de las Piedras and saw fallen pines – one of the few instances, Swetland said, when he cut down trees on his property. Seeing the fallen timber, Castro allegedly remarked, "*Que destrozo, robando la riqueza de la Patria.*"[19] Shortly thereafter, Swetland received word that his

---

[15] Kelm to Margaret Fish, October 21, 1959, Fondo: A.B. Kelm, Legajo 3, Expediente 24, AHM.
[16] Memorandum of Frederick Swetland Jr., March 7, 1961, 25, SFA.
[17] Ibid., 35.
[18] "Cuban Land for Sale," *Hartford Courant*, October 5, 1959.
[19] Roughly translated: "So destructive, robbing the nation of its resources." How Swetland knew what Castro said is unclear.

property would be "intervened" in accordance with the Agrarian Reform Law. A local official allowed him to keep some 1,500 acres of his nearly 10,000-acre property; the government expropriated the remainder.[20]

Swetland's theory about Castro's motivations may explain San Francisco's expropriation, but the process elsewhere on the Isle already had begun. The government seized the land of prominent Cuban owners first. By the end of 1959, the property of Francisco Cajigas, Gregorio "Goyo" Hernández, and Leo Leone had already been expropriated.[21] U.S. landholders came next, starting with Arthur Vining Davis's nearly 300,000 acres. Although Swetland was not the first American to lose his property to agrarian reform, he may have been the first American forced to adapt to the consequences while still living on the Isle. In retrospect, Swetland surmised that he should have seen it coming since "as the only American or Cuban landholder of any consequence left, I was bound to get it where the turkey got the axe."[22] In addition to his land, Swetland was relieved of most of his cattle; government officials in June 1960 took all but 140 of his 812 head. In August, the government seized the sawmill and half of his farm equipment. Also that month, his lot was reduced to 1,000 acres.[23] Two months later, he left the Isle.

Initially, the Cuban government's expropriation program affected only large landowners. In July 1960, however, it began a process of nationalizing all U.S.-owned property. Like the Agrarian Reform Law, owners also were entitled to compensation, though far less – and there was an important catch. Compensation would come in the form of thirty-year government bonds at 2 percent annual interest. The bonds were to be financed from profits of sugar sales to U.S. markets, anything sold above 3 million tons and 5.75 cents a pound. But the U.S. government had just significantly cut its quota of Cuban sugar purchases; in fact, the Cuban government initiated the nationalization program in response to the U.S. reduction of its sugar quota.[24] The tit-for-tat reflected increasing hostility between Washington and Havana that only grew more intense in the

---

[20] The anecdote about Castro and the Swetland property expropriation described in: Memorandum of Frederick Swetland Jr., March 7, 1961, 36–7, SFA; Swetland, *Isle of Pines*, 70.

[21] A.B. Kelm to David Browne, December 10, 1959, Fondo: A.B. Kelm, Legajo 1, Expediente 9, AHM. Given his ties to Batista, Cajigas was one of the first Cuban elites to seek exile in the United States. The fates of Hernández and Leone are unclear.

[22] Frederick Swetland Jr. to Paul Swetland, February 7, 1960, SFA.

[23] Memorandum of Frederick Swetland Jr., March 7, 1961, 40, 48–9, SFA.

[24] "Havana Is Ready to Seize More American Property," *New York Times*, July 7, 1960; "Castro Forces Carry Out Seizure of U.S. Properties," *New York Times*, August 8, 1960.

ensuing months. By mid-1960, the Eisenhower administration was in the midst of planning an invasion using Cuban exiles. In October, the United States initiated a trade embargo. Three months later, the United States severed diplomatic relations, which would remain broken until 2015.

Expropriations were not limited to individuals' properties. The American Central School – the most conspicuous example of U.S. influence on the Isle – faced closing as well. Even after the triumph of the Revolution, classes continued. Enrollment remained strong for the 1959–60 school year: 109 students, including seventy-three Cubans and twenty-three Americans. How much longer the ACS would remain American-run became a concern. The fear was heightened after the October 1959 announcement of Decree 2099, which specified the Ministry of Education's regulatory powers over education in Cuba. "Private schools have interpreted this as their death knell," one U.S. embassy official wrote.[25] Hoping to preserve an institution of American influence and stave off Cuban government intervention, the U.S. embassy encouraged the American Central School to expand its Spanish-language offerings to prepare Cuban high school students for university.[26] The rumors of the school's impending nationalization persisted, however. Williams approached a local INRA official to ask if there was any truth to it. But the man responded: "Oh, don't believe that garbage. The counter-revolutionaries are trying to stir things up."[27]

As more Americans and Cubans fled the Isle, though, keeping the school open proved difficult. Swetland, the school's director, returned to the United States in October 1960 and the U.S. Embassy in Havana lost communication with the school.[28] Consequently, the ACS no longer received Inter-American Schools Service aid. With enrollments down, the American Central School limped along for one more year. Bill Miller, who had moved to Miami after graduating from the ACS in 1959, returned to the Isle to become the high school teacher in the fall of 1960 while his mother, Marie, taught grades one through four. "I didn't have a teacher's certificate but there weren't many Americans left on the island [to

[25] John Z. Williams to U.S. Ambassador, Havana, November 13, 1959, Records of American Sponsored Schools, Box 21, Cuba – General, Record Group 59, NARA.

[26] Briefing Paper for John Z. Williams, July 23, 1959, and Summary of 400 (c) Funds Requested for American Central School, October 12, 1960, Records of American Sponsored Schools, Box 21, Cuba, Isle of Pines – American Central School, Record Group 59, NARA.

[27] Ron Williams interview with author, July 9, 2009.

[28] U.S. Embassy Memorandum, October 12, 1960, Records of American Sponsored Schools, Box 21, Cuba, Isle of Pines – American Central School, Record Group 59, NARA.

teach]," Miller recalled. "I worked more like an instructor. I did the best I could."[29] In addition to meeting the challenge of teaching for the first time, Miller had to adjust to periodic classroom visits from armed Cuban military. "They'd come in," he said. "They wouldn't say anything. They'd just come in with their guns and they'd sit in the back of the classroom and just hang out for a while and intimidate people."[30] Occasionally, the military visitors would question Miller about what he was teaching since he conducted all his classes in English. But for the most part they did not interfere, armed presence notwithstanding. In all, Miller had about ten students, five of whom were seniors who received diplomas in the school's final graduating class. Following the 1960–1 academic year, by which point U.S.–Cuban diplomatic relations had ceased and the Bay of Pigs invasion had failed, the Cuban government nationalized the school.[31]

Changing Attitudes

As tourism slowed and expropriations continued, the mood on the Isle changed starkly. Americans attributed this shift to the arrival of *barbudos*, the bearded members of Castro's rebel army like the ones who visited Miller's classroom. "They weren't exactly polite," Eli Swetland remembered.[32] Kelm in 1961 wrote that the tension U.S. citizens felt did not come from *pineros*. "Our old time Cuban friends have not changed, it's only the new ones who throw us a dirty glance now and then," he noted.[33] Frederick Swetland Jr., who described the pre-Revolution Isle as "a happy society," lamented a new spirit that bred fear and secrecy. He wrote that "the once ebullient *Pinero* was now quiet, looking over his shoulder and talking out of the corner of his mouth into a friend's tilted ear.… In any crowd there was sure to be a member or two of the secret police, an informer or two. They were there; all knew it well. There was little laughter."[34] The comments show that, to Americans at least, the Isle was no longer the same welcoming place that they had enjoyed. An anti-American sentiment that had been prevalent in mainland Cuba and co-opted by Castro and his revolutionaries now seemed to permeate the Isle.

[29] Bill Miller interview with author, August 9, 2014.
[30] Ibid.
[31] Diego Rodríguez Molina, et al., *El Verdadero Descubrimiento* (La Habana: Ediciones El Abra, 1996), 45.
[32] Eli Swetland interview with author, July 10, 2009.
[33] Kelm to William Hyland, March 29, 1961, Fondo: A.B. Kelm, Legajo 3, Expediente 27, AHM.
[34] Swetland, *Isle of Pines*, 265.

The transition was gradual. As the Revolution purged the government of *batistianos*, including the public executions of Batista-era officials across the country, those who had once supported Castro's rise became uneasy. "At first it wasn't so noticeable and people were still excited about the revolution," Sonia Martínez noted. "Then the revolution started killing people and these people were the neighbors, parents, sons, friends and school mates of residents and then it got to the point that some people were afraid to be seen with people who they had been friends with all their lives."[35] Martínez said that the Presidio Modelo's warden was one of the first to be executed on the Isle. A few months later, the warden's daughters approached Castro during one of his trips to the Hotel Colony and asked if they could open a school. Martínez overheard the conversation and Castro's brusque rebuff. "He denied them the right of opening a school and called them names ... as if whatever their father had done was their fault," she said.[36] The incident sobered her view of Castro and the revolutionary government.

In addition to opposing its tone and policies, Americans maintained that the revolutionary government failed in its primary responsibility: protecting residents. As expropriations mounted and diplomatic relations deteriorated during 1960, U.S. citizens reported no longer feeling safe in their homes. Kelm stated that many American-owned homes were robbed, not just abandoned properties but those where people still resided. "People cannot afford to leave their homes at night," he wrote.[37] In one particularly jarring incident, longtime U.S. settler Irma Smith was attacked in her home as intruders robbed the house. Her husband, Dan, found her unconscious and rushed her to the hospital in Nueva Gerona, where she needed a blood transfusion. Swetland, a friend of the Smiths, wrote that doctors found that "she had been struck, not once as she remembered, but several times. Whoever it was, how many of them, had then ransacked the house and left her to bleed to death on the tile floor of the laundry."[38] Escaped prisoners were alleged to have committed the attack, but there is no record of any arrest. Although the assault appeared to be an isolated incident, the spate of robberies suggested undercurrents of simmering anti-Americanism – or perhaps, more accurately, anti-elitism – on the Isle that the Revolution unleashed. Regardless, Americans

---

[35] Sonia Martínez e-mail message to author, May 10, 2011.
[36] Ibid.
[37] Kelm to Evelyn Haner, March 28, 1960, Fondo: A.B. Kelm, Legajo 3, Expediente 29, AHM.
[38] Swetland, *Isle of Pines*, 260–1.

had little faith in the new government's willingness to respond to reports of attacks on person or property. Swetland relayed a story of a pastor at the Lutheran church near Nueva Gerona who went to the local police to report stolen items from his office. Among the stolen items was a typewriter – the same typewriter, he noticed, that the officer was using to fill out the report.[39] True or not, the story nevertheless revealed Americans' – or at least Swetland's – lack of confidence in the new government's ability to maintain order.

Swetland's reaction to Smith's attack and the pastor's robbery underscored a rising tide of anger among Americans who did not want to leave. Longtime residents such as Kelm, the Swetlands, the Smiths, and the Sundstroms considered the Isle their home. Their tenure and their economic contributions made them feel just as invested in the Isle as any native Cuban. They resented the new government's policies that, in their view, undermined the financial and emotional ties they had made in the Isle. "It's a pioneer story, of people going off to a marginal place to make something of themselves," William Stimson later wrote. "Some of them did make something of themselves. Then the thieving and corrupt Communists came and took it all away in the end anyway."[40] Others, like Kelm, maintained that the Revolution myopically drove away the very people who had made the Isle an attractive destination. "This Isle of Pines without the American pioneers, their hard work and vast investments would still be in its backward stage.... The prosperity which developed during 1956–57 and '58 was tremendous while today there isn't a single sale of rural property and land values have declined to their lowest point," Kelm wrote in 1960.[41]

Anger gave way to resignation, and by May 1961 only thirty-five U.S. citizens remained in residence. Those who left tried to take with them as many of their valuables as they could carry. Whatever they could not take with them, they left behind either unattended or with caretakers. When Swetland departed the Isle, he left what remained of his property, including the house, with a caretaker. Four months later, he received word that authorities had seized the house and its contents.[42]

For the Miller family, who lived on the Isle for more than a half-century, leaving in 1961 was especially difficult. Bill Miller was born on

[39] Ibid, 261–2.
[40] William Stimson e-mail message to author, May 17, 2011.
[41] Kelm to E. E. Ernst, September 20, 1960, Fondo: A.B. Kelm, Legajo 2, Expediente 11, AHM.
[42] Memorandum of Frederick Swetland Jr., March 7, 1961, 49, SFA.

the Isle in February 1942 and aside from six months in Miami after he graduated from high school, it was the only home he had ever known. His mother, Marie, had also been born on the Isle of Swedish-American heritage and had spent virtually her entire life there as well. The family's roots ran deep and they knew local officials well. But as the Havana-directed expropriations continued – first with the family's farm equipment, then with their land – the Millers felt compelled to leave. The family spent a week in Havana trying to secure the proper paperwork to get out of the country. Bringing very little money and only what they could carry, Bill Miller recalled that his family were the only Americans on the plane to Miami. The U.S. government, he said, assisted the Cubans who arrived in the country but the Millers had to fend for themselves. When they arrived, their suitcases were missing and would not be found for weeks. "I had to borrow a dime to call someone I knew in Miami to get money for bus tickets to Tampa where my uncle lived," he said. His father, John C. Miller, had remained on the Isle to settle the family's affairs and joined the rest of the family in Florida about a month later. Miller said his father and brother "tried giving stuff to people who worked for them but I imagine after they left, it all went back to the government."[43]

Yet a few Americans resolved to stay. Their reasons were both practical and emotional. As Kelm pointed out, many of the last settlers were elderly and into retirement age.[44] The cost of relocating as well as the physical toll surely was a consideration. But their conviction to remain also illustrated just how deeply they identified the Isle as their home. Aside from occasional trips back to the United States to visit friends and family, some settlers had not lived there for decades. The prospect of going back held little appeal, not because of any antipathy toward their national homeland but rather a preference for living in a land they knew more intimately among neighbors with whom they were more familiar. "Everything we had was on the island – our little casita, our garden, all our things," Edith Sundstrom said. "We didn't have anything in the States – no family, no property, no money."[45] Kelm stated a similar conviction in June 1962 when he numbered just one of seventeen U.S. citizens left. "I have thought of going back to New Jersey several times, a thing my brothers have strongly suggested at various times," he wrote. "However, I have lived here for close to 46 years, my friends remain, so

---

[43] Bill Miller interview with author, August 9, 2014.
[44] Kelm to Morris Finkel, June 12, 1962, Fondo: A.B. Kelm, Legajo 2, Expediente 15, AHM.
[45] Quoted in Elinor Burkett, "The Last American," *Miami Herald*, September 4, 1988.

I would like to see the conclusion of the ball game." While Kelm remained optimistic that U.S.–Cuban relations would normalize again in the near future – indeed, up until the Cuban Missile Crisis of October 1962, many observers presumed the United States would eventually topple the Castro government – he also revealed that life on the Isle had become less tumultuous. In contrast to the antipathy settlers felt from *barbudos* during the first months of the Revolution, Kelm stated that the remaining U.S. citizens were "not molested in the least manner and the old friends haven't changed their sympathies toward our citizens."[46]

By the late 1960s, however, even holdouts like Kelm and Sundstrom reconsidered their decision to stay. For Kelm, the first signs of discontent surfaced in May 1967 when he found it increasingly difficult to procure a travel visa to leave Cuba. "This old World is growing more difficult with each passing day and I see little brightness, happiness or comfort in the future," he wrote. "You must be a tough guy these days in order to live easily, while the humble person is finding it more difficult."[47] Much of Kelm's pessimism came from his declining business prospects. As a shipping agent, he worked with various small businesses that were increasingly nationalized. By the late 1960s, he admitted that his enterprise was suffering under Cuba's socialist system. Kelm, who never remarried after his wife died in 1940, grew more despondent in his letters. One local official even suggested that he return to the United States. Kelm eventually tried to obtain an exit visa through the Swiss embassy, but for reasons unclear he never left. After he died in 1975, Cuban authorities turned his house into an "anti-imperialist museum."[48]

Sundstrom, meanwhile, resolved to live out her days on the Isle, even after her husband, Albert, died in 1978. She became a local celebrity of sorts, considered the last U.S. woman still on the Isle. Inspired by her caretaker, a *pinero* high school English teacher named Alexis Rosa, Sundstrom decided in 1987 to go back to the United States. She wanted to return for the sake of Rosa, who was himself eager to leave Cuba. After months of bureaucratic wrangling, the pair secured exit visas for the

[46] Kelm to Morris Finkel, June 12, 1962, Fondo: A.B. Kelm, Legajo 2, Expediente 15, AHM.
[47] Kelm to Clara Walkington, May 30, 1967, Fondo: A.B. Kelm, Legajo 5, Expediente 44/1, AHM.
[48] Kelm to Swiss Embassy, Havana, December 23, 1968, Fondo: A.B. Kelm, Legajo 14, Expediente 139, AHM; Kelm to Swiss Embassy, Havana, October 25, 1973, Fondo: A.B. Kelm, Legajo 14, Expediente 139, AHM; Ada Patten to Kelm, March 4, 1974, Fondo: A.B. Kelm, Legajo 12, Expediente 121, AHM. The conversion of his house reported in Burkett, "The Last American."

trip to Miami. Despite her initial excitement on returning to the United States, Sundstrom yearned for the Isle, which she still considered home. "It's so busy and noisy here," she said when she had experienced Miami. "There's so much violence, hatred and drugs. Neighbors don't even greet each other. I don't understand what has happened here.... It's very difficult. I have moments when I feel I don't belong here. I don't really know where I do belong."[49] Sundstrom, however, remained in Florida, where she died in 2001 at the age of ninety-six.[50]

Aftermath

As U.S. citizens fled the Isle, those who had their property expropriated by the Cuban government lobbied for compensation. Because this phenomenon was occurring throughout Cuba – most notably among large sugar corporations whose vast lands were being "intervened" – the U.S. government took up the protest. In the months before severing formal diplomatic relations in January 1961, the U.S. government demanded that private citizens and companies receive immediate cash compensation for lands taken. But the Castro government insisted that it did not have enough liquidity and would instead pay out in long-term bonds. For those who left their homes and businesses under duress and distrusted the Castro government, it seemed an empty promise.

In October 1964, Congress established the Cuban Claims Program for U.S. citizens to register their property losses. Administered by the Federal Claims Settlement Commission within the Department of Justice, the program received more than 8,800 claims from private citizens and corporations. It certified some 5,900 of them, valued at $1.9 billion. Corporate claims made up nearly 90 percent of the total. The commission ruled that in accordance with the International Claims Settlement Act of 1949, claimants were entitled to 6 percent annual interest from the date of expropriation to settlement, meaning that claims have accrued more than a half-century of interest. Theoretically, as the United States and Cuba continue to normalize diplomatic relations, these claims will be presented to the Cuban government for restitution.[51]

---

[49] Quoted in Burkett, "The Last American." Additional detail taken from McManus, *Cuba's Island of Dreams*, 121–3.

[50] According to one online database, someone matching Sundstrom's name and date of birth died March 9, 2001, in Miami-Dade County. No corroborating obituary could be found. www.faqs.org/people-search/sundstrom-florida/ (accessed May 11, 2016).

[51] Information about the Cuban Claims Program taken from www.justice.gov/fcsc/claims-against-cuba (accessed May 11, 2016).

U.S. settlers and entrepreneurs on the Isle submitted claims as well, albeit on a much smaller scale than in mainland Cuba. There were 233 claims totaling more than $18.2 million. Arthur Vining Davis had the largest claim, more than $4.2 million for expropriated land. Such a large claim, however, was exceptional; a majority of reported losses were for less than $10,000. Landowners who did not reside on the Isle made many of those smaller claims, absentee landlords who either had abandoned their real estate years earlier or had later inherited it. Only thirteen claims were from settlers who appeared in a 1960 registry of U.S. citizens on the Isle. Individuals rather than corporations comprised all but two of the claims. One of those corporate claims was by the Isle of Pines United Land Companies, apparently the only landholding company still in oper ation at the time of the Revolution. It cited losses of improved real estate valued at $423,000.[52]

More than fifty years later, U.S. landowners still await compensation for expropriated property. According to the Joint Corporate Committee on Cuban Claims, a private organization comprised of individual and corporate claimants, the Cuban government never issued the promised compensatory bonds or paid former owners for land that it seized.[53] There is no record as to why Cuba never paid out the promised bonds. But some reports maintain that the U.S. government rejected Cuban offers to nego-tiate the matter.[54] Regardless, a few years after he and his wife submitted their $1 million claim with the Federal Claims Settlement Commission, Frederick Swetland Jr. admitted that he never expected to receive com-pensation for his property. "Maybe my boys will get something out of it," he said. "I don't expect anything. It could come to life someday. It'll just

---

[52] www.justice.gov/sites/default/files/fcsc/docs/ccp-listofclaims.pdf (accessed May 11, 2016).

[53] For information about the Joint Corporate Committee on Cuban Claims and its asser-tion about compensation, see www.certifiedcubanclaims.org/ (accessed May 11, 2016).

[54] In September 1979, John A. Cypher Jr., a member of the Joint Corporate Committee on Cuban Claims, testified before the House Committee on Foreign Affairs that Castro in March 1964 made a $1 billion offer to settle the claims on the condition that the United States restore its sugar quota. The Lyndon B. Johnson administration, however, ignored the offer. House Committee on Foreign Affairs, *Outstanding Claims against Cuba: Hearing before the Subcommittees on International Economic Policy and Trade and on Inter-American Affairs of the Committee on Foreign Affairs*, 96th Cong., 1st sess., 1979, 9. See also Timothy Ashby, "U.S. Certified Claims against Cuba: Legal Reality and Likely Settlement Mechanisms," *University of Miami Inter-American Law Review* 40 (Spring 2009): 420–1. Ashby, a former official in the U.S. Department of Commerce, contends that Cuba in the late 1980s once again expressed interest in settling the claims, but the U.S. government did not respond to the overture.

be raw land for what it's worth or what they might be able to use it for."[55] Bill Miller also remained skeptical. His family filed five claims for land and improved real property valued at more than $300,000. "I don't ever expect to get anything," he said. "Maybe my grandkids."[56]

Almost all the Americans who left in the wake of the Revolution never saw the Isle again. The onerous U.S. policies that limited travel certainly were a contributing factor. Stimson was one of the few to return. When he did, he found the Isle scarcely recognizable. "When I went back [in 1995], I could see clear across much of the island," he stated. "All the trees had been cut. Nothing much planted. Communism. Whoever did the planning was an idiot, a real idiot. They ruined a beautiful island that could have forever been a big draw as a tourist spot."[57] Hearing those kinds of reports squelched Swetland's desire to go back. Although he once "expected to be buried" on the Isle, it was not the same place he remembered. The old house was no longer what it once was, many of the trees on the property had been cut, and the rapid population growth seemed to rob the Isle of its tranquility. "I would not, could not, go back," said Swetland, who died in 2003 in Yellow Springs, Ohio, where he resided after leaving the Isle.[58]

Despite initial plans to support tourism on the Isle, Castro changed course as he publicly embraced socialism. Indeed, the tourism industry all but vanished, replaced by communist youth camps and collective farms that drew participants from all across Cuba. As a result, the Isle's population skyrocketed, from around 11,000 people before the Cuban Revolution to roughly 84,000 in the early twenty-first century.[59] Castro also looked to turn the Isle into an education center. Boarding schools proliferated. These schools were designed not only with Cuban students in mind, but were opened to children from around the world. Many of these foreign exchange students came from elsewhere in Latin America as well as from Africa, where Cuba had militarily supported anticolonial uprisings.[60] By the mid-1980s, students attended seventy-five elementary

---

[55] Comments by Swetland made in Gruppe interview, June 21, 1971, tape 20, 4, SFA.

[56] Bill Miller interview with author, August 9, 2014.

[57] William Stimson e-mail message to author, May 16, 2011.

[58] Quoted in Peggy Shank, "A 'refugee' in his native home," *Yellow Springs News*, circa 1998.

[59] According to geographer Morton D. Winsberg's 1957 estimate, the Isle had around 9,000 residents as well as 2,000 prisoners at the Presidio Modelo. Winsberg, "Isle of Pines, Cuba: A Geographic Interpretation" (PhD diss., University of Florida, 1958), 1. For a 2012 population estimate, see www.one.cu/EstadisticaPoblacion/EstadisticaPoblacion .asp (accessed May 11, 2016).

[60] For detail about Cuba's interventions in Africa, see the work of Piero Gleijeses, including *Conflicting Missions: Havana, Washington, and Africa, 1959–1976* (Chapel Hill:

schools, forty-five junior high schools, and eight high schools; in contrast, there existed only fifteen schools on the Isle before the Revolution.[61]
In recognition of these changes and the student presence and emphasis
there, Castro officially renamed the Isle of Pines. It became the Isle of
Youth (Isla de la Juventud) in August 1978.

The changes the revolutionary government brought about were not
merely ideological. A degree of practicality was involved as well. The
Isle had had a significant amount of pro-Batista sentiment in large part
because of the *zona franca* and improvement in the Isle's economy in
the late 1950s. As native *pinero* and Cuban exile Luis Bayo maintained,
"Batista was the one president who loved the Isle of Pines and did something to help it."[62] Over the years, many *pineros* who remained in the
country were recruited into government service programs that took them
to mainland Cuba. At the same time, others from mainland Cuba came to
the Isle to institute the aforementioned reforms. This had the dual effect
of diluting lingering pro-Batista sentiment while also altering the Isle's
unique social chemistry. Nuri Anderson said that many *pineros* opposed
Castro's reforms and begrudged the influx of "volunteers" from eastern
Cuba. "We used to live with the doors open all the time," she said. "We
didn't live life with our doors closed. We didn't have to be afraid of people coming into our homes and taking things. But after Castro, we had to
close our doors and windows. There were a lot of strange people around.
You started to see more crimes."[63] The Isle's name change has bred a
lingering generational tension as well. Many of those who lived on the
Isle before the Revolution still defiantly refer to it as the Isle of Pines and
resent the younger natives of the mainland who know or care little about
the island's heritage.[64]

To Americans, the radical changes taking place on their beloved Isle
did not sit well either. Although he had left the Isle in 1925 for Tampa,
Florida, Ernest Gruppe maintained an affinity for a place he called home
for nearly twenty years. Its rapid post-Revolution population growth was
unsustainable, he argued. "The island can't support that many people,"
he said in 1971, when there were an estimated 30,000 inhabitants. "It's

University of North Carolina Press, 2002); "The First Ambassadors: Cuba's Contribution
to Guinea-Bissau's War of Independence," *Journal of Latin American Studies* 29
(February 1997): 45–88; "Cuba's First Venture in Africa: Algeria, 1961–1965," *Journal
of Latin American Studies* 28 (February 1996): 159–95.

[61] McManus, *Cuba's Island of Dreams*, 119–20; Hijuelos, et al., *Con Todo Derecho*, 79–80.

[62] Luis Bayo interview with author, August 9, 2014.

[63] Nuri Anderson interview with author, August 19, 2014.

[64] *La Isla de la Juventud*, directed by Ana Laura Calderón (Mexico: Alas Ocultas, La Casa
de Cine, 2007), DVD.

like building up Miami Beach, you can overdraw a place. That's what'll happen there with too many people."[65] Living through the changes made it no easier. Sundstrom stayed long enough to witness the stark transition. "Suddenly there were all these big, ugly buildings and people, people everywhere," she recalled. "We got roads, a great big hospital, a packing-house and all kinds of things we never had before. But something of the beauty was taken away."[66]

That remembered beauty lingered with Americans long after they left. Some recalled the Isle's rich vistas in ways akin to landholding companies' old advertisements. "It really was a paradise of nature and a wonderland of all different kinds of peoples and pursuits," Stimson recalled.[67] Others appreciated the relaxed lifestyle and the amiability it inspired among the Isle's diverse residents. In that manner, one person thought life in the United States paled in comparison. "I remember a free life, no rush, nobody was trying to kill themselves to get a dollar they didn't need because they didn't need many down there," Dan Smith said. "All the fishing, the life was more congenial. It was a place where you knew everybody – not like here in the States where you don't know your next door neighbor. It was certainly a lot more neighborly down there."[68]

For some Americans, the circumstances of their departure as well as news and rumors of what has since transpired on the Isle have tempered any desire to go back. The Swetland home, once thought to be one of the Isle's largest, was intervened by the Cuban government in 1960 and rumored to have been used by Fidel Castro. One visitor in the late 1990s said the house was still in excellent condition.[69] Eli Swetland, however, said he had no interest in seeing the house or the Isle again. "It's not like when I was a boy," he said. "And I've got memories of it. I don't want to ruin those memories."[70] Bill Miller echoed those sentiments. Unlike the Swetland home, the Millers' house was allegedly destroyed after it was intervened. "For years, I tried to put the island out of my mind because I had heard they burned our place down and they changed the names of

---

[65] Gruppe interview, June 21, 1971, tape 18, 5, SFA.

[66] Quoted in Burkett, "The Last American."

[67] William Stimson e-mail message to author, May 16, 2011.

[68] Irma and Dan Smith interview with Frederick Swetland Jr., May 28, 1969, tape 11, 6–7, SFA.

[69] Harvey Oppmann interview with author, August 16, 2014.

[70] Eli Swetland interview with author, July 10, 2009.

everything and brought all these people in," he said. "I really do not have a desire to go back and see what they've done to it. I'd rather remember it the way it was."[71]

The urge to leave the past alone was not universal among all Americans, though. Nearly a half-century later and long since settled back in his native Ohio where he spent his career as a teacher, Ron Williams still waxed emotional when talking about his one year on the Isle. The conditions in which his *pinero* friends and former students have lived continued to trouble him, particularly the limits on personal expression that have been a staple of the Castro government. Even into his seventies, Williams dreamed of one day returning. "It was ... I believe, possibly the best year of my life," he said wistfully. "The entire scene was just fantastic. I miss the food. I miss the music. I miss the rhythm of the place. I miss the easy-going way that those people had, the way that they treated me and accepted me."[72] Williams never got to go back. He died in April 2012.

After six decades, the American influence and presence on the Isle of Pines came to a rather abrupt end. U.S. citizens' cautious optimism in January 1959 toward Fidel Castro and his revolutionary movement turned to bitterness and antipathy within two years. By then, the reforms of the Cuban Revolution had taken hold and completely changed the tenor of life on the Isle. By most accounts, *pineros* – those born on the island as well as those who developed a deep affinity for the place – of the 1950s enjoyed being part of a multinational community whose friendly denizens were full of optimism that the Isle was on the verge of significant commercial growth. That spirit did not last. Instead, like other large-landowning Cubans, Americans saw their property "intervened" and their way of life challenged. Many Cubans and Americans fled to the United States. In that respect, the reforms of the Cuban Revolution did not distinguish between nationalities.

Although Americans could return to their country of origin, for many it was not familiar territory. There were a number of U.S. citizens, among them Bill Miller and Edith Sundstrom, for whom the Isle of Pines was the place with which they were most familiar. When it came time for them to leave, moving to the United States was like going to an alien world. Others, like Frederick Swetland Jr. and William Stimson, came to embrace

---

[71] Bill Miller interview with author, August 9, 2014.
[72] Ron Williams interview with author, July 9, 2009.

the Isle's culture and customs so fervently that departing the Isle bore a deep emotional impact. Especially in light of the political circumstances, Americans' departures from the Isle engendered sadness, mourning, bitterness, and anger. It was not necessarily out of a sense of nationalism or personal effrontery. Rather, their emotions stemmed from a sense of loss. After all, the Isle of Pines had been their home.

Conclusion

By the early 1960s, when only a few dozen U.S. citizens remained on the Isle of Pines, most Americans who had tried to make a home there saw their efforts as a failure. For some, there was a palpable sense of regret. Reflections of those who left in the wake of the Cuban Revolution mirrored those of early twentieth-century settlers whose enterprises never sufficiently developed. Frederick Swetland Jr., whose family had maintained a presence on the Isle since Truman Swetland purchased San Francisco de las Piedras in 1908, best expressed these feelings of failure and regret. "Of course, I blame it all on my grandfather," he wrote in 1961. "Why the hell didn't he go to Puerto Rico?"[1]

Many Americans shared Swetland's disappointment and identified a variety of scapegoats. William Stimson primarily blamed the Fidel Castro government for undermining what was shaping up to be a tourist haven. "That place could have been a tourism bonanza in perpetuity if it'd been developed in the right way," he stated. "And it could have been developed in a way that served all the populations of all the people, without endangering the unique environment."[2] Ernest Gruppe took a broader view. Having seen the rise of the U.S. colony when he resided there in the early twentieth century, he maintained that settlers' failures began long before the Cuban Revolution; they stemmed from an inability to work together more effectively. "We had an interest in the Isle of Pines because it ... had

[1] Memorandum of Frederick Swetland Jr., March 7, 1961, 49, SFA.
[2] William Stimson e-mail message to author, May 16, 2011.

some potential for the future for a real paradise. But everybody blew it. There was no coordination."[3]

Indeed, from a variety of perspectives, Americans failed to achieve many of their objectives on the Isle of Pines. For the first generation of arrivals who tried to annex the Isle to the United States during the first quarter of the twentieth century, their inability to persuade the U.S. government and the local Cuban population to go along with their scheme was a crushing blow. It was a sign that these annexationists' nineteenth-century conception of expansion – via territorial acquisition for agricultural production – was passé in a twentieth-century world. Moreover, most Americans who wanted to establish new homes and retire to a life of leisure in a tropical locale returned to the United States sorely disappointed – or worse. Only a select few managed to sustain their business ventures and withstand the challenges posed by tariffs, inadequate transportation, poor infrastructure, and tropical storms. Those who could not afford to return home often lived under hardscrabble conditions and died virtually destitute.

But the U.S. presence persisted. By the 1950s, it had clearly adapted and endured, becoming less chauvinistic and domineering than it was in the early part of the century. A new generation of Americans arrived, ignorant of the antagonisms of the Hay-Quesada era. They were more inclusive and understated than their early-century forerunners. This attitudinal shift helped to broaden the American appeal to the local population. By mid-century, the local Cuban population was actively cultivating a deeper U.S. presence. This trend stood in stark contrast to the growing anti-American sentiment in Havana during the waning days of the Batista regime. In this sense, Americans' presence on the Isle had succeeded in generating affinity for the United States from a significant segment of the Cuban population.

U.S. citizens were not alone in mourning the revolutionary changes taking place on the Isle. The country's socialist shift drove many Cuban citizens to leave as well. "After Castro, many *pineros* came to the U.S.," Nuri Anderson said. "They didn't like Castro." Anderson had deep roots on the Isle. Her maternal grandmother's family could trace its heritage there to the Spanish colonial era. Her paternal grandfather, Frank Anderson, was a U.S. citizen who had come to the Isle from Chicago in the early twentieth century. But in the years following Castro's triumph,

[3] Ernest Gruppe oral history interview with Frederick Swetland Jr., June 21, 1971, tape 18, 5, SFA.

life had become more difficult and unsatisfying. Her mother and sister as well as some cousins, nephews, and nieces eventually moved to the United States. As was the case with many other native *pineros*, they settled in Naples, Florida. Nuri Anderson would also leave Cuba in 1995 after her father procured U.S. citizenship. She first went to Miami and then to Atlanta, where she found conditions there "like the life I used to live on the Isle of Pines."[4]

Even one of the most prominent officials on the Isle during the Hay-Quesada era was not immune to the changes taking place in the 1960s. Following his twelve-year tenure as *alcalde* – during which he was one of the most vocal advocates of Cuban sovereignty and even designed the Isle's official seal – Ramon Llorca Soto went into business as an accountant. For a time, he worked for Axel Gunnar Sundstrom and after World War II bought a gas station in Nueva Gerona from Sundstrom's son. During the next two decades, Llorca Soto and his family operated the station. It catered to customers of all nationalities, which brought Llorca Soto in closer commercial and social contact with Americans. But in 1964, the Castro government expropriated the business and Llorca Soto's family was left with little means of support. Two years later, Llorca Soto made his way to the United States. His grandson, Saul Llorca, remembered that upon leaving his homeland, Llorca Soto "was understandably upset and distraught at losing thirty years of work."[5] Llorca Soto died in October 1969 in Miami, having never returned to his homeland.

The experiences and sentiments the Isle's denizens expressed underscored not only a nostalgia about life on the island, but also a sense of belonging to a broader, transnational community. Over time, the term *pinero* came to mean someone born and raised on the Isle of Pines as well as one who maintained an affinity for the place and the people who inhabited it regardless of nationality. While national citizenship remained important, by the 1950s it was not as critical a social designation as it had been in the early part of the twentieth century. Such a shift is a stark reminder about the fluidity and permeability of identity.

The attitudes of those in the final American exodus from the Isle contrasted greatly with those who had left years earlier. Settlers who departed in the 1910s and 1920s did so resignedly, having failed to secure U.S. annexation and to create sustainable commercial enterprises. They did not evince much affinity for the Cubans and foreign nationals they

---

[4] Nuri Anderson interview with author, August 19, 2014.
[5] Saul Llorca, e-mail message to author, August 26, 2014.

left behind, nor was there the level of cooperation and accommodation later generations nurtured and enjoyed. U.S. settlements were marked more by self-isolation than integration into a greater community.

The contrasting generational attitudes also revealed the differing expectations each group brought to the Isle. Among the first generation of settlers, turning a profit to afford a more comfortable standard of living was the primary objective; annexation and agrarian commercialization were considered the most effective means to that end. Among the later generation, however, expectations were more tempered. Many were retirees, looking for a quiet respite from an increasingly urbanized and industrialized society. With fewer farms and businesses, they had less need for local labor. Because the annexation question had long been resolved, new arrivals were less inclined to imprint the American way of life. With far fewer of their fellow countrymen among them, Americans of mid-century were just one of many foreign national groups, albeit still influential given their economic and cultural clout. The revival of commercialization and development in the 1950s regenerated the American community as U.S. settlers and tourists returned. By then, however, Cuban entrepreneurs had taken the lead in this activity, borrowing from the playbook of early-century U.S. entrepreneurs and spurring interest in the Isle in levels not seen since the heyday of the American presence a half-century earlier.

Those who came to the Isle were not looking to abandon their American-ness, though. Rather, they brought it with them, in the form of their styles, goods, technology, and institutions. It found a seemingly receptive audience among native Cubans, who not only worked for U.S. landowners and entrepreneurs, but also looked to cultivate Americans as potential customers. With the divisive issue of annexation off the table, a more equitable partnership was possible between Americans and Cubans. Settlers at mid-century displayed far less of a desire to Americanize the Isle than their early-century forerunners. They were content to have some American conveniences, such as goods and dwellings, while also enjoying the pace, styles, and gentility of life on the Isle. By the 1950s, Americans were more likely to enter into relationships and more widely embraced local foods and customs, including speaking Spanish. This transition illustrated that as much as American influence affected life on the Isle, so too did living on the Isle affect settlers. Undoubtedly, that made the Cuban Revolution's rejection of American-ness all the more painful.

Fleeing the Isle proved emotional for former settlers for other reasons as well. For some Americans, it was the only home they really knew. They were more familiar with the people, the pace, and the customs on the Isle than those in the United States and, as a consequence, identified more with the Isle. Such cases underscore the complexity of identity. U.S. citizens like Edith Sundstrom considered the Isle home yet never renounced their American nationality and eventually sought refuge back in the United States from the changes taking place in revolutionary-era Cuba. Nevertheless, Sundstrom's move to Florida, particularly in adjusting to new customs and the faster pace of life, was an unsettling transition.

In addition to their homes, fleeing settlers lost a degree of status. Although they embraced being part of a larger Isle community, Americans still stood apart as a distinct group who enjoyed a certain cachet by virtue of their nationality. They tended to be a bit better off socioeconomically, privileged by cheap labor and lower cost-of-living expenses. As the list of cases with the Cuban Claims Program shows, the financial toll of leaving the Isle was just as significant as the emotional one for some Americans.

The sixty-year U.S. presence on the Isle of Pines illustrated the varying modes of American expansionism – territorial, commercial, and cultural – in action on the grassroots level. Ultimately, however, this activity exposed the limits to Americans' ambitions, imposed by U.S. policymakers and Cubans alike, and served as an important twentieth-century reminder of a nineteenth-century lesson: pioneering was hard work. Ingenuity, efficiency, and pluck were not always enough to conquer an alien world. Moreover, U.S. influence was eventually rejected – a rejection not necessarily initiated by native *pineros*, but Cubans nonetheless. The U.S. presence on the Isle is an important topic of study because it serves as a counter-narrative to an otherwise successful era of American empire-building. The story reveals an unconventional method of expansion at work, one driven by non-state actors while otherwise shunned by policymakers. It was also a nonviolent bid for control of territory abroad in the midst of a very bloody anticolonial century. And in contrast to growing anti-Americanism in mainland Cuba stemming from years of U.S. hegemony, mid-century relations between Americans and *pineros* were at their most cordial. The onset of the Cuban Revolution, though, took a toll on those affairs. They were among the first casualties of the U.S.–Cuba diplomatic rupture.

After six decades, the U.S. presence on the Isle of Pines effectively came to an end. Ten years into the Revolution, fewer than a dozen Americans remained. After Harry Koenig's death in 1995, none were left. Few monuments stand to mark the bygone era. Many of the headstones at the American Cemetery are cracked or eroded, the names of the deceased lost

FIGURE C.I. The remnants of the American Central School as it stood in 2010. What was once a thriving institution that had fostered close ties between Americans and Cubans lay in decay, a fitting depiction of U.S.–Cuban relations as they stood for more than a half-century.
Source: Author's photo.

to time and nature. The building that had housed the American Central School barely stands, little more than a faded façade. What had once been a thriving institution that fostered close ties between Americans and Cubans lay in decay, a sad if fitting depiction of U.S.–Cuban relations as they stood for more than a half-century. As the history of Americans on the Isle of Pines shows, however, it was not always that way.

Bibliography

Archives and Manuscript Collections

United States
Asbury University Archives – Asbury, Kentucky
University Publications
Connecticut State Library – Hartford, Connecticut
Orville Platt Papers
Fond du Lac Historical Society – Fond du Lac, Wisconsin
Indiana Historical Society – Indianapolis, Indiana
Hester Anna Greer Papers
Library of Congress – Washington, DC
Manuscript Division
Nelson Aldrich Papers
John Hay Papers
Philip C. Jessup Papers
Records of the Olmsted Associates
Elihu Root Papers
Leonard Wood Papers
Newspaper, Periodical, and Government Publications Division
Prints and Photographs Division
National Archives – College Park, Maryland
Record Group 59 – General Records of the Department of State
Record Group 84 – Records of the Foreign Service Posts of the Department of State
Record Group 140 – Records of the Military Government of Cuba
Record Group 199 – Records of the Provisional Government of Cuba
Record Group 350 – Records of the Bureau of Insular Affairs
New York Public Library – New York, New York
Ohio Historical Society – Columbus, Ohio
Swetland Family Archives – Yellow Springs, Ohio

Wisconsin Historical Society – Madison, Wisconsin
Yates County Genealogical and Historical Society – Penn Yan, New York
E. Ben Knight Papers

Cuba

Archivo Histórico Municipal de la Isla de la Juventud – Nueva Gerona
Colección de Archivo: Donativos y Remisiones, 1886–1990
Colección Iglesias: Expedientes de Matrimonios, 1901–1918
Compañías, Sociedades, y Establecimientos de Isla de Pinos, 1905–1970
Fondo: A. B. Kelm
Hemeroteca
Juzgado de Instrucción de Isla de Pinos, 1904–1958
Juzgado de Primera Instancia de Isla de Pinos, 1904–1958
Juzgado Municipal de Isla de Pinos, 1901–1958
Papelería de Extranjeros Residentes en Isle de Pinos, 1910–1975
Archivo Nacional de Cuba – Havana
Donativos y Remisiones
Secretaria de Gobernación
Secretaria de Hacienda
Secretaria de la Presidencia, 1902–1958
Biblioteca Nacional "Jose Martí" – Havana
Instituto de Historia – Havana
Museo Municipal de la Isla de la Juventud – Nueva Gerona

Published Reports and Documentary Collections

Censo de la República de Cuba Bajo la Administración Provisional de los Estados Unidos, 1907. Washington, DC: Oficina del Censo de los Estados Unidos, 1908.
Census of the Republic of Cuba, 1919. Havana: 1920.
Cuban Society of International Law. *Statements and Documents Relative to the Isle of Pines Treaty between the United States and Cuba.* Havana: Cuban Society of International Law, 1925.
Harvard College Class of 1882, *Sixth Report of the Secretary, 1882–1907.* Boston, MA: EO Cockayne, 1908.
Quesada, Gonzalo de. *Documentos Históricos.* La Habana: Editorial de la Universidad de La Habana, 1965.
Report on the Census of Cuba, 1899. Washington, DC: Government Printing Office, 1900.
U.S. Congress. House. Committee on Foreign Affairs. *Outstanding Claims against Cuba: Hearing before the Subcommittees on International Economic Policy and Trade and on Inter-American Affairs of the Committee on Foreign Affairs.* 96th Cong., 1st sess., September 25, 1979.
U.S. Congress. Senate. Committee on Foreign Relations. *Isle of Pines: Papers Relating to the Adjustment of Title to the Ownership of the Isle of Pines.* 68th Cong., 2nd sess., 1924. S. Doc. 166.

U.S. Department of State. *Foreign Relations of the United States.* 1905–1911. Washington, DC: Government Printing Office.

U.S. Department of War. Division of Insular Affairs. "The Isle of Pines (Caribbean Sea): Its Situation, Physical Features, Inhabitants, Resources, and Industries." Washington, DC: Government Printing Office, 1902.

Speeches, Addresses, and Memoirs

Adams, James M. *Pioneering in Cuba: A Narrative of the Settlement of La Gloria, the First American Colony in Cuba, and the Early Experiences of the Pioneers.* Concord, NH: Rumford Press, 1901.

Chalmers, Stephen. *Isle of Pines: Where the Pine and Palm Tree Meet.* Nueva Gerona: Isle of Pines Chamber of Commerce, 1920.

Rice, Margaret Peggy. *Mi Vida Hasta Aquí: Las Memorias del Margaret Peggy Rice.* Translated by Guillermo Maquintoche. Nueva Gerona: Ediciones El Abra, 2009.

Rodríguez Acosta y García, Ofelia. *Apuntes de Mi Viaje a Isla de Pinos.* La Habana: Montiel y Co., 1926.

Speeches Incident to the Visit of Secretary Root to South America. Washington, DC: Government Printing Office, 1906.

Swetland Jr., Frederick L. *The Isle of Pines.* Undated. Self-published.

Torriente, Cosme de la. *Mi Misión En Washington: La Soberanía de La Isla de Pinos, 1923–1925.* Havana: University of Havana Press, 1952.

Company Prospectuses and Publications

Cañada Land & Fruit Company. "Isle of Pines: Land of Fruit and Flowers." Marinette, WI: Eagle Printing Co., 1903.

Cuba Railroad Company. "Information Concerning Cuba." New York, Undated.

Franklin, Mary Estelle. "Isle of Pines Cookbook." Boston, MA: Isle of Pines Co-Operative Fruit Co., 1914.

Hammond, Hammond & Baker. "San Pedro, Isle of Pines." Columbus, OH, Undated.

Isle of Pines Company. "The Isle of Pines: Uncle Sam's Latest Acquisition of Territory." New York, 1901.

"McKinley, Isle of Pines: A City of Orange Groves in the American District of Cuba." New York, 1911.

Isle of Pines Investment Company. "The Pineland Bulletin." Cleveland, OH, 1908.

Isle of Pines Railroad Company, Inc. "Isle of Pines Railroad Company Prospectus." New York, 1910.

San Juan Heights Land Company: "The Isle of Pines: The Garden Spot of the World." Cleveland, OH, 1914.

Santa Fe Land Company and the Isle of Pines United Land Companies. "Marvelous Isle of Pines: That Magnificent Land of Sunshine, Health and Wealth." Chicago, IL, 1914.

Tropical Development Company. "McKinley, Isle of Pines: A City of Orange Groves in the American District of Cuba." Buffalo, NY, 1906.
"McKinley in the Making." Buffalo, NY, 1906.

Newspapers and Periodicals

United States
American Magazine
American Mercury
Asbury (KY) Collegian
Biloxi Herald
Birmingham Age-Herald
Boston Evening Transcript
Butte Weekly Miner
Charlotte Observer
Chicago Daily Tribune
Coronet
Daily Northwestern (Oshkosh, WI)
Dallas Morning News
Duluth News-Tribune
Eau Claire (WI) Leader
Field & Stream
Fond du Lac (WI) Commonwealth
Fort Worth Morning Register
Fort Worth Star-Telegram
Grand Forks Herald
Grand Rapids Herald
Hartford Courant
Idaho Statesman
Janesville (WI) Daily Gazette
Kansas City Star
Lexington Herald
Marshfield (WI) Times
Miami Herald
Monroe (WI) Weekly Times
New York American
New York Times
Omaha World Herald
The Oregonian
Pawtucket Times
Philadelphia Inquirer
San Jose Mercury News
Senior Scholastic
The State (Columbia, SC)
Stevens Point (WI) Daily Journal

Stevens Point (WI) Gazette
Tacoma Daily News
Travel
Trenton Times
Wall Street Journal
Yellow Springs News

Cuba
Cuba News
Isla
Isle of Pines Appeal
Isle of Pines News
Isle of Pines Post
La Discusión
La Lucha
La Prensa
McKinley Herald
Pino Nuevo

Great Britain
The Guardian

Interviews

By Author
Anderson, Nuri – August 19, 2014
Bayo, Luis – August 9, 2014
Cepero Herrera, Elda – April 9, 2010
Miller, Bill – August 9, 2014
Oppmann, Harvey – August 16, 2014
Swetland, Eli – July 10, 2009
Williams, Ron – July 9, 2009

By Frederick Swetland Jr.
Anderson, Dorothy – June 21, 1971
Anderson, Dorothy and Tom – June 21, 1971
Barothy, Betty – March 13, 1969
Finn, Ralph – March 15, 1969
Giltner, Millie – March 13, 1969
Gruppe, Ernest – June 27, 1971
Smith, Irma and Dan – March 15, 1969
Swetland, Paula Wightman – May 10, 1970

Secondary Sources

Books

Álvarez Estévez, Rolando. *Isla De Pinos y El Tratado Hay-Quesada*. La Habana: Instituto Cubano del Libro, 1973.

Ayala, César J. *American Sugar Kingdom: The Plantation Economy of the Spanish Caribbean, 1898–1934*. Chapel Hill: University of North Carolina Press, 1999.

Bederman, Gail. *Manliness & Civilization: A Cultural History of Gender and Race in the United States, 1880–1917*. Chicago: University of Chicago Press, 1995.

Benjamin, Jules Robert. *The United States and Cuba: Hegemony and Dependent Development, 1880–1934*. Pittsburgh: University of Pittsburgh Press, 1974.

Blower, Brooke L. *Becoming Americans in Paris: Transatlantic Politics and Culture between the World Wars*. New York: Oxford University Press, 2011.

Boyce, William Dickson. *United States Colonies and Dependencies*. Chicago: Rand, McNally & Company, 1914.

Bronfman, Alejandra. *Measures of Equality: Social Science, Citizenship, and Race in Cuba, 1902–1940*. Chapel Hill: University of North Carolina Press, 2004.

Buder, Stanley. *Visionaries and Planners: The Garden City Movement and the Modern Community*. New York: Oxford University Press, 1990.

Chomsky, Aviva. *A History of the Cuban Revolution*. Malden, MA: Wiley-Blackwell, 2011.

Clark, Sydney A. *Cuban Tapestry*. New York: National Travel Club, 1936.

Cocks, Catherine. *Tropical Whites: The Rise of the Tourist South in the Americas*. Philadelphia: University of Pennsylvania Press, 2013.

Coffman Tom. *A Nation Within: The Story of America's Annexation of the Nation of Hawai'i*. Kane'ohe, HI: Epicenter Press, 1998.

Colby, Jason M. *The Business of Empire: United Fruit, Race, and U.S. Expansion in Central America*. Ithaca, NY: Cornell University Press, 2011.

Colina la Rosa, Juan. *Caimaneros y Jamaicanos en Isla de Pinos*. Nueva Gerona: El Abra, 2006.

    et al. *Síntesis Histórica Municipal: Isla de la Juventud*. La Habana: El Abra, 2011.

Conn, Steven. *Americans against the City: Anti-urbanism in the Twentieth Century*. New York: Oxford University Press, 2014.

Conniff, Michael L. *Black Labor on a White Canal: Panama, 1904–1981*. Pittsburgh: University of Pittsburgh Press, 1985.

Crane, Hart. *Complete Poems and Selected Letters*. Langdon Hammer, ed. New York: Library of America, 2006.

Daniels, Roger. *Guarding the Golden Door: American Immigration Policy and Immigrants since 1882*. New York: Hill and Wang, 2004.

Davis, William C. *Lone Star Rising: The Revolutionary Birth of the Texas Republic*. New York: Free Press, 2004.

Derr, Mark. *Some Kind of Paradise: A Chronicle of Man and the Land in Florida*. Gainesville: University Press of Florida, 1998.

Donoghue, Michael E. *Borderland on the Isthmus: Race, Culture, and the Struggle for the Canal Zone*. Durham, NC: Duke University Press, 2014.

English, T. J. *Havana Nocturne: How the Mob Owned Cuba – and then Lost It to the Revolution*. New York: William Morrow, 2008.

Ewen, Stuart. *Captains of Consciousness: Advertising and the Social Roots of the Consumer Culture*. 25th ann. ed. New York: Basic Books, 2001.

Ferrer, Ada. *Insurgent Cuba: Race, Nation, and Revolution, 1868–1898*. Chapel Hill: University of North Carolina Press, 1999.

Gannon, Michael, ed. *The New History of Florida*. Gainesville: University Press of Florida, 1996.

Garcia, Matt. *A World of Its Own: Race, Labor, and Citrus in the Making of Greater Los Angeles, 1900–1970*. Chapel Hill: University of North Carolina Press, 2001.

Gleijeses, Piero. *Conflicting Missions: Havana, Washington, and Africa, 1959–1976*. Chapel Hill: University of North Carolina Press, 2002.

Grandin, Greg. *Empire's Workshop: Latin America, the United States, and the Rise of the New Imperialism*. New York: Henry Holt, 2006.

Fordlandia: The Rise and Fall of Henry Ford's Forgotten Jungle City. New York: Picador, 2009.

Greene, Julie. *The Canal Builders: Making America's Empire at the Panama Canal*. New York: Penguin Press, 2009.

Hart, John Mason. *Empire and Revolution: The Americans in Mexico since the Civil War*. Berkeley: University of California Press, 2002.

Hazard, Samuel. *Cuba with Pen and Pencil*. Hartford, CT: Hartford Publishing Company, 1871.

Helg, Aline. *Our Rightful Share: The Afro-Cuban Struggle for Equality, 1886–1912*. Chapel Hill: University of North Carolina Press, 1995.

Henderson, Timothy J. *A Glorious Defeat: Mexico and Its War with the United States*. New York: Hill and Wang, 2007.

Hernández, María Marta, et al. *Isla de Pinos y las Compañías Norteamericanas*. La Habana: Comisión de la Escuela de Historia de la Universidad de la Habana, 1970.

Hevia, Aurelio. *Los Derechos de Cuba Sobre la Isla de Pinos*. La Habana: Imprenta El Siglo XX, 1924.

Hixson, Walter L. *American Settler Colonialism: A History*. New York: Palgrave Macmillan, 2013.

Hofstadter, Richard. *The Age of Reform: From Bryan to FDR*. New York: Vintage Books, 1955.

Hoganson, Kristin L. *Consumers Imperium: The Global Production of American Domesticity, 1865–1920*. Chapel Hill: University of North Carolina Press, 2007.

Fighting for American Manhood: How Gender Politics Provoked the Spanish-American and Philippine-American Wars. New Haven, CT: Yale University Press, 1998.

Horton, Philip. *Hart Crane: The Life of an American Poet*. New York: W. W. Norton, 1937.

Jacobson, Matthew Frye. *Whiteness of a Different Color: European Immigrants and the Alchemy of Race.* Cambridge, MA: Harvard University Press, 1998.

Jenks, Leland Hamilton. *Our Cuban Colony: A Study in Sugar.* New York: Vanguard Press, 1928.

Johnson, Chalmers. *Nemesis: The Last Days of the American Republic.* New York: Metropolitan Books, 2006.

Johnson, John J. *Latin America in Caricature.* Austin: University of Texas Press, 1980.

Kaplan, Amy. *The Anarchy of Empire in the Making of U.S. Culture.* Cambridge, MA: Harvard University Press, 2002.

Kaplan, Amy. and Donald E. Pease, eds. *Cultures of United States Imperialism.* Durham, NC: Duke University Press, 1993.

Knight, Henry. *Tropic of Hopes: California, Florida, and the Selling of American Paradise, 1869–1929.* Gainesville: University Press of Florida, 2013.

Kinzer, Stephen. *Overthrow: America's Century of Regime Change from Hawaii to Iraq.* New York: Times Books, 2006.

LaFeber, Walter. *The New Empire: An Interpretation of American Expansion, 1860–1898.* 35th ann. ed. Ithaca, NY: Cornell University Press, 1998.

Laird, Pamela. *Advertising Progress: American Business and the Rise of Consumer Marketing.* Baltimore, MD: Johns Hopkins University Press, 1998.

Lears, T.J. Jackson. *Rebirth of a Nation: The Making of Modern America, 1877–1920.* New York: HarperCollins, 2009.

Lens, Eduardo F. *La Isla Olvidada: Estudio Físico, Económico y Humano de la Isla de Pinos.* La Habana, 1942.

Lewis, Thomas S. W., ed. *Letters of Hart Crane and His Family.* New York: Columbia University Press, 1974.

Lipman, Jana K. *Guantánamo: A Working-Class History between Empire and Revolution.* Berkeley: University of California Press, 2009.

Lockmiller, David A. *Magoon in Cuba: A History of the Second Intervention, 1906–1909.* Chapel Hill: University of North Carolina Press, 1938.

Luebke, Frederick C. *Germans in the New World: Essays in the History of Immigration.* Urbana: University of Illinois Press, 1990.

Marchand, Roland. *Advertising the American Dream: Making Way for Modernity, 1920–1940.* Berkeley: University of California Press, 1985.

May, Robert E. *Manifest Destiny's Underworld: Filibustering in Antebellum America.* Chapel Hill: University of North Carolina Press, 2002.

McAvoy, Muriel. *Sugar Barons: Manuel Rionda and the Fortunes of Pre-Castro Cuba.* Gainesville: University Press of Florida, 2003.

McGillivray, Gillian. *Blazing Cane: Sugar Communities, Class, and State Formation in Cuba, 1868–1959.* Durham, NC: Duke University Press, 2009.

McManus, Jane. *Cuba's Island of Dreams: Voices from the Isle of Pines and Youth.* Gainesville: University Press of Florida, 2000.

McPherson, Alan. *Yankee No! Anti-Americanism in U.S.–Latin American Relations.* Cambridge, MA: Harvard University Press, 2003.

Medina, Waldo. *Aquí, Isla de Pinos.* La Habana, 1961.

Merrill, Dennis. *Negotiating Paradise: U.S. Tourism and Empire in Twentieth-Century Latin America.* Chapel Hill: University of North Carolina Press, 2009.

Millett, Allan Reed. *The Politics of Intervention: The Military Occupation of Cuba, 1906–1909.* Columbus: Ohio State University Press, 1968.

Moreno, Julio. *Yankee Don't Go Home!: Mexican Nationalism, American Business Culture, and the Shaping of Modern Mexico, 1920–1950.* Chapel Hill: University of North Carolina Press, 2003.

Neblett, Sterling Augustus. *Methodism's First Fifty Years in Cuba.* Wilmore, KY: Asbury Press, 1976.

Noble, David W. *The Progressive Mind, 1890–1917.* Chicago: Rand McNally, 1970.

Norris, James D. *Advertising and the Transformation of American Society, 1865–1920.* New York: Greenwood Press, 1990.

Núñez Jiménez, Antonio. *Autobiografía de Isla de Pinos.* La Habana: 1949.

   Isla de Pinos: Piratas, Colonizadores, Rebeldes. La Habana: Editorial Arte y Literatura, 1976.

   et al. *Bibliografía de Isla de Pinos.* La Habana: 1972.

Okihiro, Gary. *Pineapple Culture: A History of the Tropical and Temperate Zones.* Berkeley: University of California Press, 2009.

Oro, Julián y. *Isla de Pinos: 10 Años de Trabajo.* Guantánamo: Juan Marinello, 1978.

Ott, John Henry. *Jefferson County, Wisconsin and Its People: A Record of Settlement, Organization, Progress and Achievement.* Chicago: S. J. Clarke Publishing, 1917.

Pappademos, Melina. *Black Political Activism and the Cuban Republic.* Chapel Hill: University of North Carolina Press, 2011.

Paterson, Thomas G. *Contesting Castro: The United States and the Triumph of the Cuban Revolution.* New York: Oxford University Press, 1994.

Peña Hijuelos, Wiltse, et al. *Con Todo Derecho: Isla de la Juventud.* La Habana, 1986.

Pérez Jr., Louis A. *Cuba and the United States: Ties of Singular Intimacy.* 2nd ed. Athens: University of Georgia Press, 1997.

   Cuba: Between Reform and Revolution. 4th ed. New York: Oxford University Press, 2011.

   Cuba in the American Imagination: Metaphor and the Imperial Ethos. Chapel Hill: University of North Carolina Press, 2008.

   Cuba under the Platt Amendment, 1902–1934. Pittsburgh: University of Pittsburgh Press, 1986.

   On Becoming Cuban: Identity, Nationality, and Culture. Chapel Hill: University of North Carolina Press, 1999.

   The War of 1898: The United States and Cuba in History and Historiography. Chapel Hill: University of North Carolina Press, 1998.

Pérez, Roberto Únger, et al. *Americanos en la Isla.* Nueva Gerona: El Abra, 2004.

Pletcher, David M. *The Diplomacy of Annexation: Texas, Oregon, and the Mexican War.* Columbia: University of Missouri Press, 1973.

Risley, Reese P. and Howard S. *Fortunes in Fruit and Other Products of the Isle of Pines: A Handbook of Facts for the Settler and Investor.* Buffalo, NY: A. T. Brown Publishing House, 1904.

Rodríguez Lendián, Evelio. *El Derecho de Cuba a la Isla de Pinos Según al Tratado de Paris.* La Habana, 1925.

Rodríguez Molina, Diego, et al. *El Verdadero Descubrimiento.* La Habana: Ediciones El Abra, 1996.

Roediger, David R. *Working Toward Whiteness: How America's Immigrants Became White.* New York: Basic Books, 2005.

Rohrer, Judy. *Haoles in Hawai'i: Race and Ethnicity in Hawai'i.* Honolulu: University of Hawai'i Press, 2010.

Roig de Leuchsenring, Emilio. *Historia De La Enmienda Platt: Una Interpretación De La Realidad Cubana.* 3rd ed. La Habana: Instituto Cubano del Libro, 1973.

Rosenberg, Emily. *Spreading the American Dream: American Economic and Cultural Expansion, 1890–1945.* New York: Hill and Wang, 1982.

Sackman, Douglas Cazaux. *Orange Empire: California and the Fruits of Eden.* Berkeley: University of California Press, 2005.

Schmitz, David F. *Thank God They're on Our Side: The United States and Right-Wing Dictatorships, 1921–1965.* Chapel Hill: University of North Carolina Press, 1999.

Schoultz, Lars. *That Infernal Little Cuban Republic: The United States and the Cuban Revolution.* Chapel Hill: University of North Carolina Press, 2009.

Schwab, Stephen Irving Max. *Guantánamo, USA: The Untold History of America's Cuban Outpost.* Lawrence: University Press of Kansas, 2009.

Schwartz, Rosalie. *Pleasure Island: Tourism and Temptation in Cuba.* Lincoln: University of Nebraska Press, 1997.

Silva, Noenoe K. *Aloha Betrayed: Native Hawaiian Resistance to American Colonialism.* Durham, NC: Duke University Press, 2004.

Skwiot, Christine. *The Purposes of Paradise: U.S. Tourism and Empire in Cuba and Hawai'i.* Philadelphia: University of Pennsylvania Press, 2010.

Slotkin, Richard. *The Fatal Environment: The Myth of the Frontier in the Age of Industrialization, 1800–1890.* Norman: University of Oklahoma Press, 1985.

Gunfighter Nation: The Myth of the Frontier in Twentieth-Century America. New York: Atheneum, 1992.

Smith, Robert F. *The United States and Cuba: Business and Diplomacy, 1917–1960.* New Haven, CT: College and University Press, 1960.

Suñol, José Vega. *Norteamericanos en Cuba: Estudio Etnohistórico.* La Habana: Fundación Fernando Ortiz, 2004.

Taboada, José A. and Enrique O. González. *Hart Crane: El Poeta Perdido en Isla de Pinos.* Nueva Gerona: Ediciones El Abra, 2001.

Terry, T. Philip. *Terry's Guide to Cuba.* Boston, MA: Houghton Mifflin, 1926.

Thomas, Hugh. *Cuba, or the Pursuit of Freedom.* Updated Edition. New York: Da Capo, 1998.

Tingle, V. R. *The Isle of Pines: The Island You Should Know.* Havana: R.R. Indexo & Co., 1923.

Trask, David F. *The War with Spain in 1898.* New York: Macmillan, 1981.

Trommler, Frank and Elliott Shore, eds. *The German-American Encounter: Conflict and Cooperation between Two Cultures, 1800–2000.* New York: Berghahn Books, 2001.

Vasseur, Carlos A. *El Derecho de Soberanía Sobre la Isla de Pinos*. Panama: Star and Herald, 1925.

Veracini, Lorenzo. *Settler Colonialism: A Theoretical Overview*. New York: Palgrave Macmillan, 2010.

Verrill, A. Hyatt. *Cuba Past and Present*. Revised Edition. New York: Dodd, Mead & Company, 1920.

Washington, H. A., ed. *The Writings of Thomas Jefferson*. 9 vols. Washington, DC: Riker, Thorne, 1854.

Weber, Brom, ed. *The Letters of Hart Crane, 1916–1932*. New York: Hermitage House, 1952.

Williams, William Appleman. *The Tragedy of American Diplomacy*. New Edition. New York: W.W. Norton, 1972.

Wood, Leonard, et al. *Opportunities in the Colonies and Cuba*. New York: Lewis, Scribner & Co., 1902.

Wright, Irene A. *The Gem of the Caribbean*. Nueva Gerona: Isle of Pines Publicity Company, 1909.

Isle of Pines. Beverly, MA: Beverly Printing Company, 1910.

Wrobel, David M. *The End of American Exceptionalism: Frontier Anxiety from the Old West to the New Deal*. Lawrence: University Press of Kansas, 1993.

Ziegler, Louis W. and Herbert S. Wolfe. *Citrus Growing in Florida*. Revised Edition. Gainesville: University Press of Florida, 1975.

Articles

Academia de Ciencias de Cuba. "Serie Isla de Pinos No. 23: Latifundismo y Especulación." Delfín Rodríguez, et al., eds. La Habana: 1968.

"Serie Isla de Pinos No. 27: Situación social en Isla de Pinos antes de la Revolución." Salvador Morales, et al., eds. La Habana: 1969.

Alonso y Lugo, Miguel. "Y Para Isla de Pinos ¿Que, Dr. Grau?" La Habana: 1945.

Ashby, Timothy. "U.S. Certified Claims against Cuba: Legal Reality and Likely Settlement Mechanisms." *University of Miami Inter-American Law Review* 40 (Spring 2009): 413–31.

Browning, William. "The Isle of Pines as a Hibernaculum." *Long Island Medical Journal* (November 1910).

Carlson, F. A. "American Settlement in the Isla de Pinos, Cuba." *Geographical Review* 32 (January 1942): 21–35.

Clapp, M. E. "Have We Mislaid a Valuable Possession?" *The North American Review* 190 (September 1909): 330–7.

Davis, Collin, et al. "The Isle of Pines: A Musical Comedy." Washington, DC: Library of Congress Copyright Office, Drama Deposits, 1906.

Davis, Roy Tasco. "American Private Schools in Latin America." *National Association of Secondary-School Principals Bulletin* 29 (May 1945): 49–55.

Deere, Carmen Diana. "Here Come the Yankees! The Rise and Decline of United States Colonies in Cuba, 1898–1930." *Hispanic American Historical Review* 78 (November 1998): 729–65.

Finlay, John Huston. "The Isle of Pines." *Scribner's* 33 (1903): 174–81.

Fitzgerald, Dean T. "The Role of American Schools in Latin America." *The School Review* 63 (May 1955): 290–7.

"The Significance of American Schools in Latin America." *Comparative Education Review* 1 (October 1957): 19–22.

Frost, Janet Delavan. "Cuban–American Relations Concerning the Isle of Pines." *The Hispanic American Historical Review* 11 (August 1931): 336–50.

Gleijeses, Piero. "Cuba's First Venture in Africa: Algeria, 1961–1965." *Journal of Latin American Studies* 28 (February 1996): 159–95.

"The First Ambassadors: Cuba's Contribution to Guinea-Bissau's War of Independence." *Journal of Latin American Studies* 29 (February 1997): 45–88.

Hoernel, Robert B. "Sugar and Social Change in Oriente, Cuba, 1898–1946." *Journal of Latin American Studies* 8 (November 1976): 215–49.

López Pellón, Nivio. "Hablemos de Isla de Pinos y su régimen fiscal." La Habana: 1958.

Merritt, W. H. "The Isle of Pines." 1905.

"Pearcy v. Stranahan." *American Journal of International Law* 1 (July 1907): 784–93.

Pérez Jr., Louis A. "Incurring a Debt of Gratitude: 1898 and the Moral Sources of United States Hegemony in Cuba." *American Historical Review* 104 (April 1999): 356–98.

Quesada, Gonzalo de. "Cuba's Claims to the Isle of Pines." *North American Review* 190 (November 1909): 594–604.

Santamarina, Juan C. "The Cuba Company and the Creation of Informal Business Networks: Historiography and Archival Sources," *Cuban Studies* 35 (2004): 75–6.

"The Cuba Company and the Expansion of American Business in Cuba, 1898–1915." *Business History Review* 74 (Spring 2000): 41–83.

Scott, James Brown. "The Isle of Pines." *American Journal of International Law* 17 (January 1923): 100–4.

Swierenga, Robert P. "Land Speculation and Its Impact on American Economic Growth and Welfare: A Historiographical Review." *Western Historical Quarterly* 8 (July 1977): 283–302.

"The Isle of Pines." *National Geographic* 17 (1906): 105–8.

"Treaty between the United States and Cuba for the Adjustment of Title to the Isle of Pines." *The American Journal of International Law* 19 (July 1925): 95–8.

Vanderblue, Homer B. "The Florida Land Boom." *Journal of Land and Public Utility Economics* 3 (May 1927): 113–31.

Veracini, Lorenzo. "Introducing Settler Colonial Studies." *Settler Colonial Studies* 1 (2011): 1–12.

Williams, William Appleman. "The Frontier Thesis and American Foreign Policy." *Pacific Historical Review* 24 (November 1955): 379–95.

Winsberg, Morton D. "Costs, Tariffs, Prices and Nationalization: The Rise and Decline of the American Grapefruit Industry on the Isle of Pines, Cuba." *American Journal of Economics and Sociology* 20 (October 1961): 543–8.

Wright, Quincy. "The Isle of Pines Treaty." *The American Journal of International Law* 19 (April 1925): 340–4.

Film
La Isla de la Juventud. Directed by Ana Laura Calderón. Mexico: Alas Ocultas, La Casa de Cine, 2007. DVD, 72 minutes.

Dissertations and Theses
Avello, Julio Antonio. "The Isle of Pines as a Factor in United States–Cuban Relations." MA thesis, Southern Illinois University, 1969.

Cassidy, Caroline L. "Adjustment of Title to Isle of Pines." MA thesis, Albany State College for Teachers, 1945.

McLeod, Marc. "Undesirable Aliens: Haitians and British West Indian Immigrant Workers in Cuba, 1898 to 1940." PhD dissertation, University of Texas, 2000.

Oswald, Clarence Eugene. "The Adjustment of Title to the Ownership of the Isle of Pines." MA thesis, University of California, 1935.

Stutelberg, Hildegarde. "Relations between the United States and the Isle of Pines." MA thesis, Columbia University, 1926.

Winsberg, Morton D. "The Isle of Pines, Cuba: A Geographic Interpretation." PhD dissertation, University of Florida, 1958.

Index